D0476070

NATO ASI Series

Advanced Science Institutes Series

A series presenting the results of activities sponsored by the NATO Science Committee, which aims at the dissemination of advanced scientific and technological knowledge, with a view to strengthening links between scientific communities.

The Series is published by an international board of publishers in conjunction with the NATO Scientific Affairs Division

A Life Sciences B Physics	Plenum Publishing Corporation London and New York
C Mathematical and Physical Sciences D Behavioural and Social Sciences E Applied Sciences	Kluwer Academic Publishers Dordrecht, Boston and London
F Computer and Systems Sciences G Ecological Sciences H Cell Biology I Global Environmental Change	Springer-Verlag Berlin Heidelberg New York London Paris Tokyo Hong Kong Barcelona Budapest

PARTNERSHIP SUB-SERIES

1. Disarmament Technologies	Kluwer Academic Publishers
2. Environment	Springer-Verlag
3. High Technology	Kluwer Academic Publishers
4. Science and Technology Policy	Kluwer Academic Publishers
5. Computer Networking	Kluwer Academic Publishers

The Partnership Sub-Series incorporates activities undertaken in collaboration with NATO's Cooperation Partners, the countries of the CIS and Central and Eastern Europe, in Priority Areas of concern to those countries.

NATO-PCO DATABASE

The electronic index to the NATO ASI Series provides full bibliographical references (with keywords and/or abstracts) to about 50 000 contributions from international scientists published in all sections of the NATO ASI Series. Access to the NATO-PCO DATABASE compiled by the NATO Publication Coordination Office is possible in two ways:

- via online FILE 128 (NATO-PCO DATABASE) hosted by ESRIN, Via Galileo Galilei, I-00044 Frascati, Italy.
- via CD-ROM "NATO Science & Technology Disk" with user-friendly retrieval software in English, French and German (© WTV GmbH and DATAWARE Technologies Inc. 1992).

The CD-ROM can be ordered through any member of the Board of Publishers or through NATO-PCO, Overijse, Belgium.

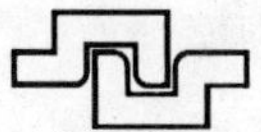

Series F: Computer and Systems Sciences, Vol. 142

The ASI Series F Books Published as a Result of Activities of the Special Programme on ADVANCED EDUCATIONAL TECHNOLOGY

This book contains the proceedings of a NATO Advanced Research Workshop held within the activities of the NATO Special Programme on Advanced Educational Technology, running from 1988 to 1993 under the auspices of the NATO Science Committee.

The volumes published so far in the Special Programme are as follows (further details are given at the end of this volume):

67: Designing Hypermedia for Learning. 1990
76: Multimedia Interface Design in Education. 1992, 2nd corr. print 1994
78: Integrating Advanced Technology into Technology Education. 1991
80: Intelligent Tutoring Systems for Foreign Language Learning. 1992
81: Cognitive Tools for Learning. 1992
84: Computer-Based Learning Environments and Problem Solving. 1992
85: Adaptive Learning Environments: Foundations and Frontiers. 1992
86: Intelligent Learning Environments and Knowledge Acquisition in Physics. 1992
87: Cognitive Modelling and Interactive Environments in Language Learning. 1992
89: Mathematical Problem Solving and New Information Technologies. 1992
90: Collaborative Learning Through Computer Conferencing. 1992
91: New Directions for Intelligent Tutoring Systems. 1992
92: Hypermedia Courseware: Structures of Communication and Intelligent Help. 1992
93: Interactive Multimedia Learning Environments. 1992
95: Comprehensive System Design: A New Educational Technology. 1993
96: New Directions in Educational Technology. 1992
97: Advanced Models of Cognition for Medical Training and Practice. 1992
104: Instructional Models in Computer-Based Learning Environments. 1992
105: Designing Environments for Constructive Learning. 1993
107: Advanced Educational Technology for Mathematics and Science. 1993
109: Advanced Educational Technology in Technology Education. 1993
111: Cognitive Models and Intelligent Environments for Learning Programming. 1993
112: Item Banking: Interactive Testing and Self-Assessment. 1993
113: Interactive Learning Technology for the Deaf. 1993
115: Learning Electricity and Electronics with Advanced Educational Technology. 1993
116: Control Technology in Elementary Education. 1993
119: Automating Instructional Design, Development, and Delivery. 1993
121: Learning from Computers: Mathematics Education and Technology. 1993
122: Simulation-Based Experiential Learning. 1993
125: Student Modelling: The Key to Individualized Knowledge-Based Instruction. 1994
128: Computer Supported Collaborative Learning. 1995
129: Human-Machine Communication for Educational Systems Design. 1994
132: Design of Mathematical Modelling Courses for Engineering Education. 1994
133: Collaborative Dialogue Technologies in Distance Learning. 1994
135: Technology Education in School and Industry. 1994
137: Technology-Based Learning Environments. 1994
140: Automating Instructional Design: Computer-Based Development and Delivery Tools. 1995
142: Dialogue and Instruction. Modeling Interaction in Intelligent Tutoring Systems. 1995

Dialogue and Instruction

Modeling Interaction in Intelligent Tutoring Systems

Edited by

Robbert-Jan Beun

Institute for Perception Research/IPO, PO Box 513
5600 MB Eindhoven, The Netherlands
E-mail: rjbeun@prl.philips.nl

Michael Baker

Centre National de la Recherche Scientifique
Laboratoire IRPEACS, Equipe COAST
Ecole Normale Supérieure de Lyon, 46 allée d'Italie
F-69364 Lyon Cedex 07, France
E-mail: michael.baker@ens.ens-lyon.fr

Miriam Reiner

Department of Education in Science and Technology
Technion – Israel Institute of Technology
Haifa, Israel 32000
E-mail: miriamr@techunix.technion.ac.il

Springer

Published in cooperation with NATO Scientific Affairs Division

Proceedings of the NATO Advanced Research Workshop on Natural Dialogue and Interactive Student Modeling, held in Varenna, Italy, October 17–20, 1992

CR Subject Classification (1991): K.3, H.5, I.2, J.4

ISBN 3-540-58834-5 Springer-Verlag Berlin Heidelberg New York

CIP data applied for

Printed in Germany

Typesetting: Camera-ready by editor
SPIN: 10486070 45/3142 – 5 4 3 2 1 0 – Printed on acid-free paper

Preface

This book derives from a workshop entitled 'Natural Dialogue and Interactive Student Modeling', held October 17-20, 1992 in the Villa Cipressi in Varenna (Italy).

The theme of the workshop focused on how approaches to natural dialogue and conversation contributed to the development of a sophisticated dialogue component in intelligent tutoring systems. Researchers from the fields of educational technology, dialogue research and user interface design were all invited to the workshop in order to ensure a broad knowledge base for the discussion of the main topic of the workshop.

The workshop included a variety of presentations, most of which are presented in this book, as well as active discussions of a number of issues related to the main topic, such as:

- the intrinsic value of a dialogue component in an intelligent tutoring system
- verbal expressions (e.g., natural language) as a successful modality in a learning setting
- the application of results from other types of dialogue, such as information or task dialogues, in models of instructional dialogue
- the role of a teacher as an intermediary who provides motivation and support in learning as opposed to the role of a teacher as someone who just presents information.

In the introductory chapter we have tried to combine these issues and link them to the papers that are presented in this volume.

It was generally agreed that successful learning critically depends on the process of meta-communication, i.e. the flow of information between sender and recipient that serves to guide and optimize the intended information transfer; simply telling students the facts rarely if ever results at all in learning. Therefore the papers in this book concentrate mainly on issues of feedback and control in dialogue. The editors are aware, however, that a thorough analysis of the role of dialogue and interaction in instructional settings is still in its infancy, but they hope that this volume at least contributes to its growth.

We acknowledge the support of NATO, which supplied funding for this workshop, and the care of the staff of the Villa Cipressi, who supplied accommodation and a most stimulating scientific environment near the shore of Lake Como.

We thank those who helped to prepare the book in one way or another; they are: Alma Schaafstal, Anita van Berkel, David Good, Don Bouwhuis, Frank Wouters, Frits Engel, Gisela Redeker, Lisette Appelo, Harry Bego, Harry Bunt, Herman Bouma, John de Vet, Maddy Brouwer, Rudy van Hoe and, of course, all workshop participants. The book was prepared in LaTeX and pictures were included in Postscript format; special thanks to Guido Leenders for doing a great job on this.

November 1994

R.J. Beun
M. Baker
M. Reiner

Table of Contents

Part 3: Natural Dialogue and Interaction Theory

Part 4: Feedback and Control in Human-Machine Communication

Editors' Introduction

Abstract. In this introductory section, a general background is sketched for the papers that are included in this book. It is discussed that dialogue plays a fundamental role in instructional environments and that knowledge about basic properties in communication is essential for building intelligent tutoring systems. Instructional dialogues are compared with more cooperation oriented dialogues, such as information dialogues. It is indicated that in the first type of dialogue the diagnostic process of correct transfer of the message plays a much more important role. Moreover, it is argued that natural language as a surface representation for the intended message in interaction can be very unnatural and that often other surface structures should be preferred. Finally, an overview is provided of all the papers contained in this book.

Keywords. Interaction, instruction, dialogue structure, information dialogue, diagnostic process

1 Background

The recent introduction of multimedia computers has led to exciting new interface techniques for educational environments. Multimedia systems such as cd-i, simulation programs and interactive animation are employed to provide a natural and realistic context for the instructional process. However, despite the progress in the interactive qualities of the tutorial domain, the development of the communicative strategies of the instructional component of so-called 'intelligent tutoring systems' is still immature. Pedagogical decisions in these systems frequently reflect unprincipled intuitions about communication, often violating well-known rules for cooperative behaviour in natural conversation.

In natural instructional settings, a tutor functions as an intermediary who transfers and activates information about the tutorial domain. This requires that she[1] takes complex pedagogical decisions and chooses from a variety of communicative acts to manage the instructional process. On the one hand, she provides for domain-related information, for instance, by introducing the tutorial topic, telling facts about the subject matter and explaining causal or other relations between these facts; on the other hand, she controls the interactional process, for instance, by managing turn taking in the classroom, posing problems, asking questions and providing feedback about the student's results.

[1] In this introductory chapter, the tutor receives female pronominalization; the student will be treated as masculine.

What type of communicative act has to be chosen at a particular moment in a learning session with a computer system and what form this act should have is, from both a fundamental and a practical point of view, still an open question. The answer requires a large amount of knowledge about communication and interaction. The purpose of this book is to link fundamental issues of communication and interaction to the more restricted domain of instructional dialogue. It is expected that insight in interactional principles, from both a theoretical and an empirical point of view, will eventually contribute to a better understanding of the communicative process in instruction and, as a result, to an improved design of the instructional component of intelligent tutoring systems.

2 Dialogue in instructional settings

The need for interaction, or what we will often call *dialogue*, in instructional situations seems to come from a fundamental property of communication: knowledge is distributed among the participants and no one has direct access to the cognitive state of another. The intended message has to pass through an error-prone communication channel, causing the sender to be uncertain whether the transmitted message will arrive correctly. This uncertainty may be reduced by feedback from the receiver about the arrival of the message (see e.g., Bouwhuis, this volume).

Even in the case of an error-free communication channel, where the intended message arrives without disturbance, a fundamental problem exists. Since the receiver's cognitive state is not directly accessible for the sender, the message has to be encoded for transfer. A speaker in a conversation, for instance, has to select relevant information, to order the information, to formulate the message into words and grammatical structure, and finally, to articulate the message to produce overt speech. In machine communication the decoding process is an exact inverse of the encoding; in human communication, however, the processes of encoding and decoding are never (inverse) identical, so important mismatches may occur between the generation and interpretation of the intended message (see Waugh and Taylor, this volume). This problem is not exclusive for natural language interaction; other modalities, such as graphics and sound, may be subject to the same deficits. Visual or auditory metaphors and symbols may be chosen inappropriately with respect to the receiver's cognitive state or may be poorly linked to an existing linguistic discourse.

In an instructional situation, the decoding of the message sent by the tutor critically depends on previous experience and knowledge of the student. Therefore, the tutor has to make careful selections in *what* to communicate and, once the message content has been chosen, in *how* to communicate the intended message. Too much information may lead to unwanted inferences; too little information may make it difficult for the student to correctly interpret the information within his frame of reference. Even worse, the student's existing model of the domain of discourse may contain inconsistencies with respect to what is taught, which may result in rejecting the new information or in building two frames of reference, for instance, an informal one for the everyday environment and a formal one for the classroom.

Clearly, monologue does not suffice in the instructional setting, because pedagogical decisions largely depend on the tutor's knowledge of the student's cognitive state and require both close observation of the student's activity and context-sensitive behaviour from the tutor in reaction to the student's performance. Therefore, in every instructional situation a method for diagnosing the student's knowledge or performance is built in. But by including the diagnostic process, the notion of dialogue has entered the instructional setting.

3 Interactional structure in instructional dialogues

If we compare the instructional situation with more cooperation oriented dialogues, such as information dialogues (e.g., where an inquirer wants specific information from an informant; see Bunt, this volume), we observe some fundamental differences. First of all, in information dialogues the basic structure is always of the form 'question of the inquirer'/'answer of the informant'/'feedback from the inquirer' (Table 1), where the question filters the range of reactions from the informant in order to adjust the information, provided in the answer, to the needs of the inquirer. Hence, in information dialogues the informant is aware of the intentions of his dialogue partner; the informant knows what the inquirer wants. In instructional dialogues, however, the tutor imposes information without knowledge about the student's actual needs and wants; the tutor wants the student to know. To put it differently, the tutor provides the information without knowing a question.

Consequently, since the tutor is committed to the successful transfer of information, the diagnostic process plays a much more important role in instructional dialogue than in information dialogue. In positive cases, the diagnostic process in information dialogues is often limited to a single feedback utterance by the inquirer, e.g. "mm", "all right" (see, for instance, papers by Allwood and Bunt in this volume), whereas the basic structure of the diagnostic process in instructional dialogues is of the form 'question of the tutor'/'answer of the student'/'feedback from the tutor'. The tutor's question provokes a reaction from the student that would probably not be given otherwise. Note that although the basic structure in the diagnostic process agrees with the basic structure of information dialogues, an important difference exists in the underlying knowledge distribution of the dialogue partners in the two types of dialogue. In the instructional dialogue, the person who asks the question knows the answer; in the information dialogue, the one who asks the question does not know the answer. The question from the tutor is only a strategy to uncover parts of the cognitive state of the student with respect to what has been taught.

It should be stressed here that the interactional sequences depicted in Table 1 reflect the basic intentions of the dialogue participants as well as the flow of information between them, and not the actual surface structure. The term 'question' indicates a particular knowledge gap in a person's cognitive state and the fact that that person wants this gap to be filled. Whatever the actual surface structure of

Table 1. Basic and diagnostic moves in information and instructional dialogues.

Interactive Moves	**Information Dialogue**	**Instructional Dialogue type I**	**Instructional Dialogue type II**
basic moves	question(inquirer) answer(informant)	information(tutor)	question(tutor)
diagnostic moves	feedback(inquirer)	question(tutor) answer(student) feedback(tutor)	answer(student) feedback(tutor)

the message will be is of no importance now, but of course some structures will be more appropriate then others to achieve the actual goal. We will return to this below.

This model of the two types of dialogue is based on an asymmetry of knowledge; the tutor and the informant are supposed to be the domain experts. It is assumed that information simply flows from one who knows to someone who does not. But, as we previously argued, the student has already acquired a substantial body of knowledge and skills before the instructional process begins (see e.g., Good, this volume), part of which may be the intended domain knowledge. In that case, the role of the tutor may change to activating the student's knowledge and skills, rather than transferring it.

Assuming background knowledge and skills has consequences for the structure of the instructional dialogue. We therefore distinguish two types of instructional dialogue (see Table 1): type I, where an explicit information-providing phase is included, and type II, where the tutor has skipped the information phase and starts by posing a problem or asking a question that has to be solved or answered by the student (e.g., Socratian dialogue). In type II, the interactional structure corresponds to the diagnostic part of the instructional dialogue of type I. Note that although the interactional sequences agree and the perlocutionary effects of both questions may result in knowledge about the student's model, the underlying primary intentions of the tutor differ. In the diagnostic part of dialogue type I, the question indicates that the tutor wants to know whether the student knows. The question in type II, however, expresses that the tutor wants to make the student aware that the student already knows and that the knowledge should be activated and made explicit. An important consequence of this is that activating the knowledge by asking a question may have the same result as simply providing information, and may even be more appropriate, since the student actively participates in the instructional process.

In practice, a mixture of different types of dialogue will often appear in the instruction, depending on the motivation, knowledge and experience of both student and tutor. For instance, when the student becomes involved with the subject matter, he may take over control and naturally start generating questions (information dialogue). The tutor may in turn respond to these questions with counter-questions to activate the student's background knowledge and skills (instructional dialogue type II) and if the activation fails, the tutor may give supplementary side-information without being asked for (instructional dialogue type I). In relation to this issue, Cheikes and Ragnemalm (this volume) distinguish between so-called *solicited* and *unsolicited* support of a training-support system, where the first type indicates support given at the request of the student and where the second type is given when the system itself decides to provide support.

As for feedback strategies, the tutor may, if possible, simply inform the student that the answer is correct or incorrect, but she may also decide to repeat the initial information, to provide extra information (see Spaai, this volume), or to ask for elaboration from the student on the subject or justification of his hypothesis (see papers by Blandford and Prince, this volume). As a result, complex interactional structures and mixed initiatives may occur. Daradoumis and Verdejo present a model for tutorial task-oriented dialogue in this volume based on Rhetorical Structure Theory. Modelling the interaction, however, requires not only theoretical knowledge about the basic concepts involved, but also a thorough empirical study of the actual information exchange between tutor and student. Guidelines for analyzing dialogues in a problem-solving environment are therefore presented in this volume by Brouwer-Janse.

So far, only one student and his tutor have been discussed in this introductory chapter. In classroom and many other instructional settings more than one student is involved. If we assume prior knowledge and experience by the students, relevant information with respect to the intended tutorial domain may be distributed among the students. Consequently, students may collaborate to find the answer or solution to an initial problem posed by the tutor; now, the tutor is not only someone who knows, but someone who provides motivation and guidance through the subject matter (see papers by diSessa, Reiner and Coleman in this volume). From a fundamental point of view, the group activity makes the instructional setting a very complex one, and raises questions such as how students co-construct a specific solution and how students establish agreement with respect to the solution. Baker's paper (this volume) is aimed at an analysis of this collaborative process viewed as a type of negotiation. Connah (this volume), taking a rigorously different view, describes the interactive process from a so-called 'situated' perspective where, in contrast to Baker, no explicit representation of beliefs and goals is required.

4 Message content and surface structure

Once the tutor has decided about the content of the message, she has to choose the appropriate final form for presentation. In the classroom, the tutor speaks, writes, draws on the blackboard, mimics, gestures, plays music, etc. and the students may respond by the same interactive means. The structure of the messages has to be rooted in both the students' and the tutor's cultures. This basically means that the (language) symbols and meaning integrated into the message by the tutor has a certain probability of being interpreted within a familiar conventional framework. Stated differently, it means that the tutor's models and the students' models somehow resonate to allow negotiation and construction of new conventions within a collaborative mutual culture of both the tutor and the students.

Dialogue may be a powerful tool to indicate direct control of the flow of information and understanding. However, verbalization may have important disadvantages. For instance, inadequate verbalization by the student does not necessarily reflect inadequate conceptualization but may be judged as such. Furthermore, many skills have to be learned by doing and may require knowledge that is difficult to verbalize. In this book we do not advocate the proposition that natural and transparent interaction is restricted to natural language (see e.g., Jacob (this volume) and, more specifically aimed at educational systems, papers by diSessa and Reiner, this volume). On the contrary, the use of keyboard and typed natural language in computer interfaces is very unnatural; natural language interaction requires at least the possibility of spoken input. However, we can learn a great deal from natural language conversation about interaction in general (see papers by Bego, Bunt, Allwood and Nivre, this volume). The papers by Erickson, Jacob, de Vet, and Wrobleski et al. (this volume) suggest that, depending on the required type of feedback and control, a substantial part of the interactional moves in human-human dialogues can be replaced by other means in human-computer dialogues, such as colour change, well-designed graphical structures, menu structures, and even eye movements.

Sad to say, the problem is more substantial than simply choosing the 'appropriate' feedback structure. Will we ever be able to relate vague external representations in multimodal environments – such as sketches and sound – to clearly definable concepts which are usable in computer systems? Lee's view (this volume) is not very optimistic, but he argues that there may be parts of the process which the computer can support in design education, especially in combination with natural language. Future research may provide satisfactory answers in some cases; for the time being, we will leave the conclusions for the reader of this volume.

5 About this book

The analysis of the notion of dialogue and instruction can be carried out along many dimensions, such as knowledge distribution, student motivation, social constraints and feedback type, and spans disciplines from psychology and artificial intelligence to ethnomethodology and, nowadays, user interface research. Although only a part of this can be covered in this book, we have tried to span a broad range of disciplines, all sharing the interest in interactive environments.

The chapters in this book have been divided into four parts. The first two parts concentrate on interaction in instructional environments. In Part 1, *Theoretical issues in instructional dialogue*, hypotheses and fundamental problems are raised and models for instruction are presented based on theoretical concepts in communication, while in Part 2, *Theory into practice: interaction in learning environments*, papers focus on actual applications.

The last two parts concentrate on general aspects of interaction, with a particular focus on issues of feedback and control in communication. Part 3, *Natural dialogue and interaction theory*, examines various aspects of human-human interaction and concentrates in particular on theoretical issues in conversation and interaction in general, while Part 4, *Feedback and control in human-machine communication*, contains papers oriented towards specific applications in human-machine interaction.

Theoretical issues in instructional dialogue

Bouwhuis' paper may be considered a general introduction on dialogue in instructional environments. In his paper he introduces basic dialogue concepts such as cooperativity, rationality, feedback and control. He argues that instructional theory, which is used to develop intelligent tutoring systems, has hardly employed dialogue theory and, vice versa, that dialogue research has neglected basic principles in instructional dialogue. Tutoring systems should, in order to become more effective, be provided with sufficient communicative power, and design should be guided by fundamental principles in interaction. He argues, however, that Gricean cooperativity maxims, such as quantity and relevance, are still too vague for concrete implementation.

The next paper, by Good, concentrates on the importance of collaboration and cooperation in instructional dialogues. It is argued that the tutor must have an adequate model of the task, skill or knowledge being taught, but that the tutor does not need to have a model of the student. To support the argumentation, an experiment by Wood and his co-workers is presented where mothers were asked to teach their children how to build a small wooden figure. It followed that adaptation of the mothers' help to the children' success clearly improved the children' performance.

Baker describes a general framework for analysing and modelling collaborative problem-solving dialogues based on viewing them as negotiations at the communication and task levels. Two specific problems are addressed: the 'co-construction problem', concerning how students interrelate their intermediary solutions so as to come to an accord, and the 'agreement problem', which involves identifying precisely when students are agreed, with respect to what, and what it means, in this context, to be agreed. The chapter concentrates on describing communicative acts and different types of relations between individual contributions for one specific negotiation strategy where students successively refine partial solutions towards agreement. In conclusion, Baker argues that given this negotiation based framework, student's interventions reflect the attitude of 'acceptance' rather than that of 'belief'.

Daradoumis and Verdejo concentrate on the problem of planning coherent tutorial dialogue in an ITS. They propose a hierarchical model, searched top-down, that reflects the tutorial task-oriented structure in six layers: conversation, pedagogy, subdialogue, exchange, move and argumentative/explanation strategy. At each level there are specific orderings of subgoals, and there are specific relations between them. The order is based on an extension of the theory of 'rhetorical relations' of Mann and Thompson, the theory of conversational structure of Clark and Schaefer, and Berry's work on exchange structures.

Lee's paper is oriented towards the education of designers. Supported by examples from a dialogue between an architect and a client, he argues that there is hardly any prospect of an intelligent tutoring system replacing a design tutor. Context-sensitivity, vagueness of the interrelation between expressions and drawings, and non-monotonocity all play dominant roles in natural multimodal dialogue. Lee states that traditional AI-research has hardly anything to offer to solve the problems involved with replicating these basic characteristics and that currently computers can replicate very little of the type of dialogue behaviour needed in design education.

In the next paper, Cheikes and Ragnemalm discuss the design implications for simulator-based tools to assist in the training of process-control operators in the paper industry. In their paper they focus on so-called troubleshooting tasks, i.e. the process which begins with the identification of a fault and ends with taking the corrective action. First, they discuss Schaafstal's task-level model of diagnosis and repair, and next, they discuss what type of adaptation the system's behaviour should take to support the student's performance. They believe four types of enhancement in interaction to be feasible and useful: explanation generation, question answering, guided exercise and skill evaluation. Finally, several different dimensions of evaluation of the effectiveness of a training tool are discussed.

Theory into practice: interaction in learning environments

In the first paper in the next part, diSessa emphasizes the collaborative aspect of learning by discussing a classroom interaction between high school students who had to design Newtonian laws of motion in the program environment BOXER. In this setting the knowledge is of a distributed nature and the teacher functions as a conceptual stimulator who controls and directs the discussion by asking questions. It is important to note that learning by the students did not come from explicitly built-in pedagogical principles in the system, but mainly from discussions among the students about the design task, the specific demands of the programming context and the guiding remarks of the teacher. DiSessa argues that programming provides a clear and precise language in which students and teacher can interact.

Reiner reports on a study of language construction in physics learning. Students had to interact with DYNAGRAMS, a dynamic, graphical multi-representational learning environment in optics. In her paper, Reiner focuses on the way students construct a symbolic system and on the constituents of such a system when applied in a discussion on optics. In Reiner's experiment the teacher was absent during the teaching session. Four types of symbols were identified: graphical symbols, mathematical symbols, verbal symbols and physical symbols. It was found that graphical symbols were introduced in the discussion more than other types of symbols and that new symbols were extensively used in the students' conversation. Reiner's research suggests that graphical environments for thought experiments play a crucial role in physics learning and should therefore be added to curricular materials in physics.

In the next paper, Coleman focuses on the collaborative learning process of co-constructing explanations by different students. Coleman suggests that students often lack effective strategies for maintaining meaningful collaborative discussions. To support discussions between students, a learning environment (CSILE) has been developed which provides information-sharing capabilities between multiple users. Various studies are presented where students had to use CSILE as medium for fostering progressive discourse. It was found that compared with face-to-face situations, students using CSILE show an important gain in the coherence of explanations and a deeper understanding of the subject matter.

Blandford describes the high-level dialogue model of an intelligent tutoring system (WOMBAT) that engages in collaborative problem-solving with a student in the domain of engineering design. The fact that in this domain there is no 'right answer', but rather a set of preferred solutions based on justified beliefs, leads to a mixed-intiative dialogue in which system and student have similar dialogue moves at their disposal, and which achieves a balance between opportunism and planning. The chapter concentrates on the problem of 'deciding what to say' from the point of view of the system. An intelligent agent architecture is proposed for this system based on an explicit representation of educational values and means-ends analysis of the likelihood of satisfying them by (dialogue) actions in a given situation.

Prince describes an intelligent tutoring system, called TEDDI, that checks concept definitions of university-level students in computer science. The system is based on the idea that the linguistic expression of a concept given by a person is a good indication of how well the knowledge about that concept has been organised. A sophisticated natural language parser is therefore required, together with conversational strategies for correcting misunderstandings or persistent failures and a dynamically updated student model. TEDDI is a specific instantiation of the CARAMEL multi-agent architecture developed in the LIMSI laboratory.

In the paper by Spaai, various types of feedback are considered in a computer-based drill for beginning readers. Spaai examines different ways in which spoken feedback facilitates learning of letter-sound correspondences. Letter-sound relations were practiced in four different conditions of feedback: control (correct or wrong), partial (control and spoken form of selected letter), elaborate (partial and visual indication) and complete (elaborate and incorrect presented before correct). It was found that learning effects are better for elaborate feedback than for other types of feedback. Spaai also found that especially poor learners seem to be in need of corrective feedback. He therefore concludes that it may be necessary to implement feedback in an adaptive way. Elaborate feedback should be given to poor performers and a combination of elaborate and partial feedback to good performers.

Natural dialogue and interaction theory

The first chapter, by Bunt, gives an overview of the different types of dialogue control that appears in natural human-human dialogues and its implications for interactive teaching systems. Two notions are central in his paper: *transparency* and *naturalness*. Transparency refers to the student's view of the system's activities concerned with the teaching activity; naturalness concerns the communicative options of both system and user, and refers to the quality of the dialogue. Bunt distinguishes between dialogue control and task-oriented dialogue acts and then concentrates on various types of dialogue control (e.g., turn management, feedback, discourse structuring). In the final section, he describes how dialogue control enhances the transparancy and naturalness of the dialogue.

In the next chapter by Waugh and Taylor, feedback is considered in a layered model of communication. In their paper they compare three layered models of interaction – Norman's theory of action, Perceptual Control Theory and Layered Protocol (LP) theory – and argue that in all three models feedback plays a crucial role. They then focus on LP theory and its role in communication between two intelligent partners. In LP theory virtual messages are transmitted from higher levels of abstraction to lower levels until the actual physical message is sent. The authors then introduce General Protocol Grammar for feedback. Feedback can be provided at each level and takes the form of virtual messages which connect the corresponding levels in each partner. Finally, they argue that feedback at the right time and the appropriate level of abstraction could allow a user, through active exploration, to develop an effective model of complex systems.

Nivre concentrates on feedback from a more philosophical point of view based on well-known studies of communicative action by Grice and the general cybernetic notion of feedback by Wiener. In line with Waugh and Taylor, he considers a hierarchy in feedback types; in Nivre's paper, however, the hierarchy is based on an explicit ranking of communicative goals. The primary goal is to evoke a certain cognitive state in the receiver (the *evocative goal*); the goal to make the evocative goal manifest to the receiver is called the *signalling goal*; and finally, the *utterance goal* involves an instance of perceptible communicative behaviour recognisable as such by the receiver. Feedback information may fall into three categories: positive, negative or neutral. Based on these notions, a first step towards a formalization of feedback is discussed.

In Bego's paper, feedback is considered as communicative acts triggered by a cognitive state change of the dialogue participants. Bego presents a simple model for interpretation and generation of feedback acts and argues that principles for generation and interpretation can be derived from default ordering of communicative function levels. In the model, two stages of feedback generation are distinguished. In the first stage, feedback acts are triggered by a process that monitors the state change of the sender of the feedback; in the second stage, the receiver's needs are taken into account. An extra input process has been added to the interpretation process that distinguishes between feedback acts and the so-called 'main message' of the sender.

In the next contribution, Allwood concentrates on management in spoken interaction. Two main kinds of management are considered: *own communication management* and *interactive communication management.* The first refers to management of the speaker's utterance with regard to the choice and change of his contribution; the latter refers to management with regard to sequencing, turn taking and feedback. He considers the role of context in the interpretation of management utterances, and then discusses the main reasons for communicative management within the perspective of communication as a species of motivated rational action. Finally, he focuses on the processes of sequencing, turn management and feedback as means to ensure the rationality and ethicalness of communication and the underlying activity.

Connah describes a new language (ABLE) for the design of artificial *situated interacting agents* that incorporates time as constitutive of agents themselves. In such systems the behaviour of a society of agents as a whole emerges from a close coupling of individual agents with the situation, and from the interaction between individual behaviours. No explicit representation of beliefs, goals or problem situations is therefore required. In conclusion he describes how situated feedback could be provided for a task where an agent makes use of visual markers to copy a pile of child's bricks which spelled out a word (a possible part of a spelling tutorial). Three types of feedback could be provided: directing the student towards an appropriate focus of attention, giving emotional feedback on problem-solving success or failure, or demonstrating if the student is having difficulty.

In the next paper Brouwer-Janse presents guidelines for analysing dialogues generated by people involved in a problem-solving situation. First, different methods to collect verbal protocol data are briefly described and next a method for analysis of the data is presented. The method is organised into two levels. First the raw data is preprocessed into codeable propositions and episodes. In the next level, a model consisting of 24 subroutines is used to code the propositions (or groups of propositions) from the previous level into labels representing the elementary processes involved in problem-solving. In her conclusions, Brouwer-Janse argues that the coding results provide knowledge about the structure of the dialogue and about the communication process of humans participating in a complex task.

Feedback and control in human-machine communication

In the first paper of Part 4, Jacob argues that properties of human dialogue such as contextual dependency and focusing should be connected to direct manipulation or graphical interaction styles in computer applications. Apart from the traditional linguistic tripartition of a syntactic, semantic and lexical level of interaction, Jacob adds the level of discourse into the direct manipulation interaction style so that different transactions can be related. An overview is given of the author's work on natural eye movements as a direct medium for human-computer communication. An important problem is the type of feedback information to be provided by the system about the user's eye position. In the final section, an overview is given of possible applications of interaction based on eye movements to perform basic operations in direct manipulation systems.

In the next paper, Erickson discusses three types of feedback that are important in graphical interfaces based on their temporal relation to the user's activity: *synchronous feedback*, *background feedback* and *completion feedback*. Synchronous feedback is coupled with the user's physical actions, background feedback gives information of the system's activity, and completion feedback indicates that an operation by the system has been completed. Erickson argues that feedback provides continuity in the interaction ('coherence') and that it allows the user to build up a mental model of the system ('portrayal'). Examples from an existing application program illustrate how the different types of feedback considerably improve the interaction with the user.

In de Vet's paper various aspects of feedback in consumer appliances are discussed. Three types of feedback are considered: *status feedback*, *corrective feedback* and *guidance*. Status feedback provides information on the current state of the system, corrective feedback are responses to inappropriate or meaningless user actions, and guidance shows the user what can be done next. Results of an empirical evaluation of two hi-fi sets are presented in the paper. It is argued that problems encountered by users of these systems can often be explained in terms of flaws in feedback from the system. In a second experiment, feedback improvements were implemented in one of the hi-fi sets. It is concluded that especially corrective feedback on inappropriate user actions seems helpful in the interaction.

In the last paper, Wroblewski, McCandless and Hill argue that conversational utterances in interaction with a machine is a method of 'last resort' because of the demands it places on the user and the problem of building an accurate model of the user in the machine. They therefore present three feedback alternatives to conversational delivery. The first one, *advertising*, draws the user's attention to work materials that bear more work. A typical example is the necessity of correction of misspelled words in a text document after a spell-checking program has indicated errors. The second type, *advertisement by proxy*, includes advertisement of invisible, logically related sources. The last type of feedback, *wear*, guides the user's activity without interrupting the user. The idea is to record information about the use of computational objects that can be displayed on future occasions. All three types of feedback seem to appear from the properties of the objects themselves rather than from an intelligent component in the system, such as a tutor or an assistant.

Part 1

Theoretical Issues in Instructional Communication

Dialogue Constraints in Instruction

Don G. Bouwhuis

Institute for Perception Research/IPO, P.O.Box 513, 5600 MB Eindhoven, The Netherlands, e-mail: bouwhuis@prl.philips.nl

Abstract. Teaching is a special kind of communication between a tutor and a student. Ideally, it seems, this communicative process should be a dialogue, but in contrast to more symmetric dialogues, tutor and student differ substantially in knowledge and skills to be acquired. Also, the tutor is assumed to take most of the initiative, and largely to control the dialogue. A regular dialogue, in addition, contains dialogue control utterances, serving to control the effective flow of information between partners, but utterances of this kind are remarkably rare in instructional dialogues. So, it appears that instructional theory has hardly ever employed dialogue theory in implementing tutoring systems, but also that dialogue research has so far neglected to cover the instructional dialogue. It is argued here that this should be urgently remedied, and that for a considerable time evaluation research on communicative and instructional success will remain necessary.

Keywords. Dialogue, dialogue control, intelligent tutoring systems, cooperation, communication, feedback, computer-assisted instruction, adaptivity

1 Instruction: a typically human endeavour

The activities of the human teacher are generally seen as the ideal form of instruction, despite the incidental and sometimes serious shortcomings that are inevitably connected with the human species of which the teacher is a member. The ideal teacher is considered to be knowledgeable in a particular field, to understand and know the student, to have various teaching strategies and to know how to deal with learning difficulties. So, it has been a particular challenge in the educational world to try and devise intelligent systems which could in principle replace a good teacher. As such, the teacher is the ultimate paragon of an effective tutoring system. One step further on, careful design has aimed at actually improving on the human teacher in limited domains by providing considerable explanatory power.

In actual practice, however, teachers are sometimes far from ideal and not always perfectly knowledgeable and may have rather limited knowledge about their students' individual proficiency. An alternate approach, then, is to implement a comprehensive tutoring system such that the observed shortcomings of human teachers can be avoided, or that the learning process can be optimized for individual students.

Lastly, multimedia technology makes it possible to demonstrate and simulate, in close interaction with the student, many phenomena that have to be learned, which may not be feasible to convey in a classical teacher-student situation. Tutoring systems with powerful simulation and reasoning tools could thus become effective discovery and teaching devices.

But, whatever the teacher may lack, the striking deficit in all implementations of tutoring systems is their very limited communicative ability as compared to the human teacher. The main assertion of this paper is that, in order to become effective, tutoring systems should above all be provided with sufficient communicative power to engage in an interesting and productive student interaction in which knowledge and skills can be acquired in a stable, correct and consistent way. Consequently, teaching and learning are placed in the perspective of a wider communicative framework. But the adoption of the communicative framework also induces practitioners to study actual learning results, rather than teaching means, in order to decide on optimal forms of tutoring systems. Obviously, the suggestion here is that teaching means have had inordinately more attention than learning results.

2 Views of education

In talking about improvement of education, it is a sobering thought that dissatisfaction with education dates back at least to the Ancient World. Criticism of the prevailing educational system has an age-old history and has not declined throughout the centuries; one may well wonder, therefore, whether any new educational system will be successful and not be subject to the same criticisms as all others before it. Chall (1967) described in a wide-ranging analysis how different methods of learning to read succeeded each other at time intervals of about twenty years. She concluded that there is a marked relationship with teacher generation. Young teachers, dissatisfied with the current methods of teaching to read, propose new ways to achieve higher literacy rates. Initially, they generally encounter mostly resistance, but gradually they gain a foothold and eventually succeed in getting their methods and views adopted throughout the reading community. By then, however, confronted with the disadvantages of the method, younger teachers start to revolt against those in power, who, after a long struggle, have become the powers of reaction and so the process starts all over again. Understandably, this evolutionary cycle has more to do with views than with facts, from many investigations it has gradually become clear that the various reading methods all lead to more or less the same result (Mathews, 1966; Reitsma et al., 1981). Important findings in this respect have been that teacher quality is by far the most important single factor in predicting reading success and that the contribution of different methods is only marginal. This is true despite the fact that reading methods can be very different; one might expect different children to benefit from different methods. However, even that seems not to be the case (Reitsma et al., 1981).

The dissatisfaction with current educational methods seems to be grounded variously in a lack of perceived logic, obvious (grave) flaws in the learning material or the manner of its presentation, the occurrence of individual difficulties, pupil failures and negative personal experiences. Unfortunately, the assessment of educational means is rarely supported by reliable statistical evidence of success, while the occurrence of spectacular failures of traditional education is frequently blown up to preposterous proportions, usually accompanied by impressively wide uncertainty margins.

Another particular difficulty is that complainants essentially already know what should be taught and reason from a different point of view than that of the naive pupils at the beginning of the training period which may span only a few weeks, but may also take many years. The ease with which some learned activities are performed by accomplished performers may easily blind them to the specific difficulties experienced by beginners. This is only one facet of the much larger issue of how learning actually takes place. What kinds of perception and memory processes are involved, how is knowledge integrated and how are skills developed? Fundamental and cohesive theory in these areas is still rather limited, although it is considerably more detailed and precise than what passes for learning theory in many educational treatises. But then what is most visible in the education and learning process is instruction, and instruction, too, is a considerably more complex and multifaceted process than many educational technologists assume.

3 Teaching and learning

Teaching denotes the process of knowledge transfer to one or more learners by a teaching source, while learning describes the process whereby the learner acquires the knowledge, presented in whatever way. Optimal teaching, then, would seem to require teaching and learning to be totally complementary, optimal learning does not necessarily imply teaching. It has been observed elsewhere (see e.g., Bouwhuis (1992)) that youngsters in particular pick up a surprising amount of knowledge spontaneously, without a process that could be called 'teaching'. To some extent, this also reflects the distinction between intentional learning and incidental learning. In intentional learning the learner is consciously involved in knowledge uptake and has learning as his or her goal. In incidental learning, however, the learner may be busy with the subject matter, but does not have the intention to learn; nevertheless, more may be learned in this way than by formal training. Take the ease with which the names and many other impressive details of team members in sports can be reproduced, which no school will deem worthy of teaching. However, similar details which are the subject of teaching in history or political science are very unlikely to be remembered with comparable accuracy. It is, therefore, erroneous to think that a learner is entirely dependent on teaching or even, for some fields, may need explicit teaching at all. Nevertheless, teaching may produce insights that would never have been acquired by an individual incidental learner. On the other hand, the contents of teaching may also have a stifling effect on knowledge application to the extent that the learner may take it for granted that there is nothing useful to be explored beyond the material taught.

One distinction is relevant here, namely that between declarative knowledge and skill and, for the present purpose we mainly concentrate on their acquisition. Declarative knowledge may be acquired in a single teaching act or learning trial, and may be successfully stored and remembered. A skill, however, cannot be 'explained' in the same way but is usually acquired by steady repetition over a long period and may still show considerable improvement with time. Inasmuch skill acquisition is largely learner controlled, formal teaching will only have a minor or marginal influence.

4 Instruction: communication and dialogue

Communication is ordinarily defined as the transfer of information from one partner to another by means of a system of symbols or codes. This definition already implies that there must exist at least one level of abstraction: a translation of the items or messages actually transferred. But this is unlikely to be sufficient for teaching applications. Despite the fact that codes in languages are in principle arbitrary, the assignment of a set of existing codes to concepts (the learning material) is not trivial. And, to make things still more difficult, the basic premise of communication is that those codes used not only are adequate representations of the originator's mental images of concepts, but will also certainly lead to corresponding mental images in the receiver.

For communication *per se* we need not suppose that two-way transfer is involved. Many communication processes proceed largely and successfully in a one-way mode; biological messages are a good case in point, as well as radio, TV and various other mass communication media. Eventual responses to messages originating from these sources in general arrive too late, and in a form too different to reshape or modify the original message to any substantial degree. In biological systems this feedback often only takes effect after multiple generations of organisms and does not have any direct effect on message dissemination. In dialogues, however, this situation is drastically changed. Figure 1 depicts the situation, in a rather schematic form, of two partners exchanging messages, and it is clear that disturbances can occur at various points of the message transmission loop.

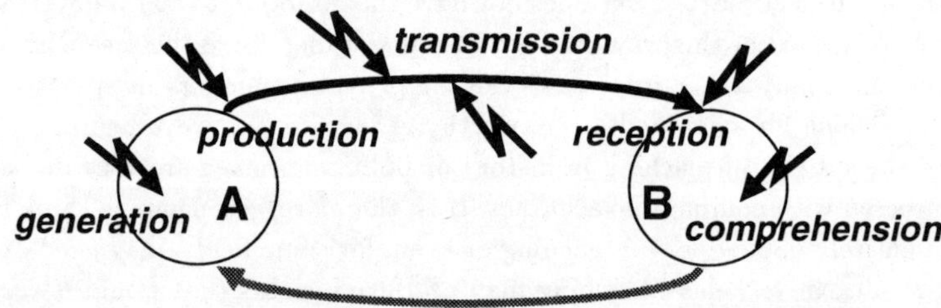

Fig. 1. Schematic depiction of the potential disturbances in the transmission path of a two-way communication process between partners A and B. Possible locations of disturbances are indicated by arrows.

First, as already stated above, psychologically represented knowledge has to be translated into natural language in order to be transmitted. This statement begs the question whether the knowledge is in a state that can be communicated successfully or correctly. Another question is whether the mapping of the mental images and concepts on to natural language words and utterances is adequate – a question that can basically only be answered by analysing the receiver's understanding. Next, pronouncing and articulating the corresponding utterances when the message is coded in speech, may occur suboptimally. The speech signal itself is by definition, like any signal during transmission, subject to noise which adversely affects its quality.

In the next step the reception of the signal is conditioned by the state of the sensory systems, while, finally, when the message has been received, it has to be understood and represented in the same way as the originator intended. Strictly speaking, it is unlikely that, considering the difficulties of transmission, the original message would come across in unmodified form. While this can be called the 'uncertainty principle' of communication, it can easily be seen that, when the receiving partner gives feedback concerning reception of the original message, the feedback message will be subject to essentially the same restrictions. This gives rise to the term 'recursive uncertainty principle' of communication. This situation is known as the Greek generals' problem, which is concerned with improving certainty of communication by means of multiple messengers. While that problem focuses on external influences, the teaching situation forces us to extend this uncertainty principle further into the minds of the originator and receiver, as these seem to be the places where the relevant processes occur.

In normal circumstances this does not seem a particular problem, since the structure of human dialogue bears testimony of being able to cope in many ways with adverse conditions. On closer inspection of what takes place in a dialogue, it becomes clear that essentially all of its properties are directed at combating the inherent uncertainty that underlies the process of information exchange.

Considering this uncertainty, it is clear that the presence of feedback is mandatory for effective communication and essentially necessitates the employment of dialogue. Inasmuch as the successful transfer of mental concepts is the principal goal of teaching, it seems necessary for feedback to be an inherent feature of the instruction process.

Frequently this is not the case. In many automatic teaching systems so much attention is given to formally structuring the learning material that analysis of the learners' responses is lags seriously behind or is lacking altogether (Bouwhuis et al., in press). Consequently, the teaching system is generally unable to direct its instructional strategies to the momentary needs of the learner, which may have several consequences, not all of them necessarily positive.

Though the classical idea of a teacher-student situation involves the notion of a mostly one-way transfer of knowledge, it will be useful to conceive of instruction as a particular kind of dialogue. Dialogue, in turn, is a special case of communication and we will first analyse how the process of human communication necessitates the particular forms in which we can observe dialogues to occur.

5 Properties of dialogue

Dialogues contain two sorts of utterances: a) the actual information bearing messages and b) control utterances that serve only to manage the dialogue and do not transmit factual information (Bunt, this volume). Allwood (this volume) distinguishes two types of dialogue management actions: 'own communication management' and 'interactive communication management', the first serving to manage the speaker's own communication with regard to processing, choice and change, while interaction management serves to structure the flow of information with respect to the listener, the other partner in the dialogue. The latter may include turn-taking, sequencing and feedback. The mere existence of clearly distinguishable management actions may be taken as an indication that dialogues do not proceed as securely as seems at first sight.

One other means of maintaining successful information transfer is the use of redundancy by the originator. Natural language, and spoken language in particular, has a high degree of redundancy on many levels of abstraction, starting with syntactic structure and proceeding down to the composition of the physical signal itself. Strictly speaking, all kinds of redundancy existing only at the originator's end; if the receiver needs all the redundant information in order to decode the message, there is no redundancy at the receiver's side.

On the positive side we may note that in most situations of spoken interaction harmful effects of suboptimal speech production, noisy channels and deficient sensory processing do not occur. Nevertheless, the basic tenet of information theory is too optimistic for language communication. Wiener's information transmission theory states that during repeated transmissions the probability that a message will ultimately be received approaches 1, irrespective of how noisy the channel is. This holds only when the carrier of the message is known beforehand and the interpretation of the message remains at the level of physical coding. In practical situations there is usually a time limit to message transfer that makes frequent repetition infeasible. The major limitations in successful message transfer, therefore, seem to be the cognitive processes responsible for message formation and understanding, processes that correspond to teaching and learning, respectively. Stating that effective teaching is difficult or, more generally, that the process of teaching is ill-understood, is a direct consequence of this principle of recursive uncertainty.

Realizing that an instructional situation is inevitably also a dialogue, it stands to reason that systematic knowledge of dialogues and dialogue protocols should necessarily be an ingredient in the design of instructional dialogues as well. One striking example is the role of dialogue control acts, mentioned above. In current interactive systems performing simple dialogues with users, there is rarely, if ever, any provision for dialogue control. The dialogue has mostly been designed in such a way that its presumed simplicity obviates the need for communicative control. In a teaching situation, however, quite a normal and acceptable dialogue utterance is one indicating whether or not the information presented has been understood. To the extent that teaching systems are designed predominantly for knowledge transfer, the need for dialogue control to guide this process adequately seems crucial. On the other hand, it appears that present-day theorizing on dialogues concentrates on actor pairs who share practically all the necessary background knowledge. In instruction, however, the natural situation is that there is a large divergence of knowledge and, as soon as the knowledge gap has been closed, the instructional dialogue will become pointless.

5.1 Driving sources of dialogue

At this point it will be useful to discuss what factors have been held responsible for driving a dialogue. It will be seen that most notions concerning the driving sources of dialogues have been evolved in the framework of spoken information dialogues, and are not always easily transferable to an instructional situation.

A branch of pragmatics, called Speech Act Theory (e.g. Searle (1969); Perrault (1989); Cohen & Levesque (1988)), holds that 'intentions' drive any dialogue, and that consecutive utterances are generated partly in response to satisfying the original intention and partly in response to the utterance of the other partners. Utterances are assumed to take into account to what extent the dialogue history has altered the states, mostly of knowledge of the partners with respect to the goal. This view reflects the rationality principle, implying that utterances are motivated by reasoning on the basis of knowledge. The limitation of this approach is that it is usually quite difficult to identify the actual intentions with any reliability, except in trivial situations. This difficulty is aggravated in an instructional framework in which the learner's state of knowledge is by definition rather uncertain.

Another theory has been put forward as Conversational Analysis, and its proponents maintain that dialogues are driven by conventions, the more so inasmuch as dialogue utterances are part of detailed "scenarios embedded in fine-grained contexts" (Schegloff, cited by Reichman (1989)). Dialogue utterances, according to this view, have to cope with so many details of the evolving scenario that they can hardly be expected to be controlled continuously by a grand plan. Not surprisingly, the topic of study of conversationalists is actual 'talk' as observed in ongoing dialogues, whereas formal linguists and speech act theorists concentrate mostly on short stretches of sentences, sometimes made up for the purpose.

A third approach, while borrowing some concepts from both of the preceding ones, states that dialogues can be modelled as games (Airenti et al., 1989). The idea is that every dialogue act is an action performed by one of the two actors and the result is shared by both. In this sense, every utterance is a move in a continuously evolving game, invoking an appropriate response from the other actor.

The game approach comes close to what has recently been proposed for fun by a number of researchers, viz. that a dialogue itself is also performed for reasons of fun. People enjoy talking to one another and a dialogue is satisfying for that reason.

It may be noted here that none of these descriptions is necessarily incompatible with the others; it is the point of observation that is different, different aspects of the dialogue being studied in all frameworks.

6 Cooperation in dialogue

For a dialogue situation it is mostly implicitly assumed that both partners are participating in it willingly and have the same possibilities for taking the initiative, or interrupting and continuing the dialogue. In addition, the partners' roles are mostly assumed to be symmetrical and utterances to bear a logical sequential relation to each other. Dialogues are thus considered to be governed also by cooperation. This is rather different from delivery in teaching where the teacher almost alone determines the course of the dialogue, which may ultimately degenerate into a monologue in which the role of the learner is reduced to passive listening. Of course, it is largely this situation which has provoked the wrath of learning theorists, insisting that superior methods of teaching should involve far more interaction, which is not only feasible but also far more effective for learning. The real problem then, however, is how the concept of cooperation employed in theoretical dialogue descriptions should be modified to fit the teaching and learning situation.

Cooperation does not just come out of the blue. Essentially, it has to satisfy a number of preconditions, which it may be worth while to explore in their own right. Entertaining a dialogue in the first place presupposes that, when one partner talks, the other listens, and vice versa. This reciprocity principle equally holds for higher levels of abstraction: speech should be recognized and understood and a reply should have a relation to what has just been said. If the reply is totally unrelated to the previous utterance, the dialogue will generally be abondoned at that point, but such cases are mostly considered to be pathological. Many dialogues do not feature any cooperative endeavour in the sense that both partners are aiming at a shared goal, but can still be conducted for protracted periods without any artificial means. An ordinary row is a good example of when the interests of the two partners conflict. Both want to impose their opinion at the cost of the other's, and actually oppose any moves of the partner, who is usually seen as the opponent. The Argument Clinic sketch by Monty Python is an instructive, and probably classical, case in point (Table 1).

It should be obvious that an argument can only exist when the two partners have contradictory goals, and try explicitly to be as uncooperative as possible. To achieve this, considerable ingenuity is employed by Mr. Barnard (Cleese), the not-so-conciliatory argument specialist, who on hearing the client's complaint "I came here for a good argument", replies "No, you came here for an argument", even denying that it is a good argument. The fact that people carry on talking for so long with inherently clashing opinions is humorous for the reason that it is recognizable: arguments can take a considerable time. The concept of rationality seems not to apply, but cooperation is by definition absent. A counter-argument on a higher level of abstraction might be that cooperation is still demonstrated by both partners inasmuch as they succeed in having an argument whith each other which functions as a common goal. Not only is this precisely the reason why this scene is absurd, but it also relegates the term 'cooperation' to describing anything, and so it would serve no useful purpose for a functional and generalizable description of what takes place in a dialogue.

Table 1. The Argument Clinic. © 1972 Buddah Records.

P: *Michael Palin, client;*
B: *Mr. Barnard (John Cleese) staff member Argument dept.*
P: *knocks on door*
B: Come in!
P: Is this the room for an argument?
B: I told you once...
P: No, you haven't.
B: Yes, I have.
P: When?
B: Just now!
P: No, you didn't.
B: I did.
P: Didn't!
B: Dìd!
P: Dìdn't!
B: I'm telling you I did.
P: You did nòt!
B: Oh, I'm sorry, just one moment. Eh, is this a five minute argument or the full half hour?
P: Oh, just the, eh, five minutes.
B: Ah, thank you. Anyway, I did.
P: You most certainly did not.
B: Look, let's get this thing clear. I quite definitely told you.
P: No, you did not!
B: Yes, I did.
P: No, you didn't.
B: Yes, I did.
P: No, you dìdn't!
B: Yes, I did.
P: You dìdn't!
B: Dìd!
P: Now, look; this isn't an argument.
B: Yes, it is.
P: No, it isn't. It is just contradiction.
B: No. it isn't.
P: It is.
B: It is not.
P: Look, you've just contradicted me.
B: I did not.
P: Oh, you did!
B: No, no, no!
P: You did just then.
B: Nonsense!
P: Oh, this is futile.
B: No, it isn't.
P: I came here for a good argument.
B: No, you didn't. No, you came here for an argument.
P: Well, an argument isn't just contradiction.
B: It can be.
P: No, it can't. An argument is a connected series of statements intended to establish a proposition.
B: No, it isn't.
P: Yes, it is. It's not just contradiction!
B: Look, if I argue with you I must take up a contrary position.
P: Yes, but that's not just saying no, it isn't.
B: Yes, it is.
P: No, it isn't. An argument is an intellectual process; contradiction is just the automatic gainsaying of any statement the other person makes.
B: No, it isn't.
P: Yes, it is.
B: Not at all.
P: Now look... *suddenly Mr B rings a little bell*
B: Good morning!
P: Whàt?
B: That's it. Good morning!
P: Well, I was just getting interested.
B: Sorry, the five minutes is up.
P: That was never five minutes! *(actually only 1'05" have passed at this moment)*
B: I'm afraid it was.
P: It wasn't.
B: I'm sorry, but I'm not allowed to argue anymore!
P: Whààt?
B: If you want me to go on arguing, you have to pay for another five minutes.
P: That was never five minutes just now; oh, come on...
B: *softly humming a melody*
P: Ridiculous!
B: I'm sorry, but I'm not allowed to argue unless you pay.
P: Oh, all right. *(hands over a one pound note)*
B: Thank you.
P: Well?
B: Well what?
P: That wasn't really five minutes just now!
B: I told you, I'm not allowed to argue unless you pay.
P: I just paid!
B: No, you didn't.
P: I did!
B: No, you didn't.
P: Eh, look; I don't want to argue about...
B: No, you didn't pay!
P: Ahà! If I didn't pay, why are you arguing. I got you!
B: No, you haven't.
P: Yes I have; if you're arguing I must have paid.
B: Not necessarily. I could be arguing in my spare time.
P: Oh, I've had enough of this.
B: No, you haven't.
P: Oh, shut up *(exits and slams door)*

It might seem easier to set up a dialogue for an instructional situation than for a more symmetric kind of language interaction, as the initiating and controlling character of the teaching partner will ordinarily be accepted as a default by the student. In addition, it is mostly known beforehand what will be communicated. Many, if not all, automatic teaching systems capitalize on this assumption by prescribing continuously what the student has to do in the interaction, and the only choices left to the student, relate to the topic of study, not the style of the dialogue. Furthermore, while feedback may well be provided in automatic teaching systems, it is almost always concerned exclusively with the status of the learning material, not with the dialogue itself. In other words, the input repertoire of the teaching system is too limited to take account of relevant behavioural features of the student, perception of which enables the dialogue to be redirected in such a way that effective information transfer ensues. An interesting exception is the TEDDI system described by Prince (this volume).

With respect to the material to be learned, the teaching system may be considered to be authoritative, but by itself this need not mean that the instructional dialogue will be effective. As a first approximation rationality seems a minimal criterion for conducting a dialogue in a meaningful way. It is, however, obvious that the rationality implied in the teaching material as such does not include all relevant behavioural phenomena conducive to successful learning.

Rationality is a necessary, but not sufficient, condition for instructional dialogues. Inasmuch as it can often only be established after the fact whether dialogue moves were rational, rationality can hardly serve as a guiding principle for effective instructional dialogues.

6.1 Gricean principles

The instructional dialogue differs in more ways from symmetric dialogue. At first sight delivery teaching and testing for knowledge seem to defy at least some Gricean maxims. The maxim of quantity, for example, not saying more than is necessary, is a questionable one in teaching. It may be quite useful to say more than is strictly necessary from a logical point of view. The concept of repetition goes directly against the maxim of quantity, but is supposed to strengthen the representation of the material on renewed exposure. The maxim of quantity, then, appears to require that the knowledge state or proficiency level of the student is exactly known before the right quantity can be established. When many presentations of the material are needed for learning, the maxim of quantity has lost most of its significance. Likewise, the large difference in domain knowledge between teacher and student makes it hard, maybe impossible to satisfy other maxims put forward by Grice (1975), like relevance and manner (perspicuous, brief, orderly, not obscure and unambiguous). The measure to which all of these properties can be realized is almost totally dependent on the understanding of the student. To know what the student understands, in turn, puts a heavy burden on feedback from the student to the teacher. Nobody will deny that these maxims are highly desirable, especially in a teaching situation; the problem is that it cannot be established when they are realized or how they could be realized. The situation is similar to that of redundancy; while the teacher, or tutoring system may take care that from the originator's side the maxims are satisfied, they need not at all be satisfied be from the learner's point of view.

In a teaching situation rules apply that are not readily accepted in a regular dialogue. This causes speech act theory, the 'intention-driven' approach (Searle, 1969), to be not directly or easily applicable to instructional dialogues. The alternative approach, whereby dialogue utterances must be seen as turns in a game, can certainly cope with a testing situation, but does not provide concrete guiding principles for the design of instructional dialogues. Stating that a dialogue is being engaged in for the purpose of fun seems to indicate the most desirable feature of an instructional dialogue, but generating fun is probably an even more elusive endeavour than implementing other approaches.

7 Diagnosticity

Uncertainty is inherent in any teaching situation in which, ideally, the student's state of knowledge has to be continuously monitored. Uncertainty is two-sided: the teacher may not know how much the student knows and the student may not understand what knowledge is to be acquired. On a deeper level the teacher may not understand why or what the student does not understand and the student may fail to communicate what remains uncertain. Advanced teaching systems, therefore, aim at interpretation of student errors in order to optimize the teaching process. The extent to which an error can be recognized and interpreted depends directly on the size of the domain model and the power of the teaching system's reasoning algorithms. The first difficulty is that students may make errors on different layers of communication in the dialogue, while the system only deals with errors in the application domain it covers. With regard to the domain, however, the knowledge and the reasoning tools are rarely sufficiently complete to cope with all student errors that occur. Designers often see this as a hit-and-miss situation, in which the hit rate has to be maximized. To the student, however, this situation looks very different. This can be explained by what we here call the decision table quandary (Table 2).

Table 2. Types of student response classification by a teaching system with incomplete coverage of the domain and/or insufficient reasoning mechanisms. Correctly scoring a student error is termed a 'hit'.

		system's error classification	
		correct	erroneous
student's response	correct	correct acceptance	false alarm
	incorrect	miss	hit

In trying to correct student errors, the teaching system operates supposedly in the area of incorrect responses, where the hit-rate obviously has to be maximized. However, as not nearly all potential student responses are covered by the system, many responses will be classified as errors, since the usage is unknown to the system, while the responses may be perfectly correct in a general sense. Therefore, the diagnostic performance of the system does not rely on the hit/miss ratio, but rather on the hit/false alarm ratio.

This can be clarified by considering the effect of student proficiency. If a student exhibits low performance, almost anything can be wrong and hopefully detected as incorrect, while at the same time there will be too few correct responses to cause a sizeable false alarm rate to develop. In such a case correct responses are relatively rare so that a 'miss', classifying an incorrect response as correct, is highly undesirable. On the other hand, it may be quite likely for an occasional correct response to be classified as incorrect, leading to an incidental false alarm. Thus, while a high hit/miss ratio might be indicated for low performers, this might lead to learning the wrong things and, at the same time, to causing appreciable frustration, in the sense that errors will be unavoidably exposed, even unjustified ones.

For high performers the situation is different. As most of their responses will be correct, the major variable of interest is the false alarm rate. Proficient students may display considerable variation of expression so that many of their responses may be classified as incorrect. Grammar checkers are a case in point. In a product evaluation test in the early nineties in the Netherlands, it was found that usually more than 50% of all grammatical errors detected by the system consisted of false alarms, mostly because the offending expression was not covered by the grammar rules of the systems. If this happens in a teaching session, students do not really learn anything new, but lose confidence in the system's ability to provide supposedly correct grammatical information. The system thus loses its authority and, with it, its role as a relevant dialogue partner. Interestingly from the student's point of view, the system violates Gricean maxims to the extent that it appears to state things which the student knows to be false.

8 Adaptivity

From the foregoing discussions it should be clear that a dialogue is inherently adaptive because, if it were not, it would be abolished as not serving the purpose it was started for. Likewise, it is widely accepted that teaching systems should be adaptive in the sense that they should monitor the student state of knowledge in order to modify the teaching material and the teaching strategy for optimal learning effects.

Two subtly different forms of adaptivity can be distinguished, namely *adaptive* systems which retain largely the same strategy, but choose the learning material in accordance with momentary needs or goals, and *adaptable* systems which may change the teaching strategy and interaction form to suit the proficiency level of the student. There may be considerable overlap between the two kinds.

Adaptivity as described here needs qualified application. In order to adapt learning material optimally to the student, an accurate assessment of what is most needed must be made. In addition, this requires a workable definition of what exactly needs to be optimized. Depending on the student's encoding and storage processes, the presentation schedules of learning items are different according to what criterion is employed (Ellerman, 1991). The criterion could be to learn a set of items in the lowest possible number of presentations, or to learn first one item to a preset criterion, then another, and so on; yet another might be to learn a limited number of items perfectly. All of these criteria lead to different presentation strategies.

Designed adaptability also has marked drawbacks, however. Adaptability gives the user the impression that the system is more intelligent than it actually is. Any ensuing disappointment can then give rise to considerable frustration and confusion. Changing the nature of the interaction as a result of adaptation may also give rise to unpredictability, making the user uncertain with regard to the type of responses to be given. Considerations such as these, which have strong empirical support (see Taylor & Hunt (1989, p. 483)) suggest that built-in adaptability should be limited and that adaptation should be sufficiently gradual not to be noticed by the student.

Assessment of what the student knows at any particular moment can, of course, only proceed on the basis of the student's response. So, any response has to be interpreted as clues of the student's knowledge, but the validity of that response with regard to the actual knowledge may be less than perfect. Take for instance the distinction between an error and a slip (Norman, 1981), where an error is thought to be the result of incomplete or erroneous knowledge necessarily leading to a wrong response. A slip is an unintentional wrong response, when the intended response was correct. Humans engaged in a dialogue have considerable leeway in handling this latter type of error that often passes unnoticed as the context is usually sufficiently restricting. An automatic teaching system, however, generally has nothing else to rely on other than the response quality proper with the concomitant hazards of misclassification and wrong interpretation, just as indicated in the decision table shown before. Adaptivity might, therefore, be frequently ill-directed.

9 Teaching declarative knowledge and training skills

In the field of learning one can distinguish between the acquisition of declarative knowledge (the learning of rules, facts and the relations between them) and the acquisition of skills. The first type of learning is addressed by means of Intelligent Tutoring Systems (ITSs) and the second by drill-and-practice systems, usually called Computer-Based Instruction (CBI). Both types also require different types of instructional dialogue. In the knowledge-acquisition case, the relative complexity of the instruction can be readily coped with by means of dialogue; errors can be detected and corrected and explanations can be provided, though misinterpretations can easily arise, as discussed above. In the skill-acquisition case, long series of responses may be entirely correct, and the main goal of the system is to provide extensive training such that responses will become automatized.

This calls for different types of feedback and interpretation, while, in addition, hardly any explanation is required. Adequate feedback, however, has to be provided in order to ensure that motivation does not decrease to a point where the practice system does not have any specific advantages over other methods of training. It seems, however, that feedback in such a case requires considerable elaboration of the learning material (see Spaai (this volume)) in order to provide a sufficiently stimulating learning environment for the student.

10 Research orientation: method or result?

Many investigators of the educational process have strong convictions about how teaching should be performed. As a result, there is a strong focus on teaching methods that are assumed to lead automatically and naturally to improved learning. Rarely are learning results evaluated in actual practice (Bouwhuis et al., in press), and generally one finds improved performance, if at all, only in the initial stages of usage of the system. The almost universal concentration on method, thus, leads to extensive theoretical development of supposedly important properties of teaching systems, of a generally high abstract level. Some examples of these have been discussed above, and they include cooperation, adaptation and rationality. Often these concepts are even stated to be guiding principles or design rules according to which the instructional dialogue should be implemented. The current position defended here is that all three concepts are interpretations of the observed behaviour after the fact – not guiding principles, but rather consequences. A similar inversion of concepts can be seen in the treatment by Connah (this volume) of autonomous agents. In Connah's system seemingly strategic behaviour can be observed where it was not built in in the first place. Cooperation can be observed and, inasmuch as the result is achieved, the behaviour is rational and seems to ensue from an intention. In reality, however, there is only behaviour of a very simple type that is completely determined by boundary conditions. As boundary conditions can vary randomly the system may even give an impression of flexibility, but that, too, has not been built in.

The status of concepts such as adaptivity has been effectively clarified by Kiss (1988). Consider, for example, the concept of road holding in a car. In contrast to other features, such as braking, lighting, heating and ventilation, it is impossible to indicate the assembly that is responsible for roadholding. Roadholding is typically a result of the cooperation of many mechanical components and modules that cannot be directly predicted from the individual assemblies. Probably nobody denies the value of intention, flexibility, cooperation and rationality in a teaching system. The real question is whether those properties will not be an automatic consequence of conducting teaching in the form of a natural dialogue with a proper use of feedback. Despite the fact that theoretical treatment of dialogues in instruction is still in its infancy, it seems clear that, if the properties of that typical human interaction form, the dialogue, are not taking into account, automatic teaching systems will remain a tantalizing challenge. For ever.

As long as systematic knowledge of the teaching and learning situation and about the usability of dialogue systems is largely absent, it seems unavoidable to guide the design of tutoring systems by the results of evaluation research. Two types of research are indicated: first, the efficiency of the dialogue system has to be investigated during the designing of the instructional dialogue. Next, the long-term educational effects of such tutoring systems have to be explored – an issue that has been largely neglected in present-day educational research. Considering the advent of the microworld approach in education (diSessa, this volume), it might also be worthwhile to study and devise dialogue systems that rely less on natural language but include substantial graphical interaction.

References

Airenti, G., Bara, B.G. & Colombetti, M. (1989) Knowledge for communication. In: Taylor, M.M., Néel, F. & Bouwhuis, D.G. (eds.) The Structure of Multimodal Dialogue. Amsterdam: North Holland.

Bouwhuis, D.G. (1992) Cognitive Modeling and Learning. In: Engel, F.L., Bouwhuis, D.G., Bösser, T. & d'Ydewalle, G. (eds.) Cognitive Modeling and Interactive Environments in Language Learning. NATO ASI Series F, Vol. 87. Berlin: Springer.

Bouwhuis, D.G., van Hoe, R. & Bouma, H. (in press) Advancing education by proper technology. Liao, T. (ed.) Proceedings of the Capstone Conference of the NATO ASI Advanced Research Workshops on Advanced Educational Technology, Grenoble, 1993. Berlin: Springer.

Chall, J. (1967) Learning to Read: the Great Debate. New York: McGraw-Hill.

Cohen, P.R. & Levesque, H. (1988) Persistence, intention and commitment. In: Cohen, P.R., Morgan, J. & Pollack, M.E. (eds.) The role of intentions and plans in communication and discourse. Cambridge, MA: MIT Press.

Ellerman, H.H. (1991) MIR: A monitor for initial reading. Ph.D. thesis, Eindhoven University of Technology.

Grice, P. (1975) Logic and Conversation. In: Cole, P. & Morgan, J.L. (eds.) Syntax and Semantics: Speech Acts. Vol. 11. New York: Academic Press, 41–58.

Kiss, G. (1988) Personal communication in a discussion at the meeting of the European Association of Cognitive Ergonomics, Cambridge, 1988.

Mathews, M.M. (1966) Teaching to Read. Chicago: University of Chicago Press.

Norman, D.A. (1981) A categorization of action slips. Psychological Review, 79, 1–21.

Perrault, C.R. (1989) Speech Acts and Multimodal Dialogues. In: Taylor, M.M., Néel, F. & Bouwhuis, D.G. (eds.) The Structure of Multimodal Dialogue. Amsterdam: Elsevier North-Holland.

Reichman, R. (1989) Convention versus intention. In: Taylor, M.M., Néel, F. & Bouwhuis, D.G. (eds.) The Structure of Multimodal Dialogue. Amsterdam: Elsevier North-Holland.

Reitsma, P., Komen, N. & Kapinga, T. (1981) Methoden voor aanvankelijk lezen: een vergelijking van leerresultaten na een jaar (Methods for initial reading: a comparison of learning results after one year) Pedagogische Studiën, 58, 174–189.

Searle, J.R. (1969) Speech Acts. Cambridge: Cambridge University Press.

Taylor, M.M. & Hunt, M.J. (1989) Flexibility versus Formality. In: Taylor, M.M., Néel, F. & Bouwhuis, D.G. (eds.) The Structure of Multimodal Dialogue. Amsterdam: Elsevier North-Holland.

Asymmetry and Accommodation in Tutorial Dialogues

David A. Good

Department of Social & Political Sciences, University of Cambridge,
Free School Lane, Cambridge CB2 3RQ, United Kingdom,
email: dg25@phoenix.cambridge.ac.uk

Abstract. This paper considers the nature of the different contributions of both tutor and tutee to tutorial dialogues. It stresses the importance of collaboration and cooperation, and of exploiting the knowledge of the teacher and the experience of ignorance of the tutee, but argues against the idea that the teacher must have a model of the tutee on the grounds that it is both impracticable and unnecessary. Instead, it is argued that the teacher needs an adequate model of the task, skill or knowledge base being taught, and a strategy for increasing or decreasing levels of help and control as a function of a tutee's varying degrees of success at any point in the dialogue. Examples and theory from work in language pathology and developmental psychology are exploited in this argument. Finally, attention is drawn to the problem of ceding too much control to the tutee, and the necessity of maintaining a tutorial demand from the tutor.

Keywords. Dialogue, tutorial systems, cooperation, Gricean maxims, repair in conversation, Vygotsky

1 Introduction

Many theories of pragmatic inference in dialogue have been influenced by the work of Grice (1975) and Grice (1989), or the many neo-Gricean descendants who have followed him. This is true irrespective of whether the concern has been with instructional, pedagogical or other kinds of dialogue, and whether or not the participants have been natural or artificial. The precise nature of the inferential machinery which does the work has always been a matter of debate, but common to the claims of both Grice and those who have used his work has been the claim that participants in a conversation will always assume that their interlocutors are cooperative or rational beings. This inviolable assumption is the basis on which many aspects of pragmatic interpretation are built. When an utterance ostensibly violates, for example, Grice's conversational maxims, and, thereby, the assumption that the speaker is rational or cooperative is challenged, hearers do not conclude that the speaker is, in fact, being uncooperative or irrational. Instead, they seek an interpretation of the utterance and a context which enables the assumption that the speaker is being cooperative or rational to be preserved. This account, in the original form in which Grice offered it, has always had a somewhat paradoxical air, because cooperation is taken to be something which isolated individuals assume, and not something which collaborative agents achieve. As an alternative to this view, I have proposed elsewhere that the assumption of cooperativity or rationality is vulnerable to challenge, and that the speaker's standing in a conversation as a cooperative or rational interlocutor is an achievement based on how he or she performs, (Good, 1991).

The data offered to support this argument came from a case study of an interaction between a thought-disordered schizophrenic and a psychologist. There, the sense that the schizophrenic was thought-disordered, and thus neither cooperative nor rational, arose in the course of an extended other-initiated repair sequence[1] where he understood, it would seem, the general demands of the exchange, but failed to provide suitable material to effect the repair which the other participant had requested. In essence, he had said something which she did not understand. She asked for clarification. He recognised that this was what she was doing, but what he said did not make his initial utterance any clearer. So, she re-initiated the repair sequence. He recognised this, but failed again to provide an adequate repair. This cycle was then repeated several times. Through the course of this sequence, his standing in the conversation seems to change, and one gets the increasing sense that he is unable to perform as a rational competent conversationalist. The reason for this would seem to lie in the specific demands of the repair in an other-initiated repair sequence, and his failure to cope with them.

A moment's reflection reveals that other-initiated repair places substantial demands on the speaker who must accomplish it. If I say something which you find unclear, then to get to the point of saying something which clarifies matters by offering a repair, I must be able to do several things. First, I must recognise that a repair sequence has been initiated, and that your repair initiation does not concern some extra-conversational material. Second, the utterance or utterance-part which needs repairing must be identified. Obviously, referring to something spoken which is unclear is not simple since it will only exist in the memory of the interlocutors; the range of things being referred to might be quite large, especially if there is a relatively late initiation of the repair; and the defining characteristic, a lack of clarity, might only be available to the repair-initiator. Finally, a repair must be formulated. For it to be an adequate repair, I need to understand what was problematic about the original item for you, and what can solve that problem. To satisfy these demands, the speaker must be able to use considerable knowledge of the addressee, and design an utterance specifically for him or her. That addressee, in turn, will be alert to this fact, or at least the quality of the utterance offered compared to his or her need, and, on the basis of that comparison draw conclusions about the speaker's willingness and ability to be a cooperative conversationalist.

Other-initiated repair sequences are a principal occasion when it is clear that an utterance is designed with a specific addressee in mind. Although it is tempting to think that all those who speak to us are always this attentive to our needs, there are reasons to believe that this is not so. The demands of real-time production are

---

[1] The classic paper on repair is Schegloff, Jefferson & Sacks (1977), and the specific type of sequence which occurred in this exchange is first discussed in Jefferson (1972).

such that we often understate our point or make it less than perfectly. As Levinson (1989) argued, the most expedient strategy in conversation is to 'understate and oversuppose' because subsequent adjustments, be they self or other initiated can be used to clarify any pragmatic failures if they occur. This suggests that there is a dimension of sartorial exactitude in conversation, and that the tailoring of utterances ranges from 'one-size-fits-all' through 'off-the-peg' to 'bespoke'. Bespoke utterances reveal a real orientation to the specific needs of the other, and the extent to which the speaker can satisfy them.

Certain implications followed from this argument concerning theory and method in the study of pragmatics. Theories which propose an inviolable assumption of rationality or cooperativity are inevitably lead to an over-estimation of the computational demands which confront the hearer because seemingly any utterance, no matter how devoid of context, nor how stripped of prosodic and paralinguistic detail, can be admitted as data. Given sufficient time, more or less any utterance can be given a reading, but this does not mean that this is a reading one could or would derive when faced with it in conversation as a real time task. Nor does it mean that the extensive cognitive resources available to derive that reading are the same as those used ordinarily. This over-estimation of the personal cognitive resources which the individual would require is allied to a failure to recognise the use which conversationalists can make of the cognitive resources provided by the other participants. This failure inevitably follows from an overly restrictive focus on single utterances as having a definite and fixed interpretation. This rules out consideration of how interpretive problems might be solved using the interlocutor's knowledge over a sequence of turns thereby establishing a collaborative cognitive solution.

This view of conversation also carries implications for the analysis and design of pedagogical dialogues of one sort or another which I believe are relevant to the idea of Interactive Student Modelling. I will begin, though, with a brief consideration of the basic metaphor which seems to underlie many conceptions of information transfer in conversation, and why we might think that teaching is impossible.

2 The building blocks of knowledge

Inevitably, instructional dialogues are based on an asymmetry of knowledge and competence. The teacher has more, the student has less, and the aim of tuition or instruction is to reduce the difference. The teacher is to increase the student's knowledge, skill or expertise, often, although by no means always, by the transfer of knowledge from teacher to student. There is a great temptation to view this process as one in which the teacher discerns the precise contours of the student's knowledge, and decides what piece of knowledge can be added most usefully. This view has a long history in education, and has pervaded much psychological theorising on human communication.

A construction or building metaphor often seems to underlie many discussions of this kind of dialogue. The role of the teacher is to add appropriately sized building blocks to whatever partial structures there are in the student's head so as to build a larger or more elaborate structure that begins to approximate that which is in the teacher's head. It is like building a free-stone wall. The problems of choosing the correct stones to add to the incomplete wall, and how to add them, parallel the problems of presenting new knowledge to a student or novice. Those who have knocked over a free-stone wall while rambling in the upland areas of the British Isles will know that such walls are very hard to build, and are equally difficult problems which face the teacher who works with this view. Indeed, it is tempting to think that the problems are so great that teaching is impossible. Amongst those which must be addressed in this process we might note the following, most of which seem fairly self-evident if one accepts the building metaphor.

First, you need to know what you know. Unless you, as the teacher, know what you know at some level, you will not have an idea of the target you are aiming at. Second, you need to know what the student knows. The classic problem in any kind of teaching is to present material that is not already known, and is neither too simple, nor too advanced. To know the right level to offer, you need to know what is already there. There is no point in building a part of the wall which is already in place, nor trying to build on a structure which is not yet in place. Third, you need to know what is a suitably sized addition to the student's structures, not too big and not too small. This is related to the previous point in that what counts as a reasonable addition depends upon the nature of the structure which is in place. It will obviously vary as a function of many factors, but again the teacher needs to know the profile of the student's knowledge.

These first three problems seem to come together in the fourth which is that you need to know what it is like to not know what you know. Not only must the teacher choose an appropriately sized and shaped addition, but it should also be remembered that what is offered to the student can be packaged in many ways. The ways in which the same thing can be said seem to be more or less without limit. The one to choose is the one which makes the package most intelligible, but to know what makes for intelligibility, the teacher needs to know what it is like to be in the student's position of both not knowing the specific thing being taught and a range of other related things. That is, a position of not knowing. Unsurprisingly, some would argue that this is an impossible mental perspective to adopt. To understand why, consider Figure 1.

This is a classic ambiguous figure of a young woman and an old woman. Many people, on first seeing it can only see one interpretation, usually the young woman, and cannot see the other. After a variable degree of advice, almost everyone can see both, and then cannot, of course, rediscover the sense of not seeing the one which was originally hard to find. Nor, most importantly can they rediscover the sense of what it is like to be given the advice on what to see when they know what is already there.

In other words, the design of an appropriate bespoke utterance by a teacher for a student depends on a model of that student which seems difficult, if not impossible, for the teacher to build. How difficult it is will depend greatly on the nature and

Fig. 1. Ambiguous portrait of a young woman and an old woman.

scope of the knowledge which is being transferred and the scale of the difference between teacher and student. However, for any reasonably large and interesting knowledge or skill base where the difference between teacher and student is not minimal, then the problems become quite unmanageable. Indeed, under this view of the process, it might seem that teaching is an impossible exercise.

However, in schools, universities and many other places this problem does not prove to be an insurmountable obstacle, and teaching is accomplished. Sometimes this is because the teacher can exploit the capacity of the students to cope with the *one-size-fits-all* or *off-the-peg* utterances mentioned above. At other times, this is because the teacher does not need to solve these communicative problems in isolation. At hand, there is the student who is the expert on those things where the teacher has the greatest difficulties. While the teacher is the expert with respect to the knowledge taught, the student is the expert in ignorance. Thus, it becomes essential to structure the dialogue as a collaborative cognitive exercise where the resources of each partner are deployed most effectively to solve the problem of designing pedagogically effective utterances. Saying this is much easier than doing it, but there are suggestions in the developmental psychology literature as to how we might approach this problem.

3 Vygotsky's blocks

These suggestions come from a series of studies by Wood and his co-workers (Wood et al., 1978) which tries to add some interactional flesh to Vygotsky's notion of the *zone of proximal development* (Vygotsky, 1962). In contrast to Piagettian analyses of cognitive development, Vygotsky was not simply concerned with understanding development as a function of an individual's current abilities, but also as a function of his or her ability to engage and work collaboratively with other more experienced people. The zone of proximal development is the difference between the individual's current competence, and the level he or she can attain when working with help from someone with greater expertise. It will vary across individuals because it depends upon the nature of the contributions which both novice and expert are able to make to the dialogue.

In the Wood et al. study, the mothers of four or five year old children were asked to teach their children how to build a small wooden figure. Different pairings of mother and child achieved this with varying degrees of ease, and by using differing conversational startegies. Wood et al. examined these, and classified the mothers' utterances to their children in line with the scheme of five levels given in Figure 2. As we move down this list from Level 1 to Level 5, the specificity of the instructions given by the mother with respect to the structure of the task increases. Correspondingly, the responsibility of the child for choosing his or her precise actions decreases. Wood et al. found that there were variations in the level adopted by different moth-

Level 1: General verbal encouragement
Level 2: Specific verbal instruction
Level 3: Assists in choice of material
Level 4: Prepares material for assembly
Level 5: Demonstrates operation

Fig. 2. Classification of mothers' utterances to their children, based on Wood et al. (1978)

ers, and in the uniformity of their choice of level over time. Some mothers went to one extreme and offered their children a lot of general encouragement (level 1), but not much else. Others gave an almost constant diet of specific demonstrations (level 5). Children who were confronted with such consistency in the type of assistance offered tended not to do well subsequently when left to their own devices, and faced with similar task demands.

Some mothers, however, adopted a variable strategy, and their children performed better when left to their own devices when working on similar tasks. These mothers, when working with their children, would intervene as a function of the child's level of success. When the child was clearly making no progress at all, they would give a specific demonstration of the part of the task that was proving problematic for the child, a level 5 type of assistance. If the child successfully copied what the mother had done, she would respond by moving up a level or two so that her instructions became less specific, and the child's responsibility for the completion of the next stage was increased. If he or she was successful again, the mother would give him or her yet more responsibility, by moving up another level. This would continue until the child began to fail at which point the mother would take a progressively more interventionist strategy.

The net result was that the child received assistance that was related to his or her own level of success, and the mother's understanding of the task, and the degrees of intervention which were possible. One could conceive of the mother as having a strategy based on a substantial model of her child's ability, but this would seem to be completely unnecessary. This is not to say, of course, that the mother is some kind of mindless automaton who has no conception of her child. She clearly needs to understand what that child responds to in general as encouragement, and how it responds to stress and difficulty, but these are not specific to this task.

4 Implications

Obviously, one cannot draw clear conclusions on the basis of one experiment such as this. Nevertheless, the suggestions it offers, and the analysis which preceded it concerning the importance of collaborative work in dialogue, and the impossibility of teaching if we take an incorrect view of tutor and student, leads to a different emphasis. The focus is then on student modelling through interaction by tutor and student rather than on student modelling by tutor as a prerequisite for interaction. If we take this focus, we can point to certain necessary elements in tutorial systems, many of which one would predict from other perspectives too, but to conclude I will focus on one aspect which seems peculiar to this vision.

It is clear that a central feature in such a system is an adequate theory of the task, skill or knowledge base being taught. This is hardly a novel observation, but the lesson from the Vygotskyan perspective is twofold. First, that an important element is a way of monitoring for success or failure in making progress, and the opportunity for the learner to seek help. Second, a hierarchy of help that varies the degree of control that is taken from the student, and the degree of specificity of the help that is offered as a function of what has gone before. Essentially, a context-sensitive tutorial that includes within it a sensitivity to the previous levels of assistance which have been offered, and the level of success of the student previously.

If one moves to a student or user centred focus, in the sense that the student's or user's behaviour plays a much greater role in driving the system, there is the prospect that the system will be built to maximise explicit user control of the instruction which is offered. Numerous systems allow users a degree of optionality in the way that they access them in the belief that this will optimise the benefits which the user can gain. In some circumstances this may be so, but it is important to bear in mind how technological developments can radically alter pre-existing author-reader, pedagogue-student, and other similar relationships, and that the changes which follow are not necessarily beneficial. An important part of the tutorial dialogue in the Vygotskyan interpretation is the way in which, in ceding control to the learner, the teacher's contribution become ever more difficult to interpret as a function of the student being successful and what the teacher knows. The importance of this relationship should not be underestimated, and in arguing for a greater focus on the task and student performance it should not be forgotten that the tutorial dialogue arises from a three part relationship between student, tutor and task.

References

Good, D.A. (1991) Repair and cooperation in conversation. In: Luff, P., Gilbert, N. & Frohlich, D. (eds.) Computers and conversation. London: Academic Press.

Grice, H.P. (1989) Studies in the way of words. Cambridge, Mass: Harvard University Press.

Grice, P. (1975) Logic and Conversation. In: Cole, P. & Morgan, J.L. (eds.) Syntax and Semantics: Speech Acts. Vol. 11. New York: Academic Press, 41–58.

Jefferson, G. (1972) Side sequences. In: Sudnow, D. (ed.) Studies in social interaction. New York: Free Press.

Levinson, S.C. (1989) Minimization and conversational inference. In: Verschueren, J. & Bertuccelli-Papi, M. (eds.) The pragmatic perspective. Amsterdam: Benjamins.

Schegloff, E.A., Jefferson, G. & Sacks, H. (1977) The preference for self-correction in the organization of repair in conversation. Language, 53, 361–382.

Vygotsky, L.S. (1962) Thought and language. Cambridge, Mass: MIT Press. Originally in Russian in 1936.

Wood, D.J., Wood, H.A. & Middleton, D.J. (1978) An Experimental Evaluation of Four Teaching Strategies. International Journal of Behavioural Development, 1(2), 131–147.

Negotiation in Collaborative Problem-Solving Dialogues

Michael J. Baker

CNRS, Laboratoire IRPEACS, Equipe "COAST", Ecole Normale Supérieure de Lyon, 46 Allée d'Italie, 69364 Lyon cedex 07, France, email: Michael.Baker@ens.ens-lyon.fr.

Abstract. Although understanding collaborative problem-solving (CPS) is currently recognised as an important problem, little research has been done on analysing/modelling dialogues produced in such contexts. An approach to analysing/modelling CPS dialogues as 'negotiations' at the domain-task level is described, based on a corpus of physics problem-solving dialogues. Two specific subproblems are addressed: the 'co-construction problem' — describing how partial intermediate solutions are interrelated in dialogue in order to converge on agreement — and the 'agreement problem' — identifying when students are agreed and with respect to what. In conclusion, it is argued that agreement should be analysed in terms of the attitude 'acceptance' rather than 'belief'.

Keywords. Collaborative problem-solving, dialogue, negotiation, belief, acceptance

1 Introduction

Understanding collaborative problem-solving (CPS) is important from a number of perspectives. However, as Barbieri & Light (1991) point out, despite an extensive research literature on peer interaction from Piagetian and Vygotskyan perspectives, 'studies in collaborative learning at the computer usually do not go into a detailed analysis of the interaction' (p. 3). One recent exception is the research of Behrend et al. (1988), where the approach was proposed of analyzing the 'Joint Problem Space', constructed by pairs of students working at a physics learning environment. In particular, this approach aimed to identify when students were collaborating and when they were not from analysis of conversational structures (for example, 'collaborative completions' of utterances). As we discuss below, several more specific problems remain to be addressed. Artificial intelligence and education research has also recently shown interest in CPS in order to construct computer-based 'co-learners' (Chan & Baskin, 1988; Chan et al., 1992; Dillenbourg & Self, 1992), this being the longer term aim of the research presented here.

When students collaborate in problem-solving they may engage in dialogue in order to co-construct jointly agreed solutions. But how do they do this? How do students co-construct solutions in dialogue, and how do they establish agreement with respect to them? Initially the answers may appear obvious: each student proposes possible partial solutions, which are then accepted or not, and so the dialogue progresses towards an agreed solution. This is oversimplified in at least two ways.

Firstly, joint solutions are not constructed by a simple accumulation of individually proposed statements since successive contributions 'build on' previous ones in different ways (successive refinement). The question therefore arises as to how, precisely, students interrelate their contributions in order to co-construct solutions (let us call this the *co-construction problem*). Secondly, *feedback* with respect to acceptance and agreement is often implicit in dialogue, which thus poses the problems of identifying when students are agreed or not, on what precisely they are agreed and even what it means, theoretically, to be 'agreed' in this context (let us call this the *agreement problem*).

We claim that viewing the processes of co-construction of problem solutions in dialogue as a type of *negotiation* can provide an approach to solving the above mentioned problems. In order to show this we shall draw on a corpus of dialogues generated by pairs of students solving simple mechanics problems in physics. The paper is structured as follows. After presenting an initial illustrative dialogue extract, an analysis of negotiation is developed. The two subsequent sections deal with analysis of specific aspects of negotiation processes, namely relations between contributions to problem solutions ('co-construction problem'), and the processes whereby agreement is established ('agreement problem'). The paper concludes with some implications for future models for CPS in dialogue.

2 An example

Our analysis method is being developed using a corpus of dialogues generated by students (aged 16–17 years) who attempted to solve simple mechanics problems in physics. The dialogues were recorded in schools in the Lyon region. The problem given was of an open-ended kind, not normally set in the curriculum, and was thus designed to provoke intensive discussion and to oblige the students to draw on and externalise their conceptions of physics concepts (energy). The students were provided with experimental materials and asked to determine a property of balls of different substances that enabled their rebound behaviour to be interpreted and hence explained in terms of the concepts of *energy*. The students were asked to produce a single solution upon which they were agreed.

The following extract is taken from the middle of a face-to-face verbal dialogue (approximately 1.5 hours long). Prior to the extract, the students had allowed two balls of the same size, one made of rubber, the other of plastic, to fall at the same time from the same height. They agreed that the rubber ball had rebounded 5 cm lower than the plastic one. S2 then put forward the explanation that the difference was due to the respective masses, S1 did not agree, and so they decided to consider what would happen in the simpler case of an inelastic impact.

Dialogue Extract 1[1]

1 S1: ...so, what can we say if there's an inelastic impact?

---

[1] The extract has been translated from the original French (see Appendix A).

2 S2: well, that the energy... all the energy...
3 S1: well, that the kinetic energy is theoretically nil
4 S2: it's nil on arrival, in fact...
5 S1: since... since the object stops, in fact, ah yes, especially since there it doesn't move, uh...
6 S2: it's nil at the start, and it's nil on arrival...... about energy... yes, but at the moment of an inelastic impact, what is it that...
7 S1: we've been doing that for a while now!
8 S2: but we've also...
9 S1: wait... inelastic impact, right, you've conservation of momentum, but... the kinetic energy isn't conserved! I think that's what we've seen... the elastic impact, by contrast, both are conserved...
10 S2: Yes, elastic impact, there's the total energy which is conserved...
11 S1: Yes...

Due to the joint explicit agreement ("Yes") in 10 and 11, most observers would probably agree that at the end of this extract the students have reached some kind of agreement. But what are they agreed on? One possible solution may be glossed as:

> 'in the case of an inelastic impact, the kinetic energy is nil on arrival and nil at the start; thus momentum but not kinetic energy is conserved; in an elastic impact both are conserved.'

However, we can not find an explicit statement of this 'gloss' in the dialogue, nor is it a simple conjunction of several statements. In fact what seems to happen is that an initially stated partial solution (2-'the energy') is successively *transformed* or *refined* by both speakers in order to lead to a composite solution on which both students can agree. For example, 2 ('the energy') is refined in 3 ('the kinetic energy is nil') by restricting the concept of energy to a specific type of energy (kinetic) and by giving a specific value for it (nil). In 4 an additional relevant feature of the problem situation is added (nil on arrival), and so the refinement process continues. From an analytical point of view, therefore, we need some principled means for describing these 'refinement' processes (the 'co-construction problem'). We shall attempt to do this by *specifying types of relations between problem solution elements in dialogue.*

Given that our intuitions concerning agreement relate to joint explicit agreement (in 10 and 11), what can we say about the middle of this extract (2-9), where there is no explicit agreement of this kind? For example, in 3 S1 completes S2's incomplete proposition: does this mean that S1 *accepts* S1's proposal, or not? In this example we might want to say that a proposition concerning 'kinetic energy' in some way presupposes acceptance of a previous one concerning 'energy'. The concept of *presupposition* is not without its difficulties in pragmatics; however, even if a clear notion of presupposition was available, we can observe large number of other cases where it is difficult to find a principled way of deciding what is agreed, how, and why, and what is not.

We can begin to address these issues by viewing collaborative co-construction of problem solutions in dialogue as a kind of *negotiation,* at the level of the problem-solving domain. The next section gives a sketch of an approach to analyzing (and eventually modelling) negotiation that can be applied in this case.

3 Negotiation

3.1 Existing views

The rôle of negotiation and dialogue in learning has recently been invoked within a number of cognitive science approaches, both from a 'traditional' AI and Education perspective, as well as within the 'situated learning' paradigm. With respect to the latter, Seely-Brown, for example, states that Intelligent Tutoring Systems should aim to '... provide initially under determined threadbare concepts to which, through conversation, *negotiation* and authentic activity, a learner adds texture.' [my italics] (Seely-Brown, 1990). Within ITS research a recent approach called 'Knowledge Negotiation' has emerged (see Moyse & Elsom-Cook (1992)) that emphasizes the need to incorporate negotiation mechanisms in tutorial dialogues, and to provide alternative 'viewpoints' on the teaching domain and students' knowledge as a basis for them. This corresponds to an epistemological shift, where knowledge is itself viewed as 'negotiable', rather than fixed in the system, ready for eventual 'transmission' to the student. However, little of this research describes negotiation processes themselves, and we therefore need to look to other domains where negotiation is a key concept — specifically, Distributed AI (DAI), language sciences and social psychology — in order to define an analysis and modelling approach. In DAI research the term 'negotiation' is generally associated with resolution of *conflicts* (usually with respect to problem-solving resource allocation). We adopt a more general definition of negotiation (see Galliers (1989)) where negotiation is a process designed to achieve agreement between agents, whether the initial starting point is one of conflict or whether it is simply one of 'absence of agreement' ('indifference' in Galliers' terms). In view of space restrictions here we shall concentrate on the most relevant language sciences research.

Within some branches of language sciences, the notion of negotiation is viewed as *constitutive* of verbal interactions, to the extent that the shared meaning of utterances is itself the object of negotiation. Thus Edmondson (1981), for example, approaches the 'indirect speech act' problem in terms of the idea of 'strategic indeterminacy' of utterances: the illocutionary force of an utterance is not 'predetermined' in some way, but is rather intrinsically indeterminate, a fact that allows for *negotiation* of its joint understanding. Thus if X says "It's cold in here" when entering Y's appartment, the illocutionary force of this utterance as an indirect request to put the heating on, a simple statement, etc. may be negotiated by X as a function of Y's response (e.g., "Shall I put the heating on?" "No no, I was only remarking"). From a cognitive perspective, Clark & Schaefer (1989) have expressed this interactionist view in terms of a *grounding criterion*: '... The contributor and the partners mutually believe that the partners have understood what the contributor meant to a criterion sufficient for current purposes.' The criterion is presented in critical opposition to most 'computational speech act' models which, it is claimed, assume that the 'common ground' in dialogue simply 'accumulates' as the result of making the right utterance at the right time. Thus specific interaction structures occur — such as 'episodes', 'repairs', 'collaborative completions', etc. — whose function is to assure grounding in these terms. The work of Roschelle and colleagues (op cit) was largely concerned with analyzing such interaction structures, as a means of identifying when students were 'really collaborating' and when they were not. They posed the problem of determining, from the interaction transcript, when a "Yes" indicated 'agreement' (*qua* 'collaboration') and when it meant simply 'turn-taking'. This is a specific case of our *agreement problem* stated earlier, in that a 'turn-taking' "Yes" could correspond to negotiation of meaning (grounding) and a 'collaborative' "Yes" to agreement. Negotiation of meaning has also been studied within the framework of a more general theory of *linguistic feedback* (Allwood et al., 1991), as will be discussed later in section 5. In this paper we concentrate on feedback at the *attitudinal level* (agreement and acceptance) rather than on the level of understanding. It is clear, however, that the two are closely related since 'real' agreement (see Nivre, this volume) with respect to something presupposes joint perception and understanding of it.

3.2 A model for negotiation in CPS dialogues

Figure 1 represents a minimal schema for negotiation of problem solutions in dialogue. It is intended to define both a *genre* of dialogue (negotiative) as well as negotiative sequences in other forms of dialogue (we shall refer to both simply as 'negotiations'), and to provide a general framework within which to pose specific research problems on the modelling of CPS as negotiation.

At the highest level, a negotiation is defined by four components:

1. an initial state;
2. a final state;
3. objects of negotiation (what is being negotiated?), and
4. negotiation processes (leading from 1 to 2).

The following are brief descriptions of each component, illustrated with respect to the corpus considered here.

1. **Initial state:** The initial state has itself four main components: mutual goals, constraints on mutual goals, individual goals, and relations between individual goals. The *defining characteristic* of negotiations is the mutual goal of attaining agreement with respect to some set of propositions. There will usually be constraints on the mutual goal state in that the agents do not want to agree on any unrelated set of propositions: constraints with respect to coherence and consistency will operate, as well as domain-specific constraints. In the present case, the propositions must be statements of physics (theory of energy) and

they must have explanatory links to an agreed set of propositions describing results. Non-necessary conditions for negotiations include specific individual beliefs and goals — for example, one or both agents may have the goal that all and only the propositions that they propose are to be in the final state (adversarial negotiation), or they may have no such goals (disinterested or 'forensic' negotiation). Finally, there may be special and mutually understood relations between individual attitudes (**Ra**), such as various forms of *conflict*. Note that we do not regard such conflict as a necessary condition for negotiation (as is the case with much DAI research): it is quite possible to have the mutual goals of negotiation for other reasons, as in the present case where reaching agreement is imposed as part of the task.

2. **A final state:** The final state is simply the state where the proposition of the mutual goal of the initial state obtains [(agree A1 A2 {p1,p2,...})]. In some cases this will be a predetermined finite set; in other more open-ended cases (such as the problem considered here), the agents must be able to judge when the set is sufficient for common purposes, and possibly when it is unlikely that they will be able to achieve further agreement. The initial state mutual goal may thus be viewed as a 'persistent goal', in the sense of Cohen & Levesque (1990), that may be dropped when a reason for having the goal no longer obtains.
3. **Objects of negotiation:** These are different types of propositions, referring to the domain of dialogue (atomic propositions), or attitudinal expressions (such as goals or beliefs). It is thus possible to extend negotiation 'backwards', for example to negotiate engaging in a negotiation about goals to pursue. Note that this will rarely be done explicitly: often a negotiative dialogue is negotiated implicitly, simply by one agent beginning to negotiate. In the present case objects of negotiation are atomic propositions referring to the problem-solving domain (e.g., "The black ball rebounded higher than the yellow one", "the mass explains the difference in rebound", etc.). Problem-solving *goals* may also be objects of negotiation (e.g., "Let's do an experiment with..."), but this is not our main concern here (see Baker (1992b)).
4. **Negotiation processes:** These include types of communicative acts or functions which may be realized jointly or singly by one or more utterances (offers and acceptances/positive or negative), and specific relations between offered propositions (**R1**, **R2**, **R3**, etc.). Clearly, in a negotiation which is going to succeed, relations should be such that a proposition is finally offered which can be accepted, and this acceptance ratified (explicit acceptance of acceptance). As we shall see, the offer and acceptance functions are rarely explicit, both often being achieved by a single utterance. Finally, specific relations may arise during the negotiation process between agents' propositional attitudes, such as *conflict of avowed opinions*. Agents may attempt to resolve them by *argumentation* subdialogues.

On the basis of this general framework for negotiation, we can now define and consider our two main problems, both of which concern *negotiation processes*: the

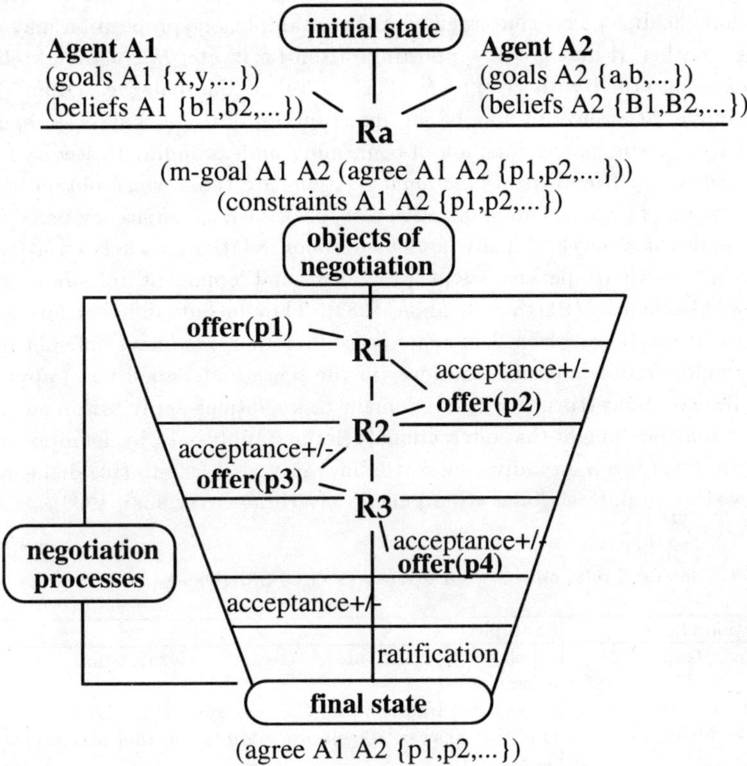

Fig. 1. Minimal schema for negotiations in CPS dialogues

co-construction problem and the agreement problem. With respect to the first problem, we concentrate here on defining the types of relations between offered propositions (section 4), and with respect to the second problem, we characterize 'offer' and 'acceptance/non-acceptance' functions of communicative acts (section 5). As we shall see, the two problems are closely related, in that one way in which acceptance may be communicated is to relate one's new contribution to the previous one in a specific way.

4 Co-construction of problem solutions in dialogue

4.1 Types of relations in dialogue

An analysis of relations between utterances in problem-solving dialogues, treated as negotiations, will show how offered solutions are constructed as a function of previous ones in order to converge on agreement. There are four main types or levels of relations between dialogue units at different levels, as shown in Table 1.

Domain-task relations obtain between propositions of the problem-solving domain that the dialogue is concerned with. For example, one proposition may 'reformulate' another, it may give a supporting reason for it, etc. *Interactional* relations are those concerned with *coordination* or *control* of the dialogue (Bunt, 1989). For example, utterance u2 may be an 'interruption' of u1, it may be a repetition of it that serves a control function of confirming understanding (a feedback function), and so on. *Hierarchical-functional* relations are those which obtain between functional units (moves, communicative acts, ...), such as 'adjacency pairs' at different hierarchical levels. Finally, *argumentational* relations are related utterances in the context where speakers adopt 'proponent' and 'opponent' rôles in a 'conflict of avowed opinions' (Barth & Krabbe, 1982). They include different forms of attack, defense and concession. Different types of relations may have different *ranges*; for example, argumentational relations (in the sense understood here) apply only across interventions (turns), whereas domain-task relations apply within and across turns. It may be thought that interactional relations apply only, by definition, across turns. However, even an individual's utterance in verbal face-to-face dialogue may be viewed as an 'interactional achievement' (Kerbrat-Orecchioni, 1990).

Table 1. Classes of relations between utterances in CPS dialogues

Relation class	Examples
Domain-task	subclass, specific-value, reason, reformulation, identity, inference.
Interactional	Repetition, Interruption, Continuation, Floor-hold
Hierarchical-functional	Question-answer, affirmation-acceptance, offer-acceptance/rejection
Argumentational	Attack, counter-attack, protective defense, counteractive defense

Describing relations between dialogue units on different levels in this way highlights important differences with respect to the work of Mann & Thompson (1988) on *rhetorical relations*. It is not surprising that there should be differences since the latter work was developed for relations between segments in *texts*, although there have been attempts to extend this work to modelling dialogue (see e.g., Daradoumis & Verdejo, this volume). The major differences are:

- there are types of relations in dialogue which do not apply in texts, and
- between two segments in dialogue, relations on most or all of the levels described above will apply *simultaneously*, whereas in rhetorical relation theory, there is a single unique relation between two text segments (although different analyses may predict different single relations between segments).

With respect to the first point, for example, argumentational relations in the specific (dialectic) sense in which we understand them, are quite unlike relations of 'justification' in text (in a text the writer's goal is not to win an interactive argumentative game). More obviously, texts are simply not interactional. With respect to the second point, we consider (with many other writers) that dialogue utterances are *multifunctional*; i.e., an utterance may perform a number of communicative functions, contribute to a solution, express argumentational opposition or agreement, etc. Analytically separable levels of analysis are therefore preferable in order to study subsequently their interaction.

We shall concentrate here on *domain-task relations* since they express how solutions themselves are co-constructed (an adequate treatment of other types of relations — argumentation, interaction structures, etc. — would require separate paper(s)).

4.2 Domain-task relations

In general, there are four main things that an agent participating in CPS can 'do' with a previously offered partial solution (C1), thereby establishing a specific relation with the new (C2) contribution:

1. C2 can describe *foundations* for C1 (explanation, reasons for and against);
2. C2 can *expand* C1 (add a new relevant feature of the concrete situation described, draw inferences from it, categorise it, state its superclass);
3. C2 can *contract* C1 (give it a specific value, subtract a proposition from the set described, state a specific subclass) and
4. C2 can be *neutral* with respect to the content of C1 (it may be a reformulation, have identical content, be an alternative or opposite case).

These actions correspond to classes of domain-task relations[2], shown in Figure 2.

It must be noted that an utterance which establishes a specific relation with a previous one at the domain-task level, will also establish a relation (perform a function) at other levels. For example, 'identity' relations often occur at the end of sequences, as *repetitions* (interactive level), or summaries of what has been said and agreed, offered for the confirmation of the other. Or again, *negative reasons* (domain-task) may, of course, occur as *attacks* at the argumentative level, although this is not necessarily the case (negative reasons may be given without argumentation taking place). We do not have space here to discuss each specific relation in detail here, and so shall simply give one example of their use in analyzing Dialogue Extract 1, shown earlier. From the graphical layout of Figure 3 we can see how the jointly agreed partial solution was co-constructed, at least at the level of the domain. It may be described as: in 2 adds a new description (add-sit) of the situation described in 1, and then generalizes this; 3 contracts 2 to its subclass, then gives a specific value for this class, etc., and so on. Note that *higher-order relations* do occur, but have not been marked here. For example, 2–9 may be viewed as an explanation for 1.

Even for such a short extract a quite complex picture emerges of joint problem-solving, where students build on the solutions of the other, on their own previous

[2] Some of these classes of relations are similar to 'coherence relations' in text described in the earlier work of Hobbs (Hobbs, 1982).

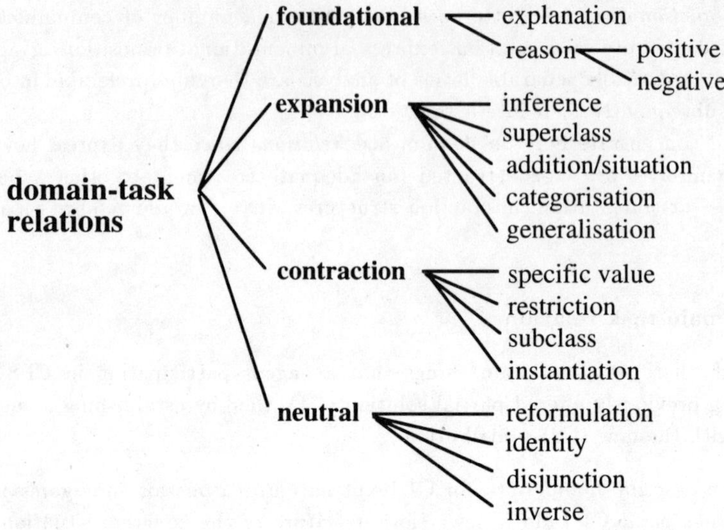

Fig. 2. Classes of domain-task relations in CPS dialogue

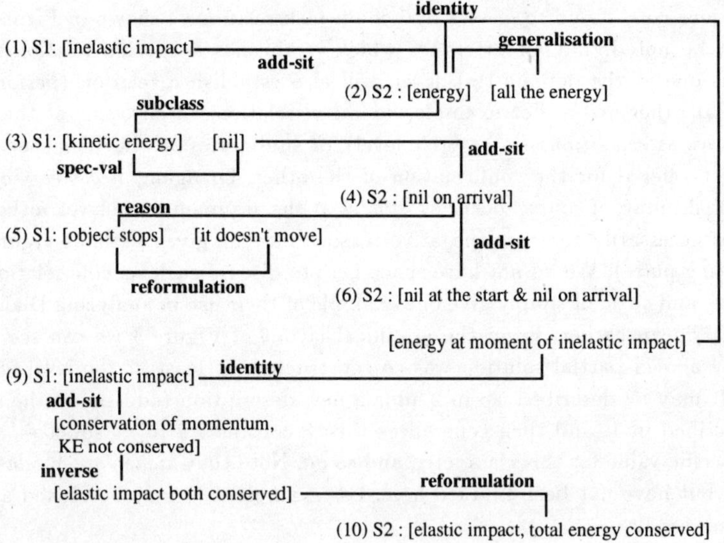

Fig. 3. Analysis of domain-task relations in Dialogue Extract 1

solutions, and develop their own contributions to a greater or lesser extent. Analysis of this kind can thus help us to give precise answers to more specific questions relating to co-construction, such as *who contributed the most?* and *to what extent are the students collaborating?* (rather than resolving in parallel). We can answer this to some extent by counting relations to self and to other across turns, and within turns, as shown in Table 2.

For such a small extract the figures are not of course significant; we can however remark that in this extract S1 develops his own solution to a greater extent than S2, and that S2 builds on his own previous contributions more than S1.

Finally, we may ask to what extent these relations may generalize to other domains. We have not yet applied the defined relations to other collaborative tasks since the analysis approach is currently under development. However, it seems that such very general classes as 'inference', 'explanation', etc. are likely to apply elsewhere, and that specific domains and tasks will emphasize one type of relation rather than another. In the task we consider here, a number of the relations have a special significance. The students' task is effectively one of *modelling*, to the extent that they must select relevant facts in the experimental situations, and 'translate' them into a language of physics terms (see Greeno (1989); Tiberghien (1993); Chi, Feltovich & Glaser (1981)). The *reformulation* relation is thus very important, since students must take descriptions of the experimental situation at an 'objects and events' level, and translate them into physics terms. For example 'weight' becomes 'mass'. The *addition-situation* relation is also important since this corresponds to enumeration of relevant facts in the experimental situation. The general point to be made is that in specific domains, specific types of relations can be reinterpreted in the light of an available *cognitive model* for problem solving.

Table 2. Number of domain task relations for Dialogue Extract 1

		S1	S2
To self:	within turn	4	1
	across turn	0	2
To other (across turn)		3	4
Total		7	7

5 Agreement in dialogue: feedback, belief and acceptance

In the previous section we described sequences within which initially offered partial solutions are successively refined towards (explicit) agreement. Such sequences at the *transaction* level (Moeschler, 1985) are typical of this corpus (and of other corpora). CPS dialogues may thus be analyzed as *iterations* on solution elements, where the 'output' agreed solution of one negotiation sequence may be input to further sequences. In order to identify when interlocutors are agreed, and thus on what they are agreed, we need some way of analyzing the way in which *feedback* on the level of the attitudes '*agreement*' or '*non-agreement*' is communicated. There are two main cases to be addressed: *explicit agreement* and *implicit agreement*. Both presuppose some notion of what agreement is, so this will be dealt with first.

After a long (in AI terms) preoccupation with 'knowledge representation', research on computational models of language and communication has more recently given a privileged position to the epistemic attitude of 'belief', beginning with the work of the 'Toronto School' (notably Cohen & Perrault (1979); Allen & Perrault (1980); Cohen, Morgan and Pollack (1990)). Thus the illocutionary point of an 'inform' communicative act is the addition of a belief to the hearer's set of propositional attitudes to the effect that the speaker believes the expressed proposition, and so on. A natural extension of this approach would be to analyze the primitive 'agree' in Figure 1 as a *mutual belief* with respect to a set of propositions (part of the 'common ground' established in dialogue). Leaving aside technical problems associated with mutual attitudes (such as infinite regression), we would make the following claim: *the propositional attitude of 'belief' alone is inadequate for modelling attitudes of speakers in dialogue.* We do not have the space to argue fully for this claim here, and so shall give a brief summary of the general view adopted.

Consider the case of a completed argumentation sequence in dialogue. In such a case there is no a priori reason why the 'loser' should adopt a *belief* with respect to the proponent's argued thesis. We should rather say that the 'loser' has *conceded* the statements advanced. Dennett (1981) describes this situation as follows:

> '...somebody corners me and proceeds to present me with an argument of great persuasiveness, of *irresistible* logic, step by step. I can think of nothing to say against any of the steps. I get to the conclusion and can think of no reason to deny the conclusion, *but I don't believe it!*' (p. 308).

A more 'mundane' case is that where a sequence simply reaches *closure* — a state which may imply nothing more for speakers than 'it is unlikely that we can progress further together on this point, the solution is acceptable enough as far as it goes at present'. In general, therefore, we are obliged to admit a larger set of attitudes associated with dialogue, including *belief, opinion, concession, commitment* and *acceptance.* We adopt the approach of analyzing *agreement as joint acceptance.* In Cohen's (1992) terms, 'acceptance' of a proposition differs from belief in that 'Belief is a disposition to feel, acceptance a policy for reasoning' (op cit, p. 5). We would argue that this provides a more plausible analysis of students' attitudes in CPS dialogues to the extent that students accept offered partial solutions as part of a common reasoning process, rather than (primarily) adopting beliefs with respect to them during the dialogue. We describe acceptance as 'joint' rather than 'mutual' since we adopt the following view: what is *said* is important in collaborative dialogue, not what is *believed*', i.e., 'acceptance' of a proposition means making some utterance that is mutually understood to give feedback on acceptance (such as "Yes" or "Ok": see Allwood et al (1991)), and 'joint acceptance' simply means that utterances of this kind have been made by both interlocutors.

The above discussion indicates an approach for dealing with explicit feedback on agreement (*qua* acceptance). It is restricted to the simple (and prevalent) case where *positive* feedback is given with respect to utterances that have *positive polarity* (Allwood et al., 1991). As Allwood and co-workers have shown, *explicit* feedback expressions (such as "yes", "mm", "no", "ok") are 'highly dependent on context for a precise determination of their meaning' (op cit p. 13), and specifically on the polarity, mood (speech act) and information status of preceding utterances. As we describe below, the *relation* between the information 'content' of an utterance (u1) and the information content of one that follows it (u2) is also important in determining the type of *implicit* feedback communicated. This establishes a close link between the two main problems considered here.

We now consider *implicit* agreement *qua* acceptance. Why is joint acceptance signalled explicitly at the end of Dialogue Extract 1 (10-11) whereas it may be viewed as signalled implicitly throughout (2-9)? Consider the following three interventions from the above Dialogue Extract 1:

		...
2	S2:	well, that the energy... all the energy...
3	S1:	well, that the kinetic energy is theoretically nil [implicitly accepts 2 'as far as it goes...']
4	S2:	it's nil on arrival, in fact... [implicitly accepts 3]
		...

Intuitively we want to say that in uttering 3, S1 accepts 2 'as far as it goes' (i.e. 'it is acceptable that the *energy* is... but we can say something even more specific, about *kinetic* energy'), and that in uttering 4 S2 accepts 3 implicitly, since 4 has a specific content (domain-task) relation with 3 (it 'builds on' 3 and does not contradict it). How can we give substance to these intuitions? There seem to be three main possibilities, which we can only sketch here.

The first possibility is to show how 'offers' can communicate acceptance by characterizing them as *communicative functions* (Gazdar, 1981; Bunt, 1989). Thus, following Edmondson (1981) offers can be viewed as *conditional acceptances*: an offer with respect to a proposition p1, realized by agent A1 directed towards A2 in dialogue, updates the epistemic states of A1 and A2 with (at least) the element:

((accepts A1 p1) if (accepts A2 p1));

or as Edmondson (op cit) puts it, a 'propose' (offer) illocution expresses 'I will if you will' (p. 142).

The second approach is to combine an analysis of offers in terms of communicative functions with our analysis of domain-task *relations* between successively offered propositions. For example, if we have the following utterances and (minimal) updates of knowledge states of both agents:

(u1) A1: (offer A1 p1) [=update → ((accepts A1 p1) if (accepts A2 p1))]
(u2) A2: (offer A2 p2) [=update → ((accepts A2 p2) if (accepts A1 p2))]

given certain values for the relation R between p1 and p2 (such as that p2 *presupposes*[3] p1), we can derive from u2:

((accepts A2 p1) if (accepts A1 p1)).

This puts the agents in the somewhat curious situation where each will accept a proposition if the other will (!). Now, in subsequent utterances this process of joint conditional acceptance can continue, thus building up a *stack* of propositions. Our model therefore predicts that the stack build-up will stop when each agent makes an explicit non-conditional acceptance; and this is precisely what occurs (the joint explicit acceptance described earlier, also shown as explicit acceptance / ratification in Figure 1). The remaining problem is to provide a rigorous analysis of how specific domain-task relations between utterances function with respect to implicit feedback. We leave this problem for future research.

There is a third relevant approach to analyzing acceptance, that has been described by Hamblin (1971) and Mackenzie (1981; 1985). The approach consists in positing a dialogue rule for updating a 'commitment slate', whereby *acceptance is assumed* with respect to a statement in the absence of explicit *denial* or *retraction*. As Mackenzie (1985) puts it '...in this [dialogic] game silence means assent.' (p. 333). This approach has been developed with respect to highly idealized mathematical models for dialogue, consisting of successions of logical statements (see also Barth & Krabbe (1982)). The problem is that in real dialogues,denial or retraction is not always explicit. This approach is therefore of some application, but requires extension to take into account specific relations between utterances in the type of dialogue considered here and the rôle of implicit and explicit feedback.

6 Conclusion

This paper has been concerned with two main problems that arise in analysis and modelling of dialogues produced in the context of CPS:

1. modelling how joint solutions are co-constructed, and
2. determining when students are agreed and with respect to what.

Our responses to both problems are situated within a more general model of CPS in dialogue as *negotiation*, the principal defining characteristic of which is the mutual goal of achieving agreement with respect to a set of propositions. Thus, our approach to addressing the first problem was to define a set of relations between offered partial solutions at the domain-task level, as they converge towards agreement. This enabled us subsequently to address one specific part of the second problem — that of analyzing the implicit feedback communicated (acceptance-non- acceptance dimension) by an offered proposition that follows another. In this case, our hypothesis

[3] We recognise that invoking the notion of presupposition introduces a large number of theoretical problems (see Levinson (1983)). Our aim is simply to indicate other areas of research in pragmatics that are relevant to the problems considered here.

is that the kind of feedback communicated depends on the content relation between the offers. With respect to the second problem we described how problem solutions are co-constructed within iterative transaction units, 'punctuated' by the kind of joint explicit acceptance described by Allwood and co-workers (op cit). Finally, we described the necessity to extend the range of epistemic states incorporated in communicative act models, beyond 'belief' to 'acceptance', 'opinion' and 'concession'. Such a project requires exploration of the logical properties of acceptance, to an extent which has been performed for knowledge and belief.

The analysis model has not yet been systematically applied to the whole corpus, largely because a number of important and difficult theoretical issues remain to be addressed. The relations and feedback elements described have, however, proved sufficient for analyzing one case study (dialogue of one and a half hour's length). It is therefore not yet clear to what extent the relations described will extend to other domains, although we may make this conjecture given their highly general nature. Note that we have not considered analysis of argumentation sequences in this paper, although their rôle in conceptual change is clearly important (see Baker (1991; 1992a)).

A number of theoretical problems remain for further research, the most important of which include: communicative act models based on acceptance rather than belief; a thorough explanation of the logical properties of acceptance; and the detailed analysis of the rôle of content relations in implicit acceptance. Given that progress can be made in these directions, the negotiation-based analysis approach described here does appear promising as a means of increasing our understanding of collaborative problem solving in dialogue.

Acknowledgements

I would like to thank Andrée Tiberghien and Françoise Langlois for providing the dialogues analyzed in this paper. This research has been supported in part by the C.N.R.S. "Cognisciences" programme and the Rhône-Alpes Region research programme "Intelligence Artificielle — Systèmes Experts et Applications".

A Original of Dialogue Extract 1

1	S1:	donc qu'est ce qu'on peut dire si il y a un choc mou?
2	S2:	bein que l'énergie... toute l'énergie...
3	S1:	bein que l'énergie cintique à priori est nulle!
4	S2:	elle est nulle à l'arrivee, enfin...
5	S1:	puisque... puisque l'objet s'arrête, enfin, ah oui, surtout là il ne bouge pas ah...
6	S2:	elle est nulle au départ, et c'est nulle à l'arrivée... d'énergie... oui mais lors d'un choc mou, qu'est ce que...
7	S1:	ça fait un moment qu'on l'a fait ça!
8	S2:	mais on a aussi...

9 S1: attends... choc mou, bon t'as conservation de la quantité de mouvement mais... l'énergie cinétique ne se conserve pas! je crois que c'est ca qu'on a vu... choc élastique par contre, les deux se conservent...
10 S2: oui, choc élastique, il y a l'énergie totale qui se conserve
11 S1: oui
...

References

Allen, J. & Perrault, C.R. (1980) Analysing Intention in Utterances. Artificial Intelligence, 15, 148–178.

Allwood, J., Nivre, J. & Ahlsén, E. (1991) On the Semantics and Pragmatics of Linguistic Feedback. Gothenburg Papers in Theoretical Linguistics 64. University of Gothenburg, Department of Linguistics, Sweden.

Baker, M.J. (1991) The influence of dialogue processes on students' collaborative generation of explanations for simple physical phenomena. Proceedings of the International Conference on the Learning Sciences. Northwestern University, Illinois USA, Evanston, Illinois, 9–19.

Baker, M.J. (1992a) An analysis of cooperation and conflict in students' collaborative explanations for phenomena in mechanics. In: Tiberghien, A. & Mandl, H. (eds.) Intelligent Learning Environments and Knowledge Acquisition in Physics. NATO ASI Series F, Vol. 86. Berlin: Springer-Verlag.

Baker, M.J. (1992b) Modelling Negotiation in Intelligent Teaching Dialogues. In: Elsom-Cook, M. & Moyse, R. (eds.) Knowledge Negotiation. London: Paul Chapman Publishing, 199–240.

Barbieri, M.S. & Light, P. (1991) Interaction, gender and performance on a computer-based problem-solving task. To appear in International Journal of Educational Research.

Barth, E.M. & Krabbe, E.C.W. (1982) From Axiom to Dialogue: A philosophical study of logics and argumentation. Berlin: Walter de Gruyter.

Behrend, S., Singer, J. & Roschelle, J. (1988) A Methodology for the Analysis of Collaborative Learning in a Physics Microworld. Proceedings of ITS-88, 48–53.

Bunt, H.C. (1989) Information Dialogues as communicative action in relation to partner modelling and information processing. In: Taylor, M.M., Néel, F. & Bouwhuis, D.G. (eds.) The Structure of Multimodal Dialogue. Amsterdam: Elsevier North-Holland.

Chan, T. & Baskin, A.B. (1988) Studying with the Prince: The Computer Companion as a Learning Companion. Proceedings of ITS-88. Montréal.

Chan, T., Chung, I., Ho, R., Hou, W. & Lin, G. (1992) Distributed Learning Companion: WEST Revisited. In: Intelligent Tutoring Systems. Second International Conference, ITS'92, Montreal, Canada. Lecture Notes in Computer Science, Vol 608. Berlin: Springer-Verlag.

Chi, M.T.H., Feltovich, P.J. & Glaser, R. (1981) Categorization and Representation of Physics Problems by Experts and Novices. Cognitive Science, 2, 121–152.

Clark, H.H. & Schaefer, E.F. (1989) Contributing to Discourse. Cognitive Science, 13, 259–294.

Cohen, L.J. (1992) An Essay on Belief and Acceptance. Oxford: Clarendon Press.

Cohen, P.R. & Perrault, C.R. (1979) Elements of a plan-based theory of speech acts. Cognitive Science, 3, 177–212.

Cohen, P.R., Morgan, J. & Pollack, M.E. (eds.) (1990) Intentions in Communication. Cambridge, Mass: MIT Press.

Dennett, D.C. (1981) How to Change your Mind. In: Brainstorms: Philosophical Essays on Mind and Psychology. Brighton, UK: Harvester Press, 300–309.

Dillenbourg, P. & Self, J. (1992) People Power: a human-computer collaborative learning system. In: Intelligent Tutoring Systems. Second International Conference, ITS'92, Montreal, Canada. Lecture Notes in Computer Science, Vol 608. Berlin: Springer-Verlag, 651–660.

Edmondson, W. (1981) Spoken Discourse: A model for analysis. London: Longman.

Galliers, J.R. (1989) A Theoretical Framework for Computer Models of Cooperative Dialogue, Acknowledging Multi-Agent Conflict. Ph.D. thesis, Human Cognition Research Laboratory, The Open University (UK) unpublished.

Gazdar, G. (1981) Speech act assignment. In: Joshi, A.K., Webber, B.L. & Sag, I.A. (eds.) Elements of Discourse Understanding. Cambridge (UK): Cambridge University Press, 64–83.

Greeno, J. (1989) Situations, mental models and generative knowledge. In: Votovsky, K. (ed.) Complex Information Processing: The Impact of H.A. Simon. Hillsdale, NJ: Lawrence Erlbaum Associates, 285–318.

Hamblin, C.L. (1971) Mathematical models of dialogue. Théoria, 2, 130–155.

Hobbs, J.R. (1982) Towards and Understanding of Coherence in Discourse. In: Lehnert, W.G. & Ringle, M.H. (eds.) Strategies for Natural Language Processing. Hillsdale, NJ: Lawrence Erlbaum Associates, 223–244.

Kerbrat-Orecchioni, C. (1990) Les Interactions Verbales, Tome 1. Paris: Armand Colin.

Levinson, S.C. (1983) Pragmatics. Cambridge: Cambridge University Press.

MacKenzie, J.D. (1981) The dialectics of logic. Logique et Analyse, 24, 159–177.

MacKenzie, J.D. (1985) No logic before Friday. Synthèse, 63, 329–341.

Mann, W.C. & Thompson, S.A. (1988) Rhetorical Structure Theory: Toward a functional theory of text organisation. Text, 8(3), 243–281.

Moeschler, J. (1985) Argumentation et Conversation: Eléments pour une analyse pragmatique du discourse. Paris: Crédif-Hatier.

Moyse, R. & Elsom-Cook, M. (1992) Knowledge Negotiation. London: Academic Press.

Seely-Brown, J. (1990) Toward a new epistemology for learning. In: Frasson, C. & Gauthier, G. (eds.) Intelligent Tutoring Systems: At the crossroad of artificial intelligence and education. Norwood New Jersey: Ablex.

Tiberghien, A. (1993) Modelling As a Basis for Analysing Teaching-Learning Situations. Learning and Instruction. (to appear).

Using Rhetorical Relations in Building a Coherent Conversational Teaching Session

Thanasis Daradoumis[1] and M.Felisa Verdejo[2]

[1] Departamento de Lenguajes y Sistemas Informaticos, UPC, Pau Gargallo 5, 08028 Barcelona, Spain, email: daradoumis@lsi.upc.es
[2] Escuela Tecnica Superior de Ingenieros Industriales, U.N.E.D., Avda Complutense s/n, 28080 Madrid, Spain, email: felisa@toledo.uucp

Abstract. We propose a model of an intentional (tutorial task-oriented) structure for a natural-language interface to carry out the student-understanding and system-generation tasks needed to support a tutorial dialogue between a student and a guided-learning environment. The model reveals the different general-purpose explanation strategies used and the rhetorical relations implicit in the dialogue and may be used to generate largely coherent, lengthy and complex dialogues.

Keywords. Natural language, tutorial dialogues, rhetorical relations

1 Introduction

Research in Artificial Intelligence has clearly revealed the necessity to treat discourse as a planned activity. The distinction Grosz & Sidner (1986) have made between the three structural components (i.e., linguistic, intentional and attentional) is also widely accepted. The intentional component identifies segment units and their structure. The segmentation of a discourse accounts for the intentional behaviour, which means that each segment reflects a particular intention. Segments are linked by either *dominance* or *satisfaction-precedence* compositional relations. In task-oriented dialogues a further distinction is needed between the structure of the non-linguistic task and that of the dialogue engaged while doing the task.

Tutorial dialogues are a kind of task-oriented dialogue. We assume a tutor and a student involved in a cooperative and negotiative activity to reach a shared objective. The learning process will be guided by the system(tutor), but the initiative can be taken by both the system and the student. This means that the structure of the dialogue should account for phenomena such as interruptions for clarification or negotiation.

Most guided-learning environments do not provide natural-language interfaces, which means that tutorial discourse is fully generated by the guide component and is shown by either a pre-formated, menu-like interface or a direct interface. However, natural-language tutorial dialogues, as stated before, require both to distinguish the communication functionality of the interface from the tutorial functionality of the system and to establish the shared knowledge needed for a dialogue.

In this paper we propose a model of an intentional (tutorial task-oriented) structure for a natural-language interface to carry out the student-understanding and system-generation tasks needed to support a tutorial dialogue between a student and a guided-learning environment.

Our environment includes a Tutor Strategist capable of dynamically building a plan to reach a learning goal, adapted to a particular student. Relevant parts of this instructional plan are included in the dialogue model, i.e. are known by the interface.

The proposed dialogue model enhances the work done by Grosz and Sidner in two ways: first, it provides a set of rhetorical relations for representing in a more accurate way not only the intentional but also the pedagogical and instructional behaviour inherent in tutorial dialogues; these tutoring-based influencing factors result in particular classes of relations, such as *pedagogical* or *instructional* relations, based on the generally common function and scope of a relation class. Secondly, the work provides a layered model of discourse and a rich dialogue structure using these relations.

Mann & Thompson (1988) developed the Rhetorical Structure Theory (RST) as a descriptive tool for text analysis by identifying a number of rhetorical relations that can be used to coherently relate the various (small and large) units containing a text. In the area of language generation, various researchers have suggested top-down planning mechanisms that automatically construct RST trees which in turn give rise to the generation of coherent texts (for example, Hovy (1988); Moore & Paris (1989); van der Linden et al. (1992)). In spite of its wide application to written monologues, its suitability for representing interactive discourse has not been tested yet.

To that end, we propose to build a hierarchical model of dialogue consisting of six levels, i.e. conversation, dialogue, subdialogue, exchange, move and linguistic act, which conforms to the fundamentals of the Rhetorical Structure Theory:

- The phenomenon of nuclearity: a text unit consists of a nucleus and one or more satellite parts connected to one another by relations.
- The dialogue planner works with the constraints on the applicability of RST relations. These constraints concern the nucleus, the satellites and their combination. It also works with the effect a particular relation may have on the participants' (tutor's and student's) state of mind.
- The dialogue can be represented by a tree structure. The RST tree is based on: pedagogical/instructional principles as well as teaching/rhetorical goals of style as provided by the lesson (curriculum) plan of a Tutoring Strategist, the domain structure encoded in the KB and the student model. Initially, the tutor's lesson plan mirrors the structure of the domain knowledge. In turn, the dialogue structure mirrors the task-oriented structure of the lesson plan at hand.

This 'classical' RST framework will be further extended and adapted to the emerging necessities of interactive discourse to result in a model and theory that can fully represent and build a dynamic model of dialogue.

The structure of the paper is as follows: we will first present the hierarchical model of dialogue that results from a lesson plan proposed by the tutor. Then we will discuss the model of the dialogue by examining each level and determining the kind of relations that can appropriately relate the individual segments of a level. Furthermore, the model will be illustrated with the aid of a selected simplified example that will clearly show the rich (sophisticated) dialogue structure produced. Finally, the exchange level of the model will be highlighted and its structure will be discussed and represented by means of the extended RST theory, which will prove to provide an initial but sufficient and promising formalism for modelling exchanges.

2 Building a hierarchical model of dialogue out of a lesson plan

We have mentioned above that natural-language tutorial dialogues must distinguish the tutorial functionality of the system from the communication functionality of the interface and must also establish the correspondence between the levels of the tutorial task structure (intentional structure) and the levels of the dialogue structure.

The tutorial conversations studied here actually represent a complete instantiation of a general lesson (curriculum) plan proposed by a Tutoring Strategist. The conversation itself may consist of six levels as mentioned above (see Figure 1, section 4). The three upper levels of conversation (conversation, dialogue, subdialogue) correspond to (follow precisely) the tutorial task-related levels of the lesson plan structure.

In particular, each of these conversational levels is marked from the top by a specific goal (conversation, pedagogical and teaching, respectively) and from the bottom by the subgoals into which that goal is decomposed. In other words, these goals delimit and constrain the scope of a conversational level by indicating its start (first appearance of the goal) and its termination (accomplishment of the subgoals). Or, if the goal cannot be accomplished, its corresponding conversational part is also considered uncompleted (temporarily suspended) or aborted in the extreme case.

The distinction, then, between the structure of the non-linguistic task and that of the dialogue is detected precisely at the exchange level. It is at that level that conversation really begins, that participants' interactions occur and that interruptions — a dynamic phenomenon — are handled. Thus, dialogue is initiated dynamically, which means that any participant has the opportunity to initiate it (mixed initiative dialogues).

Let us first examine and describe the three upper levels of our dialogue model: conversation, dialogue and subdialogue. In a later section (section 5), we will discuss the purely linguistic task of our model, the exchange level, and will focus on the representation of the exchange structure. The three upper levels will initially be described in terms of the kind of discourse intentions of a conversational part. In section 3, we will propose a new approach for structuring these levels by means of rhetorical relations. Since the lower boundary of these levels is delimited by the discourse goals which mark the exchange level, we will begin with the conversational level which constitutes the *middle level* in our hierarchical model of dialogue.

Completion of an *exchange* means accomplishment of the discourse goal (for example: 'explain concept', 'verify understanding') that the exchange refers to (Grosz & Sidner, 1986; Carberry, 1990). Discourse goals in an Intelligent Tutoring System (Fernandez et al., 1988), of which our dialogue model is part, usually constitute related steps (subgoals) of higher-level goals, called *teaching goals*. In other words, information needed for teaching goals is obtained through discourse goals and therefore discourse goals can be reached in order to accomplish teaching goals.

A teaching goal may consist of two or more discourse goals, i.e. a teaching goal may take two or more exchanges to be achieved. Since teaching goals constitute a separate level in the tutorial task-related structure, we will also define a higher level in our model that represents a conversational structure consisting of two or more related exchanges, which we will call *subdialogue*. It constitutes the *low-upper level* in our model.

Furthermore, in the tutorial task-related structure, teaching goals constitute related steps (subgoals) of higher-level goals, called *pedagogical goals*. In other words, pedagogical goals are achieved through teaching goals, so teaching goals have to be executed before pedagogical goals can ultimately be performed.

As before, a pedagogical goal may consist of two or more teaching goals; that is, a pedagogical goal may take two or more subdialogues to be achieved. Thus, pedagogical goals, which represent the *high-upper level* of the tutorial task-related structure, can then correspond to a distinct level that constitutes the high-upper level in our model. This level represents a conversational structure consisting of two or more related subdialogues, which we will call *dialogue*.

We can also consider a *top level* structure in our hierarchical model of dialogue that stands above all the dialogues that constitute the dialogue level and which we will call *conversation*. A tutor's top-level goal characterizes the scope of the intended tutorial conversation.

Thus, our dialogue model is constructed incrementally by relating the tutorial task-oriented levels (intentional structure) to corresponding conversational levels (dialogue structure). Finally, we will complete the model with two more level structures: the first, forming the *lower level* of our model, is called *move* and is part of the exchange; the other, called *speech act*, forms the *bottom level* and is part of the move. These two levels, together with the exchange level, constitute the pure linguistic (dialogic) part of our model.

3 Use of rhetorical relations for the general structuring of a conversational teaching session as an RST tree

Our conversation structure is constructed incrementally as we move depth-first through a lesson plan and execute the steps (goals) of each level of the plan. Our model of conversation is thus a hierarchical model that reflects the tutorial task-oriented structure (intentional structure) that a tutor builds. Then, goals at each level form a tree structure in which each node represents a different task or goal (which can be a pedagogical, teaching or discourse goal, depending on the level considered) that the tutor is performing and wishes to achieve. The children of a node represent the subgoals pursued in order to perform (accomplish) the parent goal.

Therefore, at any level of the tutorial (intentional) structure, the children of a node are all part of an overall goal at the next level up and they together contribute towards the accomplishment of the latter. Thus, the children of a node are *related* in some way and we should be able to identify that relation as well as the role that each of them plays with respect to the other and to the higher goal it contributes to. These relations can then be used to model, i.e. coherently relate, the parts of the conversation to which these goals correspond.

The ability to determine rhetorical relations between any parts in the conversation makes it possible to the whole conversation in a coherent manner and enables us to identify at any moment what function each part has (dialogue, subdialogue, exchange) in relation to other parts at the same level.

Thus, in addition to the *dominance* intentional relation of Grosz & Sidner (1986) that is used to identify relationships between goals on adjacent levels, in the case of dialogue generation we substitute the other *satisfaction-precedence* intentional relation by an appropriate set of rhetorical relations that relate goals (intentions) and identify their role in the dialogue while being at the same conversational level. The substitution of this relation — which Grosz and Sidner used as a unique relation for all levels of discourse — by a set of specific rhetorical relations results in a richer dialogue structure and a generally coherent conversation.

Furthermore, our conversation structure is a combination of different particular discourse structures provided by the rhetorical relations identified at each conversational level. Each of these structures serves to reflect the sources it results from and a partial ordering on discourse. Thus, in tutorial dialogues, rhetorical relations can be grouped into different classes of relations according to their pedagogical, instructional, dialogic, interpersonal or ideational (informational) sources.

In particular, at the conversation level of our dialogue model, the relationships recognized between the intentions (pedagogical goals into which a tutorial conversation goal is decomposed) form a set of *pedagogical relations* and provide the *pedagogical structure* of the discourse according to a pedagogical theory of comprehension and learning principles for tutoring.

Similarly, at the dialogue and subdialogue levels, the relationships between the intentions (teaching/discourse goals) that mark the lower boundaries of these levels form another set of *instructional relations* and provide the *instructional structure* according to a theory of what instructional steps are usually followed in interactive tutoring.

Figure 1 (section 4) presents the conversation structure and the relations that model it. For instance, the *enablement* relation is a top-level *pedagogical* relation that is used to relate two dialogues (pedagogical goals) by thus building the top level of the conversational structure. Moreover, the *enablement-using* relation is a high-upper level *instructional* relation that models a dialogue by coherently relating two of its subdialogues (teaching goals). Finally, the *support-understanding* relation is a low-upper level *instructional* relation that coherently connects two exchanges (discourse goals) of a subdialogue. Further illustrations of the dialogue structure and other relations (dialogic, interpersonal/ideational) used to model its middle and lower levels (exchange and move) are presented in sections 4 and 5.

The above leads to the following conclusions. On the one hand, the RST-tree represents the *macrostructure* of dialogue: the pedagogical and instructional relations between the different upper levels of conversation. In other words, the dialogue macrostructure reflects the tutoring activity engaged by the tutor. On the other hand, the RST-tree also represents, as in monologues, the *microstructure* of dialogue (the *move structure* at the lower levels of conversation): the *interpersonal/ideational* RST-relations that give rise to an argumentative/explanation strategy used to accomplish a move (i.e. a move's interpersonal/ informative goal), as well as those local RST-relations between acts.

Finally, at the middle level of conversation (exchange level), specific *dialogic relations* are used to represent the *exchange structure* and identify the relationships between the exchange units (moves) — see section 5 for more details. It is at this level that student activities are reflected and form part of the exchange either by contributing towards the exchange's (tutor's goal) completion or prompting in by causing an interruption.

Tables 1 to 5 present the main types of relations we are currently working with. The relations are classified according to the class they belong to and the conversational level they operate. A brief description explains the scope and function of each relation. At this point we would like to underline that there are more of these relations. In particular, we use further specific relations that model dynamic phenomena in dialogue such as interruptions, and thus provide the means for building a dynamic model of exchange, as described in Daradoumis (1993a); Daradoumis (1993b).

4 The dialogue model

We will illustrate the dialogue model and the way it is used to model a tutorial conversation. In order to build the dialogue model, we will present, as a starting point, a lesson plan proposed by the Tutoring Strategist. Following the task-oriented structure of the lesson plan, we will identify the levels of the conversation and will relate them to the corresponding levels of the intentional structure of the lesson plan. The relations that link related dialogues of the conversation session, related subdialogues of a dialogue and related exchanges of a subdialogue will be explained and justified. Thus, the dialogue (conversation) will be rhetorically analysed and explained from the conversation down to the act level.

The following simplified example presents an exchange by which the tutor intends to remind the student of a previously learned concept by using a specific explanation strategy (*analogy*).

tutor: Repeating... a simple output element of a function has a similar definition as the simple input element defined before. In particular, it also consists of a name and domain as the simple input element does.
student: Oh, I see.
tutor: Good.

The above exchange is actually the result of a lesson plan generated by the Tutoring Strategist and is shown in Figure 1. The exchange is identified by its discourse goal (*recall*). This lesson plan is one of several plans that may be generated during a tutor-student interaction given a student model and the context of the teaching session. For further details of how lesson plans are generated see Fernandez et al. (1988).

Table 1. Types of relations and their function at the conversation level

Conversation level - Pedagogical relations	Functional Description
Enablement	The student is asked to prove her expertise on a given concept, which will enable the tutor to continue teaching properly.
Background-specific	Specific background information should be checked with the student before the real teaching begins.
Background-general	General background information is to be presented briefly to the student before the real teaching begins.
Support-learning	The student is asked to provide evidence of understanding as regards certain concept(s) learned, which supports(assesses) the underlying Learning process.
Elaboration	The student is directly involved in the real teaching process and her knowledge is further elaborated and extended.
Identification	The teaching process (and the tutor itself) is introduced to the student before the real teaching begins.
Conclusion	The current teaching process reaches an end.

Figure 1 presents a lesson plan annotated with the pedagogical, instructional, dialogic and ideational relations, identified for this plan at each conversational level, and with the specific discourse structures produced on application of these relations.

When we examine this lesson plan we see that *enablement* is a rhetorical relation between the intentions underlying the pedagogical tasks of 'briefly reminding the student of a known concept' and another pedagogical task, possibly 'introducing

Table 2. Types of relations and their function at the dialogue/subdialogue level

Dialogue/Subdialogue level - Instructional relations	Functional Description
Enablement-understanding	The tutor gives the student a problem to solve, which enables the tutor to assess the student's understanding of the concept.
Enablement-using	The tutor conveys to the student the necessary information about a concept (including an initial checking of the student's understanding). Successful completion of this plan(step) enables the tutor to give the student a problem to solve, which allows the tutor to verify whether the student knows how to use the concept or not.
Background-prerequisite	The tutor explains any unknown prerequisites of a concept before presenting it.
Support-understanding	The tutor explains a concept to the student and then requires student's evidence of support(understanding).
Elaboration-subconcepts	The tutor explains a concept by first describing the subconcepts of the concept.
Elaboration-synoptic	The student is informed of the concept(s) she is going to learn in more detail afterwards.
Sequence	The tutor continues with the next teaching activity as the student knows the current concept.

Table 3. Types of relations and their function at the exchange level

Exchange level - Dialogic relations	Functional Description
Consent	The tutor gives(presents) some information to the student and expects to obtain the student's consent as regards the suitability of the info conveyed.
Elicitation	The tutor elicits the information it needs to know about the student's state of mind.
Ascertainment	The tutor attempts to ascertain and evaluate the student's state of mind.

new concepts'. This background-type relation is thus a specific relation that models (relates) the discourse intentions that refer to two pedagogical plans and will thus belong to the class of relations that we called *pedagogical relations*. Both pedagogical tasks are said to represent two complete dialogue parts of the conversation session and thus belong to the dialogue level of the conversation. The 'remind' dialogue provides the background information needed by the student to understand the concept so that the tutor will *be able* to continue the teaching session.

On the other hand, the *enablement-using* is another specific rhetorical relation that relates the two subdialogues (teaching goals) 'recall concept' and 'verify concept with problem' that form part of the 'remind' dialogue. This relation belongs to the class of *instructional relations* since it links two instructional plans (steps) to be followed in this order so that the tutor will be able to achieve the above pedagog-

Table 4. Types of relations and their function at the move level

Move level - Interpersonal/Ideational relations	Functional Description
Motivation	The tutor motivates(convinces) the student to perform an act or accept the current goal/activity.
Justification	The tutor justifies the necessity of a goal/activity for the current purposes of the teaching process.
Supporting evidence	The tutor explains a concept by giving an example associated with the concept.
Supporting antithesis	The tutor explains a concept by giving a counter-example associated with the concept.
Comparative	The tutor explains a concept by presenting an analogous concept with which the student is familiar.
Elaboration part	The tutor explains a concept by identifying and explaining each of the parts of the concept.
Elaboration object	The tutor explains(describes) a concept by giving basic information without details.
Elaboration generality	The tutor explains(describes) a concept by giving quite detailed information about it.
Identification	The tutor explains(describes) a concept briefly.

ical (dialogue) goal. In particular, by carrying out the 'recall concept' subdialogue first, the tutor conveys to the student the necessary information about the concept at hand (including an initial checking of the student's understanding). Successful completion of this plan (step) *enables* the tutor to give student a problem to solve, which allows the tutor to verify whether the student knows how to use the concept or not.

Similarly, *support-understanding* is a specific type of *support* relation that relates two exchanges (discourse goals) and it is also a kind of *instructional relation*. More specifically, the tutor provides some information ('recall') and expects the student's *support* or not when the tutor intends to verify the student's *understanding* at the next step-exchange ('verify understanding').

Finally, the two lower levels of dialogue structure — move and act — are also represented as interfering with an appropriate explanation strategy, resulting from the application of the *comparative ideational* rhetorical relation, necessary for the 'recalling' move of the tutor. A rhetorical relation, *similarity*, is also shown between the tutor's two 'inform-similarity' and 'inform-analogy' acts.

This illustration of our dialogue model shows that the evolution of the rhetorical relations, from the dialogue level down to the act level, follows the same traversal process of discourse relations depicted at the relation networks of Maier & Hovy (1991), i.e. from general to specific relations as we move from the highest to the lowest level of a network. This results in the design of a new approach to dialogue planning that conforms to several of the ideas presented in the new text planner architecture of Hovy et al. (1992).

At this point we do not claim that a certain set of relations is exclusive: the

Table 5. Types of *local RST relations* and their function at the move level

Move level - Local RST relations	Functional Description
Consequential	The tutor explains that the current goal/activity is the consequence of a higher-level purpose and should thus be performed as such.
Means	The tutor explains that the goal/activity used constitutes the right means to achieve the current purpose.
Supporting example	The tutor gives an example which contributes to the student's understanding of the concept at hand.
Supporting counter-example	The tutor gives a counter-example which contributes to the student's understanding of the concept at hand.
Similarity	The tutor explains a concept by describing its similarities with respect to a familiar concept.
Contrast	The tutor explains a concept by describing its differences with a familiar concept.
Whole-part	The tutor explains the main concept and its parts by using the same method(explanation strategy), with the same amount of detail.
Set member	The tutor explains the main concept for using a certain method and amount of detail. Then it chooses an optimally different method to explain each part using, however, the same amount of detail for all of them.
Process step	The tutor explains the main concept and its parts independently (by using different methods and amount of detail).
Domain-dependent attributes	The tutor explains a concept by stating the properties(attributes) ascribed to the concept.
Abstract instance	The tutor explains a concept by identifying and describing a familiar subconcept and then abstracting this subconcept to a superconcept that (subsequently) introduces the concept.
General-specific	The tutor explains a concept by describing its defining characteristics (different and similar attributes) with respect to its generic concept; i.e. by specializing a more general (super)concept.
Identify	The tutor presents a simple description of the concept.

same relation may belong to two different sets (e.g., it may be both pedagogical and instructional). However, even if this is the case — further investigation of more tutorial dialogues will prove whether this is true or not — their effects on subsequent decisions will be different since they belong to different levels of the dialogue model and their scope and function are distinct at each of these levels. Such relations, though having the same name, thus belong to different classes and must consequently be considered seperately at any decision point at the lower levels which they affect.

Pedagogical structure is the top-level structure of a tutorial conversation or lesson plan that clearly defines the main pedagogical tasks performed during a teaching session. Most importantly, it gives the *general coherence* of the conversation as a whole by means of the pedagogical relation that models the conversation. This re-

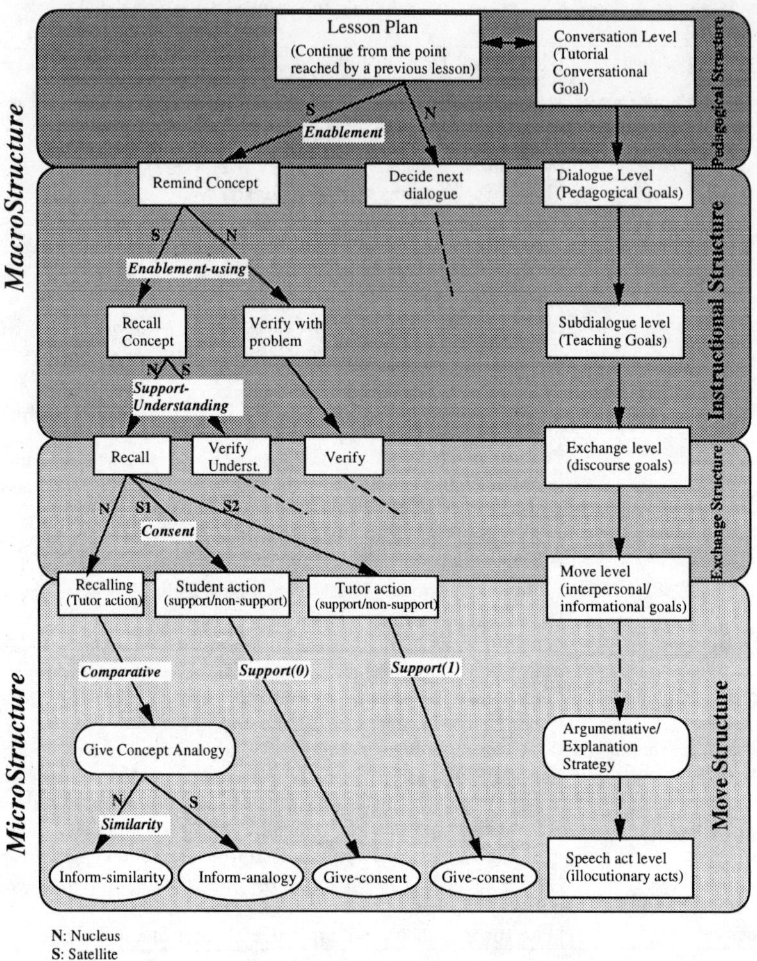

Fig. 1. Annotated lesson plan generated for a teaching session

lation also annotates a partial *ordering* on discourse (by ordering the pedagogical (dialogue) intentions into which the conversation goal is decomposed). Further ordering is provided by the instructional relations that operate on the dialogue and subdialogue levels and build the instructional structure of the dialogue. These relations annotate the order according to which instructional steps have to be carried out so that the corresponding higher-level pedagogical or teaching tasks can be reasonably and successfully completed (e.g., first you describe a concept via an explanation text and then the student's confirmation of comprehension is sought by means of a verification question).

As a consequence, ordering relations facilitate the comprehension, reconstruction, acceptance and retention of the material included. Furthermore, at the exchange level, further ordering relations dictate the way an exchange is unfolded under normal conditions (i.e., when no interruptions occur). Finally, other lower levels (move and act), which actually belong to a text planning facility, further ordering is provided by other rhetorical relations derived from other sources, such as ideational (conceptual) and interpersonal sources. Ordering is also derived from the focus of attention.

5 Exchange representation

We will now turn to the linguistic part of our model, the exchange level, and will focus on the representation of its structure. Exchange is one of the most important parts of conversation level (see justification of this point at the beginning of section 2) as well as the point in the dialogue at which text generation actually begins. Thus it deserves particular attention as well as a neat and precise representation of its structure.

An exchange, as a structure, consists of moves and can be initiated by both parties in the dialogue (mixed initiative). In other words, 'it gains its name from the fact that it is the unit in which some commodity — either information (knowledge) or action — passes from one participant to the other' (O'Donell, 1990).

Our exchange model is based on linguistic work on exchange structure and dynamics as described in Martin (1992), who also took initial work of Berry (1981) as a point of departure.

Following Berry, Martin developed an exchange model, called 'negotiation', which classifies exchanges into two types: *action* exchanges as opposed to *knowledge* (*information*) ones, and exchanges initiated by the Primary Actor/Knower as opposed to those initiated by the Secondary Actor/Knower.[1]

A general representation of an exchange of any type is the following:

$$((dX1) \wedge X2) \wedge X1 \wedge (aX1) \wedge (X2f) \wedge (X1f)$$

where () indicate optional elements and $\wedge$ linear order. Those labels were introduced by Berry: d stands for delay, a for accept, f for follow-up.

$X1$ is called the *obligatory move* in the sense that it must be provided (explicitly or implicitly) so that the exchange (discourse goal) can be successfully completed. The rest of the moves are called *optional moves* in the sense that their realization depends on the kind of exchange produced and on the attitude of the participants. X is substituted for K or A depending on whether the exchange is a knowledge or action type of exchange.

[1] The Primary Actor is defined as the person who is actually going to carry out the action and the Primary Knower as the person who already knows the information which is the basis of exchange. On the other hand, the Secondary Actor or Knower is the person who is supposed to receive the action or information. Exchanges can be initiated by both (Berry, 1981).

For instance, our example presented at the beginning of section 4 is a specific knowledge exchange ('give-information'). The tutor's initial proposition constitutes the $K1$ move, while the other two moves (the student's and the tutor's) are follow-up moves which could be generated or not. Thus the exchange structure of this example is represented by: $K1 \wedge K2f \wedge K1f$.

Another example of a knowledge class exchange ('ascertain-information') is the following:

$dK1$	Do you know what this denotes?
$K2$	This is a function declaration.
$K1$	That's right.
$aK1$	This is how a function is declared.
$K2f$	All right.
$K1f$	OK.

As noted, the exchange structure of the above example is also provided by Berry's labels. In fact, $aK1$ is an additional move that we added since it is used in tutorial dialogues particularly as an extension of the $K1$ move. Thus, exchanges consisting of up to six moves are proposed.

Our ultimate purpose is to define appropriate rhetorical relations that will be used to model (represent and build) the exchange structure presented here in terms of an extended RST theory and will thus replace the opaque labels of Berry (see O'Donell (1990) for problems with these labels).

In particular, we claim that the $X1$ move of the exchange can play the role of the nucleus, as defined in the RST theory, perfectly. On the other hand, the optional moves can act as the satellites, whose function is to either contribute towards or support the success (completion) of the nucleus (i.e., of the exchange goal).

As a consequence, an exchange can be perfectly represented by a new, particular kind of rhetorical relation, called *dialogic rhetorical relation*, that has the same characteristics as the kind of exchange it models. Berry's labels, then, are no longer useful, since each part (move) of an exchange is represented by the corresponding nucleus/satellite part of the relation that models the exchange. The nucleus and satellite parts of a relation contain all the knowledge necessary to describe and represent the exchange context in much detail. This knowledge is contained in the *constraints* and *effects* definitions of a relation that take the participants' mental states (knowledge, beliefs, attitudes, etc.) into account. *Constraints* are used to decide on the applicability of a move option whereas *effects* describe the effect of a move on the exchange context.

The particular type of dialogic rhetorical relation that models the kind of exchange presented in our example in this section is called *Ascertainment relation*. Its name denotes the specific kind of exchange it models as well as the goal the exchange is to achieve. Exchange structure, then, is represented by the following application diagram of this relation definition (Figure 2).

In the exchange structure, moves are represented by horizontal lines and are labelled N or S. N is the *obligatory move*, which is said to contain the *point of the exchange*, i.e. it either carries or indicates the completion of the illocutionary intent of the exchange. Thus, this move plays the role of the nucleus (N) in the exchange structure. All the other moves play, in principle, the role of the satellite (S), by either *contributing* to the initial completion of the nucleus (being on the left of N) or by simply *supporting* the ultimate successful completion of the nucleus (being on the right of N). The *contribution* and *support* relations are actually based on the theory of 'discourse contributions' as developed by Clark & Schaefer (1989). The discourse goal of the exchange is accomplished only when the exchange (in fact its nucleus) has been completed by the *contribution* relations and has been successfully backed by the *support* relations.

Each dialogic relation clearly specifies how the constituents (moves) of the exchange co-occur, how they relate to one another, how the nucleus of the relation is related to the whole collection — its satellites, and also the (*changing*) role of each move in the exchange structure. All this important knowledge constitutes what we call the *rhetorical structure* of the exchange and is necessary for identifying how the different units of the exchange relate to each other and to the exchange goal (and subgoals) these units contribute to. Moreover, it accounts for coherence, maintains a record of the contributing and supporting relations chosen to achieve the current goals and generates linguistic information (clausal connectives, lexical cues) (Moore & Paris, 1989; Redeker, 1991). For more details on the exchange model see Daradoumis (1993a).

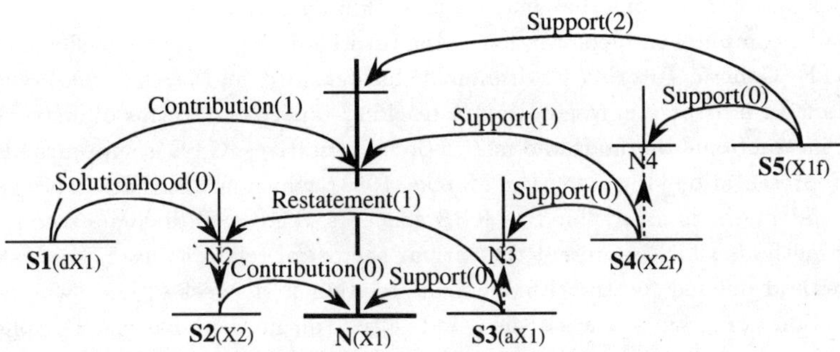

Fig. 2. The ascertainment dialogic relation (schema type)

6 Conclusions

We have made an attempt to build a rich (sophisticated) dialogue structure for tutorial dialogues by means of rhetorical relations which can be identified at each conversational level between the individual parts of a level. This dialogue organization closely follows the tutorial task structure by providing a clear correspondence between the levels of the tutorial task structure (intentional structure) and the levels of the dialogue structure.

At this point we should note that it is the ITS, of which our dialogue model forms part, that initially decides upon the general tutoring strategy to be followed and on its decomposition into adequate steps. According to this strategy, the student is allowed to take the initiative to pursue a goal of her own; however, the whole process is always controlled by the tutor. So, in certain cases, such as when serious conflicts arise between the tutor's and the student's goals, the tutor may completely re-plan its general strategy to resolve the conflict.

Consequently, our dialogue model serves to cover the whole tutoring process derived and to associate its intentional task-oriented structure with the dialogue structure by means of the rhetorical relations used to model the conversation produced. It further identifies the particular structures (e.g., pedagogical, instructional) of which tutorial dialogues may consist. The model reveals the different general-purpose explanation strategies used and the rhetorical relations implicit in the dialogue, and may be used to generate largely coherent, lengthy and complex dialogues.

This demonstrates that the 'classical' RST theory, initially developed and applied for monologues only, can also be used for modelling dialogues. It also illustrates the principal idea distinguishing this model from all other models of dialogues developed so far: the use of discourse (rhetorical) relations, identified at each level of dialogue planning, to model the whole conversation. Discourse relations will then be dialogue planning methods which will be applied to structure the entire conversation from the conversation level down to the speech-act level and, as we also believe, to model any type of interruptions that may occur within an exchange.

Finally, computer implementation of the tutorial dialogue model is effected using the GTE (Generic Tutoring Environment) formalism (van Marcke, 1990), which is based on an in-depth representation of teaching expertise in terms of instructional tasks, instructional methods and instructional primitives. GTE is supported by the KRS representation language (van Marcke, 1988), which means that GTE's generic tasks and methods are defined as KRS concepts. The RST dialogue tree is built up by methods which represent the various rhetorical relations used. For instance, the method defined for the 'Enablement' relation first checks to see whether its application constraints are satisfied and, after the method has been applied, it determines how the effects of the relation cause the student model to be updated accordingly.

References

Berry, M. (1981) Towards layers of exchange structure for directive exchanges. Network, 2, 23–32.

Carberry, S. (1990) Plan recognition in natural language dialogue. Cambridge, Mass.: The MIT Press.

Clark, H.H. & Schaefer, E.F. (1989) Contributing to Discourse. Cognitive Science, 13, 259–294.

Daradoumis, T. (1993a) Building a dynamic RST-based grammar of coherent interactive dialogues. Proceedings of the 4th European Workshop on Natural Language Generation, Pisa, Italy, 91–101.

Daradoumis, T. (1993b) Managing interruptions in tutorial dialogues by means of an extended RST-based model. Proceedings of the AI-ED 93 World Conference on Artificial Intelligence in Education, Edingburgh, Scotland, 121–128.

Fernandez, I., Diaz, A. & Verdejo, M. (1988) A cooperative architecture for tutoring tasks. Proceedings of the 8th Int. Workshop on Expert Systems and their application (volume 2), Avignon.

Grosz, B.J. & Sidner, C.L. (1986) Attention, Intention and the Structure of Discourse. Computational Linguistics, 12(3), 175–204.

Hovy, E. (1988) Planning coherent multisentential text. Proceedings of the 28th Annual Meeting of the ACL, Buffalo, NY, 163–169.

Hovy, E., Lavid, J., Maier, E., Mittal, V. & Paris, C. (1992) Employing knowledge resources in a new text planner architecture. In: Dale, R., Hovy, E., Rösner, D. & Stock, O. (eds.) Aspects of Automated Natural Language Generation, Lecture Notes in Aritificial Intelligence 587. Berlin: Springer-Verlag, 57–72.

Maier, E. & Hovy, E. (1991) A metafunctionally motivated taxonomy for discourse structure relations. Proceedings of the 3rd European WS on Language Generation, Judenstein, Austria, 38–45.

Mann, W.C. & Thompson, S.A. (1988) Rhetorical Structure Theory: Toward a functional theory of text organisation. Text, 8(3), 243–281.

Martin, J. (1992) English Text: System and Structure. Amsterdam: Benjamin Press.

Moore, J. & Paris, C. (1989) Planning text for advisory dialogues. Proceedings of the 27th Annual Meeting of the ACL, 203–211.

O'Donell, M. (1990) A dynamic model of exchange. WORD: Journal of the International Linguistic Association, 41(3).

Redeker, G. (1991) Lexical markers of discourse structure. Linguistics, 29.

van der Linden, K., Cumming, S. & Martin, J. (1992) Using systems networks to build rhetorical structures. In: Dale, R., Hovy, E., Rösner, D. & Stock, O. (eds.) Aspects of Automated Natural Language Generation. Berlin: Springer-Verlag.

van Marcke, K. (1988) KRS User Manual. Memo 88-15. VUB AI LAB, Brussels, Belgium.

van Marcke, K. (1990) GTE-1 User Manual. Tech. report. Knowledge Technologies C.V., Brussels, Belgium.

Graphics and Natural Language in Design and Instruction

John R. Lee

EdCAAD, Dept. of Architecture, University of Edinburgh, 20 Chambers Street, Edinburgh EH1 1JZ, Scotland, U.K., email: john@caad.ed.ac.uk

Abstract. The education of designers (e.g. architects) is typically quite different from many other instructional situations. As argued e.g. by Donald Schön, the 'studio' method has many distinctive characteristics. These have serious implications for any possibility of applying intelligent tutoring systems in such domains. For several reasons, there is evidently no prospect at all of the system replacing a design tutor: it will never have the breadth of experientially acquired knowledge; it will never possess the inherently unformalisable criteria of architectural criticism; and it will never be able to understand drawings well enough. This last point is, however, related to the general question of in what ways and to what extent a computer system might assist in design education. Integrated natural language and graphics dialogue systems have been proposed as an environment for designers, and perhaps students learning e.g. redesign tasks. This paper describes some research into the properties of such dialogues and considers computational and other implications.

Keywords. Design, 'studio' education, NL dialogue, drawing, knowledge representation

1 Introduction

It was suggested at the inception of this workshop that instructional dialogues are mainly or centrally about the transference of information. However, even if it may appear at first sight that this is the case, examination soon reveals it to be an oversimplification. Certainly, the student will need to acquire information, but typically much else as well, being in general concerned also with the development of a skill (or set of skills). Dialogues in instructional situations will therefore have a number of complex and interlocking components, many of which are concerned with performances of various kinds by the student, interrupted only if necessary by the tutor. This is particularly true, of course, in domains where much of the knowledge relevant to the exercise of a skill is not usually (and perhaps cannot be) made explicit or formalised or codified in recognisable ways.

Design is archetypal of this kind of domain; but it should be recognised that there is more similarity than is sometimes thought between design skills and those involved in many other less obviously 'intuitive' practices. In fact, whereas design is often (quite unconvincingly) characterised as formal 'problem solving' — especially in the AI literature — the converse is the case: problem solving in almost all real situations involves a substantial amount of activity which very closely resembles design. That is to say, the identification of a path towards the solution of a problem, and indeed the characterisation of the problem itself, is rarely something that can be addressed by formal methods in advance of some kind of sifting process guided by an 'intuitive' grasp of the issues involved. While instruction must of course be able to convey the basic information which will be used in solving a problem, it must also provide for the development of the skills needed to use that information effectively. A dialogue between an instructor and a student will thus often have to be a development in which components of information-transfer are interwoven with relatively informal analysis and some kind of practical application of the knowledge. What is called for here is a flexible system, where structure is established by tacit agreement between the participants, rather than a highly restrictive dialogue with a predetermined structure, as one much more commonly sees in HCI.

Design dialogues are notable for their high degree of *multimodality*, especially the use of drawings. This is, of course, a feature shared by many natural instructional dialogues, as witness the commonplace uses made of blackboards and other visual aids. An important aspect of drawings in these situations is that they are relatively informal and not predefined by complex sets of constraints; a central component of the dialogue is therefore concerned with establishing and maintaining a shared interpretation by the participants of the drawings involved. The analysis of instructional dialogues of such kinds will have to take account of this, and be able to distinguish between the various functions of different parts of the dialogue. These remarks help to establish one of the main ideas behind this paper, which is that although the emphasis is on possible uses of computers in design education, instructional dialogues in many other contexts often need to be thought of as two-way multimodal conversations about things hard to formalise; hence dialogues which arise in the context of design are worth looking at for what they may tell us about such conversations in general.

I propose here to consider, not so much whether there ever could (or should) be such a thing as an intelligent tutoring system for design, but rather more general issues arising in the context of design education. Although it seems clear that a computer system will never replace the design tutor, for reasons which we will consider below, there may be aspects and parts of the design education process which computers can in some way help with. We should try not to prejudge the extent to which these will benefit from attempts to emulate human-human dialogue phenomena; the latter are studied more in the expectation that they will reveal something of value about the structure of dialogue and the process of design, than in the hope that such discoveries will be immediately applicable. There exist, for instance, systems which provide the design student with ways to 'play with shapes', perhaps using a shape-grammar formalism. Such systems may be extremely useful in developing, say, the spatial imagination of the student, but although it is quite likely that the interface will condition their utility we do not know enough about how it may do this. It is at least plausible that elaborate dialogues will be unnecessary, if not actually undesirable.

2 Instructional dialogues and design

The nature of dialogues which bring many of the above-mentioned aspects together in a specific instructional situation — the architectural design studio — has been discussed in some detail by Donald Schön (1987). His main concern is to develop an argument showing how all practical professions (medicine, law, management) will benefit from recognising the strong element of design-like 'artistry' in their problem-solving. He treats the design studio dialogue as a prototype for a kind of dialogue which he believes should be developed for education in all such professions. His emphasis is at a fairly high level, on indicating how successes and breakdowns in communication between student and tutor reveal the complex nature of the relationship between their different ways of knowing or conceiving of a design and the design process.

The objective is to show that the student is not told how to design, but rather is gradually moulded into a way of doing, thinking and talking about things that results in his becoming a designer. It is necessary that this is the case, according to Schön's view (which, however, reflects the orthodox among designers, at least architects), because design is a skill which cannot be explained. Clear reasons cannot be given for the judgements that a design tutor gives of the student's efforts. Analogously with the Platonic paradox of knowledge (as expressed in the *Meno*), it is claimed, only a designer can recognise the basis for a design judgement, and hence it is impossible that the student should understand until he has become a designer himself (at which point the learning process is in some sense over). By extension, Schön thinks, it's important to recognise this element of inexplicability in other fields of professional judgement, and he is led to advocate the explicit adoption of a 'studio' teaching method in such fields.

There are two things to be said about this position. On the one hand, it seems to be overstated. At least from the viewpoint of the non-designer or, frequently, the design student (and there is perhaps no completely unbiased viewpoint to be taken), design critics could often do much more to articulate the basis of their judgements, and seem even to hide behind the inexplicability thesis to avoid having to examine them too closely or to flesh them out more fully. On the other hand, to go even further than Schön, we might say that other skills in general — not just 'professional' skills — also seem to have a strong aspect of being learned 'by experience', or 'through doing', even those not usually thought of as 'practical', whether constructing logical proofs and philosophical arguments, solving differential equations or 'algebra word problems', criticising literature, analysing proteins, etc. There's an extent to which no amount of explanation, however cogently put together, is ever a substitute for (usually repetitive) practical experience in acquiring any skill, whether physical, cognitive, judgemental or whatever. Schön's concept of 'reflection-in-action' applies equally to their application.

The most important claim of Schön's that we clearly have to sustain, however, is that the criteria for evaluating the quality of a design cannot be formalised in such a way as to be mechanically checkable (something that has also been forcefully argued in the CAD context by Bijl (1989)). This suffices to establish the impossibility of a full-scale computerised design tutor. But it remains conceivable that an intelligent tutoring system should at least be able to offer advice on various aspects of the evolution of a design, especially if we observe that a tutor, to be useful, need not be an ultimate arbiter or a complete expert; vaguely appropriate hints may often be quite valuable. This is just as well, since it seems likely that a great many other tasks to which one might want to apply tutoring systems will also have no computable 'correctness' conditions.

Our discussion has emphasised that an important part of an instructional dialogue, involved at some stage in learning almost anything, will be to allow the student to practise some activity under the watchful eye of the tutor, who will intervene if requested or if it appears necessary to help the student out of some difficulty. The tutor thus needs to be able to follow and interpret the behaviour of the student, even when it is relatively ill-defined, as for instance when based on the development of a rough drawing. Computer-based tutoring systems seem on the one hand particularly well suited to this kind of role, since it requires long periods of attention and should ideally be available whenever it suits the convenience of the student; but on the other hand little is known about the analysis of the kinds of dialogues needed to support such activity in general. This observation again helps to motivate the investigation of design dialogues in the general context of interfaces to instructional systems, by emphasising their relevance to the general issues raised by ill-structured multimodal dialogue situations where it is necessary to allow for the dynamic development of the dialogue in a direction which must be open to flexible interactive control jointly by the participants.

Of course, a great many existing tutoring systems embody a practice-based strategy; they provide the student with a large supply of problems and then, in more or less sophisticated ways, supervise attempts to solve them. In many cases, it is possible to subsume the entire learning process in a particular domain, say of mathematical problems, under this scheme. A danger here is that such systems may, through offering the student an impoverished interface or simplified interactions, artificially constrain the student's approach to the problem, or impose formalisation of an inappropriate level or nature upon it. Even in a domain of formal problems, the student may wish to develop a direction different from that presumed in the design of the system, and this is something that requires a responsiveness and flexibility, in the elaboration of dialogues, which is not found in current interfaces (as is confirmed by a glance through the comprehensive survey provided by Wenger (1987)).

In an attempt to illuminate these issues, the present paper offers some observations deriving from the study of a dialogue in which natural language and graphics act together to provide an integrated 'channel' which is used by the participants in a highly dynamic way (although there is nothing specifically 'instructional' about the particular dialogue in question). The study was conducted as part of a research programme into the integration of graphics and natural language in general, the goal being to draw morals for the development of advanced HCI systems. The above arguments suggest that some of the lessons will be rather relevant in the context of HCI for instructional applications, in particular given the emphasis which emerges on the fact that a drawing, however it is used, has to be seen as embedded in a whole activity, which may be quite complex even when the drawing is relatively simple. In uses of graphics in teaching e.g. mathematics and logic, we find that usually very simple diagrams are used, which nonetheless support a rather complex interaction. The drawings used by Schön's subjects are similarly often simple, but interpreted in a rather rich framework, and this is reflected also in the drawings produced in the dialogue discussed below.

3 Integrating graphics and natural language

Whereas Schön's discussion is conducted at a rather high level and in quite broad terms, an interest in HCI compels us to focus on quite specific details of interactions. We also want to pick up the issues of knowledge representation which are relevant to the support of this kind of dialogue. The question is: what kind of system would one need, to support the phenomena observed here? Can current approaches be modified, easily or at all, to provide the basis for a remotely 'realistic' graphics/language dialogue? And, in any case, how realistic would one want a dialogue in HCI to be, in these terms?

We need to look firstly at the uses of linguistic and graphical expressions. It is easy to be too simplistic about these. Expressions are used to convey information, declaratively, but also have many other functions. In extant natural language (NL), and in some cases multimodal interface systems, some of these are of course codified and implemented, e.g. asking questions of different kinds, giving instructions, etc. — various kinds of *communicative acts* (Maybury, 1992). An important function which is not usually addressed in such systems is *giving a meaning* to or for some other expression. A sentence can be used to explain or define the meaning of another, e.g. one containing a technical term unfamiliar to the other party in the dialogue; and similarly, a sentence can supply an interpretation for a drawing. This can be extremely important in applications such as instruction, where unfamiliar terms are perhaps especially likely to be introduced, and in design, where the meanings of drawings are generally not available from pre-existing conventions and drawings are often potentially highly ambiguous.

In most current systems that have graphical interfaces, the interface exploits a fixed set of graphical objects — primitives such as lines, rectangles and circles — which can be composed by the user in various completely pre-defined ways. If the system is able to interpret the resulting configuration at all, then usually it can only do so in terms of a rigidly fixed schema, which is either beyond the control of the user or at best manipulable only as simple, direct assignments of relationships between graphical objects and objects in some domain. This can result in something like a graphical (or visual) programming language, but is too inflexible for many less clearly formalised applications. Our hope is that NL can be harnessed to the task of providing a context within which graphical expressions can acquire a meaning in a more flexible way, a prospect which derives from the power of NL to operate at a very high level of abstraction. It is unlikely that a formal language (visual or otherwise) can be defined, which would have comparable power and yet be sufficiently learnable etc. for non-specialised use (cf. discussion in Lee (1991)). What we also need to be able to do is exploit NL in this way within a framework which in addition allows a naturally flexible use of graphics, rather than an artificially constrained set of primitives and operations. Such a goal is of course highly ambitious and perhaps even in principle unrealisable. It is too early to judge this issue yet, however, since the structure of natural dialogue using NL and graphics is far too ill-understood.

Much of the limited amount of work that has been done in integrating graphics and natural language has approached the matter by identifying *deictic* links between language and graphics: 'pointing' actions associated with the use of certain indexical terms such as *this*, *that*, etc. Interfaces can therefore be created which allow the user to make declarations of the form *This is a* ..., introducing the intended interpretation for (part of) a drawing. These kinds of sentences have commonly been taken as typical of the linking which occurs between graphics and language, and have been implemented in a number of systems attempting to integrate these modalities for purposes such as knowledge-base querying and update (Kobsa & Allgayer, 1986; Neal et al., 1988; Lee et al., 1989; Lee & Zeevat, 1990; Lee, 1992a), and intelligent computer-aided design (cf. Pineda (1989)).

The originators of such systems, including the present author, typically have not investigated whether the assumptions they make are justified by what happens in real dialogues. Very often, explicit deictic relationships are taken to be paradigmatic of the binding between graphics and natural language, simply because (characteristically of popular AI techniques) they are very successful in limited contexts and are relatively easy to implement, being quite congenial to an analysis of graphics as consisting of discrete objects built up into compositions. But in fact very little is known about the real structure of integrated graphics/language dialogues, at least at a level where the kinds of issues we are interested in here can be addressed.

The observations reported below [1] attempt to remedy this situation by examining a real dialogue conducted between an architect and a client about the redesign of the client's kitchen. The dialogue, of some 2 hours duration, was videotaped and transcribed with detailed attention to the drawings and gestures as well as the language (Neilson, 1991). It is discussed in considerable detail in Neilson & Lee (1994). We were concerned to see how language and graphics interrelate and what kinds of things affect the interpretation of the two media. The dialogue was not restricted by any artificial constraints; the architect was able to use pencil, eraser and overlay draughting paper, and was given no special instructions about how to behave. It should be recognised that at present the issues of integrated dialogue have to be addressed in a preliminary and exploratory fashion, and that our concern is with rather general questions about the types of dialogue phenomena that arise. There is no suggestion that anything specific in the dialogue discussed here is or is not appropriate in other kinds of situations, e.g. dialogue between tutor and student.

[1] Made by Irene Neilson at EdCAAD.

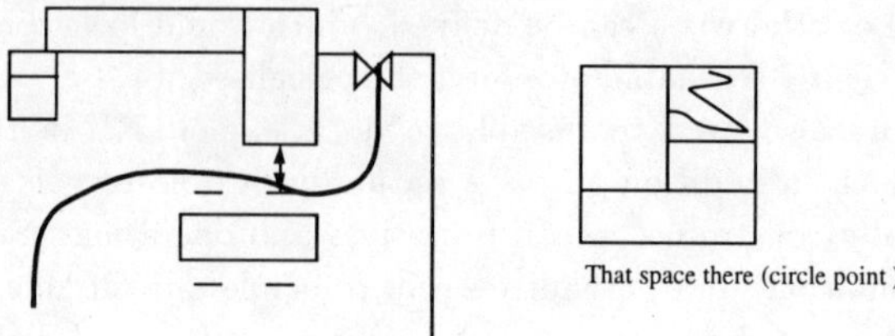

Fig. 1.

One of the first things to emerge from these observations was that, where they are used, explicit deictic relationships between language and drawing are considerably more complex than is generally acknowledged (see Neilson and Leslie (1991), for a detailed discussion). It tends to be assumed that specific well-defined objects will be pointed at, and that these can be identified in the drawing and named, perhaps with a little use of contextual information. This assumption seems to reflect a view about how deixis operates in practice, although it also happens to coincide with what current programming techniques allow easily to be implemented. The 'targets' of pointing actions linked to deictic expressions in our observations were, however, often *not* clearly identifiable objects; they were, for instance, spaces, parts of objects, objects that had not yet been completely defined, invisible constructs such as routes between objects, etc. (Fig. 1).

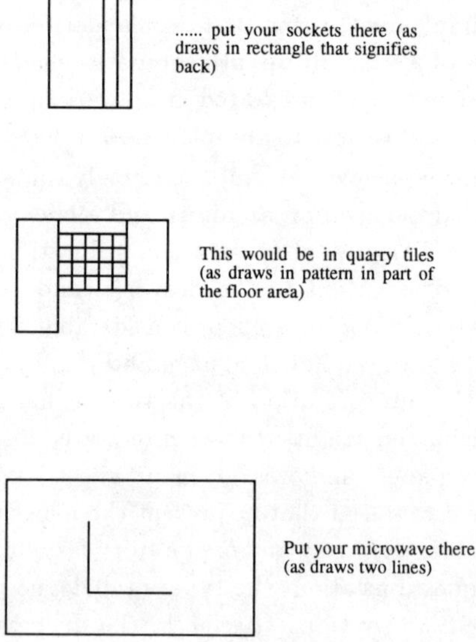

...... put your sockets there (as draws in rectangle that signifies back)
This would be in quarry tiles (as draws in pattern in part of the floor area)
Put your microwave there (as draws two lines)

Fig. 2.

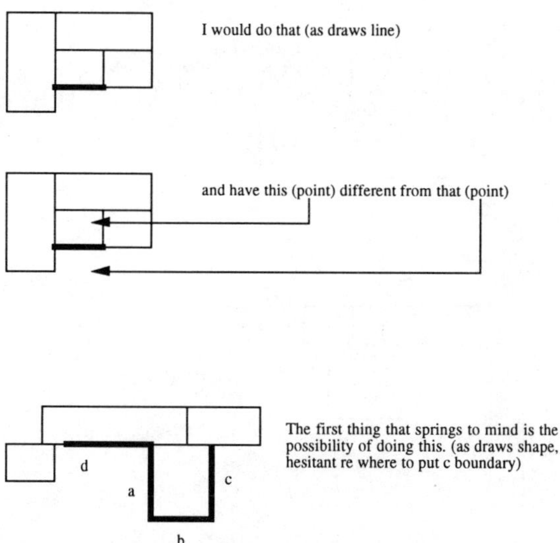

Fig. 3.

Other pointing actions singled out no kind of object at all, but instead were often gestures, related to no particular word or phrase, which served mainly to localise the context of the immediately surrounding part of the discussion. And where deictic definitions were used in something like the conventionally assumed way, the associated action was very often not a pointing action but something else, such as a drawing action (Fig. 2), which itself might become the referent of the deictic expression (Fig. 3).

Many of the relationships between graphics and language are not established or maintained by the use of any explicit or specialised expressions or actions (Neilson & Lee (1994), *op. cit.*). What happens, instead, is that the two modalities fuse together into a combined communication system from which neither component can be extracted and seen to work independently. Talking and drawing lean on background knowledge to create a context in which each gives signification to the other, often quite indirectly.

The example in Fig. 4 shows this rather clearly: the drawing itself is too sketchy to have a determinate meaning outside the context of the discussion; the introduction of the circle would be at best quite unclear aside from the designer's accompanying remark; and the remark would be incoherent without the context and the drawing.

Similarly, in Fig. 5, there is no reference at all, anywhere in the interaction, to *chairs* (or stools); yet we know immediately that this is what the two lines are intended to represent. The understanding of the picture and its components is immediately changed, as the sentence brings a new idea to bear and ties it to previously un-needed parts of background knowledge about kitchen furniture and behaviour.

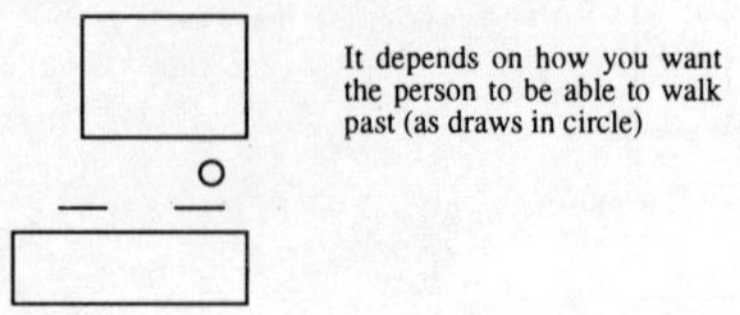

It depends on how you want the person to be able to walk past (as draws in circle)

Fig. 4.

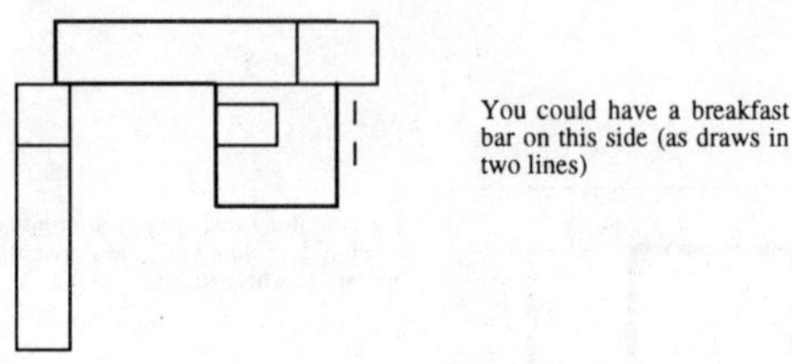

You could have a breakfast bar on this side (as draws in two lines)

Fig. 5.

In computer interfaces, it is usually assumed to be most important to maintain consistency between the graphical display and the knowledge or data that it represents. A good deal of work goes into developing feedback and other mechanisms which can establish what changes need to be made either to the picture or the knowledge representation, in consequence of some move in the interaction. In the observed dialogue, by contrast, the picture often became inconsistent with what is clearly the intended state of the depicted object (the kitchen, or some part of it), without this causing any difficulty for either participant. As a reflection of this, it is notable that the eraser was used *only once* in the entire dialogue (although of course the use of overlays is important here). The example in Fig. 6 and 7, for instance, shows how an inconsistency in the drawing can be disregarded. This relates to the question, raised again below, of how closely we might expect or want computer interfaces to resemble natural dialogue.

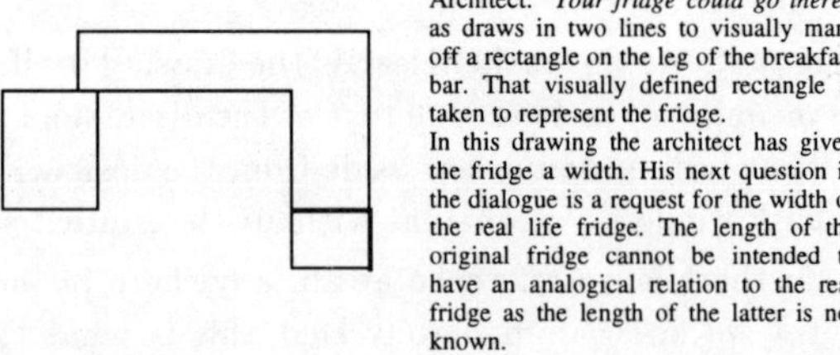

Architect: *"Your fridge could go there"* as draws in two lines to visually mark off a rectangle on the leg of the breakfast bar. That visually defined rectangle is taken to represent the fridge.
In this drawing the architect has given the fridge a width. His next question in the dialogue is a request for the width of the real life fridge. The length of the original fridge cannot be intended to have an analogical relation to the real fridge as the length of the latter is not known.

Fig. 6.

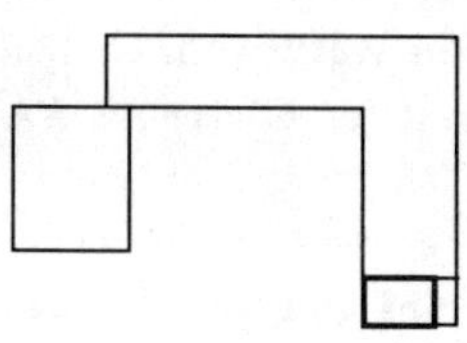

"You could have the fridge ... Yes, cos I have made this (the breakfast bar) wider than the width of the fridge. The fridge is actually going to be there" as draws in lines 1, 2, 3, 4. He darkens these lines. This seems to be being used by the architect to signify that the fridge is boxed in though the client is not aware of this. The two lines which indicated the previous position of the fridge are not removed: they are simply ignored.

Fig. 7.

4 Knowledge and representation

Although, obviously, a great deal of further, more directed research is required into the kinds of phenomena we here see starting to be revealed, we have nonetheless already drawn some morals for the support of such dialogues in intelligent systems (Neilson & Lee (1994) *op. cit.*, Lee (1992b)). Foremost among these is the primacy of contextual knowledge in accounting for the development of the dialogue; many and varied moves take place which cannot be made sense of simply with respect to the preceding utterances, or to anything in an existing interpretation of the drawing — instead, a new orientation is required which seems to be available only by relating the expressions to previously unused aspects of background knowledge of the situation under discussion. But we can also make some observations about the kind of structure needed in the representations that relate to such knowledge. One which classifies its subject matter into a domain of discrete objects with specific properties may well be too rigid. Often, the dialogue concerns incompletely specified objects; it concerns representations which are not clearly of any particular object, but may perhaps constitute various possible sets of subparts of various different objects. A typical knowledge-representation ontology will have trouble with these things — interpretational mappings will frequently have to be undone and redone, decompositions of structure will be only transiently valid. The unsolved problems of nonmonotonicity become oppressively dominant and vicious.

It would be premature to conclude that traditional AI has nothing to offer in these circumstances, but equally it would be wrong to shrug off the problems as ones which will submit to a standard object-and-rule-based approach given time. New and more flexible notions of structure need to be sought; but at present there are few pointers to likely-looking candidates.

5 Conclusions

As stated at the outset, the objective of this paper has been mainly to raise the issues of multimodal dialogue in a rather general way, in the hope that they can be made relevant to the context of instructional systems. There are, of course, many other respects in which the use of graphics has great instructional potential. Pictures of various kinds can be used as a presentation system, to show information about, among many other things, the domain which is the subject of instruction (e.g., a device which has to be operated, as in WIP; André and Rist (1992)) or an explanation of a piece of reasoning related to it (cf. GUIDON-WATCH; Richer and Clancey (1985)). Diagrams can be used as external representations which might relate to mental models used in inferential processes, so that their construction and manipulation can be used as a basis for reasoning and teaching logic (cf. Barwise and Etchemendy (1990), Wang and Lee (1993), Stenning and Oberlander (to appear)).

In a natural dialogue, these different kinds of uses of pictures are switched between frequently and without warning — something which causes the participants no difficulties but adds enormously to the inferential problems besetting an AI system which tries to follow them. It is therefore common to limit systems' use of graphics to one or another of these aspects, and severely to restrict the range of dialogue. This may well be entirely appropriate, and it would be obviously absurd to suggest that natural dialogue should be used in all situations. Perhaps, in fact, it should be used in none. As was mentioned above, we should not assume that HCI ought to mimic human-human interaction even where 'natural language' is being exploited, and even where one has the ambition to link it to 'natural' uses of graphics. At present, we can only pose questions about whether and when these things would be useful.

These final remarks rather echo the remarks of Wenger (1987), who in drawing towards a conclusion of his assessment of existing tutoring systems, makes the following observations:

> Bringing more intelligence into knowledge communication requires an understanding of the communication environment in which it takes place. In other words, intelligence is relative to an environment. ...the communication environment created by two people and that created by a person and a machine are not likely to be the same, and the terms of the cooperation required for successful communication may differ in fundamental ways. Hence, computational models of knowledge communication will require new theories of knowledge communication, as computer-based systems evolve and as research in artificial intelligence and related disciplines provides more powerful models (p. 426).

If there is a point of divergence between this paper and Wenger's view here, it resides in his emphasis on 'knowledge communication'. What we began by noting, and found emphasised most strongly by Schön, is that teaching very often, and not only (even though perhaps most obviously) in design, is not clearly describable in these terms; and neither is the activity that takes place in the dialogue we observed. There is much that is not clearly defined 'knowledge', and there are many things occurring besides 'communication', at least unless both these notions are understood in a much wider sense than is usual in attempts to characterise them in terms of formal theory. While we can make a solid enough start by focussing on these analytical triangulation points, we should not assume that they exhaust the whole area.

Acknowledgements

The author is especially indebted to Irene Neilson, who carried out and analysed the observational study described and has contributed in many other ways to the development of the ideas. This research has been conducted under the auspices of projects funded at EdCAAD, the Centre for Cognitive Science, and the Human Communication Research Centre, University of Edinburgh, by the UK Joint Research Councils' Initiative in Cognitive Science and HCI (SPG8826213, *Foundations for Intelligent Graphical Interfaces*; SPG8919793, *Structure of Drawings for Picture-Oriented HCI*; and SPG69018050 *Specificity of Information in Graphics and Natural Language*), and by ESPRIT Basic Research (6296, *Graphical Communication in HCI — GRACE*).

References

André, E. & Rist, T. (1992) The Design of Illustrated Documents as a Planning Task. In: Maybury, M.T. (ed.) Intelligent Multimedia Interfaces. Menlo Park, CA: AAAI Press.

Barwise, J. & Etchemendy, J. (1990) Information, Infons and Inference.

Bijl, A. (1989) Computer Discipline and Design Practice — Shaping our Future. Edinburgh: Edinburgh University Press.

Kobsa, A. & Allgayer, J. (1986) Combining deictic gestures and natural languages for referent identification. XTRA project report 7. University of Saarbrücken.

Lee, J.R. (1991) Intelligent Interfaces and UIMS. In: Duce, D.A., Hopgood, F.R.A., Gomes, M.R. & Lee, J.R. (eds.) User Interface Management and Design. Berlin: Springer-Verlag. (EurographicSeminars).

Lee, J.R. (1992a) Graphics and Dialogue. In: Bès, G.G. (ed.) The Construction of a Natural Language and Graphic Interface: results and perspectives from the ACORD project. Berlin: Springer-Verlag.

Lee, J.R. (1992b) Graphics and Natural Language in Multi-Modal Dialogues. In: Taylor, M.M., Néel, F. & Bouwhuis, D.G. (eds.) The Structure of Multimodal Dialogue. Amsterdam: North-Holland. (in preparation).

Lee, J.R. & Zeevat, H.W. (1990) Integrating Graphics and Natural Language in Dialogue. Proceeding INTERACT 90. Amsterdam: North-Holland.

Lee, J.R., Kemp, B. & Manz, T. (1989) Knowledge-based Graphical Dialogue: a strategy and architecture. In: ESPRIT 89, ed. CEC-DGXIII. Dordrecht: Kluwer Academic, 321–333.

Maybury, M.T. (1992) Communicative Acts for Multimedia and Multimodal Dialogue. In: Taylor, M.M., Néel, F. & Bouwhuis, D.G. (eds.) The Structure of Multimodal Dialogue. Amsterdam: North-Holland. (in preparation).

Neal, J.G., Dobes, Z., Bettinger, K.E. & Byoun, J.S. (1988) Multi-modal references in human-computer dialogue. Proceedings AAAI-88, 819–823.

Neilson, I. (1991) Natural Language Dialogue Centred on a Drawing. EdCAAD working paper (transcript). Dept. Of Architecture, University of Edinburgh.

Neilson, I. & Lee, J.R. (1994) Conversations with Graphics: implications for the design of natural language/graphics interfaces. International Journal of Human-Computer Studies, 40, 509–541.

Neilson, I. & Leslie, N. (1991) Shared Frameworks in Interactive Design. Proceedings InterSymp '91. Baden-Baden, Germany, 12–18 August 1991.

Pineda, L.A. (1989) GRAFLOG: A theory of semantics for graphics with applications to human-computer interaction and CAD systems. Ph.D. thesis, University of Edinburgh.

Richer, M.H. & Clancey, W.J. (1985) GUIDON-WATCH: a graphic interface for viewing a knowledge-based system. IEEE Computer Graphics and Applications, 5(11), 51–64.

Schön, D.A. (1987) Educating the Reflective Practitioner. San Francisco, CA: Jossey-Bass Publishers.

Stenning, K. & Oberlander, J. (to appear) A cognitive theory of graphical and linguistic reasoning: logic and implementation. To appear in Cognitive Science. Preliminary version available as: research report HCRC/RP-20. Human Communication Research Centre, University of Edinburgh.

Wang, D. & Lee, J. (1993) Visual Reasoning: its formal semantics and applications. Journal of Visual Languages and Computing, 4(4), 327–356.

Wenger, E. (1987) Artificial Intelligence and Tutoring Systems. Los Altos, CA: Morgan Kaufmann.

Simulator-Based Training-Support Tools for Process-Control Operators

Brant A. Cheikes[1] and Eva L. Ragnemalm[2]

[1] The MITRE Corporation, 202 Burlington Road, M/SK 302, Bedford, MA 01730, USA, email: brant@linus.mitre.org
[2] Department of Computer and Information Science, University of Linköping, S-581 83 Linköping, Sweden, email: evalu@ida.liu.se

Abstract. Dynamic process simulators are increasingly being used in industry to support employee education and training. For nearly as many years as the field of Artificial Intelligence (AI) has existed, researchers in AI and Education have been investigating designs for computer-based tutoring and training systems, with the aim of developing instructional systems comparable in their effectiveness to expert human instructors. Only in the last few years, however, have simulator-based training system designs begun to be seriously explored. This article describes a research project focusing on the design of simulator-based tools to assist the training of process-control operators in the paper industry. In particular, we discuss the design of tools that operators could use to improve their skills in diagnosis and repair tasks.

Keywords. Simulators, education and training, intelligent tutoring systems, diagnosis and repair, artificial intelligence

1 Introduction

Dynamic process simulators are increasingly being used in industry to support employee education and training. For more than a decade, high-fidelity simulators have been used in the training of, among others, airline pilots and nuclear power plant operators. Allowing personnel to develop and hone their skills on simulators has been shown to have numerous benefits, including increased training effectiveness and substantially reduced training periods and costs (Baines et al., 1992; Lajoie & Lesgold, 1989; Woodward et al., 1988). Cohen, for example, cites a case from the nuclear power industry in which an extremely unlikely equipment failure was treated as if it were a routine event, primarily because the plant operators had successfully handled such incidents dozens of times earlier on the plant simulator (Cohen, 1988).

In industries such as nuclear power and commercial aviation, it has been considered essential for simulators to have *face validity*, meaning that their interfaces mimic the corresponding work environments as closely as possible. Nuclear power plant simulators thus have the look and feel of power plant control rooms, and aircraft simulators have the look and feel of aircraft cockpits. Training on such simulators is highly effective in terms of the directness with which students are able to transfer their simulator-developed skills to the actual work environment, but this effectiveness comes at a formidable cost. In the case of nuclear plant simulators, one reference places the cost per simulator in the range of $10 million to $15 million (Cohen, 1988).

In many industrial settings, however, as well as in other learning environments such as secondary schools and universities, useful education and training goals may still be achieved using simulators that lack face validity yet otherwise faithfully model the dynamic behavior of the processes of interest. Given advances in microprocessor technology that have brought mainframe-quality computing power to low-cost laptop personal computers (PCs), it is now possible to develop computationally demanding simulator-based methods and apply them to a wide variety of education and training tasks.

In industries such as paper manufacturing and pharmaceutical production where teams of operators control complex dynamic processes, the needs for improved training programs and methods have grown along with advances in technology. As Bainbridge has observed, automatic-control systems often make the operator's job more difficult rather than easier, by eliminating the straightforward aspects of the job and leaving to the operators only the cognitively demanding tasks (Bainbridge, 1987). For these industries, the use of simulators in training offers great hope as a means of helping operators develop the knowledge and skills necessary for effective performance. The question of exactly *how* to incorporate simulators in training has recently inspired substantial research interest.

This article describes an on-going research project—begun in consultation with a Swedish manufacturer of equipment for the pulp and paper industry—whose goal is to develop and evaluate principles and methods for the design of simulator-based training tools that operate on PCs. The project has been conducted under the auspices of a government-sponsored research initiative whose goal is to foster the development of improved training methods for the process industry. Our work started when our industrial contact was completing implementation of elaborate PC-based graphical simulators modeling different stages and configurations of their pulp-processing equipment. One of the company's concerns was how they might advantageously integrate these simulators into the training programs they offer to their customers. While the simulators clearly could be used in classroom settings under the guidance of expert human instructors, it also seemed reasonable, in view of the long history of research in Artificial Intelligence (AI) and Education, to investigate how such PC-based graphical process simulators might be invested with 'intelligent' training abilities to create effective standalone training tools.

This research vision immediately presented us with two broad questions: (1) What useful training goals could be achieved with such standalone tools? (2) For a given set of training goals, what principles and techniques from AI and cognitive science could be used (or must be developed) in the design, implementation and evaluation of the corresponding tool?

This article presents the results of our work to date on these questions. In particular, we will discuss the design of simulator-based tools that trainee operators could work with at their own convenience to improve their skills at diagnosis and repair. In the next subsection, we summarize the general training problems of concern in the pulp and paper industry, then discuss the particular training niche that we are aiming to provide tools to fill.

1.1 Current training practices in the pulp and paper industry

The process of converting wood chips into paper pulp involves complex, expensive machinery and can take anywhere from several hours to several days to complete. Before the advent of computer-driven automatic control technology, pulp mills employed hundreds of operators, in shifts of dozens. Operators were stationed throughout the physical plant, often under hazardous conditions, each one manually controlling a small portion of the overall process.

In modern pulp mills, automatic control technology has made it possible to remove operators from the machine rooms and place them instead in safe, centralized control rooms. From these areas, operators now manage day-to-day activities by monitoring and manipulating graphical computer displays. The conversion to computer-controlled operations has had three effects: (1) it has drastically reduced the number of operators needed per shift from dozens to a handful; (2) it has placed greater responsibility in the hands of individual operators, since they control larger portions of the process than they did before; and (3) it has profoundly altered the very nature of the operator's job, from 'hands-on', physical work to mental, intellective work (a phenomenon analyzed and documented by Zuboff (1988)).

The modern process-control operator has four general tasks (Schaafstal, 1991):

1. **Control:** Routine monitoring of gauges, interpreting the signs and signals emanating from the physical plant, responding to observed deviations from desired production parameters (e.g., reductions in pulp brightness), diagnosing and repairing incorrect device settings and equipment failures.
2. **Special procedures and drills:** Certain operations, such as plant startup, shutdown, and emergency procedures, occur infrequently and thus must be practiced periodically in order to maintain adequate levels of preparation.
3. **Routine maintenance and cleaning:** Equipment must be regularly cleaned, tested and adjusted to reduce the chance of breakdown.
4. **Recording and reporting:** Special actions, alterations to process-control parameters, observed changes in process state, etc., need to be logged and communicated both to management and to subsequent operator shifts.

Procedures for training operators to perform these tasks vary widely from mill to mill. Most commonly, limited on-site classroom training is combined with *apprenticeship*, in which less-skilled operators are paired with seasoned experts who are expected to provide one-on-one instruction and guidance for as long as necessary.

In practice, this approach to training is adequate in the sense that apprentice operators do, ultimately, become skilled and able to carry out their tasks independently. It is far from satisfactory, however. Four deficiencies with the apprenticeship method have been identified which might be addressed by the introduction of appropriate computer-based training technology:

1. Expertise in process operation does not necessarily correlate with expertise in teaching and training, thus the quality and effectiveness of an apprenticeship varies with the expert's interest, enthusiasm and skills.
2. While apprenticeship may be quite effective for training operators in routine activities, rare events (such as low-probability equipment failures) may be missed during the apprenticeship period, leaving the trainee unprepared when such an event finally strikes.[1]
3. Many tasks, both frequent and rare, demand periods of intense concentration and activity. These tasks are particularly hard to train by means of apprenticeship, since at these times the expert is usually too busy to explain what is happening, how he is responding to changes in the plant, and why. After-the-fact discussions can help, but this depends on accuracy of recall, and important details can easily be confused or lost. (This problem is also noted by Lajoie & Lesgold (1989).)
4. When additions or replacements of equipment occur in the physical plant, the effectiveness of experts as mentors may be reduced while they themselves adjust to the new working conditions.

We believe that simulator-based training tools can help in all four areas. First, training tools operating on computers can be designed to behave in a consistent manner with all students. (*Consistent* behavior also includes *adaptive* behavior, in the sense that systems can be designed to adapt their training methods in predictable ways to individual student needs.) Second, with simulators, uncommon events can be reproduced at will. Moreover, using computer technology one can encode libraries of events with which operators need to be familiar. Then, the training of individual operators could be tracked with respect to these libraries, enabling the system to ensure that, over time, each operator learns (or at least is exposed to) the knowledge and skills needed to respond properly to each recorded event. The *Sherlock* system, for example, has a fixed training 'curriculum' represented in its knowledge base (Lajoie & Lesgold, 1989), and Wasson and McCalla have been developing methods for dynamic generation of instructional plans (Wasson, 1990; McCalla & Wasson, 1991).

Third, unlike real paper mills, simulations can be suspended at any time, permitting analysis and discussion of observed events and possible responses, free of time pressure. Fourth and last, simulators can often be made available well in advance of the installation of new equipment,[2] permitting operators to begin training early and thereby be familiar with the equipment by the time it becomes operational (Baines et al., 1992).

---

[1] Consider that most automobile drivers are, due to lack of prior experience, completely unprepared to handle skids on ice.

[2] Our industrial contact has built their simulators using a simulator-building toolbox of their own design. This has greatly simplified and expedited the task of simulator construction for new pulp-processing machinery.

1.2 Training tools versus training-support tools

Computer-aided instruction (CAI), an active field of investigation in its own right, has also motivated research in several branches of AI, including natural-language dialogue, user modeling, planning and plan recognition, fault diagnosis and qualitative reasoning.

Many AI-oriented researchers in CAI look into the future and see autonomous tutoring and training systems able to engage students in natural dialogue and intelligently combine written and/or spoken language with graphics, sound, animated video, and other communication media. Some of these researchers envisage a world in which such advanced computer systems can effectively take the place of experienced human instructors. For example, Kassianides and Macchietto have described their work developing a system intended to provide 'comprehensive computer-based training' for process-plant operators where 'the overall objective is to enable a complete novice to become fully proficient in the use of the plant under normal operation, and to identify the most common operational problems' (Kassianides & Macchietto, 1990).

While these goals are both exciting and visionary, ours are more modest. We recognize the many potential applications of AI technology to education and training, but believe that at least for the immediate future, expert human instructors are irreplaceable resources. Great strides in standalone training system technology have certainly been achieved, most notably by the *Steamer* (Hollan et al., 1987) and *Sherlock* (Lajoie & Lesgold, 1989) systems. In *Sherlock*'s case, however, making these strides was 'a massive undertaking' (Lajoie & Lesgold, 1989, p. 26) involving the efforts of more than two dozen scientists over several years.

Rather than supplanting experienced human instructors, the computer systems that we envisage serve instead as *training-support tools*, tools that assist human instructors to perform their tasks more effectively. It is the concept and design of tools of this sort that we intend to concentrate on in this project. We believe that by focusing on practical tools whose design, implementation and deployment are feasible in the near term, we will be better able to evaluate our achievements and progress. (We will return to the subject of evaluation in Section 3.4.)

1.3 Outline of paper

The rest of this document is organized as follows: In Section 2, we discuss the theoretical aspects of our research project. Section 3 examines several basic research problems to be faced in the design of an out-of-class study (cf. Section 2.1) tool intended to help process-control operators improve their diagnosis and repair skills. Conclusions and summary remarks are presented in Section 4.

2 Theoretical framework

This section presents the theoretical framework for the proposed research project. We distinguish two aspects of instruction and identify the aspect which we intend to develop tools to support (Section 2.1), state the research questions with which this project is generally concerned (Section 2.2), and outline our intended research focus (Section 2.3).

2.1 In-class and out-of-class study

Traditional education methods distinguish two complementary components of instruction, which we will call *in-class* and *out-of-class* study. In-class study takes place under the supervision of an instructor. The instructor prepares, organizes and directs the learning activities, which typically include lectures and practice sessions. Out-of-class study (commonly called 'homework') takes place at the student's own convenience, without an instructor present, and consists of, e.g., assigned readings and written exercises.

In this research project, we focus on developing simulator-based training tools to support out-of-class study. To justify this choice, it is necessary first to mention some of the enhancements to process simulators that we believe to be both technologically feasible and potentially useful and which may be worthy of investigation:

- **Explanation generation:** When requested, an enhanced simulator could provide explanations of observed changes to the state of the simulated process, e.g., allowing students to interrupt the simulation at any point and ask, in effect, "What's happening?" or "What just happened and why?";
- **Question answering:** An enhanced simulator could answer a variety of questions about the function of plant components (e.g., "What is the purpose of pump P147?") and their influence on the process (e.g., "How does closing valve V425 affect pulp viscosity in tank E2?");
- **Guided exercises:** An enhanced simulator could systematically guide a student operator through pre-designed training scenarios (e.g., plant startup or shutdown) and provide guidance and feedback when and where appropriate (cf. *Sherlock* (Lajoie & Lesgold, 1989));
- **Skill evaluation:** An enhanced simulator could monitor student responses to a simulated system failure and provide instructive critique, e.g., suggesting improvements, pointing out forgotten steps, and affirming correct responses (this could also influence the choice of the next exercise presented to the student, in order to allow him/her to practice and overcome weak points).

These all appear to be interesting dimensions into which process simulators could be extended. In settings where an expert instructor is readily available, however, we have doubts that there is a real need for the computer to possess any of the above capabilities. The human instructor could provide all these functions and more, easily, flexibly, and probably with higher quality and effectiveness (including cost-effectiveness) than current computer-based methods permit.[3]

[3] One might, however, imagine such a need in settings where instructors are assigned to *groups* of students, rather than to individuals. In these situations, it might be useful if a student could obtain helpful feedback from the system while the instructor was otherwise occupied.

On the other hand, economic and scheduling constraints will more than likely mean that expert instructors cannot be present whenever an individual process-control operator has the time and inclination to work on skill development. We believe that productive learning should nevertheless be possible during these periods. Therefore we feel that out-of-class study tools are most likely to have real value and impact in the near term, and thus are particularly deserving of research interest.

2.2 Research questions

Given our chosen focus on out-of-class study tools, we see the following three questions as fundamental to our program of research:

1. What sorts of simulator-based out-of-class study activities would be beneficial as part of a training program for process-control operators in the paper industry?
2. What sorts of enhancements to process simulators would be *necessary* in order to make those activities possible?
3. What sorts of enhancements to process simulators could make those activities *more effective*?

Clearly, an answer to the first question is a prerequisite for any further progress. Its importance cannot be overemphasized. Too often it seems that research on intelligent tutoring and training is motivated less by considerations of what functionality would actually be useful or desirable in a system than by each researcher's personal notion of what theoretical problems are 'interesting.' It is our goal to develop an understanding of the training needs in the domain *first*, before designing any algorithms or implementing any software.

The second question assumes that some of the desirable out-of-class training activities will demand a process simulator that has been enhanced in one or more ways. For example, to help operators improve their diagnostic reasoning skills, we might want to design a training system that allows students to perform diagnostic tests on a (simulated) process. Some of these tests may involve little more than checking a variable on the display and comparing it with its process-specific limits. Other tests, however, may involve checking plant components or conditions that ordinarily would not be part of the simulation, e.g., the physical appearance of fuses in a fuse box (to determine whether or not any have blown), or the temperature of the exterior metal case of a pump. To build an adequate training system, it might turn out to be necessary to introduce variables into the simulation that would not be necessary otherwise.

The third question supposes that the addition of certain facilities to a simulator could improve the effectiveness of out-of-class exercises. For example, although not strictly necessary, if the diagnosis-training system that was suggested in the previous paragraph were also able to explain *why* a particular equipment failure gave rise to the observed changes (alarms, activation of safety interlocks, reductions in pulp brightness, etc.) in the state of the process, the student would have the opportunity to learn relevant details at a timely moment, thereby increasing the value of the overall training exercise.

2.3 Focus on troubleshooting tasks

In partial answer to the first question above, we have decided to further focus our work on the design of a simulator-based training-support system whose purpose is to give pulp-mill operators practice on troubleshooting tasks. By 'troubleshooting', we mean the entire process from the initial identification of the symptoms indicating the existence of a fault to the taking of corrective action.

We had three reasons for this choice. First, developing expertise in troubleshooting takes time and extensive practice. Whereas the classroom is the best place for learning diagnostic principles and related domain knowledge, practice work designed to reinforce classroom instruction is best performed outside the classroom. Simulator-based tools appear ideally suited to this purpose.

Second, related research indicates that good diagnosis and repair skills are essential for an operator to be judged well qualified. Indeed, Schaafstal has argued that 'diagnostic skill is one of the most important factors underlying efficient operator behavior' (Schaafstal, 1991, p. 1). Thus there seems to be a pressing need to develop tools and techniques to improve operators' troubleshooting abilities.

Finally, Schaafstal's recent dissertation provides a promising theoretical framework in the form of a task-level analysis of the diagnosis and repair process. (We review Schaafstal's work in Section 3.1 below.) Based on her studies of expert-novice differences in diagnosis and repair tasks, she recommends that more effort be put into the training of explicit task-level diagnostic strategies, since novices appear to lack the kinds of efficient strategies demonstrated by experts. From a theoretical point of view, we would like to evaluate Schaafstal's task-level model and assess its utility as a basis for the design of a simulator-based training-support system.

3 On the design of a training system for diagnosis and repair

Perhaps the two most basic questions confronting any would-be training-system designer are these: What is to be the system's overall training goal, and with what techniques is it to achieve that goal? One reasonable answer to the first question is that the tool should strive both to habituate the student to an effective problem-solving method, and to communicate the principles and knowledge that the student needs in order to be able to properly apply that method to a given troubleshooting task. We have only begun to investigate the second question; this section discusses the major issues we have been studying. We begin with a summary of Schaafstal's task-level model of diagnosis (Section 3.1), since it is the most plausible candidate for the training system's problem-solving paradigm. In Section 3.2 we discuss the need for training systems to adapt their behavior to the skills and knowledge of their students. Section 3.3 considers different sorts of problem-solving support that out-of-class study tools ought to be able to provide, and Section 3.4 examines several dimensions along which the value or effectiveness of training systems might be measured.

3.1 Schaafstal's task-level model of diagnosis and repair

In her recent doctoral dissertation, Schaafstal examines the domain knowledge and reasoning skills that contribute to expertise in diagnosis and repair tasks (Schaafstal, 1991). She claims that 'in general, skilled behavior may be attributed to well-structured declarative domain knowledge, coupled with efficient problem-solving strategies' (p. 133). She offers the following nine-part[4] task-level model of diagnosis and repair, intended to characterize the general problem-solving strategy of expert operators:

1. **Identification of symptoms:** Symptoms such as alarms and safety-interlock activations indicate that something is wrong in the process. Since alarms often set off other alarms in a chain reaction, it is important to be able to distinguish root symptoms from all the others.
2. **Judgment of problem seriousness:** It may be critical to quickly judge how serious the problem is. Problems with potentially disastrous consequences may demand immediate action, whereas less serious problems may allow time for careful thought as to the best repair strategy.
3. **Determination of possible faults:** Any given set of symptoms may have a set of possible underlying faults.
4. **Ordering of faults:** Since fault hypotheses are explored in sequence, some order for the exploration must be selected.[5] One possible ordering principle would be to rank fault hypotheses in decreasing order of probability that the fault exists given the symptoms.
5. **Testing:** Testing is used to rule out as many candidate fault hypotheses as possible.
6. **Determination of repairs:** Depending on the fault that has been identified, different repair methods may be appropriate. These differ between *local repairs*—repairs that apply precisely to the fault at hand—and *global repairs*—repairs that work in many situations and which sometimes can be applied in the absence of a complete diagnosis.
7. **Determination of repair consequences:** Reasoning about the possible side-effects of a given repair strategy may influence the choice of which one to actually use.

[4] Her initial model actually has only eight parts. However, after analyzing the results of her experiments, she concludes that an additional 'ordering of repairs' step is needed.

[5] Schaafstal did not actually find empirical support for the existence of this step. Yet she still felt that such a step was taken, and simply not verbalized by her subjects during the thinking-aloud experiments.

8. **Ordering of repairs:** When several possible repair options exist, experts appear to rank them in order of desirability of their consequences.
9. **Evaluation of post-repair conditions:** The last step in the diagnosis and repair process is to evaluate the situation after the repair has been made and decide whether the problem has in fact been corrected.

Although experts are generally expected to proceed through these steps in order, Schaafstal has found that several deviations from strict sequence are common. Most significantly, while the above model is biased towards breadth-first exploration of hypotheses, empirical evidence shows that experts often reason in a depth-first manner, e.g., jumping from step 7 back to 3 after they have completed consideration of a fault hypothesis.

With respect to the question of what domain knowledge is used during troubleshooting, Schaafstal has identified eight general types:

1. knowledge about process flow;
2. knowledge about the topographical location of parts of the process;
3. knowledge about how the process is controlled;
4. knowledge about the general function of parts of the installation;
5. knowledge about the process of paper making, i.e., the influence of process parameters on the quality of paper;
6. knowledge about normal values of process parameters;
7. knowledge about process dynamics;
8. knowledge about the current functioning of parts of the installation.

Furthermore, she has found that different sets of these knowledge types are involved at each stage of troubleshooting.

Although Schaafstal's task-level model appears promising as a problem-solving paradigm for troubleshooting, it is not obvious how to design a simulator-based training system that would either teach such a step-by-step method to students, or at least enforce its rules. The principal problem is that most of the steps are 'invisible' in the sense that, given observations of the actions of a student working with a simulator, one could not normally deduce what symptoms the student had identified, what seriousness ranking he had made, what fault ordering he had chosen, and so forth. Schaafstal used thinking-aloud experiments to force operators to verbalize their thought processes. If her model is to be successfully built into a training system, some means must be found for the system to obtain the same sorts of information from student users that the thinking-aloud protocols yielded.

One approach we have been considering is to design a kind of 'thinking-aloud' user interface, in which students are able to explicitly signal each problem-solving step that they take. Such an interface could prompt students to specify, e.g., the symptoms they have identified, their judgments of problem seriousness, fault hypotheses, etc. An expected advantage of such an approach is that repeated use of the system would presumably lead students to develop methodical problem-solving habits in accordance with the task-level model. (In a related vein, Lajoie discusses how the menu-oriented interface to *Sherlock* provides a kind of 'cognitive template' for the desired problem-solving strategy (Lajoie & Lesgold, 1989, p. 19).) A possible disadvantage is that such an interface might be judged intrusive, meaning that the students find themselves spending more time dealing with the interface than working on the problem itself. (Arguably, this may be time well spent, since through their interactions with the interface, students will indirectly be focusing on important aspects of the troubleshooting task structure.)

Another method that we are considering to encourage the student to 'think aloud' is to design the training system as a *learning companion* (Chan & Baskin, 1990). A learning companion (LC) acts as a fellow student, engaging the human student in a dialogue centered on the current problem, and forcing the student both to express and explain his reasoning and to 'listen' to and evaluate another student's point of view. It is also possible for the LC to guide the student indirectly through the steps of the diagnostic procedure by asking questions (the Socratic method) or pointing out important considerations that are in danger of being overlooked.

A LC framework has the advantage that it would make the educational situation more like the real one, since troubleshooting in paper mills is typically performed by teams of operators rather than by individuals. As a result, one critical skill that operators must develop is that of working together effectively. A LC approach may foster the development of cooperative work skills, since it accustoms students to the need to present, defend and possibly revise their ideas and suggestions during group activity. The main potential disadvantage of the LC approach is its computational complexity, especially regarding dialogue processing. It remains an open question as to whether an adequate yet constrained sub-language can be designed allowing us to avoid the need for sophisticated natural language processing technology.

3.2 Adaptive behavior in tutoring and training

Good instructors are skilled at tailoring their behavior to the particular skill level of students and to both the quality and quantity of students' knowledge. This adaptation takes several forms, including:

- varying the information content of descriptions and explanations;
- varying the degree of detail of descriptions and explanations;
- varying the aspects of the problem that they focus on during a given exercise;
- gradually broadening and deepening the student's knowledge in a way that builds upon and refines the student's existing knowledge;
- overlooking student mistakes that involve principles which the instructor judges the student to be unprepared to comprehend.

Tools for training or training support such as we envisage will need to possess similar sorts of adaptation skills if they are to be effective. This demands that we develop an understanding of these skills at a level of formality sufficient for encoding in computer algorithms. Work on the first two forms of adaptation has already been carried out by researchers in natural-language processing; see, e.g., Maybury (1990), Paris (1988) and Reiter (1990). Work by Wasson and McCalla on instructional planning seems relevant to the third point (Wasson, 1990; McCalla & Wasson, 1991), in particular their distinction between *factual*, *analytic* and *synthetic* domain knowledge. The *Sherlock* system appears capable of the fourth type of adaptation, since it takes students through a graded series of problem-solving tasks (Lajoie & Lesgold, 1989); note, however, that the 'curriculum' represented by that graded series was created by a human domain expert, such that the system does not have any explicit representation of the factors that make one problem more or less difficult to solve than another. We are not aware of any work relevant to the fifth type of adaptation.

Some of these problems may be simplified in the case of out-of-class study tools, since these tools are seen as only one element of a larger educational program comprising in-class, instructor-guided education (where the student learns basic concepts and principles), out-of-class independent study (where he/she systematically applies and practices concepts and principles learned in class), and on-the-job apprenticeship (where the student both relates classroom and simulator-based learning to the 'real world' of the workplace, and learns detailed 'real world' issues and procedures that might not be covered elsewhere). For example, it might not be so critical for the system to be able to generate highly-customized natural language explanations of process behavior (where much research is needed before the necessary technology can be realized). 'Canned' explanations might suffice (demanding little or no additional research work), since students could always seek clarification from the instructor if they are not satisfied with the system's output.

We currently see the fourth type of adaptation—gradual broadening and deepening of knowledge—as perhaps the most critical form needed in the diagnosis and repair training-support systems that we envisage. We conceive of these systems as operating by posing problems for students to solve using the simulator. The training-support component of the system monitors the student's problem-solving activities and intervenes and offers guidance when the student appears unable to make progress on the problem, or when he appears to have become lost. (In addition, certain facilities ought to be available that allow the student to take the initiative, e.g., by requesting hints or suggestions for the next problem-solving step; we return to this topic in Section 3.3.)

Clearly, such a system will need to be able to pose a variety of problems for the student to solve. Thus it will need to have access to a training corpus of troubleshooting problems. These problems will need to be ranked in some manner. Several dimensions for ranking could be considered:

- according to the number of repair actions required to solve the problem;
- according to the speed with which repairs must be effected;
- according to the number of alternative hypotheses that must be explored;
- according to the number of tests that must be performed to identify the fault;
- according to the part(s) of the physical plant that must be understood in order to solve the problem;
- according to the length of the causal chains that must be understood in order to select appropriate repairs;

- according to the number of conflicting goals that must be balanced in choosing a repair.

Assuming we are able to define a set of rating metrics, the next question will be how to use them to order problems according to level of difficulty. That is, we would like the system to be able to first present students with relatively easy problems, then gradually increase the difficulty level as the students' skills improve. This design goal will demand that we develop rules relating student performance monitoring to problem selection. Relevant questions include:[6]

- When is a student allowed to proceed from one level of difficulty to the next?
- How should slower students be handled?
- Could the training program be adaptable with respect to both the number of exercises and the type of exercises?

We have only begun to explore these issues. We feel that being able to define a principled set of problem-difficulty levels would be a valuable accomplishment, since we would have gained insight into the divisions along the scale from 'novice' to 'expert'.

3.3 Supporting the student during problem solving

The question we consider here is this: What sorts of support should a simulator-based tool for training diagnosis and repair be capable of providing to students during problem solving? By support we mean all types of advice and critique the student needs in order to solve the exercises while at the same time learning more about the troubleshooting process.

Two general forms of support can be distinguished: *solicited* or *unsolicited*. Solicited support is given upon request, unsolicited support is given when the system itself decides that the student needs guidance. So far, we have identified three types of support that we feel ought to be available:

1. question-answering capabilities on both system components and process states (e.g., answering "What is the purpose of pump P138?", "Why does the level in tank T11 keep rising?");
2. guidance in the diagnosis and repair process, both unsolicited (intervening to offer hints when the student appears blocked during problem solving) and solicited (e.g., answering "What do I do next (and why)?" questions);
3. post-exercise evaluation of the student's activities.

Question-answering support is needed when students forget details that were learned in class, for example, the function of various plant components, their role in the overall process, and the possible faults associated with them. Students should be able to point to any object displayed on the simulator interface and ask questions about it. (To avoid problems of natural-language understanding, questioning can

[6] Suggested by A. Schaafstal (personal communication).

be performed using menus, since there is only a small number of questions relevant to each device in a pulp-processing plant.)

The second form of guidance addresses the possibility that a student who does not really understand the problem he is faced with may waste lots of time exploring incorrect hypotheses, trying out repair methods that are ultimately ineffectual, etc. Consequently, the training-support system ought to be able to intervene and offer hints and suggestions when the student no longer seems to be making progress. Of course, training systems also must somehow strike a balance between intervening the moment that students err, and permitting them to make errors and thereby learn, a point well argued by Burton and Brown (1982). It may, however, be difficult for a system to decide when intervention is appropriate. Thus students must also be given the opportunity to ask for help when they feel they need it. (Munro et al. strongly claim that intrusive feedback during dynamic skill training may actually be harmful, and recommend that students be permitted to decide themselves when to accept feedback (Munro et al., 1985).)

The third type of support is like the more classical critique of a teacher, an after-the-fact evaluation of the student's performance (cf. Miller (1986) on so-called expert critiquing systems). This has the advantage of being one of the least intrusive forms of support, and if it is done in combination with simulator replays, it can avoid the problem of the student forgetting the problem situation.

A preliminary study on the feasibility of tracking student interactions with a simulator has been performed by Cowperthwait (1991). A PC-based commercial process simulator was connected to a Sun Sparcstation running a monitoring program. The study showed that it is possible to provide exercises and monitor the student's actions, to give unsolicited critiques based on system states, and to perform post-exercise evaluation of student performance. It also suggested that when the simulator and the tutoring component are run on separate display screens, the tutoring component must make special effort to alert the student (using, e.g., sound signals) to the fact that it has information to convey.

A practical problem that will have to be solved in order to be able to provide the kinds of support described here concerns the communication bandwidth between the simulator and the training component. In Cowperthwait's study, all simulator variables (numbering twelve) were monitored. Simulators seriously intended for use in operator training, however, will have on the order of thousands of variables, making comprehensive monitoring computationally infeasible. This means that a more intelligent communication protocol must be developed.

3.4 Evaluation

One of the most vexing problems concerning the design of educational tools of any sort is that of *evaluation*. That is, how do we assess the value or effectiveness of a tutoring or training tool? There seem to be several different dimensions of evaluation for a training tool, among them these:

- **Raw improvement:** Are students any better at problem solving after working with the tool, and if so, is their improvement attributable to the training component or is it merely a natural result of practice using the simulator?

- **Improved understanding:** Are students better able to *explain* and *justify* their problem-solving behavior after working with the tool, and if so, is their improvement attributable to the training component or is it merely a natural result of practice using the simulator?
- **Functionality:** Does the tool provide adequate guidance for problem solving? Are there any support features which students feel are missing? Are there any support features that are rarely or never used?
- **Intrusiveness:** Does the tool behave in ways that students find intrusive? Does it strike a good balance between, on the one hand, permitting students to make mistakes and learn from them, and on the other hand, intervening and providing corrective feedback when they seem to have lost their way?
- **Impact on classroom activity:** For out-of-class study tools, what effect, if any, does student use of the tool have on their in-class activities? For example, is the instructor able to spend more time helping students to understand general principles and high-level problem-solving strategies while relying on out-of-class tool use to give students an understanding of the details?

Clearly, the most difficult task will be devising reliable means for measuring the above properties. Raw improvement, for example, might be measurable by, e.g., (1) creating two versions of the training-support tool, both with the ability to pose troubleshooting problems at a fixed level of difficulty, but one with all guidance facilities enabled, and the other with all such facilities disabled; (2) assigning each version of the tool to a distinct group of trainee operators and permitting them to work with it; and (3) testing each group's pre- and post-tool-use performance on a problem not within the tool's training corpus (though at the same level of difficulty). Other properties could be measured using questionnaires and structured interviews of students and/or instructors.

A thorough discussion of evaluation criteria and measurement methods is beyond the scope of the present paper. We want merely to underscore the necessity of evaluation studies as part of any effort to develop tutoring or training tools.

4 Concluding remarks

Demands for improved training methods to cope with the increasing complexity of the workplace, coupled with dramatic drops in the cost of computing power, have greatly expanded the potential range of applications for simulator-based training technology. In this paper, we have examined a range of research questions related to the design of effective training tools, in particular, tools to support out-of-class study on diagnosis and repair problems.

Perhaps the broadest conclusion to be drawn from the work reported here is that there exist many challenging problems to be solved on the road to truly useful simulator-based training-support tools, despite many years' accumulation of related theoretical results in the AI/CAI community.

The one problem we currently see as both interesting and perhaps most theoretically significant is that of defining a principled scale for ordering problems according to difficulty level (cf. Section 3.2). We hope to make progress in that direction as we continue to develop the ideas discussed herein.

Acknowledgements

This research has been supported by a grant from NUTEK (Swedish National Board for Industrial and Technical Development) and a post-doctoral research fellowship from the Department of Computer and Information Science at the University of Linköping. Comments from Alma Schaafstal were very helpful in improving the content of this report.

References

Bainbridge, Lisanne (1987) Ironies of Automation. In: Rasmussen, J., Duncan, K. & Leplat, J. (eds.) New technology and human error. New York: John Wiley & Sons.

Baines, Glenn H., Gunseor, Frank D., Haynes, Jim B. & Scheldorf, Jay J. (1992) Benefits of using a high-fidelity process simulation for operator training and control checkout. Tappi journal, 75, 133–136.

Burton, Richard R. & Brown, John Seely (1982) An investigation of computer coaching for informal learning activities. In: Sleeman, D. & Brown, J.S. (eds.) Intelligent Tutoring Systems. New York: Academic Press, 79–98.

Chan, Tak-Wai & Baskin, Arthur B. (1990) Learning Companion Systems. In: Frasson, C. & Gauthier, G. (eds.) Intelligent tutoring systems: at the crossroads of Artificial Intelligence and Education. New Jersey: Ablex, 6–33.

Cohen, Jon (1988) Simulators: Tough Training for Top Operators. EPRI journal, 22–29.

Cowperthwait, Christopher (1991) A Prototype Implementation of a Tutoring System for an Evaporator Simulator. Tech. rept. LiTH-IDA-Ex-9140. Department of Computer and Information Science, University of Linköping, Sweden.

Hollan, James D., Hutchins, Edwin L. & Weitzman, Louis M. (1987) STEAMER: An Interactive, Inspectable, Simulation-Based Training System. In: Kearsley, G. P. (ed.) Artificial Intelligence and Instruction: Applications and methods. Reading: Addison-Wesley, 113–134.

Kassianides, Symeon & Macchietto, Sandro (1990) A Simulation Based System for Operator Training. In: Bussemaker, H.T. & Iedema, P.D. (eds.) Computer Applications in Chemical Engineering. Amsterdam: Elsevier North-Holland, 203–208.

Lajoie, Susanne P. & Lesgold, Alan (1989) Apprenticeship Training in the Workplace: Computer-Coached Practice Environment as a New Form of Apprenticeship. Machine-Mediated Learning, 3(1), 7–28.

Maybury, Mark T. (1990) Custom explanations: Exploiting user models to plan multisentential text. Proceedings of the Second International Workshop on User Modeling, University of Honolulu, Hawaii.

McCalla, Gordon I. & Wasson, Barbara J. (1991) Negotiated Tutoring Needs, Student Modelling and Instructional Planning. In: Moyse, R. & Elsom-Cook, M. (eds.) Negotiated Learning. London: Chapman.

Miller, Perry L. (1986) Expert Critiquing Systems: Practice-Based Medical Consultation by Computer. New York: Springer-Verlag.

Munro, Allen, Fehling, Michael R. & Towne, Douglas M. (1985) Instruction Intrusiveness in Dynamic Simulation Training. J. Computer-Based Instruction, 12(2), 50–53.

Paris, Cecile L. (1988) Tailoring object descriptions to a user's level of expertise. Computational Linguistics, 14(3), 64–78.

Reiter, Ehud (1990) Generating descriptions that exploit a user's domain knowledge. In: Dale, R., Mellish, C. & Zock, M. (eds.) Current Research in Natural Language Generation. New York: Academic Press, 257–285.

Schaafstal, Alma M. (1991) Diagnostic Skill in Process Operation: A Comparison Between Experts and Novices. Ph.D. thesis, University of Groningen, The Netherlands.

Wasson, Barbara Jane (1990) Determining the Focus of Instruction: Content Planning for Intelligent Tutoring Systems. Ph.D. thesis, Department of Computational Science, University of Saskatchewan, Saskatoon, Saskatchewan, Canada.

Woodward, Dale C., Poulin, Dominique, Marin, Andre & Terrell, Jennifer (1988) Training simulators for the pulp and paper industry. Tappi journal, 71(12), 109–113.

Zuboff, Shoshana (1988) In the Age of the Smart Machine: The Future of Work and Power. New York: Basic Books.

Part 2

Theory into Practice: Interaction in Learning Environments

Designing Newton's Laws: Patterns of Social and Representational Feedback in a Learning Task

Andrea A. diSessa

Graduate School of Education, University of California, Berkeley, CA94720, USA.
email: disessa@soe.berkeley.edu

Abstract. We describe a classroom group discussion in which high school students were asked to 'design Newtonian laws of motion' expressed in programming terms. We trace the success of this design activity to properties of the representational medium used (programming), together with the feedback and feed forward patterns of communication that that medium fostered.

Keywords. Computational medium, extended literacy, Boxer, programming representation, communication patterns, feedback, design task

1 Introduction

The Boxer Project at the University of California at Berkeley is dedicated to exploring the possibility of extending human intelligence and learning potential by placing flexible computer power in everyone's hands for their own expressive purposes. We believe that intellectual capability is in a real and important sense external and material as well being, like ideas, internal and insubstantial. That is, people think, learn and achieve in important measure based on the external representational and symbolic systems they have developed. They think by writing and reflecting on the stable inscriptions thus produced. They revise and ultimately throw away drafts, keep and distribute 'final text'. They reason by writing down principles and carefully argued conclusions. They express scientific theories in algebraic form, and calculate to derive and check implications of those theories. Literacy, in its broadest meaning, is the name we give to 'material intelligence'.

The transition from pen-and-paper technology to computer-based technology can be accompanied by an extension of literacy to much more visually expressive, dynamic and interactive forms. The implications may be far-reaching. For one, human's native spatial and dynamic reasoning capabilities may be engaged and developed. Too much of school is based on competence with language in a narrow sense. For another, new subjects or very different approaches to old ones may become accessible, 'easy to talk about' in a new written 'language'.

The Boxer Group has developed an interim version of a computational medium to serve as the basis for experimenting with learning within a new literacy. Boxer contains easy-to-learn capabilities for:

1. text and hypertext processing;
2. organizing personal or professional data into forms that are both easy to peruse, but also computationally accessible (as with database queries);
3. dynamic and interactive graphics; and
4. programming.

The last of these, programming, is especially important in our view as it brings process and non-verbal interaction, two modes that are almost inaccessible for written text, within the expressive range of the medium. We will not describe Boxer here in any detail. For more on Boxer, the reader is referred to diSessa & Abelson (1986) and diSessa, Abelson & Ploger (1991).

This paper develops a case study of the use of Boxer as a representational language in instructing students in Newton's laws of motion. In fact, the task we set for students was basically to design Newton's laws in the form of a program. We want to examine some of the ways in which representational systems, especially computationally enhanced representational systems, work to make some school subjects more accessible and even fun. In particular, we will concentrate on the ways in which the medium fosters effective communication feedback patterns from students to teacher and back, and from students to other students. A more extended version of the analysis presented here is given in Sherin, diSessa & Hammer (1993).

Before entering into the empirical analysis that is the core of this work, we prepare for it in three ways. First, we explain a bit more about our perspective on computational literacy, highlighting important general themes of this work. Second, we describe in more detail the task we posed for students. Third, we introduce our framework for understanding how students learned from this task; it is a framework describing forms of feedback.

2 Themes in this work

Figure 1 schematizes several important lines in our prior work that play important roles here. At the top is the umbrella concept of a new literacy, implicating many changes in learning patterns and everyday intellectual work for teachers and students. Beneath that concept, on the right hand side of the figure, are the changed ways in which a new symbolic system presents what students learn. In the present case, the underlying conceptual content, Newton's laws, is quite familiar. In other cases new media may bring with them new domains and targets of instruction as well. What is new in this case is the face that Newton's laws present to students. There are two main aspects of this new face. First, students may interact with ideas like Newton's laws in simulations or other forms that directly engage dynamic and kinesthetic intuitions of motion. This plays a role in what happened in our classroom. What is more prominent, however, is that we have replaced the precise and compact representational forms traditionally associated with physics, namely algebra, with programming. This leads to substantially altered forms of feedback to students, as we shall see.

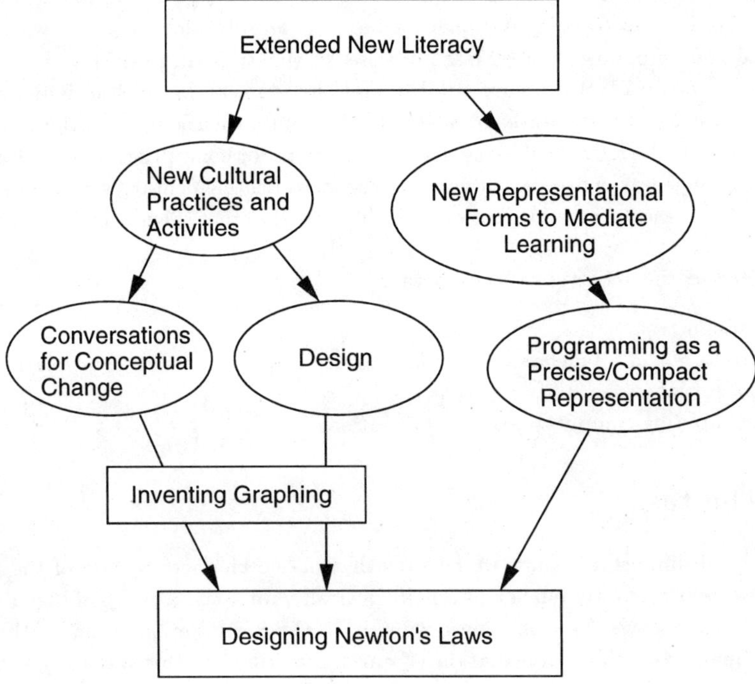

Fig. 1. Under the umbrella concept of a 'new literacy,' the themes 'new and improved activities' and 'new representational forms' played into the success of Designing Newton's Laws.

On the left side of Figure 1, we pick out a different slice of what a new literacy entails—the new cultural practices and activities that can be developed with support from the new medium. Paper and pencil literacy leads to practices like note-taking, essays, written exams and so forth. Paper and print lead to text books, state mandated standards for texts, reading assignments and all the rest that is familiar in current schools based on print literacy.

Among the new activity patterns computational media can foster are student construction of concept maps and knowledge spaces, which are hypertext organizations of a domain aimed at visually showing the relational structure of ideas in a field (diSessa, 1990). More central to this work, and highlighted in Figure 1, we believe that student design can be a much more prominent form of learning with computational media. Simply put, computers are the most flexible and easily mastered medium for design. Design has some especially nice properties with respect to student engagement and motivation, and learning through design activities becomes immensely more practical and attractive in the presence of computers.

The other activity highlighted in Figure 1 is 'conversations for conceptual change'. What we have in mind are teacher-led full-class discussions that are aimed at provoking conceptual change. Unlike other categories in the figure, this one bears less direct relationship to computational media. It is an 'old idea', but one with substantial contemporary interest (e.g., diSessa & Minstrell (in press)). It is also an activity form we advocate, have studied, and one that can be substantially altered by the presence of computational media. In the figure, we also note a prior study of ours that joined a focus on design with conversations for conceptual change. 'Inventing Graphing' was a five-day design exercise in which elementary school students designed representations for motion. See diSessa, Hammer, Sherin & Kolpakowski (1991).

So, in net, the activity we study here is

1. a design task,
2. carried out in a fullclass discussion organized by a teacher to focus on difficult conceptual issues, and
3. mediated by computational representations.

3 The task

To make an important point, we begin with a biased characterization of the task, which we will promptly refine and repair. Basically, we asked a group of high school students to discover Newton's laws, roughly in the form familiar from textbooks, force equals mass times acceleration (F=ma). Described in this way, this appears to be an absurdly difficult assignment. How could more-or-less average high school students, roughly ten weeks into a physics course, possibly duplicate the hard work and genius of Newton within the course of a two-day discussion? These students did not even have calculus available to them, which Newton had to invent to express his laws.

Even more, a host of research suggests that students come to physics classes with deep-seated misconceptions about the relation between force and motion. For example, most students seem strongly to believe that an object moves only when there is an imbalance of forces on it, and it moves in the direction of the imbalance at a speed proportional to the net force. Most students also believe that in the absence of force, motion gradually dies away of its own accord. In contrast, Newton discovered that motion is perpetual and constant in the presence of no forces (or, equivalently, whenever forces balance), and force does not directly determine either the direction or magnitude of motion. Instead, force determines acceleration, the 'a' in F=ma, which is the change in velocity of an object.

We need to unveil the 'tricks' we used to make 'discovering F=ma' a plausible and doable task. First, we couched this as a design task in a *semi-concrete situation*. Instead of asking students to discover laws of motion, we asked them to 'design a program to simulate a space ship with impulse engines that work in short bursts'. This transformation entails a number of simplifications. First, we have picked a physical situation that is very nearly ideal for Newton's laws, separated from many complications like air friction. Second, the *design context* puts students in a situation in which 'guess and repair' strategies seem natural and (we know) will be productive. Students have designed and built many things before, from drawing pictures to making tree houses. This task is close enough to 'make a video game' to seem familiar and motivating for students—far more so than discovering an essential truth of the universe.

Finally, we have provided a medium of expression, programming, that has two important properties. First, it is comprehensible enough that students can master it relatively easily. Compared to the conceptual rigors of calculus, programming with a language that is designed for comprehensibility is quite accessible. Though many students in the class had no programming experience entering our physics course, most of the class were easily fluent enough to accomplish the programming entailed in this design.

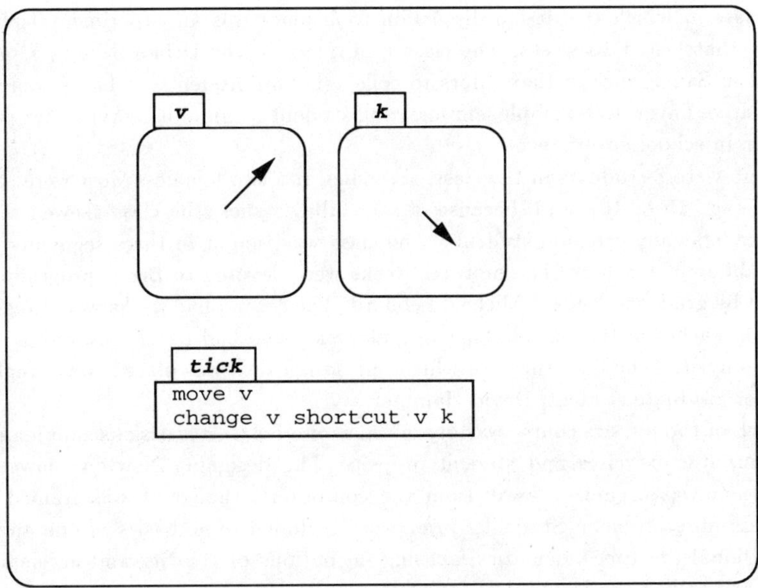

Fig. 2. The 'tick model' replaces F=ma with a programming equivalent.

To be clearer on what we hoped students might accomplish, Figure 2 shows the textbook-pure version of F=ma we intended to teach in this course. This is the form we hoped students might even be able to design for themselves. The boxes with rounded corners, `v` (for velocity) and `k` (for kick) are vector variables in Boxer. Students had used vectors in Boxer and were familiar with their properties: Vector arrows could be re-aimed and lengthened or shortened by clicking on them and moving a mouse. Vectors could cause motion with the `move` command, which instructs a graphical object (the mass implied in F=ma) to move along a vector. Repeatedly executing `move v` causes an object to move across the computer screen in the direction of `v` with a speed proportional to the length of `v`. One additional command involves vectors. Vector addition combines two vectors into a resultant vector in the usual head-to-tail way. Our students knew this operation by the name `shortcut`, implying that if you move along one vector, then along another, you could as easily achieve the same result by running along a shortcut directly from start to the final position.

The `tick` procedure in Figure 2 is meant to be executed once each 'tick of the clock'. It shows both how `v` effects an object, and it also shows how `k` (kick), a discrete and simplified version of Newtonian force, affects velocity. Taken together, this trio of boxes defines velocity and shows how kicks (forces) influence it.[1]

4 The classroom context of the task

The class in which the design discussion took place was an experimental physics course that lasted 15 weeks. The class took place in the Urban School, a private school in San Francisco that caters to college-bound students. It has a somewhat alternative flavor, for example, emphasizing student community service and participation in school governance.

There were 8 students in the class, six males and two females. Most were sophomores (age 15 or 16), and, because of scheduling issues, the class skewed toward less academically oriented students. The class was taught in three segments, with three different teachers. The first five weeks were devoted to Boxer programming, taught by graduate student Michael Leonard. The second five weeks were taught by a math teacher in the school, Tina Kolpakowski, who had previously worked with Boxer physics. The final third, in which our design task was placed, was taught by another graduate student, David Hammer.

Much of the physics course was organized around class discussions supplemented by computer exercises and student projects. The designing Newton's laws class discussion was organized away from the computers, though it was framed as a programming problem. Students' prior work included some basics of one and two dimensional (vector) kinematics focusing on notions of velocity and acceleration. They had talked about and done computer work on relative motion.

5 Analytic framework

Figure 3 shows a schematic of the paths of feedback and feed forward that we believe account for many of the empirically observed properties of the classroom design of F=ma. We will argue that these paths help explain how this activity came to a successful conclusion. In the center of the diagram is the process of design in which our students and teacher participated. At the bottom is the product or 'net result' of that process, notably a working program that students could either inspect to think about force and motion, or run to experiment with them. At the top of

[1] To maintain a short and relatively simple exposition, we are suppressing a number of details about how this represents F=ma. See Sherin (1992).

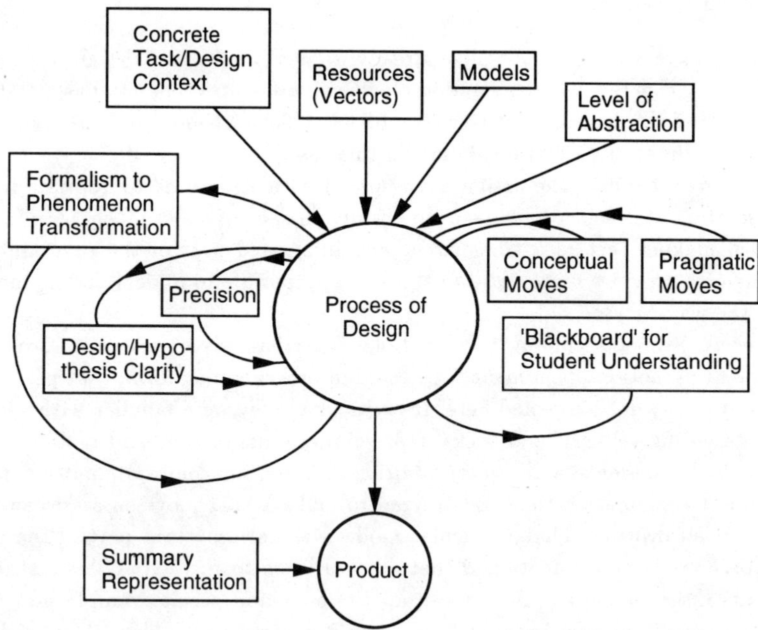

Fig. 3. Various paths of feedback and feed forward, mediated by programming, contributed to the process of design.

the diagram are sources of feed forward, aspects of the conceptual and practical landscape of the task that we set up deliberately to enhance chances of success for students. On the left hand side of the diagram are forms of feedback that primarily operated among students and the progressing design. On the right hand side are forms of feedback that primarily involved the teacher in monitoring and helping the design process.

In the following listing, it will be helpful to keep in mind that these paths of feedback and feed forward fall, generally, into two different but somewhat overlapping categories. *Conceptual pathways* directly provide content-specific help to the process. For example, providing vectors as an available means of representation is effective because, since Newton, we have understood that they are exactly the right language to use to describe motion compactly and precisely in Newtonian terms. *Pragmatic pathways* provide more general, less content-specific help to foster an effective process that converges on a useful and socially consentual product. Any feedback that helps participants be clear on the state of their ongoing design or the degree of agreement or disagreement among them would count as pragmatic. Conceptual and pragmatic feedback are useful constructs to help focus our attention on different aspects of communicative situations or, more generally, situations that involve intellectual work.

5.1 Feed forward

1. *Concrete task context.* We have already argued briefly that design, especially involving concrete products and easily visualized contexts of use, has attractive properties as a learning activity. See diSessa (1992) for more general arguments and Sherin et al. (1993) for details in this case.
2. *Resources.* Loading the design environment with structures appropriate to the resolution of design problems is an effective means of fostering success. In this case, making vectors a transparent and integrated part of the programming language provides representational forms appropriate to understanding motion in the way Newton did.
3. *Models.* Students coming to this design task had experience with two prior models of motion phenomena, expressed in programming form, that played directly into what happened here. In particular, they were familiar with vectors representing velocity, and 'ticks' representing units of time and motion. They also had experience with vector addition representing composite motion in the form of a simulation they constructed to make a boat move on an ocean that was itself drifting. That particular model was an important part of the prior experience these students had that allowed them to succeed at this task. Students inserted the specific code from the boat and ocean example into their spaceship simulation because they knew it was relevant. Then they modified the code appropriately for the new context. These actions show the role of programming in making prior work effective in a new context.
4. *Level of abstraction.* Pointing out the appropriate level of abstraction at which an effective conceptualization of a phenomenon may be achieved is an immense help toward formulating that conceptualization. In this case, numbers, vectors and move commands all suggest an appropriate level of abstraction for a Newtonian view of motion. For example, these rule out overt anthropomorphism and concentrate on geometry, to the relative exclusion of many concrete features, such as the shape of the spaceship and properties of the surrounding vacuum.

5.2 Student feedback

5. *Precision.* Programming carries with it a natural level of precision, that at which a program will work. It happens that natural language is much more vague about issues of motion than this. Time and time again we saw students pushed to make their ideas more precise in order to satisfy the obvious demands of the programming context. In non-programming contexts, we believe we saw discussions that sufficed to the students' own level of satisfaction while riding roughshod over important distinctions that were brought out in the programming context. For example, in a non-programming discussion, students agreed and were satisfied with the description that a kick combines with existing motion, without getting to the key distinctions on how they combine that formed the core of the discussion here.

6. *Formalism to phenomenon transformation.* Programming representations have one critical property that is missing in essentially all other representations—they may be run. This provided a critical feedback path linking hypotheses about motion formulated as programming statements to students' commonsense knowledge about motion. Students frequently simulated the running of their design, ascertained properties of the resulting motion, then affirmed or corrected their program as a result. Algebraic, verbal and written natural language, by and large, cannot support this feedback path as well as programming can.
7. *Hypothesis and design state clarity.* In order to foster better cooperation and mutual understanding in a group, it is often helpful to have a clear and unambiguous language in which to frame hypotheses. Although students frequently had trouble understanding each other's natural language explanations, there was rarely a disagreement over what was meant by a particular segment of code. Similarly, the current state of design, expressed in programming terms, constituted a clear landmark against which one could measure successes and failures, and with respect to which changes (new hypotheses) could be suggested.

5.3 Teacher feedback

8. *A window on student understanding.* As in 7, fragments of program code produced by students constituted clear and unusually helpful information for the teacher about students' states of mind. Armed with a view of where students stood, the teacher could use programming in order to make many kinds of conceptual or pragmatic moves, as in the following examples.
9. *Pragmatic teacher moves.* In order to clarify the state of the design, the teacher could, and frequently did, ask students to run the program mentally and assess its adequacy. Similarly, the teacher could focus attention on various issues for various reasons by selecting a piece of code to attend to. "Let's look at student X's idea..."
10. *Conceptual teacher moves.* In the same way, the teacher can add information and ideas in relatively clear and frequently unobtrusive ways by suggesting programming ideas. "What if we used a vector to represent velocity?"

5.4 Summary feed forward

11. *A concise summary language.* Aphorisms like 'to every action there is an equal and opposite reaction' or even 'F=ma' serve as useful summaries of a line of conceptual inquiry. Programs also can serve such mnemonic functions. In this case, students brought in knowledge gained from prior learning in the form of pieces of code — for example, the line of code that combined two component motions, mentioned in item 3. Similarly, we hoped students would retain some of their understanding of F=ma pretty much in the literal form

of the tick model, Figure 2. This is a summary feed-forward mechanism of carrying learning from one task into another.

6 Designing F=ma

The aim of this section is two-fold. First, we want to provide a sketch of the design conversation to give readers a sense of how it actually took place. We will have to be brief here; again, refer to Sherin et al. (1993) for details. Our second aim is to provide some data in support of many, but not all, of the feedback functions for the programming representation we listed above.

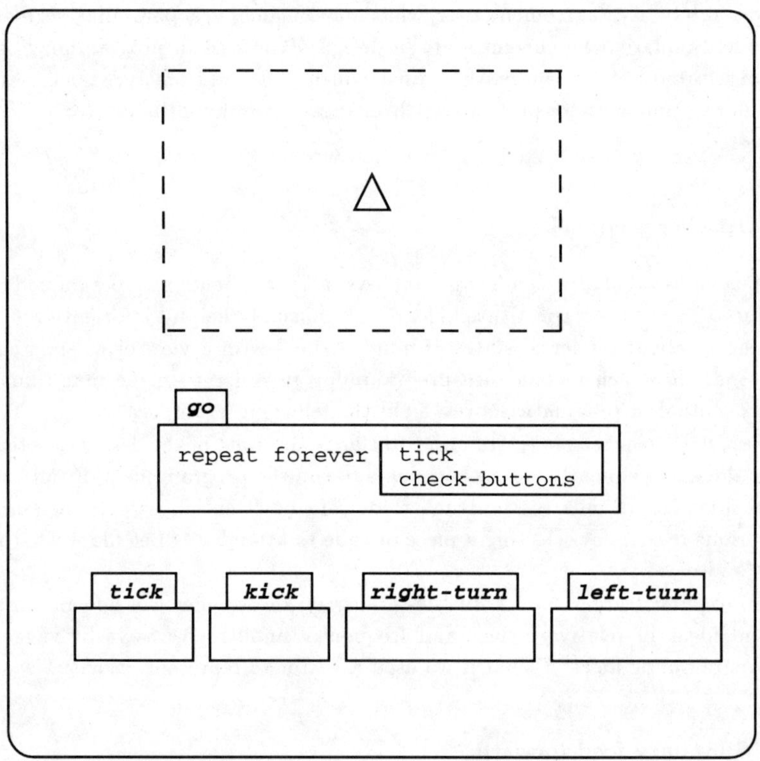

Fig. 4. The template initially provided students involved GO (overall iterative control) and templates to fill in for TICK (motion without a force), KICK (how force affects motion), and RIGHT and LEFT TURNs (re-aim force). The dashed box at the top contains the moving spaceship.

Figure 4 shows the starting point of the discussion and design. It is a template that already is aimed at focusing students' attention on the key physical aspects of the design. The `go` loop repeats over and over `tick` and `check-buttons`. `Tick` corresponds to what the spaceship does constantly when there is no intervention (via button presses). It is the place where students should place the programming equivalent of Newton's first law: 'An object in motion travels indefinitely in a straight line at constant speed unless acted upon by an outside force'. The command `kick` is executed by `check-buttons` if the middle button on the mouse is pressed. This is where students need to place a version of Newton's second law, which describes how an object's motion responds to external forces. The commands `right-turn` and `left-turn` describe how the ship should be reoriented when left or right mouse buttons are pressed; they re-aim the force, which should be used in `kick`.

Right away, students began exploring the template by filling in simple pieces. In the following selection, the teacher focuses attention by pointing to a particular box. He asks students phenomenologically what should happen with `right-turn`, then more precisely how to make that happen with programming. The students follow this line flawlessly, and they spontaneously run the suggested code mentally to check that it has the appropriate behaviour. This shows how programming here is used

1. to focus students' attention on particular issues,
2. to ask for more detailed ('how') explanations, and
3. it shows how students run the program to get phenomenological feedback on what their formal expressions mean.

In the following, ellipses denote segments of the discussion that have been deleted.

Teacher:	... So, what will turn-right do? (1)
Jim:	Make it turn right.
Teacher:	How? ... What should be the command, what should it say inside this box? (2)
Jeffrey:	'R' 'T' 1.
Teacher:	'R' 'T' 1. [Writes it in.]
Orson:	Does that mean you're going to have to — Wait. So that means — yeah! ... (3)
Jeffrey:	If you keep it down, it'll go like this. [Motions a gradual turn.] (3)
Teacher:	If you hold it down, it'll pivot. [Nods.]
Adam:	It'll go more like this. [Motions very slowly.] (3)
Orson:	Super slow. (3)

The next issue to be solved, spontaneously raised by the students, was how to get the spaceship to move constantly. One student, Jim, explained that `kick` was not the place for constant motion commands. This is a critical conceptual point, motion does not need a constant intervention (kick) to perpetuate itself. In the following, notice how programming serves the teacher to make clear

1. what is being discussed,
2. what a student's hypothesis is, and
3. what needs to be decided.

Notice especially that Jim's explanation implicitly refers at once to what ought to happen, to the code, and to the result of running the code.

Lori:	I don't understand what the problem is. I mean, why can't you say, you know, forward one?
Teacher:	Where? (1)
Adam:	In kick.
Lori:	In kick.
Teacher:	In kick?
Lori:	Yeah.
Teacher:	OK, so let's just put let's say forward one in kick. [Writes fd 1 in kick.]... (2, 3)
Jim:	I can explain why it doesn't do that. [To teacher.]
Teacher:	You want to explain?
Jim:	You turn the thing, right? So you hit the button and you turn, right? And you want to give it, you want to give it a thrust, right? And a thrust in space, you're going to give it a thrust, it'll keep going in that motion, there's nothing there to stop it, unless acted upon by a separate force, right? Now the way you're setting it up, you hit kick, it's gonna go forward once like blup. [Makes a sound and gesture to show a very short movement.]
Lori:	Oh! So, it's supposed to keep going?

The last line shows the exchange was successful. Lori has understood the critical claim Jim is making. The students settled on an interim design, placing `forward 1` in `tick`.

Shortly thereafter, the students pinpointed a second key conceptual point that was to occupy much of the rest of the discussion. In the following, Kelly and Jim note, quite vaguely, that they need some way of combining kicks with existing motion; they need Newton's second law. Kelly initially describes both influences (kick and prior motion) incorrectly as forces, and she describes their composition as canceling.

Kelly:	...what you needed is a formula to cancel out the two different forces that you put on it.
Teacher:	To cancel out– what are the two different forces you put on it?
Kelly:	The way it was going and the way you just turned it. [She gestures a kind of shove.]
Jim:	I think you want to combine 'em.
Teacher:	The way it was going and the way you just turned it, those are the two forces.
Kelly:	Right... [inaudible]

Teacher: Right, so we need to figure out some way to get this — If this is moving in some direction and then you add a kick, you have to figure out how to add that kick in. Is what you're saying. Mmmm, no?

Jim: I think you have to add all of them, you have to combine them. You have to combine like—If you hit kick like you have to figure out some way to be able to like combine kick with right [right-turn], kick with left [left-turn], and kick with tick.

In the following, the students make a first try at a more specific way to combine motion with kick. Note that the need for a more precise combining is clear in the programming context. Note that Adam's hypothesis (first line below) is made explicit and the focus of the group's attention by writing the code down. The teacher prompts attention to details by, in effect, suggesting mentally running the code. In this case, Adam's hypothesis fails for syntactic reasons (Jeffrey is correct), but in other cases the issue of 'does it do the right thing if we run it?' predominated.

Adam: Kick needs to be like tick + 5.

Teacher: Kick need to be tick + 5? [Writes it in.]

Kelly: Well, why doesn't it just go forward 15?

Lori: Yeah, what's wrong with that?

Teacher: What happened, what does — How does the computer understand tick + 5?

Adam: But if we use — ... That wouldn't really work.

Teacher: How does the computer understand—it's gonna run a tick, so it's gonna go forward 10, and then it's gonna get plus 5, and it's gonna say: plus what with 5?

Jeffrey: It's gonna output 5 in a do-it—in a data box.

In following conversation, Kelly argues that the program needed some way to 'remember' both speed and direction of the ship prior to a kick, so that it could be combined with the kick. This is essentially the notion of momentum, and the teacher seized the moment to make a strong conceptual move. He suggested representing that motion with a vector, which students accepted. The students called the vector `George`.

The conversation entered an extended confusing period where students debated how the ship should face with respect to `George`, its velocity. No resolution emerged, but the teacher occasionally brought order to the conversation by reminding students of the state of their program, what it did and did not do. Below is one example of this.

Teacher: With this program, the way it's set up right now, if I hit the left button, what will we see? Will the ship move in a different direction, or will it just pivot?

Lori: It'll just pivot. We need to do a kick thing for it to move, right?

Teacher: Now why do you say it'll just pivot?

Adam: Because...

Lori: Because George is—the vector, is set at that.

Students returned to the central conceptual issue, combining kicks with motion. In the following, Adam introduces a key new idea with encouragement from the teacher. `George` (the velocity) must be affected by `kick`. If an object is to change its motion, kicks not only combine with prior motion, but also that combination must replace the old velocity. In the following, we believe students, particularly Adam, are keeping hold of the meaning of terms (notably `George`) by running the program mentally. In addition, note that Jim immediately jumps on Adam's suggestion, which is qualitatively correct, but does not represent the kind of influence Jim has in mind for `kick`. This level of precision is in stark contrast to non-computer mediated discussions where students were frequently satisfied and claimed agreement on the basis of extremely vague descriptions. For example, only a few days earlier students had a non-computer mediated discussion on hits affecting the path of a hockey puck. They agreed the motion of the puck would be deflected, but they were not at all concerned with exactly how deflection took place. Here, Adam suggests deflection (re-aimed motion); Jim says that is not precisely what is needed.

Adam: Okay, I have a question. I don't quite understand. I know that Jim just said something to this effect but— It's moving along, this is George right now. The motion that it's going at is George.

Teacher: George is a vector that way.

Adam: Right, is George now a vector that way? [points in the new direction] Or is George still —

Teacher: George has to—If we want it to move in the new direction, George has to change to be the vector that way. That's very good.

Jim: But—

Adam: Okay, well then change—tell George to turn-left and turn-right degrees would work.

Jim: But we want it to add to it, we don't want it to — I don't think— we don't want it to just to change George or our whole problem would be solved. We want it to add George to whichever way we want it to turn so it keeps moving in that motion, but it's going like this, until you give it thrust. We want to add to the thrust one is the one we wanted to add to George.

After an extended discussion about the effects of pushes on objects like cars, spaceships and video game spaceships, Jim suggested that the influence of motion, the kick, needed to be represented by another vector. Now, in physicists' eyes, force has become a vector, and the ground is fully prepared for F=ma in programming form. The teacher intervened to rename the two key vectors: `George` is velocity, and the group settled on `thrust` to name the kick (force) vector.

In the following two segments, Kelly provides the final pieces of the puzzle. She first remarks that velocity and thrust should be combined with vector addition (`shortcut`) and then that the result of that combination is the new velocity. Notice here the following:

1. The teacher is again steering the conversation by asking questions about code.
2. Progress is not made in natural language terms, like 'acceleration' and 'thrust' that have unstable and probably idiosyncratic meanings for these students.
3. Progress is made in terms of new code.
4. The final step, changing velocity, is taken only after an initial guess is written down and students appear to run the program mentally to see that it is not quite right.

Teacher:	What should happen in kick? What should kick do? (1)
Orson:	It should be like a thrust. (2, *here and below four lines*)
Lori:	It should be acceleration.
Orson:	No, it should be the thrust.
Teacher:	It should be the acceleration. It should be the acceleration meaning the change in velocity.
Orson:	I think it should be the thrust. [With teacher above.]
Kelly:	It should move shortcut velocity thrust. (3, *here and below*)
Rusty:	Wait, the thrust and —
Teacher:	Kick should say [writes] move shortcut velocity thrust.

Shortly later:

Jeffrey:	The velocity keeps —that's just going to say that—It's never going to really—I don't know...
Kelly:	The velocity wouldn't change.
Teacher:	According to this the velocity wouldn't change.
Jeffrey:	Uh-huh. And it would if you had thrust...
Teacher:	Okay. And if it had a thrust that would change its velocity. So this needs to be fixed. [Points to kick.] ...
Adam:	Shortcut velocity thrust return velocity.
Kelly:	Change velocity to shortcut velocity thrust. [Teacher starts to write this.] (4)
Jeffrey:	Yes, that's it, that's it! Yeah, I think so.

7 Reflections

In order to help calibrate the results of this experiment we pose and answer some questions about it.

Aren't algebra and calculus at least as clear and precise as programming? They are, provided learners understand these 'languages'. Calculus, however, was beyond the mathematical preparation of these students. Instead, a short, 5 week introduction to programming allowed them to consider many of the same issues treated in calculus by using simple, iterative programs. In a course similar to the one described here given to sixth grade students, students did not even know algebra, yet programming still supported learning physics. See, for example, diSessa (1993). In addition, programming is mentally runnable, which neither algebra nor calculus share and which played an important role in this context.

Shouldn't much of the credit for this episode go to the mathematical concept of vector, rather than to programming or Boxer? Vectors are not built into Boxer but were programmed in Boxer as a resource for teaching physics. The same resources of Boxer can be used to add graphical objects to the programming language that may be valuable for teaching other subjects. This is not possible with other programming languages. In addition, we believed students learned about vectors substantially by experimenting with them in small, but interesting programs. So the programming context helped students understand vectors in the first place. Finally, conventional vectors are not runnable in the programming sense that proved helpful in this design episode.

To what extent could these students 'transfer' what they learned via programming to a non-programming context? Program design was only one context in which these students learned about motion. On other occasions, they observed and discussed physical experiments, or took measurements from them to analyze on a computer. Overall, we took pains to make sure that these students knew the physics they were learning applies to the world, and that they could apply it. We did not expect this single activity to do all that work. Evidence from the course convinced us beyond any doubt that students learned about real-world physics. But the credit does not go to programming per se.

How do we know students really learned from this activity? As part of an ongoing class, we did not pre- and post-test students, nor did we have a control group with which to compare. On the other hand, we believe video tape analysis provides data, within limits, to support the case that these students learned. See Sherin et al. (1993) for details. Given the extensive research that shows how difficult learning about Newton's laws is, we believe we have demonstrated at least a promising avenue of future pursuit.

How do we sort out the differential contributions of the various aspects of this activity: semi-concrete situation, design context, programming as a representational medium, student collaboration and the skill of the teacher? Separating out the effects of individual components of an educational activity is possible only to a limited extent. Effective educational practice involves synergistic combination of multiple components, not a linear cumulative effect. Nonetheless, cumulative experience with multiple examples and careful analysis of learning patterns can lead to some helpful generalizations. For example, collaborative work is often productive when a single child, by him or herself, is unlikely to come up with the breadth of ideas necessary for certain accomplishments. Discussion is also valuable, sometimes, for its own sake—to help students learn to communicate with and learn from others. The representational attributes of programming, especially runnability, pay dividends in non-collaborative contexts as well. See, for example, articles in a special issue of the *Journal of Mathematical Behavior* (The Boxer Group, 1991).

8 Conclusion

Familiar forms of representation, like talk and print, are so commonplace that one may easily forget that they have particular properties and characteristics, and not others. In this paper we have argued and tried to show that programming has some important properties that can foster excellent conversations about scientific matters. Among the more critical characteristics for the success of the discussion described here are that: Programming provides a clear and unusually precise language in terms of which students and teachers can phrase hypotheses, maintain focus and assess group agreement, and state summary results to be incorporated into later work. We have pointed out that programming is unique in allowing students both compact and precise expression, yet it also allows them to draw phenomenological conclusions easily by mentally running their code. Programming is an excellent tool for teachers as well. It helps them monitor students' ideas, and it provides easy means to make effective conceptual and pragmatic moves. "How about using a vector?" "What does this do — what *should* it do?" "Why don't we call this variable velocity?"

We believe that the design discussion described here could not have taken place successfully without using programming as a means of expression. It allowed us to transform the task from an impossible one for high school students, divining Newton's laws unaided, into a 'scaffolded reconstruction' that set an excellent context for students to think about force and motion. With important help from the teacher, the task context and the representational form, students were able to find the resources within themselves to design F=ma.

The broader implications of this work are more important than one successful class activity. Educationally, it alerts us to how much things may change in the presence of computational media. Old assumptions and common sense may need to be questioned and new possibilities tried. Scientifically, this work reminds us that the micro-structure of representation, activity, and conceptual change is rich and surprising. It behooves us to look carefully and study more.

Acknowledgments

The author wishes to acknowledge the support of the National Science Foundation under grant numbers MDR-88-50363 and RED-92-52725. The opinions expressed are those of the author and do not necessarily reflect those of the Foundation. The original analysis of data presented here was developed collaboratively with Bruce Sherin and David Hammer. Thanks are due also to an anonymous reviewer for helpful comments on an earlier draft.

References

diSessa, A.A. (1990) Social niches for future software. Gardner, M., Greeno, J., Reif, F., Schoenfeld, A., diSessa, A. & Stage, E. (eds.) Toward a Scientific Practice of Science Education. Hillsdale, NJ: Lawrence Erlbaum Associates, 301–322.

diSessa, A.A. (1992) Images of Learning. Corte, E. De, Linn, M.C., Mandl, H. & Verschaffel, L. (eds.) Computer-based learning environments and problem solving. NATO ASI Series F, Vol. 84. Berlin: Springer-Verlag.

diSessa, A.A. (1993) The many faces of a computational medium. Jaworski, B. (ed.) Proceedings of the international conference on technology and mathematics teaching. Birmingham, UK: University of Birmingham, 23–38.

diSessa, A.A. & Abelson, H. (1986) Boxer: A reconstructible computational medium. Communications of the ACM, 29(9), 859–868.

diSessa, A.A. & Minstrell, J. (in press) Cultivating conceptual change via benchmark lessons. Greeno, J.G. (ed.) Thinking Practices. Hillsdale, NJ: Lawrence Erlbaum Associates.

diSessa, A.A., Abelson, H. & Ploger, D. (1991) An Overview of Boxer. Journal of Mathematical Behavior, 10(1), 3–15.

Sherin, B. (1992) Programming as a language for learning physics. Boxer Technical Report G7. University of California, School of Education, Berkeley, CA.

Sherin, B., diSessa, A.A. & Hammer, D.M. (1993) Dynaturtle revisited: Learning physics through collaborative design of a computer model. Interactive Learning Environments, 3(2), 91–118.

The Boxer Group (1991) Special issue on Boxer. Journal of Mathematical Behavior, 10(1,2).

Learning by Explaining: Fostering Collaborative Progressive Discourse in Science

Elaine B. Coleman

University of Delaware, College of Education, Dept. of Educational Studies, Newark, DE 19716, USA, email: elainec@brahms.udel.edu

Abstract. There has been an impressive body of work on conversational analysis and turn-taking exchange systems. The present paper is more interested in discussions mediated towards learning. Various ways of examining students' scientific discourse are presented with a particular emphasis on the role of 'co-constructing' explanations to foster deeper conceptual understanding of scientific phenomena. These investigations have been undertaken as part of a major line of research examining ways to promote the coherence of students' scientific beliefs. Methods include 'inquiry-driven' discussions mediated by a Computer Supported Intentional Learning Environment (CSILE), the analysis of natural classroom dialogues, and controlled face-to-face interactions in quasi-experimental settings. The implications for research examining students' discourse in the classroom are discussed.

Keywords. Collaboration, discourse, explanation, science learning

1 Introduction

The enthusiasm for collaborative learning has become so widespread that most researchers and educators believe that students learn better when they work in groups as compared to when they work autonomously. This enthusiasm is partially based on the belief that learning will emerge through children's natural discourse as they work collaboratively to solve a problem.

However, research on argumentation and collaborative discourse in science has found that students' discourse strategies are inappropriate for making inferences or drawing conclusions based on evidence (Kuhn et al., 1988; Linn & Burbules, in press). They rarely produce explanations or justifications for their answers (Forman, in press), they tend to make and defend vacuous claims rather than refine the problems collaboratively (Eichinger et al., 1991), and they routinely criticize or dismiss each other's ideas leading to what some observers have called the 'Social Destruction of Knowledge' (Coleman, 1992). These findings suggest that students do not communicate effectively, they do not monitor the group's progress and consensus of ideas usually rests on the status of the individuals rather than their discourse (Coleman, 1992). Consequently, good ideas are routinely lost or rejected (Eichinger et al., 1991).

The reason for this failure may be that students lack effective strategies for entering into and sustaining meaningful collaborative discussion. It is believed that if students are supported to engage in scientific inquiry and discussion so that during their search for meaning an attempt to construct explanations is made (Miller, 1987), then deeper learning should occur. By deeper learning it is meant that the knowledge is accessible and therefore more likely to be used by the learner rather than becoming inert.

Advancing students' ideas through their discussions with others has theoretical support from both the Vygotskian notion of 'scaffolding' and the Piagetian notion of 'cognitive conflict'. For Vygotsky, speech during social interactions between a child and parent is taken over by the child and internalized and continues to mediate the child's cognitive development (Wertsch, 1985). For Piaget, a mechanism for cognitive development was cognitive conflict. The conflict arises through the interactions between the contradictions between subject's anticipated actions and what he/she observes as the outcome of those actions (stressing an intra-individual conflict) (Inhelder et al., 1974).

Socio-cognitive conflict theorists have extended Piaget's mechanism for cognitive development by stating that intellectual development arises from the resolution of conflictual crises between individuals, as opposed to within. Taken together, these views hold that argumentation and conflict between individuals (inter- individual) as well as within themselves (intra-individual) are the precursors for belief revision (Baker, 1991; Gilly, 1990).

The purpose of this chapter is to review some of the findings from research on students' discourse that has been conducted at the Centre for Applied Cognitive Science in Toronto as well as to discuss the merits of CSILE, a Computer Supported Intentional Learning Environment. The chapter is divided into three main parts: Part one includes a review of some empirical studies which provide a rationale for the design of CSILE. Part two provides a description of CSILE with an example of some students' work. Part three includes a review of some of the empirical studies validating CSILE as a technical knowledge medium for facilitating students' inquiry and scientific discourse in the classroom.

2 Facilitating progressive discourse in science: A goal for science classrooms

One approach to science learning is to help students achieve understanding by restructuring the classroom discourse from an individually centered to a collaboratively centered place. Here, the emphasis and value is placed on building from each other's ideas and advancing the knowledge of the entire class, instead of placing value only on individual achievement (Scardamalia & Bereiter, in press). When this occurs, students work together and share ideas with the goal to promote the progress of ideas for the entire class. This behaviour is referred to as engaging in a progressive discourse and it is believed to be essential for collaborative knowledge building or deeper learning to occur in science (Bereiter, 1994).

During a progressive discourse in science, students actively engage in a questioning and explanation process in which they evaluate each others' queries, pose their own questions, select and build upon information or data previously mentioned, and relate new information to what is previously known (e.g., to general principles of the domain they are learning). This is designed in the effort that they will collaboratively revise their own theories and beliefs about phenomena in the world that they have been trying to understand as well as to begin to evaluate their own epistemological commitments. Students displaying these characteristics are sometimes referred to as having a passionate mind (Shulman, 1991) or taking an intentional approach toward learning (Bereiter & Scardamalia, 1989). Here, learning is viewed as a cyclical process of identifying and solving new problems in order to construct new knowledge as opposed to having a rote learning approach, in which learning is viewed as identifying the facts and memorizing them.

It is often difficult to assess or recognize when students are advancing their understanding in science. In a progressive discourse, progress is viewed as a consensual advance in understanding made between individuals who previously held differing views (Bereiter, in press). Progress thus defined does not avoid the problem that students' misconceptions (e.g., confuse evidence from theory) in science may remain as part of their ongoing discourse and may even propagate. However, some student misconceptions may facilitate progressive discourse or at least not impede it and may eventually lead to emerging scientific beliefs and theories.

3 Part I: Empirical studies examining students' discourse: A rationale for a Computer Supported Intentional Learning Environment (CSILE)

One way to understand how to facilitate students' learning in CSILE is to describe how students' discourse evolves and monitor when progressive discourse moves are made. A series of studies were conducted in order to examine the nature of students' discussions in science. For instance, Chan (1992) followed the pattern of discourse of five pairs of students as they worked collaboratively to comment upon and rate controversial hypothetical statements about evolution. By monitoring the flow of information (i.e., discourse and knowledge-building moves), as well as students' belief change, she identified whether information is taken up by another person, whether it is rejected, stonewalled, compromised too readily or whether a deeper explanation is required of them. Chan subsequently connected the students' patterns of discourse to their conceptual advances made about theories on evolution. Her preliminary findings suggest that the progressive moves found in the students' discourse are often centered around a problem or a knowledge conflict (i.e., they notice a discrepancy or an inconsistency, or they present a lingering doubt that they hold) and are not concerned with superficial or literal meanings of the statements given. For example, students are discussing which variables effect evolution and one student noticed a discrepancy between his/her belief and the new information that was being presented, and stated the following:

"Well, its just the fact that I still think that the environment has an effect on evolution and it's saying that it's not?"

Chan's results also suggest that students' construction and use of elaborative explanations and analogies leads to new understanding, especially during their search for mechanistic explanations about how evolution occurs. This observation is supported by other studies in which students who generate elaborative explanations achieve greater understanding of the domain they are attempting to learn (Chi et al., 1989; Pressley et al., 1992).

4 Using explanation to foster deeper levels of processing

Fostering deeper levels of inquiry in students scientific discussions and in learning in general has been found through the process of explanation (Orsolini & Pontecorvo, 1992; Pressley et al., 1992; Webb, 1989). It is believed that the role of explanation, if viewed as a mechanism of group learning or as part of an ongoing process of negotiation (O'Malley, 1987), will help students co-construct understanding.

Getting students to construct explanations for how things work or fail to work has been a promising direction for encouraging deeper levels of inquiry in students. In one study, Burtis et al. (1992) constructed a hypercard version of an animation program which was based on a 'cartoon-like' frame by frame principle. Students were asked to construct animations to represent the scientific phenomena that they were learning in class (e.g., the flow of electricity). Upon interviewing the students and asking them to explain their animations, several believed that their animations led them to particular problems that they had never considered previously. It appears that having students generate animations may be a useful way to enhance scientific explanations.

If explanatory knowledge is indicative of deeper level inquiry, then one way of supporting this type of behaviour is to design an intervention that requires students to construct and apply their explanations to understand natural phenomena. In another study, an Intervention group was provided with 'procedural facilitation prompts' which were in the form of written questions or prompts that the students asked themselves or asked other members of their group at various intervals as they worked collaboratively to solve photosynthesis problems (Coleman, 1992; Coleman, 1993). The notion of 'procedural facilitation prompts' was adapted from Scardamalia et al., (1984), and Scardamalia and Bereiter's work on procedural facilitation.

This research extends the use of procedural facilitation and focuses on the use of explanation to foster progressive discourse which, in turn, acts as a mechanism for advancing students' conceptual knowledge of photosynthesis. In particular, this research evaluated the effects of a scaffolded explanation-based instructional intervention which was designed to promote changes in students' beliefs as they work collaboratively to advance their own understanding of photosynthesis. The intervention is based on the view that learning science is 'problematic'. The scaffolding consists of instruction and prompts encouraging students to explain, justify, compare and contrast their personal knowledge with the 'scientific' knowledge acquired. For example, the Intervention group was provided with procedural learning prompts while they solved the photosynthesis problems. These prompts were developed to:

1. convey that it is important to evaluate your own thinking or understanding by constructing explanations, (*example prompt: "Can you explain this in your own words?"*);
2. convey that it is important to justify any evaluations of their own work or another's responses with an explanation, (*example prompt: "Explain why you believe that your answer is correct or wrong."*);
3. convey that their explanations should be based on conceptions that they have been learning in class and not on their everyday knowledge (*example prompt: "Can you explain this using the 'scientific' information that we learned in class?"*).
4. convey that there are 'scientific' ways of thinking about functions of concepts as well as everyday definitions of those same concepts (*example prompt: "Is that explanation a 'scientific' explanation or an everyday explanation?"*).

Essentially, these explanation prompts were designed as 'conversational aids' to move the students' discourse. They were not prompts in the standard sense because they are context dependent, intended only to influence the discourse and be mastered by the students. These prompts act in ways similar to the *'dialogue control acts'* described by Bunt (this volume) in which these dialogue acts serve to monitor and evaluate the dialogues by signalling misunderstandings and attempting to repair them.

The following is an excerpt of discourse where an explanation is constructed by a fifth grade student as he attempts to draw an analogy between a plant without carbon dioxide and a flame without oxygen. This discussion is elicited by a prompt while they are working on their explanation to the following question:

> *"Some plants were put in soil, given water and placed in a tightly sealed bottle so they could not get any air. Will the plants in the jar have a food source? Explain."*

(After several minutes of discussion)

(*Prompt*) D: *"Can you compare how you used to think about this with how you think about it now?"*
S: "um..."
D: "I never really thought of it"
S: "Well I always seemed to know that plants um...do need like um... fire if you know those big long things and they are used to..."
D: "Matches?"
S: "No not matches...you know they are called "stuffers" and they have this little sort of container on the top and you put it over the fire and it cuts off the air"

J: "Oh those things"

S: "And when you take it up it's dead...so it is sort of like the plant"

J: *"Now I can compare how I used to think"*

S: "I always believed that like I always thought that they need carbon dioxide and without carbon dioxide they can't live, it can't make its food"

D: "Well I never heard of carbon dioxide before"

The excerpt illustrates how the explanation prompts were being used by the students and how they appeared to elicit further discussion and sharing of ideas that would probably not have occurred otherwise. The prompts gave the students ample opportunity to justify their own beliefs about photosynthesis as well as to use what they have been learning in class.

The results of this research indicated that the explanation prompts used in the intervention played an important role in facilitating students' cognitive processing by advancing their conceptual understanding of photosynthesis. The students who received the explanation prompts constructed conceptually more advanced explanations about photosynthesis and acquired and retained more information about photosynthesis as measured by their scores on the comprehension posttests, and other tasks evaluating structural change compared to the students who did not receive the Intervention (Coleman, 1992; Coleman, 1993).

Furthermore, these results provide some support for the process of explanation as one of the rudimentary structures of argumentation which acts as a mechanism for advancing students' understanding about photosynthesis. By emphasizing the communicative aspect of collaborative learning, it assumed that participants must offer explanations, justifications, questions and resolutions when discussing and working on a task with each other (Brown, 1989; Draper, 1988; Linn & Burbules, in press), and it assumed that using one's knowledge in the context of explanation and argumentation is a useful instructional practice (Voss, 1990). Moreover, it assumed that the nature of the participants' discussion would have an overall effect on the groups' learning outcomes.

The studies presented so far highlight the importance of students' discourse for advancing their own learning and understanding in science. Students who were actively engaged in discussions where students articulated explanations, justified their responses or offered elaborations while reasoning through problems in science, performed greater than students who did not. In addition, students' discussions which focussed on problems (e.g., underlying causes or mechanisms) rather than on topics in science elicited greater understanding. One challenge is to build upon and use some of these empirical findings to design a system which will sustain and support students' discussions in their classrooms and give priority to processes of inquiry and explanation.

5 Part II: CSILE as a knowledge medium for progressive discourse

CSILE (Computer Supported Intentional Learning Environment) is a knowledge-medium which provides information-sharing capabilities between multiple users. It is best viewed as a discourse medium where students ideas are written down, recorded and shared with other students in the class. A central feature of CSILE is its student-generated communal database into which students can enter both written notes and graphics. At present, CSILE is being used in classrooms in the United States and Canada. The usual configuration is eight networked computers to a classroom.

The research reported in this chapter only refers to studies conducted at four elementary classrooms in a school in Toronto, Ontario. Here, elementary students have been using CSILE as a central, cross curricular environment in which they individually or collaboratively author written notes and graphics, and share their ideas through commenting and notification facilities. Students can comment on each other's notes, and authors are notified when comments have been made. Students write comments for various reasons. Sometimes they suggest new information, or ask for clarifications from other students, but often they challenge each other's ideas by presenting them with new facts or problems that need to be considered. When this occurs, it is often the starting point for further discussion. Students' written notes and graphics are stored and are accessible through a communal database situated across a local area network. Students' written entries are individually stored with assigned keywords which makes them accessible to other users. Students learn to search and browse through the database using the keywords as a way to keep up with all of the new information that has been created by other students.

Students use CSILE as part of their on-going study of science, mathematics, history, geography, art, social studies, and physics (Hewitt & Webb, 1992; Scardamalia et al., 1989; Scardamalia et al., 1992b). For example, most students do not view mathematics as a subject for discussion. However, in a study conducted by Lamon (1992), fifth and sixth grade students worked on an activity centering on argument and discussion of the following mathematical problem: "Using only nickels and dimes, how many ways can you make 85 cents?"

Students were asked to solve the problem on CSILE and to search the database for one solution which agreed with their answer and one which disagreed. They were also asked to send comments to the authors of the solutions chosen. Many of their comments were evaluative and led to further discussions comparing various approaches to solving the problem. An interesting discussion about permutations and combinations emerged on CSILE when the students realized that the solution to the problem depended on how the word 'and' was interpreted (Lamon, 1992).

6 Part III: Empirical studies validating CSILE

Studies comparing students' natural discourse on and off CSILE have also been influential in the design of CSILE as a medium for fostering progressive discourse.

Recently, in a pilot study conducted by Cohen (1992), the face-to-face natural discourse of a group of university students was compared with the discourse of students using CSILE as both groups collaborate to solve a physics problem. He examined the types of conjectures made by the students, whether they explicitly mention the variables necessary to solve the physics problems, whether those variables are linked to prior knowledge and whether they contribute additional information that advances the collective knowledge of the group. Although the CSILE students did not communicate their ideas more often then the face-to-face group, they provided more justifications for their ideas as compared to those made by the face-to-face interaction group. Student entries and input in the CSILE group were more evenly distributed across high and low performing students whereas individual students tended to dominate in the face-to-face discussions. It is possible that making written entries into CSILE in order to comment upon other students' notes, requires more reflection and justification than would face-to-face verbal interaction. Students using CSILE have also been found to outperform classmates working in face-to-face groups while solving math problems. CSILE students were able to sustain high-level goals over a lengthier period of time (Lamon, 1992).

An important question for research on CSILE is whether altering particular features of the system which were designed to guide students' discussions would promote greater scientific inquiry. The specific nature of these features required to advance and support students' scientific understanding is under study in some of our more recent research.

Hewitt and Webb (1992) have been experimenting with a new CSILE facility called the 'discussion note' which encourages students to focus on a particular problem. A series of individual notes are attached chronologically with the most recent note appended to the end creating a linear stream of discourse. These notes are identified by author and assigned specific prefixes or 'thinking types' by the students as an indicator of the kind of entry they are constructing. Although, 'thinking types' have been part of the original CSILE design, (Scardamalia & Bereiter, 1991), Hewitt has been experimenting with five new thinking types that are designed to promote students discourse by engaging them in cognitive processes that are deemed necessary for making knowledge advances. Students can choose from the following five prefixes: *Problem (P), My Theory (MT), I Need To Understand (INTU), Comment (C), and New Information (NI).* For example, as students work on a problem of different blood types posed by one of their classmates, students respond by stating their own theories, and provide new information.

Problem (P): "How do different blood types affect different people?" (RS)

My Theory (MT): "I think that different types of blood are inherited and that is what is different in the bodies of people. I think I once heard that if somebody receives a blood transfusion of a different blood types, that clumping takes place and can block blood vessels and lead to serious illness or possibly death. Therefore I think that just like DNA blood type can affect a person's health if it doesn't match." (RS)

My Theory (MT): "I think that if people are born with a certain type of blood they can live but if people are given a different kind of blood their body try to destroy it and then they wouldn't have enough blood to survive on." (RD)

New Information (NI): "When a patient receives donated blood for any reason the doctors have to match up their blood type. Certain blood types match even if they are different types. If they don't match, the blood clumps (sticks together) and blocks the blood vessels. This could lead to serious illness or even death." (RS)

I Need To Understand (INTU): "What types of blood are there?" (RS)

My Theory (MT): "I think there are a number of blood types. I think that the different types of blood are expressed with letters. (for example type A, AB)." (RS)

The above example illustrates that having students 'prefix' their written entries with a 'thinking types' may have externalized some of the cognitive processes which are fundamental for advancing their learning (i.e., referring to prior knowledge, stating a theory or belief, monitoring the group's progress, and advancing the collective knowledge with new information). It also serves to guide their discourse by requiring a sense of relevance, continuation and fluidity of their ideas that is essential for any progressive discourse to occur— i.e., it keeps the discourse relevant and on track. Although this has not been empirically tested, the hope is that it will foster deeper and more sustained inquiry where students revise their beliefs in response to comments made by other students (Scardamalia et al., 1992a).

Lastly, a challenge for research on CSILE has been to examine whether learning on CSILE transfers to other learning situations. One study examined whether drawing on CSILE for explanatory purposes would transfer to other media. Fifth and sixth grade CSILE students' graphical and causal explanations of continental drift, were compared to those of control students who did not use CSILE. It was hypothesized that using multiple representations, i.e., graphic and textual, which are non-redundant in terms of the information they present, would facilitate a causal or 'dynamic' view of continental drift since it requires an integration of the descriptive aspects with the causal and dynamic information embodied in this domain (Gobert et al., 1993).

All of the students were required to convey their understanding of continental drift through the use of paper and pencil to eliminate a possible advantage for the CSILE users. Overall, the CSILE students constructed more advanced causal explanations and constructed diagrams which contained more causal/dynamic information than the students who did not use CSILE. Both of these findings reflect a deeper understanding of the domain and point to the usefulness of explanatory knowledge (both written and graphical) as measures of greater understanding in science (Gobert et al., 1993).

In summary, having CSILE in the classroom has encouraged students to focus on the growing body of knowledge they acquire collaboratively and to decide what is left to be learned or which problems remain to be solved. Students in CSILE classrooms have been found to show significant gains in the coherence of their explanations and elaborated answers, generate more knowledge advancing and 'wonderment' questions, use more mental state verbs such as 'wonder', 'belief', 'understand', and 'hypothesize' than their non-CSILE peers (Scardamalia & Bereiter, 1992; Scardamalia et al., 1992a). In addition, CSILE students perform significantly greater than controls on standardized achievement tests of basic language skills. (See Scardamalia et al. (1992b) for more information on the evaluation of the cognitive effects of using CSILE in the classroom.)

7 Conclusions

Learning will not be manifested through all types of discussion. If collaborative discourse is going to lead to learning, then students need help to sustain deeper levels of inquiry. For the most part, students are too ready to close a sequence of dialogue for reasons which are not greatly understood. (Coleman, 1992; Baker, this volume). Supporting sustained inquiry and progressive discourse has been done by implementing instructional and technical designs as supportive interventions.

Efforts have focussed on the patterns of discourse moves which appear to sustain inquiry-driven reasoning. Results suggest that a query-explanation process which extends students' discourse by making them more likely to justify their points of view, and build upon previous statements, fosters deeper and more sustained inquiry (Orsolini & Pontecorvo, 1992). Moreover, students' discussions seem to flourish when they are centered around problems in which they are searching for explanations and noticing discrepancies among each other's statements.

These strategies are illustrated in research investigating classrooms designed as communities of learners (Brown & Campione, 1990). When thinking and reasoning are part of the school curriculum, then the classroom is a useful place for students to gain repeated experience in argumentation and sustained inquiry. Within these classrooms, students discuss while they work collaboratively in order to advance on a particular topic. They learn to argue, justify claims, use evidence and theories and eventually come to adopt these critical strategies as their own. One of the purposes of this research is to identify collaborative learning situations which promote students' conceptual change and belief revision through their discussions.

Various designs and interventions have been described which attempt to facilitate knowledge-advancing discourses through CSILE and in face-to-face conditions. Findings suggest that CSILE plays an important role in developing and sustaining students' understanding. What has been most impressive is that students work collaboratively to advance the collective knowledge of the class in a way that surpasses any individual effort. It appears that explanatory knowledge or elaboration is an important factor for facilitating, producing and sustaining useful dialogues for learning. More research is needed which can 'unpack' the explanation process in order to understand what happens (cognitively speaking) when one constructs an explanation in a progressive discourse.

Acknowledgements

Preparation for this paper was supported by the James S. McDonnell Foundation. I am grateful to Marlene Scardamalia, Carl Bereiter, Stellan Ohlsson and Amy Shapiro for their helpful comments.

References

Baker, M.J. (1991) The influence of dialogue processes on students' collaborative generation of explanations for simple physical phenomena. Proceedings of the International Conference on the Learning Sciences. Northwestern University, Illinois USA, Evanston, Illinois, 9–19.

Bereiter, C. (1994) Implications of postmodernism for science, or, Science as progressive discourse. Educational Psychologist, 29(1), 3–12.

Bereiter, C. & Scardamalia, M. (1989) Intentional learning as a goal for instruction. In: Resnick, L.B. (ed.) Knowing, learning, and instruction: Essays in honor of Robert Glaser. Hillsdale, NJ: Erlbaum, 361–392.

Brown, A.L. (1989) Analogical learning and transfer: What develops? In: Vosniadou, S. & Ortony, A. (eds.) Similarity and analogical reasoning. Cambridge, MA: Cambridge University Press.

Brown, A.L. & Campione, J.C. (1990) Communities of learning and thinking or a context by any other name. Contributions to Human Development, 21, 108–126.

Burtis, J., Bereiter, C., Scardamalia, M. & Rowley, P. (1992) Children's understanding of mechanisms. Interim report to the Ontario Ministry of Education on Problem-Centered Knowledge Appendix D.

Chan, C. (1992) Collaborative knowledge building and progressive discourse in students' understanding of evolution. Interim report to the Ontario Ministry of Education on Problem-Centered Knowledge Appendix C.

Chi, M.T.H., Bassok, M., Lewis, M.W., Reimann, P. & Glaser, R. (1989) Self-explanations: How students study and use examples in learning to solve problems. Cognitive Science, 13, 145–182.

Cohen, A. (1992) Using CSILE in a progressive discourse in physics. Paper presented at the annual meeting of the American Educational Research association, San Francisco, CA.

Coleman, E.B. (1992) Facilitating conceptual understanding in science: A collaborative explanation-based approach. Unpublished doctoral dissertation, University of Toronto, Toronto.

Coleman, E.B. (1993) Inducing a shift from intuitive to scientific knowledge with inquiry training. Proceedings of the Fifteenth Annual Conference of the Cognitive Science Society. Boulder Co., 347–352.

Draper, S.W. (1988) What's going on in everyday explanations. In: Antaki, C. (ed.) Analysing everyday explanation: a casebook of methods. London: Sage publications, 15–31.

Eichinger, D.C., Anderson, C.W., Palincsar, A.S. & David, Y.M. (1991) An illustration of the roles of content knowledge, scientific argument, and social norms in collaborative problem solving. Paper presented at the annual meeting of the American Education Research Association, Chicago, IL.

Forman, E. (in press) Discourse, intersubjectivity and the development of peer collaboration: A vygotskian approach. In: Winegar, L.T. & Valsiner, J. (eds.) Children's development within a social context. Hillsdale, NJ: Erlbaum.

Gilly, M. (1990) The psychosocial mechanisms of cognitive constructions: Experimental research and teaching perspectives. In: Perret-Clermont, A.N. & Schubauer-Leoni, M.L. (eds.) Social Factors in Learning and Instruction. London: Academic Press, 607–621.

Gobert, J.D., Coleman, E.B., Scardamalia, M. & Bereiter, C. (1993) Restructuring the classroom: Implementing Knowledge Building Via CSILE. Presented at the Annual Meeting of the Educational Research Association, Atlanta, GA.

Hewitt, J. & Webb, J. (1992) Designs to encourage discourse in the OISE CSILE system. Poster session conducted at the ACM Conference on Human Factors in Computing Systems (CHI'92), Monterey, CA.

Inhelder, B., Sinclair, H. & Bovet, M. (1974) Learning and the development of cognition. Cambridge, MA: Harvard University Press.

Kuhn, D., Amsel, E.D. & O'Loughlin, M. (1988) The development of scientific thinking skills. San Diego: Academic Press.

Lamon, M. (1992) Learning environments and macrocontexts: Using multimedia for understanding mathematics. Grounding mathematical problem solving in meaningful contexts: Research implications and outcomes. Symposium presented at the meeting of the American Educational Research Association, San Francisco.

Linn, M.C. & Burbules, N. (in press) Construction of knowledge and group learning. In: Tobin, K. (ed.) Constructivism and applications in mathematics and science. Washington, DC: American Association for the Advancement of Science (AAAS).

Miller, M. (1987) Argumentation and cognition. In: Hickman, M. (ed.) Social and functional approaches to language and thought. New York: Academic, 225–249.

O'Malley, C. (1987) Understanding explanation. Cognitive Science Research Report CSRP-88. University of Sussex.

Orsolini, M. & Pontecorvo, C. (1992) Children's talk in classroom discourse. Cognition and Instruction, 9(2), 113–136.

Pressley, M., Wood, E., Woloshyn, V., Martin, V., King, A. & Menke, D. (1992) Encouraging mindful use of prior knowledge: Attempting to construct explanatory answers facilitates learning. Educational Psychologist, 27(1), 91–109.

Scardamalia, M. & Bereiter, C. (1991) Higher levels of agency for children in knowledge building: A challenge for the design of new knowledge media. The Journal of the Learning Sciences, 1(1), 37–68.

Scardamalia, M. & Bereiter, C. (1992) Text-based and knowledge-based questioning by children. Cognition and Instruction, 9(3), 177–199.

Scardamalia, M. & Bereiter, C. (in press) Technologies for knowledge building discourse. CACM Special Issue: Technology in Education.

Scardamalia, M., Bereiter, C. & Steinbach, R. (1984) Teachability of the reflective process in written comprehension. Cognitive Science, 8, 173–190.

Scardamalia, M., Bereiter, C., McLean, R., Swallow, J. & Woodruff, E. (1989) Computer-supported intentional learning environments. Journal of Educational Computing Research, 5, 51–68.

Scardamalia, M., Bereiter, C. & Lamon, M. (1992a) The CSILE project: Trying to bring the classroom into world 3. Paper presented to the McDonnell Foundation.

Scardamalia, M., Bereiter, C., Brett, C., Burtis, J., Calhoun, C. & Smith Lea, N. (1992b) Educational applications of a networked database. Interactive Learning Environments, 2(1), 45–71.

Shulman, M. (1991) The passionate mind. New York: Macmillan: The Free Press.

Voss, J. (1990) Reasoning by argumentation. In: Mandl, H., de Corte, E., Bennet, S.N. & Frederich, H.F. (eds.) Learning & Instruction: European Research in an International Context, vol.2:1 Social and Cognitive Aspects of Learning and Instruction. Oxford: Pergamon, 305–319.

Webb, N. (1989) Peer interaction and learning in small groups. International Journal of Educational Research, 13, 21–39.

Wertsch, J.V. (1985) Vygotsky and the formation of mind. Cambridge, MA: Harvard University Press.

Tools for Collaborative Learning in Optics

Miriam Reiner

Department of Education in Science and Technology, Technion, Haifa 32000, Israel,
email: miriamr@techunix.technion.ac.il

Abstract. The core problem discussed in this paper is the construction of communication and reasoning symbols involved in collaborative physics learning. First we discuss three aspects of the crucial role of the 'physics language': the individual learner, the collaborative learning set-up, and the language embedded in the domain of physics. Following this we report on a study of physics language construction while students interact with a rule-based, dynamic, learning environment in optics. The learning environment is designed to provide symbols as tools for collaborative visualization and comunication on physics. We look at how students construct a physics language during a session of collaborative problem solving in optics, and how this is related to the learning environment. We also examine the rate of change of new symbols in the discussion and how this is related to the learning situation. Four types of symbols were gradually introduced by students: graphical symbols: static or dynamic, mathematical symbols: letters, numbers or expressions, verbal symbols, physical symbols: objects and/or procedures. It seems that students found graphical symbols the most powerful tools within this environment.

Keywords. Communication, symbolic system, collaborative learning, optics, microworld

1 Introduction

Much of the recent research on physics learning has focused on the various ways in which students' conceptualize physics. Processes of conceptual change are treated mainly from the content and psychological point of view. Despite an extensive literature on conceptualization in physics, only few looked at the way physics-language is constructed.

Communication and reasoning in physics are based on a set of symbols unfamiliar to everyday language. Knowing, thinking and discussing physics means to acquire and apply new tools for representation, reasoning and communication, which must be consistent with the tools used by the scientific community (Pimm, 1987).

The core problem discussed in this paper is the construction of communication and reasoning symbols involved in physics learning. First we discuss three aspects of the crucial role of the 'physics language': the individual learner, the collaborative learning set-up, and the language embedded in the domain of physics. Following this we report on a study of physics language construction, while students interact with a dynamic, graphical, multi-representational learning environment in optics.

2 Language construction in physics learning

2.1 The individual's point of view

Extensive research on students' ideas has changed the accepted view of what physics learning is. Understanding of the role of students' ideas in physics learning has lead to a rejection of the 'objectivist' representation of physics knowledge in which the student is seen as acceptor and teacher as provider of 'objective' knowledge (Von-Glasersfeld, 1992). A widely accepted view favors a learning environment that supports the gradual construction of physics concepts, based upon students' preconceptions, understandings, ideas and interests (Minstrell, 1992). This involves an ongoing process of re-examination of the physical concept against personal experience as a basis for successive conceptual refinement. Learning involves the bridging of formal physics representations to students' experience, and integration of multiple representations, appealing to students' various perception channels.

Above all it involves the development of a language rooted within the epistemology and 'culture' of the discipline. The process of construction of a language begins with the meaning of words and phrases. According to radical constructivism, 'knowing' the word optical 'image' for instance, means that the learner must see an image at least once, experience the situation in which the image is created, and associate the word 'image' with this experience (Von-Glasersfeld, 1987). To know what others mean by the word 'image' means to experience situations experienced by others.

The learner constructs a general concept of an 'image' to fit different experienced situations. This means that various situations related to an 'image' are associated with this concept. Concepts are constructed by the individual, on the basis of personal experience (Gibson, 1979). Therefore, a word cannot represent an objective concept, no matter how large and extensive an individual's experience, or how much she/he interacted and negotiated meanings with others. Hence language cannot transfer objective conceptual entities. Agreed upon words can only trigger the learner's personal experience associated with the word. If some of the experience is shared by the discussing group, communication is made possible. Successive negotiation furthers refines the various aspects of the word (Brown, 1989). If experience associated with the word differs dramatically, communication may become inefficient. This may often happen when members of two very different cultures meet. Communication becomes even more complex when the communicating persons did not yet construct labels of their personal experience. These may still be absent from the learners linguistic inventory and tools to construct such labels are necessary. In the following we suggest that a graphical-dynamic learning environment may provide tools for the individual to construct labels that share some common features with other learners or teachers.

2.2 A social point of view

Label construction is meaningless if it is not accompanied by a social agreement. This does not mean that all members (teacher and students) share identical conceptual structures. It means there is a common core of personal experience agreed upon by the collaborating members.

The Wittgensteinian view of learning (Wittgenstein, 1953) takes a social approach, folding language, interaction and communication into the process of learning. According to this view, language is not a private endeavor. It is rooted in a social activity. The labels learners create are inherent in their social understanding of the community that practices the discipline, in this case physics. Furthermore, labels are negotiated and refined so that they match the learner's understanding of the practice and conventions of the discipline, as defined by the community (Pea, 1987). Participating and interacting with a community means further tracing of the various meanings of a label, its applications and related activities.

Questioning, negotiation and argumentation are means for refinement of meanings. They are social activities, and conversation is a mechanism by means of which individuals engage in the social construction of meaning. Eckert (1989) suggests that learning is a lifelong process in which a learner becomes a member of different 'communities of practice'. The members of a community of practice share similar goals, procedures, concepts and language, ways of recognizing evidence, argumentation processes and technical, hands-on procedures.

Indeed, collaborative learning set-ups have been found to be advantageous to learning: they improve academic performance, self esteem, social relations and attitudes towards science (Hamm & Adams, 1992). Only few studies go into detailed analysis of group interaction. Roschelle (1992) is one recent exception: he demonstrates a convergent process of collaborative conceptual change on acceleration and velocity. Baker (this volume) studies the process of agreement in a collaborating group on physics problem solving. Wenger (1993) looks at technology for the work place: he argues that technology should be designed in a way which supports communication between members of a social community. Learning collaboratively involves the ability to participate in the 'language games' (Wittgenstein, 1953), which frame the interaction within a 'community of practice' (Lave & Wenger, 1991). According to this view, language is relative to a specific community. As Wittgenstein pointed out 'If a lion could talk, we could not understand him' (Wittgenstein (1953) p.223). Sometimes a physicist's talk is a 'lions talk'. Language, terminology and symbolic systems for communication are situated in the culture of a specific community (ibid. p.223; Brown et al. (1989)). A 'mass point moving with a constant velocity' triggers a whole web of interrelated associations in a physicists mind, totally different from the one triggered in the mind of an actor, or of a naive physics student. Language construction is therefore a socially shared process.

Tools for sharing information are frequently established in most communities. Journals, workshops, conferences, meetings, discussions and brain-storming are all means created by communities for mutual learning. Yet school learning, especially in science, only seldom provides learning environments which encourage collaborative learning.

2.3 A disciplinary point of view

Physics learning is viewed here as a process of adaptation of a new symbolic system, necessary for communication and reasoning about physical phenomena. It is strongly associated with the notion of discovery *'what sort of demonstration will justify us in agreeing that whereas this was not previously known, it can now be regarded as known?'* (Toulmin (1960) p.17)

The core of the discovery, a *'transition from the state-of-affairs in which this was not known to that in which it was known, was a double one: it comprised the development of a technique for representing optical phenomena which was found to fit a wide range of facts, and the adoption along with this technique of a new model, a new way of regarding these phenomena and of understanding why they are as they are'* (Toulmin (1960) p.29)

Communication and reasoning about natural processes, analysis of observations, nature of evidence, epistemological aspects of data, mental dynamical images and thought experiments are not compatible with every-day terminology. The nature of representations is related to habits of thought about physical phenomena. One of the major 'habits' of thought is related to experimentation – both hands-on and thought experiments.

2.3.1 Experimentation in physics learning

Physics is seen by science educators as an empirical discipline. Therefore one of the major tools in generating physics knowledge is experimentation of various kinds: hands-on experimentation with actual equipment in a physical environment, and thought experiments involving symbolic representations in a mental imaginary environment. The first is widely refered to in physics education projects and curriculum materials (e.g., Physical Science Study Committee (1987); Purcell (1965)). Most teaching efforts address the empirical aspect of knowledge generation in physics, namely lab experimentation. The second, cognitive processes in which an 'imaginary world' is constructed and imaginary 'experiments' are carried out, is only seldom recognized as a tool for learning about physical phenomena. Yet it is a necessary component in physics reasoning.

3 Terminology: Meaning negotiation, symbols and representations

Meaning negotiation is considered here as the process of communication in a group in which at least two different representations of a particular concept are associated, or alternatively, as a communication process in which symbols are attached to meaning. A segment of student discussion follows, recorded a short time after students had started working. The question which students spontaneously raised was related to the function of the lens in the eye. They decided to construct a bigger lens in the micro world and to examine the impact of the lens on the 'lines' (rays of light). Figure 1 shows the rays and lens on the computer screen.

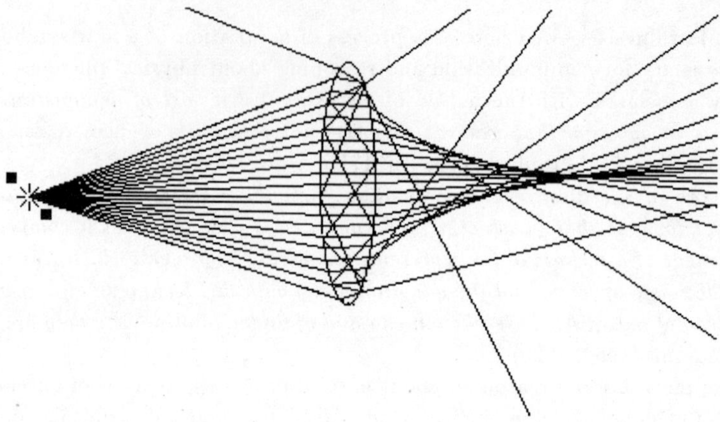

Fig. 1. Diagram present on the screen during students' conversation on lens and light source.

Student A: `...all lines get to the same place ...` *(points at one point)*
Student B: `Ah, not really ...` *(points at one line which is totally internally reflected)*
Student A: `They come from different points on that circular object` *(The interface labels a varying lens as a circular object)*
Student C: `How come these lines get to one place ...`
Student B: `The lines don't come from different points on that object they just hit different places on the object`
Student B: `All lines come from one point, what did you call it?`
Student A: `It says it's a light source ...` *(The word light source is explicitly written in the menu on the screen)*
Student B: `Yeah, light from the light source`

Various symbols are involved here: a dark point on the screen from which lines originate is labeled as a light source. The light source is represented as a point from which lines originate (see the last statement by Student B). Therefore the physics meaning attached to the point is that of a source of light. Once the word light source is recognized it may bear additional associations, based on personal experience and conceptual constructs. For instance, following the identification of the point as a light source, student B now uses the term light rather than line. The symbol of a line stands for the concept of light.

The symbol of a 'circular object' is explicitly present on the screen, and stands for something which is met by lines (light). It changes the direction of these 'lines' so that they all reach the same 'place' - a symbol that still does not represent a concept in physics. The concept of 'lens' is still absent, though a preliminary meaning, the impact of a circular object on the 'lines' is constructed.

The concept of an image of the source represented by the point at which lines cross each other (labeled in the conversation as the 'place') is constructed later on, after recognizing the geometrical similarities between the light source and the point at which lines cross each other. One general comment is that in most cases in school, students work mainly with the symbol structures, ignoring the conceptual level (Pea et al., 1991).

Communication about optics is constrained by the symbols available to the students. Since physics events are poorly described by everyday language, an additional symbolic system is made available in the software. This symbolic system is consistent with that of the physics community. Symbols are considered here as the construction blocks of representations. Reasoning and communicating information about representations of the behaviour of the mirror, such as reflection, demands a set of agreed upon symbols. Students examine events, predict situations and outcomes, test hypotheses, raise questions, construct explanatory models and epistemological arguments by means of the constructed symbols. These processes act as a basis for the construction of representations.

The distinction between representations and symbols is somewhat tricky. Generally stated, both terms construct a correspondence between some aspects of the representing (symbolizing) entity and the represented (symbolized) entity. Any particular specified representation should describe five entities (Kaput, 1987):

1. The represented entity
2. The representing entity
3. Aspects of the represented entity
4. Aspects of the representing entity
5. The correspondence between the two entities

Whereas a symbol relates the 'material' aspect of one world, in which no meaning is attached (a letter, a line, etc.), to a world in which a meaning is attached, a representation relates semantic aspects of two worlds. Basically, a symbol in itself has no meaning within the domain of optics. The meaning attached to it arises from the fact that it signifies a concept. A representation is constructed by a mapping function which attaches one meaning to another, e.g.: the representation of light as a wave is constructed by attaching the concept of a wave and the concept of electromagnetic radiation (visible light). A symbol is similarly constructed by a mapping function – it attaches a conceptually empty figure to a conceptual entity.

Any representation is constructed of symbols. As such, symbols may constitute the building blocks of a representation, just as letters (symbols) when combined, under the correct syntax, construct meaningful words and sentences (representations).

However, unlike the technical role of letters which impose no meaning on a word, a symbol in physics may be chosen as such because of its properties. For instance, the symbol of an arrow is chosen for light because of its vector properties. The symbol of a line is not as powerful as that of an arrow. An arrow in itself, though, has a mathematical meaning, it has no physics meaning. It retains its meaning (within the domain of optics) from the fact that it is related to light.

The meaning of a symbol used in a conversation is constructed gradually. For instance, an arrow as a symbol of light, once accepted as a symbol relevant to the discussion, has a preliminary meaning attached to it. This meaning, through linkage to additional symbols, may be abstracted and extended to various representations of light behaviour acting as tool for thought. Such tools when carefully chosen, because of their properties, act as triggers for progressive conceptual refinement.

The experiment described here uses a learning environment in Optics. It is designed to provide symbols as tools for collaborative visualization of thought experiments and communication on physics. We look at how students use symbols provided on the screen to discuss Optics. The learning environment is now described, followed by a description of the learning experiment, results and conclusion.

4 The problem: A graphical learning environment for collaborative construction of communication tools

'Speaking physics' is then a major component in physics learning. The individual constructs concepts by labeling and communicates to negotiate meaning in a social set-up. This leads towards an agreed upon set of conventions. The conventions are represented by means of a particular language, which allows communication on mental images and thought experiments.

The hypothesis tested here is that a graphical learning environment provides tools for labeling phenomena, collaborating and describing mental images in a manner consistent with the discipline of physics. The main research question is: how students construct a symbolic system, and what are the constituents of such a system when applied in discussions on optics.

5 The structure of the optics learning environment

Dynagrams[1] is a rule-based 'micro world' in optics, based on a direct manipulation graphical interface consistent with conventional representations in physics (Pea et al., 1991).

Legitimate processes in the software are dominated by an internal set of physics rules on light-matter interaction in the domain of refraction and reflection. The range of legitimate values allowed for each variable is extended beyond that existing in nature. Hence, the learning environment provides interested learners with tools for reasoning about imaginary physics situations.

Each event in the micro world is generated by a specific combination of the variables defining the situation represented. Since the range of the variables is continuous, the number of possible states in the micro world is infinite.

---

[1] Dynagrams was developed at IRL by Allen S., Goldman S., Jul S., Pea R., Reiner M., Sipusic M. and Slavin, E. under NSF grant #MDR 88-55582.

5.1 Modes of representation in the learning environment

Since one of the major goals of the learning environment is to facilitate discussion, graphical representations are provided to allow communication about light behaviour which cannot be represented in a static diagram or a hands-on experiment. For example: the quality of an image is a function of the sharpness of the point where all the rays cross each other. If they cross each other at one point the image is sharp, otherwise it is blurred. The behaviour of light which results in a blurred image, is represented in a dynamical simulation, which provides students with the graphical tools to construct a causal explanation of what sort of light-matter interaction may result in a blurred image.

5.2 The Dynagrams software

The software allows students to collaboratively construct objects with various shapes of transformed spheres. These objects have certain properties: absorption, reflection, transmission and index of refraction. Numerical values of the variables are controlled by the student through a friendly interface. The range of the values is not restricted by the range of the actual values in the natural world. Thus, students can construct imaginative set-ups in which visualization of hypothetical situations are possible.

6 Method

The learning experiment took place in an eleventh grade of a well established high school. Students participating were described by the school system as low achievers in mathematics. The experiment took place during the summer vacation in a lab at the university. Prior to the experimental instruction, students were asked to respond to a paper and pencil questionnaire. Overall, 12 students participated in the study. Only 9 of those who took the posttest also took the pretest and participated in the whole experiment. Thus all of the analysis is done on this group of students.

The participating teacher is a very well respected physics teacher. He participated in the development of the activities based on the software, and helped designing the research, but was not present during the teaching sessions.

The teaching period was divided into two parts. In the first part, the activities of the day were described, general information was given on technical matters such as the equipment and interface, and students' questions were dealt with. In the second part, students separated freely into groups of two or three, and a guide moved freely among them providing assistance wherever requested. The basis for activity was a daily sheet collected after the session. The students activity reported here was to examine the periscope. A periscope is essentially made of two parallel plane mirrors. In this activity the students was asked to rotate the upper part of the periscope around its axis until the image observed turns upside down. It is not explained to the student that this simply means revolving the upper mirror through 90 degrees.

Students were asked to construct this situation in the micro world, and to explain why the image is reversed.

Collaborative work was taped by two cameras. One focused on the screen of the computer and the lab equipment on the table, another on the learners. Pre- and posttests were administered.

7 Results: Collaborative construction of a symbolic system

Some of the symbols available in the learning environment are meaningless in the students' framework. Therefore they are not considered to exist as symbols until a need to deal with the symbol is dictated by the problem students are attempting to solve. Indeed results show that the longer students interact with the learning environment, the more they use the symbolic system (see Table 1). The rate of new symbols integrated in the discussion increases as the interaction time increases, up to a particular peak. At this point, the rate of new symbols involved decreases, though the total number increases. Four types of symbols were identified:

- graphical symbols: static or dynamic
- mathematical symbols: letters, numbers and expressions
- verbal symbols
- physical symbols: objects and procedures.

Graphical symbols are used either by copying them on paper or in 'the air', pointing at them on the screen or on paper, or tracing symbols on the screen (extended pointing). Dynamical graphical symbols are addressed by a verbal pointer, asking for attention, or a tracing procedure (rays are traced on the screen) in which changes in the state are emphasized.

Verbal representations are somewhat tricky. Since any word is a symbol, all words used in the discussion in the first few sentences are 'new' in the discussion. Not all of these are of any interest in this paper. Therefore, only physics-related new verbal labels are considered, e.g.: point source, line object, circular object, lens, ray, light source, distance, image, picture, shadow, light intensity. Most students have a prior 'naive' meaning already attached to a symbol. Furthermore, students frequently share a common understanding, a convention-related symbol. In this sense, the verbal representation, unlike graphical or mathematical symbols, is already associated with a semantic level. Physical objects or events are used when these are given in the situation stated in the problem, and they force the students to use the actual hands-on experiment in order to communicate about it. It seems that once an additional symbol is attached to a phenomenon, discussion about the phenomenon is made possible.

Mathematical symbols are rarely used, and can probably be explained by the letters attached to the measuring tools in the software or to students' ideas about symbols that should be used in physics. Numbers are symbols of a unique nature: once a number is used for communication it bears an implicit meaning of size attached to the symbol. The process of attaching size to a physical representation on the screen (such as the point on the screen where all refracted parallel rays cross each other – which physicists would label focal length) is part of the construction of meaning of the concept of focal length.

Table 1 presents the frequency of integration of new symbols in a group discussion. The three sessions, lasting a total of roughly 240 minutes, were divided into periods of 10 minutes each. The number of new symbols used in each period of 10 minutes was counted. Frequency here is the number of new symbols introduced by the three students of group A, for each 10 minutes of student interaction, in the second, third and fourth of 12 sessions. The second meeting was actually the first during which they interacted with the software. We had 23 measures for each group. Results for group A are presented in the following. The list of numbers shows the frequency of symbols integrated in the discussion for the first time, at intervals of 10 minutes. Figure 2 presents the rate of change of the number of new graphical symbols students used in their discussion. The term 'new' means that the symbol has not been mentioned before. For instance, in the fifth period of 10 minutes, students introduced 4 new graphical symbols.

Table 1. Rate of change of symbols integrated in the discussion.

Graphical		Mathematical			Verbal	Physical	
static	dynamic	letters	expressions	numbers		objects	procedures
0	0	0	0	0	2	0	0
1	0	0	0	0	5	0	0
1	0	0	0	0	2	0	0
2	0	0	0	0	2	0	0
4	0	0	0	0	2	0	0
6	1	0	0	0	5	0	0
9	1	0	0	0	6	0	0
12	1	2	0	0	6	0	0
15	1	0	0	0	8	0	0
19	2	1	0	2	13	0	0
20	2	0	0	1	13	0	0
20	3	1	0	2	8	0	0
18	2	1	0	1	7	3	0
19	3	0	0	2	5	4	1
18	3	1	0	0	5	3	0
15	2	1	0	2	3	4	0
12	2	2	1	3	5	4	0
13	3	2	0	4	5	0	0
13	4	1	0	4	4	0	0
14	7	2	1	6	3	2	0
15	11	5	3	3	3	3	1
16	15	5	3	3	3	4	0
14	5	5	1	3	2	2	0

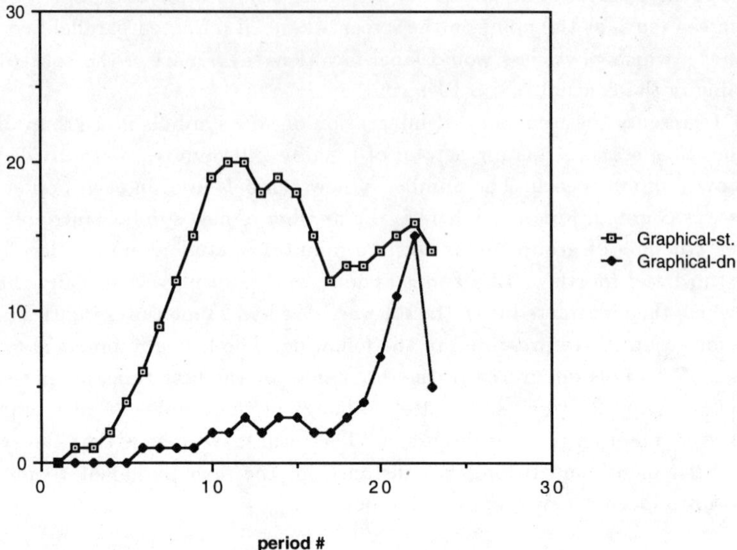

Fig. 2. Distribution of new graphical symbols (static and dynamic) integrated by students in the discussion.

Not surprisingly, the frequency of the new symbols introduced, increases with time. It is low in the first few periods until some practice is gained. Once practice is established the rate of new graphical symbols employed increases, until it attains a specific peak, and then gradually decreases. Eventually it decreases to zero, once no more symbols are required for communication about Optics.

Dynamical symbols sometimes turn into icons that symbolize a process in physics. For instance, a ray emitted from the source and reflected when it meets an object was used by students as a symbol of reflection. This symbol is sometimes used in physics for reflection.

Students increase the number of dynamical symbols they use in the discussion. The rate of increase is far smaller than that of static symbols. The relation between the two is interesting: the peak of employment of new dynamic symbols comes shortly after the peak for static symbols. This may suggest that student need static symbols as a preliminary basis for dynamic symbols.

Mathematical symbols are far less popular during student discussions than are graphical symbols, but cannot be ignored (see Figure 3). Students sometimes use letters. They sometimes use expressions such as "d is 10" for the magnitude of distance, or "R is bigger for this lens" for the curvature of a lens, even if the curve is not a part of a circle. 'D' and 'R' are symbols used in the software. Most letters are taken from the problem itself or from the software 'measuring toolbox' and are extended to other situations. Numbers are used sometimes, especially when the need for comparison arises. They are never used to calculate quantitative values though the qualitative analysis required to respond to the problems could be based

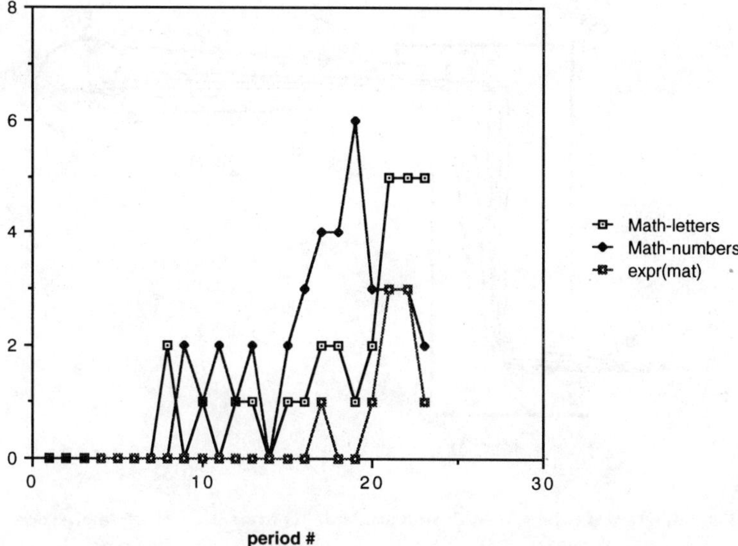

Fig. 3. Distribution of new mathematical symbols integrated in the discussion.

on a calculus approach.

Mathematical expressions are even less frequently used. These are mostly used when dynamical graphical symbols are used, as exemplified in the following segment of discussion. Students discuss the point at which they need to 'put' the 'eye' in order to observe a specific object through the periscope. Mathematical expressions are bold. Figure 4 presents the diagram on the screen.

Student A: `You need to make the light bounce off the mirror so it hits the eye.`

Student B: `...hits the eye ...You need to put the light closer to the mirror` *(in the periscope)*

Student C: `Noooo ...`

Student B: `watch this ...` *(grabs the mouse, moves the light source closer to the mirror. Sends a light ray towards the mirror, which is reflected by the first mirror and then reflected by the second mirror, hits the eye)*

Student B: `The closer the source ...`**`the bigger the angle is`**` ...and it gets into the eye.`

Student A: `You are looking at the wrong ...`**`the angle is really more important.`**

Student B: `What angle?`

Student A: `I mean ...`**`relative to the mirror`** *(points at the source, and an imaginary line to the mirror) ... (grabs the mouse and puts the source further away and emits a light ray that hits both mirrors at a similar angle of incidence, and finally hits the eye)* ...**`This angle is equal to this angle`**

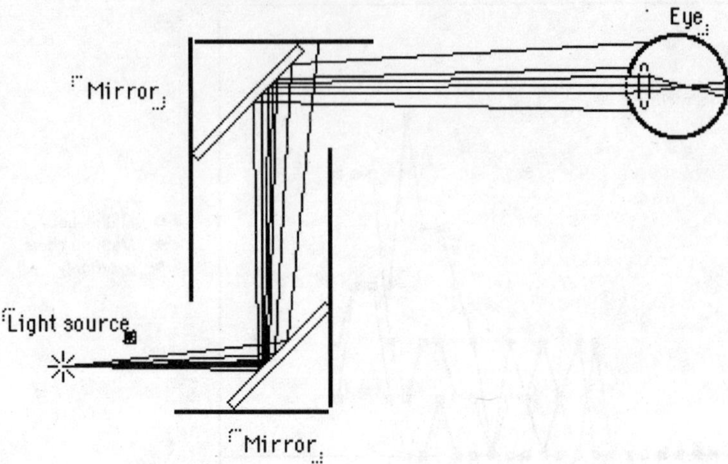

Fig. 4. Basic diagram on the screen during students' conversation on the periscope.

... *(points at the angles of incidence and reflection),* **light is bounced off ...it's ...nice symmetry**

Student C: **You can do it at any distance ...as long as the ray gets here** *(points at the first mirror)* **at this angle.**

Student A: **...if you put the source just a little bit to the left ...** *(points at the screen part left to the source)*

Student A: **mean like this ...upwards ...** *(points at the area above the light source)* **It changes the whole thing, light is blocked,** *(points at the point where light is absorbed)* **it does not hit the eye ...**

Student B: **you moved the source only one pixel ...**

Student C: **The mirror** *(points at the second mirror)* **makes it bounce off** *(points at the ray)* **...this angle**
(points at the angle of reflection) **is bigger ...it doubles it ...** *(points at angle)*

Note that the mathematical expressions here are of the kind described by verbal concepts, not necessarily by mathematical symbols. The words used in this discussion have an optics meaning. For instance, students use the term 'light rays', rather than lines. This means that students already constructed some verbal labels which match graphical symbols on the screen. Graphical symbols are frequently integrated in the discussion through pointing. Students discuss the symbols on the screen using conceptual terminology.

The overall number of verbal symbols (Figure 5) introduced is about a third of the number of graphical symbols students use (117 verbal symbols as compared with 344 graphical symbols). The peaks of both verbal and graphical-static symbols occur at about the same time, which may suggest that the situation involved required

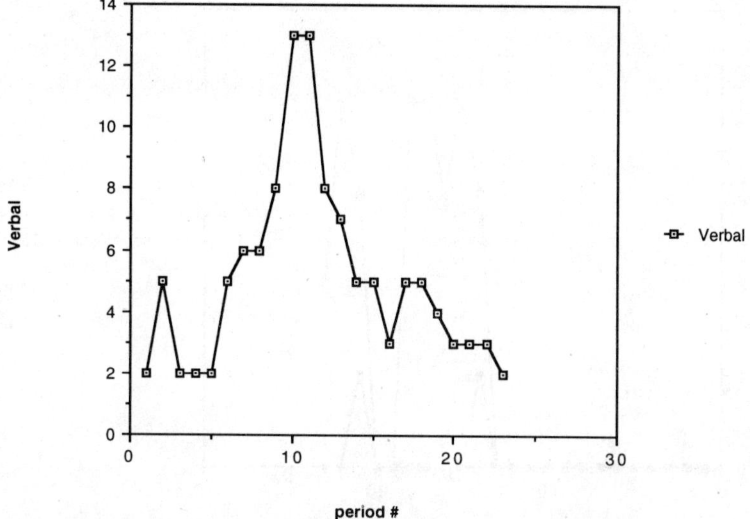

Fig. 5. Distribution of new verbal symbols integrated in the discussion.

new symbols as a precondition of coping with it. Most verbal symbols used have an everyday meaning and are sometimes attached to a graphical symbol. This explains the fact that the peaks occur at the same time.

Physical objects were used as symbols by pointing at them or referring to one of their properties. This, in order to verbally direct attention to the object. The periscope for instance was named the "blue cylinder", "thing", "the two pipes" or "this toy", accompanied by pointing or showing the periscope. Though the word periscope was explicitly printed in the problem, students seldom used the explicit word. Only two physical procedures were used. These were actual demonstrations of a physical phenomenon. The student used the periscope to explain what a field of vision was. He moved around with the periscope on his eye, to show how his field of vision changed when he changed the relative position of his eye, the periscope and the objects in the environment. Then another student changed the position of an object on the desk, and left the periscope in a constant position to show what the conditions were for an object to be seen. During the two demonstrations, the largest number of physical objects were used as symbols – a glance at the graph shows that the two peaks of the actual lab work are simultaneous with the peaks of physical symbols (Figure 6).

8 Conclusion

We examined language construction in the context of interpersonal symbol processing: speaking, listening, sense-making, 'reading' symbols, and labeling. Results

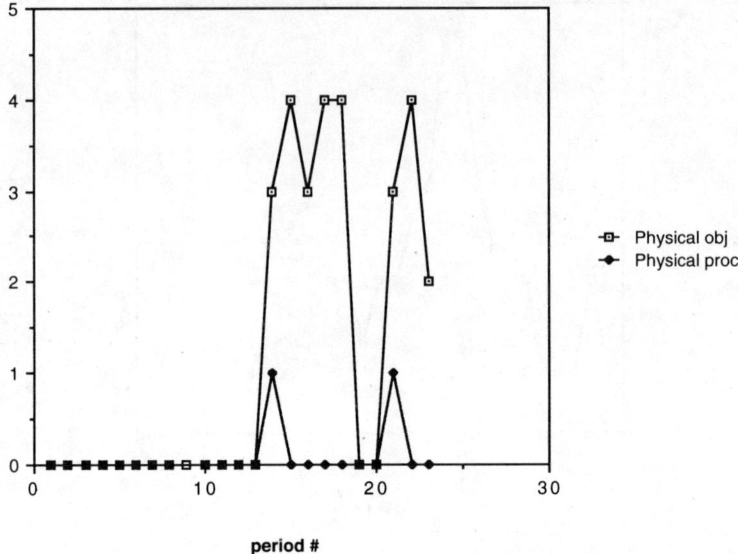

Fig. 6. Distribution of physical objects and procedures integrated in the discussion.

show that a symbolic system is indeed constructed and heavily introduced in discussions. The impact of constructing a physics-language on reasoning in physics is not completely clear. This is because the role of language in thinking is not entirely clear. Three alternative views describe the relations between thought and language (Dewey, 1910): first is that they are identical, second is that words are tools for communication only, not essential for thought, and third is that language is necessary for communication and thought but not identical. The term language itself is somewhat ambiguous . The position taken here is adopted from Newell & Simon:

1. *The generation or processing of symbol structures that are isomorphic with the strings of natural language or with their surface structures is essential to human problem solving.*
2. *The internal symbol structures that represent problems and information about problems are synonymous with the linguist's deep structure. If 'language' means deep structure then language is essential to thinking and problem solving.* (Newell & Simon, 1972)

Our intention in the paper was to relate the language deep structure and the language surface structure in reasoning in physics. The learning experiment reported here is an attempt to provide students with the symbols (constituents of the surface structure) necessary for labeling. Labeling attaches a meaning to a symbol, therefore it is located within the framework of the deep structure of language. It is related to the various meanings and representations one constructs through interaction with other members or through interaction with the learning environment. The first layer, the symbolic surface structure, is preliminary to the second – there is no way to think of or communicate about a concept unless it is recognized as such, and a symbol for is associated with it. In order to develop a preliminary system of symbols, one needs a learning environment which will provide the symbols that match the processes in physics. Results of this experiment show that the coupling of a symbol and a concept in the learning environment allows students to introduce systematically various types of new symbols in the discussion.

Graphical symbols are introduced in the discussion more than other types of symbols. This is partly due to the fact that graphical symbols are intrinsically integrated in physics, therefore any representation of physics content is naturally based on diagrams and other graphical symbols. The qualitative approach to optics, implemented in Dynagrams dictates a very limited involvement of mathematical formal symbols. This may explain why students rarely introduce mathematical expressions.

The extensive use of new symbols in the conversations during the learning experiment shows that these are absent from the symbolic system available in every-day life, and that once available, students take advantage of them: they construct a correspondence between a symbol (surface structure) and a meaning (deep structure) for and during conversation. The 'correctness' of the concept is irrelevant to this discussion. It is the process of coupling itself we focus on.

Most curricular materials in physics introduce a high density of disciplinary concepts, which for students act as mere surface symbols. Sometimes, sense making processes lead to a construction of misconcepts, or thin concepts. Classroom teaching also frequently starts from the second layer – the conceptual meaning of physics, before the symbols of the physics language are established. It is therefore not surprising that deep structure representations, understanding and conceptual familiarity, are hardly achieved by conventional.

The manipulation of symbols does not guarantee insight into conceptual deep structure of these symbols. Manipulating a point that emits lines aimed at a target, have nothing to do with optics. It is the awareness of the underlying concepts that we are interested in. We have found that by manipulation of symbols, these become progressively more transparent. Transparency means that after a while, the student looks at, and manipulates the symbol but discusses, or 'sees', and reasons about the underlying concepts. The following statements are a few examples of how students talk about the concept while manipulating the symbol:

Move the light source closer to the mirror *(moves the point closer to the line representing the periscope mirror)*
The focal point of the eye-lens is too big ...the light does not get to ... *(changes the curvature of the circular object inside the circle which stand for an eye) ... (another student)* **better move the light source ...it is like old people, need special glasses for short distances.**
Who says the two mirrors have to be parallel? *(changes the angle of the mirror) ...* **You can make a smart periscope if you allow the two mirrors to rotate ...** *(another student)* **you can capture a bigger field of view ...this**

`light source,` *(puts a new point for light source on the screen)* `you could not see it, now you can` *(rotates the second mirror, and emits a ray from the new source that hits the eye)*

Students communication is within the framework of the deep layer: They manipulate symbols but discuss concepts and construct situations which they see in their mind's eye. Students use symbols and events on the monitor to experiment with ideas in mind: a smart periscope, a short-sighted person, increasing the view of field. They solve problems, bridge events on the screen to their experience. In this sense, manipulating graphical symbols in a symbolic learning environment possibly means conceptual construction.

The results of this study show that the largest number of physical objects acting as symbols are used when a dynamical hands-on experiment is performed (see Figure 6). This is due to the fact that hands on activities demand manipulation of objects. The interrelations between the properties and situation of the object and the results of the experiment constitute the deep linguistic structure. The opportunity to manipulate objects may trigger a deep structure language. Though students did not manipulate physical objects and the graphical symbols on the software at the same time, they used mostly graphical symbols to communicate about the hands-on experiment (see Figure 7). Sometimes they did this by drawing diagrams in space, on paper, or by simulating the hands-on experiment in the software. The graphical symbols allow students to actually 'see' the unseen: the path of the rays of light. The event in the 'micro world', and the graphical and hands-on representations are coupled. The two matching peaks (Figure 7) suggest that graphical symbols are needed to discuss and negotiate hands-on experiments, and that the process of meaning negotiation is related to coupling between graphical and hands-on activities. Schools normally introduce hands-on activities, but most curricular materials do not provide graphical language to make sense of the experiment. This study shows that students may gain more if they have the tools which allow them to construct alternative representations (e.g., graphical).

Figure 8 shows that all types of symbols are used simultaneously. This suggests that the coupling of multiple representations – physical objects and procedures, verbal and graphical, dynamic and static, may happen simultaneously. This suggests that coupling representations is necessary for, or equal to, sense making.

One finding made clear in Figure 8, is that the number of graphical symbols is far larger than any other type, including the frequent everyday language (see Figure 8). This suggests that graphical representations are powerful in the sense that students prefer them to any other type of communication tool.

The mode of interaction with all the components of the learning environment is based mainly on problem solving activities. We do not know if a free-goal environment would bring about similar processes of language construction. In case discussed here, language is 'naturally' developed through various levels of problem solving. There is no need to 'teach' the language.

Discussions have a crucial role in the argument that physics language is essential to physics learning: It forces one to look for tools in his environment that allow the

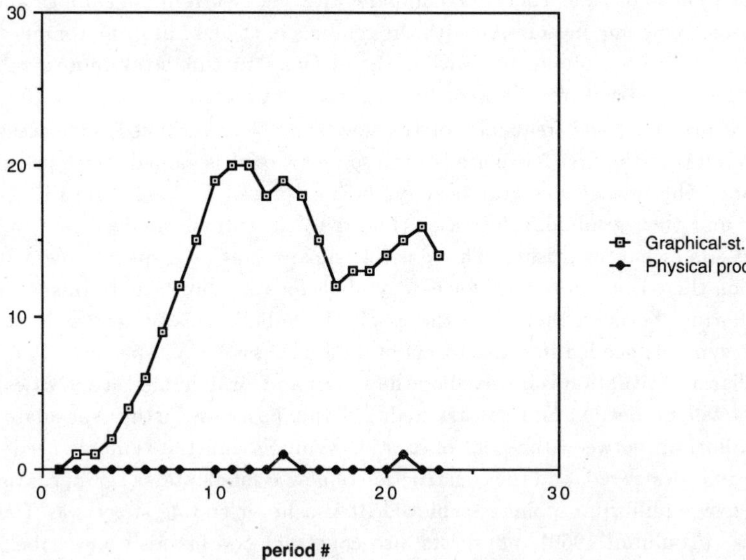

Fig. 7. Distribution of graphical symbols and physical procedures in the discussion.

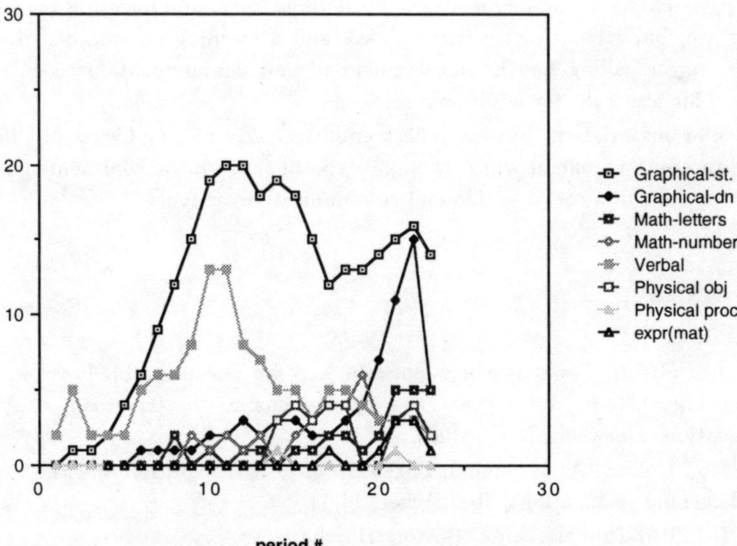

Fig. 8. Distribution of new symbols in the discussion.

best, most accurate way to communicate. It also forces one to listen to others and thus make sense of their concepts, compare with his own refine meanings and set conventions. Ongoing interaction with the symbols in the learning environment provide new ways to communicate – with in the surface structure level (more symbols) and in the deep structure level (conceptual representations).

Not surprisingly, the frequency of the new symbols introduced, increases with time. It is low in the first few periods until some practice is gained. Once practice is established the rate of new graphical symbols employed increases, until it reaches a peak, and then gradually decreases (Figure 6). Eventually it decreases to zero, which is somewhat surprising. This possibly means that at a specific point in the discussion there is no more need for new symbols for communication. This is a point of equilibrium between the size of the 'pool' of symbols already used at least once and the symbols needed in order to maintain a discussion. We speculate that if an unfamiliar new situation is involved on the screen and/or in hands on activities, new symbols will be needed and constructed. On this basis we further speculate that the equilibrium between the pool of existing symbols and the symbols needed for discussion is destroyed, and the construction of new symbols starts again, continuing until a new equilibrium point is achieved. It is a never ending story – as Toulmin suggests (Toulmin, 1960), physicists also construct continuously new labels and symbols to help them talk about new phenomena or look at old phenomena in a new way. The equilibrium points are those at which learners are familiar with symbols and the main activity is devoted to the extension of meaning – the deep structure of the symbol. No evidence is available for this speculation in this study, and more research is needed.

This research shows how crucial graphical tools for communication on physics learning are, but what exactly turns a task and a learning environment into an effective trigger calling for the development of new communication tools, is not obvious. This also calls for additional research.

Curricular materials in physics reflect empirical aspects of physics but do not provide an environment in which thought experiments can be represented on the screen by means of a set of visible and communicative symbols.

References

Brown, J.S. (1989) Towards a new epistemology for learning. In: Frasson, C. & Gauthiar, J. (eds.) Intelligent Tutoring Systems: at the crossroads of AI and education. Norwood, N.J.: Ablex.

Brown, J.S., Collins, A. & Duguid, P. (1989) Situated Cognition and the Culture of Learning. Educational Researcher, 18(1).

Dewey, J. (1910) How we think. Boston: Heath.

Eckert, P. (1989) Jocks and burnouts. New York: Teachers College Press.

Gibson, J. (1979) The ecological approach to visual perception. Boston: Houghton Mifflin.

Hamm, M. & Adams, D. (1992) The Collaborative Dimensions of Learning. Norwood, NJ: Ablex Publishing Co.

Kaput, J. (1987) Representation system and mathematics. In: Janvier, C. (ed.) Problems of representation in the teaching and learning of mathematics. Hillsdale: Lawrence Erlbaum.

Lave, J. & Wenger, E. (1991) Situated Learning: legitimate peripheral participation. New York: Cambridge University Press.

Minstrell, J. (1992) Facets of students' knowledge and relevant instruction. In: Duit, R., Goldberg, F. & Niedderer, H. (eds.) Research in Physics Learning: theoretical issues and empirical studies. Kiel: IPN, Institute for Science Education.

Newell, A. & Simon, H. (1972) Human Problem Solving. Englewood Cliffs: Prentice Hall, Inc.

Pea, R.D. (1987) Socializing the knowledge transfer problem. The Int. Jrnl. of Education Research, 2(6), 639–663.

Pea, R.D., Allen, S., Goldman, S., Jul, S., Reiner, M., Shulman, D., Sipusic, M. & Slavin, E. (1991) Designing classroom discourse resources for conceptual change in science: Dynagrams. Tech. rept. Institute for Research on Learning, Palo Alto. Final project report for NSF grant MDR-88-55582.

Pimm, D. (1987) Speaking Mathematically. Language Education and Society Series. London: Routledge and Kegan Paul.

PSSC (1987) Physics. Boston: Heath and Company. (Physical Science Study Committee).

Purcell, M. E. (1965) Berkeley Physics Course. McGraw Hill.

Roschelle, J. (1992) Learning by Collaboration: Convergent conceptual change. The Jrnl. of the Learning Sciences, 2(3).

Toulmin, S. (1960) The Philosophy of Science. New York: Harper and Row.

Von-Glasersfeld, E. (1987) Learning as a Constructive Activity. In: Janvier, C. (ed.) Problems of Representation in the Teaching and Learning of Mathematics. Hillsdale, NJ: Lawrence Erlbaum.

Von-Glasersfeld, E. (1992) A Constructivist View of Learning and Teaching. In: Duit, R., Goldberg, F. & Niedderer, H. (eds.) Research in Physics Learning: theoretical issues and empirical studies. Kiel: IPN, Institute for Science Education.

Wenger, E. (1993) Communities of Practice. Ph.D. thesis, Department of Computer Science.

Wittgenstein, L. (1953) Philosophical Investigations. Oxford: Basil Blackwell and Mott.

Deciding What to Say: An Agent-Theoretic Approach to Tutorial Dialogue

Ann E. Blandford

MRC Applied Psychology Unit, 15, Chaucer Road, Cambridge, CB2 2EF, United Kingdom, email: ann.blandford@mrc-apu.cam.ac.uk

Abstract. Natural dialogue is a form of joint action in which two autonomous agents participate in pursuit of both individual and mutual goals. Within the dialogue what an agent chooses to say, and how it chooses to say it, depends on its goals, beliefs and values. In developing systems to support learning, one of the requirements is that the system must respond appropriately to the student. The system should be able to both react to input from the student and prompt the student into thinking about the topic more deeply. This requires that the system should have its own goals and beliefs, a repertoire of interaction styles, and the ability to decide what to say or do at any point in the interaction. In this chapter, I present the design of a computer-based agent which has such teaching expertise and describe a prototype implementation in the domain of design decision making.

Keywords. Agent architectures, design education, intelligent tutoring, ITS, interaction styles, mixed-initiative dialogue, teaching strategies

1 Introduction

In this chapter, we consider not the detailed structure of a single utterance or feedback act (as discussed, for example, by Bego and by Bunt in this volume), but the higher level structure of the tutorial dialogue. We are also not concerned with describing or analysing existing tutorial interactions but with defining how a computer-based agent can participate in — be a creative partner in — new tutorial interactions within its domain of expertise.

In a tutorial interaction the participating agents (students and teacher) each have their own goals — to survive the lesson, to gain or promote understanding, etc. However, in the context of their interaction they are also involved in joint activity, mediated by dialogue. For example, in a problem-solving domain, finding a solution to the problem is a goal which is held by all parties, while in a domain where the acquisition of information or ideas is important, common goals include exploring the domain effectively. Different agents will take different roles in the joint activity, reflected in their different roles within the dialogue, but nevertheless there is a joint activity in pursuit of a common goal (see for example the discussion by Grosz and Sidner (1986) of the 'common discourse purpose').

What a tutor chooses to say in a teaching context is clearly influenced by the common goal — whether this defines the syllabus in a knowledge-transfer domain, or the problem-solving steps in a problem-solving domain. This can lead to a 'planning' approach to interaction (e.g., Shadbolt (1989), Daradoumis & Verdejo, this volume). The obvious disadvantage of planning beyond the current utterance is that it fails to take account of the goals and beliefs of the student, and that if the student is granted any autonomy in the interaction then there will need to be frequent re-planning in the course of that interaction. Conversely, if the tutor simply reacts to the student's input — even with a rich student model to guide the tutor in what to say next — then the interaction can become rather aimless.

In this chapter, I present an approach which seeks to achieve a reasonable balance between addressing the teaching aims of the system and reacting appropriately to the student's input. Some teaching aims are regarded as being achievable (cover this syllabus, solve these problems, ...) while others are inherently unachievable — for example, keeping the student motivated and interested, as discussed by Lepper and Chabay (1988), and encouraging the student to be more reflective, analytical, and creative. Many established approaches deal adequately with the former; few seek to address the latter explicitly.

To focus the discussion, let us take as an example an extract from an interaction between a user and a prototype Intelligent Educational System called WOMBAT. WOMBAT is designed to support learning about decision making in design. As Lee (this volume) outlines, in such a domain, it is clearly inappropriate to deal with information as 'knowledge'; the system has no more of a monopoly of the truth than the student does, and the student is required to view the system's suggestions critically. For the purposes of prototype implementation, the domain has been characterised as justified beliefs ('I believe X', 'I believe X because Y', etc.). The approach taken is to engage the student in collaborative problem solving; tutor and student discuss together both how they should go about the decision making and what criteria the decision should be based on. In the example presented here, the problem is to select the best design from a set of 6 pre-defined designs for a car which is to be marketed as a family car, with an emphasis on safety features and comfort and with a maximum retail price of 8000. Having already eliminated one alternative (as being too expensive to produce) and explicitly agreed to take safety and comfort into account in their decision making, the interaction proceeds:

1. user: `What shall we do next?`

2. system: `I think we should agree additional objectives. Do you agree that we should agree additional objectives?`

3. user: `Why do you think we should agree additional objectives?`

4. system: `I think we should agree additional objectives because that way we take account of the purchaser. Do you agree that we should agree additional objectives?`

5. user: `Yes, I do.`

6. system: `Let us agree some more objectives. Can you suggest some objectives?`

7. *user:* `I think we should include pollution. I think we should include fuel economy. I think we should include internal size. I think we should include luggage capacity. I think we should include 4 doors. I think we should include flexibility. I think we should include reliability. I think we should include colour.`
8. *system:* `I agree that we should include 4 doors as an objective because people in back. I do not agree that we should include flexibility as an objective. I agree that we should include reliability as an objective. I do not agree that we should include colour as an objective because various colours available. Why do you think we should include colour as an objective?`
9. *user:* `I've changed my mind about that.`
10. *system:* `I agree that we should not include colour as an objective. I do not agree that we should include flexibility as an objective because unimportant most of the time. Why do you think we should include flexibility as an objective?`
11. *user:* `Because wind surfing.`
12. *system:* `I don't know about wind surfing being a reason for considering flexibility as an objective. I do not agree that we should include flexibility as an objective. Do you really think we should include flexibility as an objective?`
13. *user:* `Yes, I do!`

This interaction is clearly not full natural language, but is as it appears on the screen (Figure 1). It is not generated 'from first principles', but is made up of phrases which convey the semantic content of the utterance. System output appears in one window; user input is constructed by pressing buttons and typing free-form phrases in another. Although it is obviously less rich and expressive than natural language, this interaction has many of the qualities we require for rich tutorial dialogue.

Firstly, it is mixed-initiative; neither tutor nor student is always in charge; both can challenge and question and make suggestions. This is not the case for systems employing fixed teaching strategies such as Socratic tutoring, coaching (Burton & Brown, 1979) or critiquing (Miller, 1984). It is symmetric, in the sense that the same dialogue moves are available to both participants, though the participants have different roles within the interaction. For example, in utterance 8 the system presents a justification for a proposition which both parties have agreed about, because it believes that doing so helps the student's understanding of the problem; an agent which did not have this role would be unlikely to do this.

Secondly, it is coherent, in that it makes sense to the participants. Each utterance is made in the context of the preceding dialogue, and can be seen to follow on from what has gone before. Each utterance fits in with the currently open topics of conversation, and is relevant to the current activity (e.g. agreeing additional objectives, from utterance 6 onwards). It is jointly constructed, in the sense that the utterances made by one participant cannot be separated out from those made by the other. Of the indefinite number of possible dialogues which could have evolved

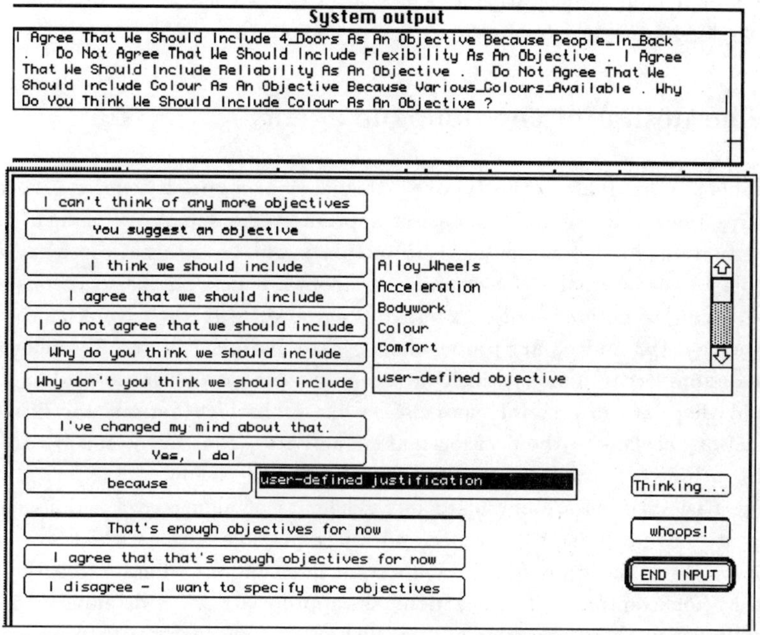

Fig. 1. Screen as it appears after utterance 8.

from the same starting position, this is the particular one constructed by these two dialogue participants.

Thirdly, it is purposeful in two ways, both in terms of the problem solving — progress is being made towards a solution — and in terms of the system's teaching aims. For example, in utterance 4 the system aims to inform the user by justifying its suggestion; in utterance 6 it aims to provoke thought through its questioning; in utterances 8 and 10 it challenges the user's ideas and asks him to justify his position. (This interaction took place between the system and a male design educator.) Although in this particular extract there are no examples of it, the system also sometimes asks the user to justify propositions over which there is no disagreement on the premise that, as discussed by Coleman (this volume), students benefit from being challenged to question their assumptions and think more deeply about the problem.

Less obviously, the criteria on which the system chooses what to say next include motivational ones such as keeping the interaction varied (not repeatedly using the same dialogue moves) and allowing the user to retain ultimate control (e.g. in utterance 13 the user gets the final say over whether or not to include flexibility as a decision criterion).

A feature of the implementation which is important, but only apparent in utterance 6 in this example, is the system's ability to extend the discussion by asking a question or making a suggestion which is not a direct response to anything which has gone before but which is relevant in the context.

2 The design of the dialogue agent

To be able to participate in this type of dialogue, an agent needs to have a repertoire of basic actions and the ability to select appropriate combinations of them in any given situation. In this context, a basic action might be external — to say or do something — or internal — for example, to adopt a belief. The basic actions which involve saying something — for example, 'I agree with *p*1' or 'I think *p*2, because *p*3', where *p*1, *p*2 and *p*3 are propositions — are discussed more fully below. The external, non-verbal, actions which the agent can perform all involve adding to or manipulating data in a simple spreadsheet-like tool which permits the display of information relevant to the decision-making activity (Blandford, 1993b). Internal actions such as belief maintenance are discussed briefly below.

These basic actions are organised into schemata of higher-level actions so that the agent does not have to consider and reject possible actions which are totally inappropriate at the time. (This is important in situations where interaction time matters.) For example, different actions are appropriate when listening and when responding, and there are prerequisites such as it being necessary to understand a proposition stated by the user before the system can assess it (i.e. form its own opinion about the proposition).

Put simply, once the system is engaged in collaborative problem solving with a student, it engages in dialogue which involves listening to, then responding to the user repeatedly until both participants agree to finish the interaction (or the user just walks off!).

Listening involves several steps (Blandford, 1993a), including assessing each proposition made, or question asked, by the user. If the user has stated a proposition, *p*, then the system assumes sincerity, and notes that it believes that the user believes *p*. For each proposition or question, the system applies a simple reasoning mechanism to a database of possible beliefs. It then updates its own beliefs appropriately (to note that it believes *p*, believes (*not p*), or whatever). It then notes what general class of response it wishes to make; the possibilities are:

- note agreement,
- resolve a conflict,
- note user's expectation (e.g. of an answer to a question),
- note that it doesn't know about the proposition, or
- note that the sentence is incomprehensible

Each of these relates to a particular proposition (or sentence). The system chooses between these possibilities based largely on the built-in design constraint that it should remain coherent, and respond appropriately. At this stage (as part of listening to and assessing the user's input), it does not plan *how* to respond to each proposition, in terms of what to say, but simply notes what goal it will try to satisfy in responding. So for example, when assessing utterance 1 in the example above, the system notes that it should consider addressing the goal of responding to the user's expectation as part of its response. A short time later, when constructing its response, it addresses this goal; it knows of three possible ways of addressing it - to simply answer the question, to answer the question and justify that answer, or to explicitly decline to answer the question. In this case (utterance 2) it chooses to simply answer the question; this involves first adopting an appropriate belief (that they should agree additional objectives based on the likely lifestyle of the target purchaser) and then imparting it.

In the last section, it was noted that there are things the system is trying to achieve at different levels — for example, in terms of solving the problem and enhancing learning. At this point it is worth making a clear distinction between goals, which are achievable, and another class of attitudes, which we will call values (Kiss, 1989), which are unattainable but influence decisions about how to act, including what to say. Goals may be individual or joint; for example, in the above example solving the problem (choosing a car) is a joint goal, whereas reaching a resolution to a detected conflict (over flexibility or the choice of colours) or being explicit about agreements is an individual goal of the agent. In deciding what to say, the agent considers all the possible ways it knows of addressing the current goal, and selects between them on the basis of its values.

The agent's values are derived from the very general value of being an effective teacher. This general value can be expressed in more specific terms to deal with particular situations. For example, in deciding what to say, one important value is 'don't ask too many questions' — i.e., do not fire multiple questions at the user in one utterance, because the user is unlikely to be able to consider and answer them all effectively, and is unlikely to gain maximum benefit from considering the issues involved. In principle, the agent would acquire these more specific values, and establish their relative importance, over time — by learning through experience. In practice, the values, together with numerical weights to reflect their relative importance, have been hand coded by the system designer, and simply reflect intuitions about what values are important in given situations. An example giving the values relevant to one particular decision is included in the next section.

3 Deciding what to say

When deciding what to say or do next, the agent considers all possible actions which it believes address the current goal, and selects the one which has the maximum expected utility. It does this on the basis of its values, each of which has a numerical weight to reflect its relative importance to the system, and means-ends beliefs about whether particular actions are likely to satisfy given values in the current situation. The expected utility of an action is the sum of the weights of the values which that action is expected to address in the current situation. (The use of numerical calculations is clearly unattractive if the agent design is viewed as having any psychological plausibility, but it allows relatively speedy decision making to be performed — again, important in the context of implementing a practical tutoring system which is capable of operating in real time.) The mechanism is illustrated by means of an example showing how the values, their numerical weights, means-ends beliefs and relevance functions affect the course of an interaction. For the purposes of this example, attention is focused on how the agent addresses the goal of resolving a conflict. When addressing this goal, the values which are relevant, and their weights, are:

don't ask too many questions	50
encourage reflection	11
make conflict explicit	23
user develops their understanding of the problem	18
make progress towards a solution	28
vary interaction	8
avoid repetition	10

Some of the basic dialogue actions are currently defined to be fairly complex. In the current implementation the possible actions which address the goal of resolving a conflict are:

- impart disagreement ('I disagree about *p*')
- elicit justification ('Why do you think *p*?')
- impart disagreement and elicit justification ('I disagree about *p*. Why do you think that?')
- impart disagreement, impart justification and elicit agreement ('I disagree about *p* because *q*. Don't you agree?')
- impart disagreement, impart justification, elicit justification ('I disagree about *p* because *q*. Why do you think *p*?')
- impart disagreement, impart alternative belief ('I disagree about *p*. Instead I think *q*.')
- impart disagreement, elicit confirmation ('I disagree about *p*. Do you really think *p*?')

As discussed earlier, one pedagogical principle (to do with control) is that the user should always get the final say, so while it would be possible to have a conflict-resolution tactic called 'insist on my view', this has not been implemented.

The agent has means-ends beliefs about how these possible actions satisfy the values:

- any action which does not involve eliciting satisfies the value of not asking too many questions in the situation where it has already decided to ask a question as part of the current utterance.

- any action which involves eliciting a justification satisfies the value of encouraging reflection. However, the system also checks whether it knows of justifications for both views before it asks the user to justify her position (so that there is a possibility of it agreeing with the user's justification even though it disagrees with the proposition, and so that the system has a counter argument ready). Arguably this is an unnecessary restriction, as the user should be encouraged to express views whether or not the system is equipped to form its own view on them.
- any action which includes imparting disagreement makes the conflict explicit.
- any action which includes imparting a justification helps to improve the user's understanding of the problem (but is only possible if the system knows of a justification to impart).
- any action which does not involve further justifications helps to make progress towards a solution, except for simply imparting disagreement.
- any action which has not just been done avoids repetition, and any which has not been done recently helps to vary the interaction.

In this illustration, attention is focused on the decisions which are made as part of the system constructing its response to the user's utterance, and in particular those which relate to resolving the conflicts detected while listening to utterance 7 in the example dialogue:

7. *user:* `I think we should include pollution. I think we should include fuel economy. I think we should include internal size. I think we should include luggage capacity. I think we should include 4 doors. I think we should include flexibility. I think we should include reliability. I think we should include colour.`
8. *system:* `I agree that we should include 4 doors as an objective because people in back. I do not agree that we should include flexibility as an objective. I agree that we should include reliability as an objective. I do not agree that we should include colour as an objective because various colours available. Why do you think we should include colour as an objective?`

While listening to this utterance (which includes a large number of propositions), the system decided that it agreed with the first 5 propositions and about reliability, but that it disagreed about flexibility and the choice of colours. In the interests of verbal economy, it only dealt explicitly with some of these propositions in its response, leaving several of the agreements implicit. The first goal it addressed in constructing its response (which appears as the last part of the utterance) was that of resolving the conflict over whether or not the range of colours is important. It can be seen that this goal is addressed by imparting disagreement, imparting a justification and eliciting a justification, for which the calculated expected utility was 120 (50 + 11 + 23 + 18 + 10 + 8), since all the values except that of making progress towards a solution are satisfied. In contrast, when the system addresses the goal of dealing with the conflict over flexibility, because it has already decided on one question for the current utterance the action with maximum expected utility this time is that of simply imparting disagreement.

This illustration of the detailed mechanics of the current implementation shows how effective a very simple approach can be. There are clearly many ways in which the basic mechanism could be refined and improved — for example, increasing the system's repertoire of utterance types or refining the values and means-ends beliefs. Additionally, it should be possible to combine the smaller basic units (those which impart or elicit one proposition) in novel ways.

Little use is made of an explicit user model. In fact, the only beliefs about the user which are maintained are those about the user's beliefs about the problem. No inferences are made about the user's level of expertise in this type of problem solving (selection between alternatives), their knowledge about this artefact (cars), or any other user characteristics. The system is sensitive to the user only in that a user who asks more questions and seeks more help is guided more than one who does not. In the evaluation study of the system (Blandford, 1993b), it was found that users were confident in their discussions about criteria for selecting a car, but less so in their discussions about how to make the decision. For the latter, additional support is required, but it is not currently clear whether or not this actually requires a fuller student model — with all the computational overheads that maintaining such a model entails (see for example (Self, 1990)) — or whether the simple provision of a wider range of explanation facilities is all that is required, so that students who are unsure can ask more questions and receive appropriate explanations, as discussed by Pilkington (1992).

4 Discussion

In this chapter, some aspects of the design of a tutoring system which can engage a user in collaborative problem solving have been described. The system has several important features, including the fact that it does not assume that either participant — and that includes itself — knows all the answers, that it can accept responses which contain propositions which it does not know about, and that it allows the user to retain ultimate control. The basic architecture emphasises the importance of general teaching aims such as keeping students motivated and encouraging reflection, rather than focusing on imparting knowledge, and recognises that a teacher is trying to achieve many things, on different time scales, simultaneously.

The system is clearly not sufficiently well developed to be able to present any measures of educational effectiveness of the approach, or of the implementation. It has, however, been used by 10 subjects as part of a formative evaluation. The main conclusions of that study were that the system can engage in an extended mixed-initiative dialogue which remains largely coherent and reasonable; the principal cause of shortcomings in this respect is the system's impoverished representation of problem-solving in the domain — a subject which is beyond the scope of this chapter. As to its educational potential: the general conclusion was that this seems like a reasonable approach, though there is clearly a long way to go before any potential is realised! It was felt that the system is not able to vary its level of guidance sufficiently — that it should offer more to start with, and reduce its level of intervention as the user became more competent. This would necessitate the system having a much richer student model than it does at present.

Clearly, the approach which has been taken has been influenced by the domain of application. There is a much more obvious need for an opportunistic, argumentative style of interaction, in which both participants have access to the same dialogue moves and both can take the initiative, in this type of domain than in the more traditional problem solving and concept formation domains which have been the focus of most previous research. However, it seems likely that there would be (as yet untested) benefits of applying this more flexible approach even in domains for which it is less obviously necessary. In problem solving domains there is generally not one unique way of solving problems although some solution methods may be better (more efficient or less prone to error) than others (see for example (Devi, 1992) on the development of basic arithmetic skills); for more sophisticated learners, the relative strengths and weaknesses of different approaches can be discussed, though a simpler strategy would be more likely to be successful with younger children. Similarly, in domains involving the teaching of concepts, the choices of concepts to be taught and the means of presentation could be made in a much more dynamic (or opportunistic) way in response to the abilities, pre-existing knowledge or preferences of the student. In long-term future developments, it is possible to imagine teaching systems equipped to adopt strategies in a way which is much better adapted to the needs of the individual student. However, this must, for now, remain in the realm of speculation.

Although currently limited, and only tested in one domain of application, the WOMBAT prototype exists, and demonstrates the feasibility of the approach; it allows the user to express their view (unlike — for example — critiquing systems, which do not accommodate the user answering back) and treats the user as a responsible partner in their own learning. It is equipped with a basic structure which allows it to respond appropriately to everything the user has said in the context of the preceding dialogue, and it can also extend the discussion to cover new topics as and when this is seen to be appropriate. The system maintains a balance between reaction to what has gone before — necessary to retain coherence — and taking the initiative — helpful for keeping the discussion focused and purposeful. It also accommodates aims at different levels. As such, it provides an appropriate base for further research on interaction and teaching styles.

References

Blandford, A.E. (1993a) An agent-theoretic approach to computer participation in dialogue. International Journal of Man-Machine Studies, 39(6), 965–998.

Blandford, A.E. (1993b) Applying the WOM to WOMBAT: evaluation of a tool to support learning about design evaluation. Design Studies, 14(3), 228–246.

Burton, R.R. & Brown, J.S. (1979) An investigation of computer coaching for informal learning activities. International Journal of Man-Machine Studies, 11, 5–24.

Devi, R. (1992) Modelling children's arithmetic strategies. In: Moyse, R. & Elsom-Cook, M.T. (eds.) Knowledge Negotiation. London: Academic Press.

Grosz, B.J. & Sidner, C.L. (1986) Attention, Intention and the Structure of Discourse. Computational Linguistics, 12(3), 175–204.

Kiss, G. (1989) Some Aspects of Agent Theory. Proceedings of International Joint Conference on Artificial Intelligence. Detroit, IJCAI.

Lepper, M.R. & Chabay, R.W. (1988) Socialising the Intelligent Tutor: Bringing Empathy to Computer Tutors. In: Mandl, H. & Lesgold, A. (eds.) Learning Issues for Intelligent Tutoring Systems. New York: Springer Verlag.

Miller, P.L. (1984) A critiquing approach to export computer advice: ATTENDING. London: Pitman Publishing.

Pilkington, R.M. (1992) Intelligent help: Communicating with knowledge-based systems. London: Paul Chapman Publishing.

Self, J.A. (1990) Bypassing the intractable problem of student modelling. In: Frasson, C. & Gauthier, G. (eds.) Intelligent Tutoring Systems: At the Crossroads of Artificial Intelligence and Education. Norwood: Ablex.

Shadbolt, N. (1989) Speaking about plans. In: Smeaton, A. & McDermott, G. (eds.) AI and Cognitive Science '89. London: Springer-Verlag.

Feedback in Computer-Assisted Instruction: Complexity and Corrective Efficiency

Gerard W.G. Spaai

Institute for Perception Research/IPO, P.O. Box 513, Eindhoven, The Netherlands, email: spaai@prl.philips.nl

Abstract. Feedback is considered to be an important factor in learning optimization. Although the problem of feedback is a long-standing one in educational research, little is known on how to structure feedback exactly as to quantity, nature and timing. In the present study the effectiveness was determined of different forms of spoken feedback content used in a computer-based drill for beginning readers. The subjects' task was to select a letter from among alternative letters on a computer screen after the spoken form of the letter had been presented by the computer. The spoken information fed back in the case of an error was varied depending on the selected answer and the correct answer. The results showed that feedback containing limited information about the correctness of an answer in terms of right or wrong and an indication of the right answer when an error is made, was most effective. Also, especially poor learners benefit from extensive forms of feedback. It is suggested that feedback should be presented in an adaptive way.

Keywords. Feedback, speech, computer-assisted instruction, beginning readers

1 Introduction

Learning to conceive speech as a sequence of discrete elements and learning how to relate sound segments to units of print is acknowledged to be an important component of learning to read alphabetic languages (Samuels, 1972). One of the essential ingredients of formal reading instruction is therefore teaching the relationships between graphemes and phonemes (Anderson et al., 1985).

Acquiring knowledge of letter-sound correspondences is not easy, mainly because correspondences between letters and sounds are often arbitrary and quite abstract (Ehri et al., 1984). In order to achieve fluency in associating letters with sounds, extensive practise and instruction are needed (Calfee et al., 1972), especially in the case of poor learners. For practical reasons, however, the amount of time available for reading instruction and teacher-guided practice in school is often limited. A possible solution to make up for this lack of practice is the use of a computer-based system that provides support in independent practice in associating letters with their pronunciation.

In order to use such a system, it is necessary to employ speech. This is necessary for providing instructions which tell the reader what actions should be performed and for presenting the learning materials. Furthermore, the use of speech is necessary for providing comments on reader's responses what is also known as feedback.[1] The issue of this paper is to determine the spoken feedback content which is most beneficial for promoting skill in associating letters with sounds.

The structure of the paper is as follows. The first section describes different ways in which feedback can affect learning. Furthermore, factors related to the way feedback is processed by the learner are discussed. In the second section spoken feedback content is investigated in a search for what is most facilitative when practising letter-sound correspondences. Children are instructed to select a letter on the screen after its spoken form has been provided by the computer. The spoken information fed back to the learner in the case of a response error is varied depending on the selected answer and the correct answer. In the final section the experimental results are discussed in terms of their implications for the appropriate use of spoken feedback in computer-based reading exercises for beginners.

2 Feedback and learning

In educational psychology the term feedback is used to refer to the confirmation or correction of a student response, supplied by for instance the teacher or by an 'answer key' to a test or an exercise. The importance of providing feedback has often been demonstrated in human learning in general, as well as in classroom. Feedback may lead to improvement in learning in two different ways: *cognitively* and *affectively*. Cognitively, providing feedback is necessary to enable the learner to realize whether performance is correct or not. It furnishes information according to which mistakes can be corrected and adjustments can be made to improve performance (Roth, 1985; Anderson et al., 1980). Affectively, feedback can encourage or discourage learners and influence their motivation to continue (Andrews & Debus, 1978).

Whether the improvement in learning is the result of motivational or informational consequences, whether the feedback should contain only a limited amount of information and whether the presentation of the feedback should be delayed or not, depend in part on the type of learning task under consideration. Schimmel (1988) suggested that 'minimal, immediate feedback' may be more appropriate for skill learning and 'elaborate, delayed feedback' for abstract, higher-level learning. When the learning task is verbal and meets the definition of meaningful learning frequently seen in the classroom, the informational consequences appear to predominate. For example, Kulhavy & Anderson (1972) have gathered evidence for the role of informative feedback in the facilitation of classroom learning through

[1] The use of speech has three other advantages that apply to instructional programs in general and make the use of speech preferable over any other presentation mode (Bouwhuis, 1993). Firstly, speech seems to invite a much more interactive dialogue in a sense that it has a more demanding or inviting character. A visual message can be ignored. Secondly, by virtue of its temporal structure and its intonation, a spoken message can convey its meaning and intention more clearly than a visual message. Thirdly, speech is a natural component of a multimodal dialogue. It provides natural means for often subtle forms of control and feedback and offers a clear temporal structure for turn-taking.

the correction of previous errors with little effect on correct responses. This finding contradicts most behaviouristic theories of learning that feedback acts mainly as a reinforcer of correct responses.

The fact that feedback *can* facilitate learning does not imply that it will *always* facilitate learning. For instance, presearch availability of feedback lowers the facilitating effects feedback can have on learning. Kulhavy (1977) used this term to describe the availability of feedback to answers in instructional materials before students construct their own answers to questions. When presearch availability is high, students simply copy the correct answers and pay no attention to the instructional materials. The availability hypothesis has been tested in a study by Anderson, Kulhavy and Andre (1972). In this study students received various forms of feedback in a computer-controlled lesson. In one feedback condition, called PEEK, the correct answer to each program frame was visible on the computer screen during the entire time that the item was exposed. The results showed that students in the PEEK condition used less time to complete the lesson, made fewer errors but had significantly lower scores in a posttest compared with students receiving feedback *after* every frame.

3 Feedback: Timing and content

The effect of feedback on subsequent performance is determined by the way feedback is processed (Carroll, 1976). A recent model of feedback suggests that a learner's initial confidence in a response is a useful indicator of subsequent feedback processing and later performance in a posttest (Kulhavy & Stock, 1989). Therefore, if the student's confidence in the correctness of a response is high and the student's response is incorrect the student will spend more time studying the feedback on that response and will thereby increase the likelihood of an error response being corrected although in some cases the modification of deeply rooted knowledge can be troublesome. Furthermore, if the response certainty is low and the student's response is incorrect, the student will probably not spend much time studying the feedback, which will decrease the likelihood of the incorrect response being replaced by the correct one. Other factors that can affect the way feedback is processed are related to the timing of its presentation and the type of information provided (Kulik & Kulik, 1988).

3.1 Timing of feedback presentation

There is evidence that delaying feedback for one day or more is at least as effective as immediate feedback, provided the material is meaningful (Sassenrath, 1975). Several studies even suggest that delayed feedback is superior to immediate feedback, especially when delayed retention tests are used. A widely accepted theoretical explanation for this has been proposed by Kulhavy & Anderson (1972). The explanation is known as the interference-perseveration theory, which postulates that incorrect responses tend to be forgotten during a delay period, and are not available to interfere with the learning of correct responses in a delayed-feedback trial; evidence supporting this explanation is, however, lacking. A second possible explanation has been postulated by Kulik & Kulik (1988). They state that in delayed-feedback studies the test item presentation is often repeated at the end of the test which means that feedback is exposed for twice as long as when feedback is presented immediately. Alternatively, Sassenrath and Yonge (1968) suggested that learners are able to rehearse the subject of tuition internally in the period of feedback delay.

From a meta-analysis of feedback studies, Kulik & Kulik (1988) concluded that immediate feedback was best for most learning situations, but that delayed feedback was superior in 'test-acquisition' studies, in which test questions are used as the instructional materials. They concluded that delayed feedback is only superior for tasks and materials requiring longer processing. However, for the acquisition of motor skills and for the immediate retention of less cognitive verbal materials, such as paired associates, the provision of immediate feedback is superior to delayed feedback. Furthermore, in all these studies feedback was given in written form. It is suggested that when feedback is presented in spoken form, for example in interactive reading programs for beginners, it should be presented immediately after the learning trial to enable students to consider the information carefully (Spaai, forthcoming).

3.2 Feedback content

The amount of information the feedback contains is also an important determinant of feedback effects. According to Kulhavy (1977) the content of feedback may be considered along a continuum. The simplest feedback content provides a simple Correct or Incorrect supply while the most complex feedback may present considerable instruction-specific remedial information (elaborate feedback). It is often implicitly assumed that the more information the feedback contains, the greater the chance incorrect responses being replaced by correct ones. In some studies (Hudson, 1981) feedback containing information about the correctness of responses has been shown to coincide with learning with no-feedback practise formats (Kulhavy, 1977) and feedback procedures providing the correct answer itself have been shown to be superior to feedback procedures containing merely information about the correctness of the answer. However, no such effects were found in other studies (Wentling, 1973). Furthermore, no extra learning effects were found in the case of more elaborate feedback procedures (e.g., Kulhavy et al. (1985)). Kulhavy and his colleagues assumed that the lack of positive effects for elaborate forms of feedback is due to the fact that learners tend to process the elaborate feedback at a shallower level. It is assumed that people tend to better remember information that is processed at a semantic level within the cognitive system. The depth at which new information is processed is reflected by the amount of effort spend on encoding and by the number of meaningful elaborations produced during learning. Low-level processing, however, might yield longer reading times but would do little to increase the number of correct responses; it could even have the effect of reducing feedback effectivity, because more information has to be processed (Kulhavy et al., 1985).

In summary, it can be concluded that no conclusive evidence is yet available about the amount and type of information the feedback should contain to be beneficial for learning. Furthermore, in all the studies described above, feedback was provided in written form only. Hence, little experimental evidence is available for the effects of the informativeness of feedback in spoken form. Research into the effects of the informativeness of spoken feedback on performance is therefore necessary for the development of computer-based reading programs for beginners.

4 Experiment

In the present experiment, the spoken feedback content for facilitating the learning of letter-sound correspondences was studied. The task for the children participating in this experiment was to select a letter from a set of letters on the computer screen, after the letter had been pronounced by the computer. Corrective feedback was presented in spoken form. In order to enable the learner to process the information optimally, speech feedback was presented almost immediately after the learning event.

Letter-sound relations were practised in four different conditions. Practise conditions differed in the detail of the spoken information supplied. In the *control* condition children received information about the correctness of the answers in terms of right or wrong only. In the *partial-feedback* condition spoken information about the correctness of the answer was given by the computer as right or wrong and the selected letter was subsequently presented in spoken form too. In the *elaborate-feedback* condition spoken information about the correctness of the selection was provided and whenever an error was made the correct letter was indicated visually and was also pronounced. The *complete-feedback* condition was comparable with the elaborate-feedback condition, the only difference being that whenever a response error was made, the spoken form of the incorrectly selected letter was presented before the correct selection was presented.

No a-priori hypotheses were made regarding possible differences in learning effects, although it was expected that providing corrective feedback whenever an error was made would help the pupils to direct their attention to the correct response (Tait et al., 1973). It was also expected that the extra information provided in the case of errors might be helpful in discriminating between the correct response and the incorrect response. It remains questionable, however, whether novice learners can process the extra information presented in the complete-feedback condition (Kim & Phillips, 1991).

4.1 Method

4.1.1 Procedure and design

Four different groups of children practised letter-sound correspondences, each under a different practise condition. The children were instructed to select a letter from among four others on a computer screen after the letter has been pronounced by the computer (e.g., "Wijs aan de ... /w/" ("Point at the ... /w/")). The vowels and the fricative consonants were pronounced in isolation, whereas the stop consonants were always followed by a short segment of the vowel 'schwa' in order to make these phonemes pronounceable. Furthermore, in all cases a pause of 0.7 sec preceded the presentation of the spoken form of the letter. That way the letter sound could be clearly distinguished. The letters were pseudo-randomly displayed in different parts of the screen. The child had to select the pronounced letter from the others on the screen by positioning the cursor on the letter with the aid of a mouse and giving a click response. After clicking, the selected answer could not be changed. Furthermore, when a child did not answer within 15 seconds, the letters were removed from the screen and two seconds later a new set appeared and a next letter was pronounced by the computer. When a child pointed at a place where there was no letter, the computer provided further instruction in spoken form. After a child had selected a letter on the screen, a rectangle was drawn around that letter to inform the child that his or her answer had been registered by the computer.

Each child participated in three learning sessions on consecutive days. The learning sessions took place in the classroom during ordinary classroom lessons. Children received spoken instructions and feedback through headphones. During the learning sessions, the teacher ensured that the programs were used according to the rules; an experimenter was not present. The computer told the child what to do by giving spoken instructions at all times. That way the child could work with the computer independently and did not need the assistance of the teacher. A learning session could be started by inserting a diskette into its drive and pointing at a picture of a door on the screen. Spoken instruction was available from the moment the door appeared on the screen. During the learning sessions the computer registered response times and response errors. After all the letters had been presented twice in a learning session, the session stopped automatically and the learning session was concluded with a suitable construction. The average length of each learning session was about 7 minutes.

The letters were presented in separate tests, i.e. the pretest and the posttest, on the day before and the day after the learning sessions. The children were instructed to select the pronounced letter on the computer screen and did not receive any information about the correctness of the selected letter. The letters were presented in different random orders in the pretest and the posttest while response errors and response times were registered. The children did a practise set of three trials during the learning sessions, the pretest, and the posttest in order to become familiar with the experimental procedure. Learning effects were determined as differences in response times and response errors between pretest and posttest results.

4.1.2 Subjects

Seventy-two first-graders (34 boys and 38 girls) from four normal primary schools participated in the experiment. The children were 6.4 to 6.6 years old. At the time the study was conducted (September-October), all the children had received about

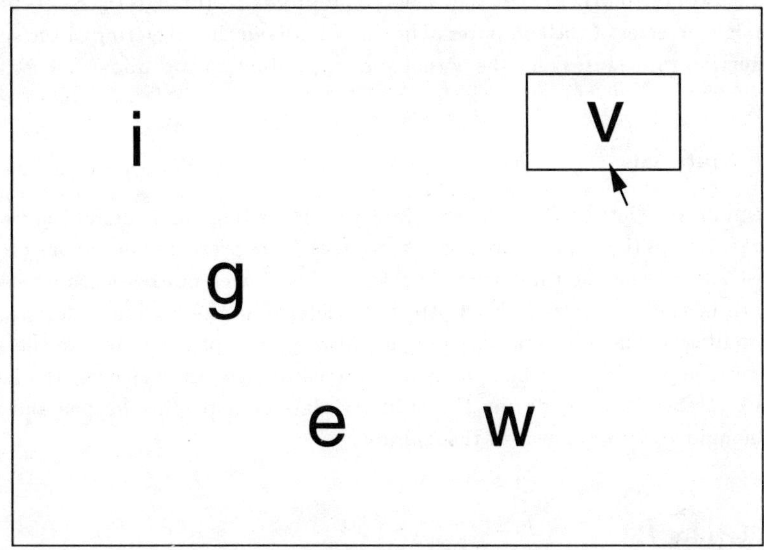

Fig. 1. Screen layout for the SPELL exercise. The child had to select the letter on the screen matching a letter sound presented by the computer.

three weeks of reading instruction. All the schools used the same reading method. Prior to the experiment the children were given a letter pronunciation test in order to measure their active knowledge of letter-phoneme relations.

Subjects were matched in groups of four, on the basis of their scores in the letter-pronunciation test. Within each group subjects were randomly assigned to one of the four practise conditions. Because some children were not able to participate in all experimental sessions the four groups could not be kept equal in number. The numbers of children participating in the control condition, the partial-feedback condition, the elaborate-feedback condition and the complete-feedback condition were 18, 15, 15 and 16, respectively. The average scores in the letter pronunciation test of the children in the control condition, the partial-feedback condition, the elaborate-feedback condition and the complete-feedback condition were 12.4 (sd=3.8), 13.5 (sd=3.9), 12.6 (sd=3.5) and 12.3 (sd=3.0), respectively.

4.1.3 Equipment

The letters were presented pseudo-randomly in black on white in lower-case on the screen of a Macintosh-Plus microcomputer. Using software tools for bit-mapped graphics, an alphabet was created that closely resembled the font and character size children were acquainted with in their regular reading materials (see Figure 1). The speech sounds used for instructions and feedback were first pronounced by an experienced male speaker and recorded on tape and were then digitized at a sampling rate of 10 kHz so that they could be reproduced through the 8-bit-digital-to-analog converter of the computer. The delay between the triggering of the speech reproduction procedures and the actual speech production was about 0.8 sec.

4.1.4 Materials

The stimuli were letters from the standard Dutch reading curriculum. Ten letters, the target letters (i.e., v, k, aa, oo, ee, i, g, w, u, e), were presented in the pretest, the posttest and during the three training sessions (i.e., twice in each learning session and once in the pretest and the posttest) to determine the learning effects in the four conditions. These letters were taught in two groups of five letters in the same way as in the ordinary reading curriculum. According to the teachers, the letters had not yet been taught during the ordinary classroom reading lessons and they were thought to be unknown to the children.

4.2 Results

4.2.1 Response times

Table 1 presents the average response times for the target letters with correct responses in the pretest and posttest for the four experimental conditions. The pretest scores did not differ significantly for the conditions ($F < 1$). The mean response times for correct responses in the pretest and the posttest were 2.9 sec (sd=1.2) and 2.4 sec (sd=1.1), respectively. Response times for correct responses were significantly shorter in the posttest than in the pretest ($F(1,53) = 9.54$; $p < 0.05$). No differential effect of condition was found on the decrease in response times ($F < 1$).

The differences in scores for pretest and posttest response accuracy were separately subjected to an analysis of covariance with the pretest score as a covariate. The effect of the covariate was significant ($F(1,51) = 36.59$; $p < 0.05$) in that there was a tendency for the decrease in response times to be greater for the poor performers. This tendency was found in all conditions. Again, no differential effect of condition was found ($F(3,51) = 1.86$; $p < 0.10$).

Table 1. Mean response times in seconds for correct target letters in the pretest and the posttest in the four conditions (with standard deviations in parentheses).

Condition	Pretest	Posttest	Pretest-Posttest
Control	2.8 (1.2)	2.3 (0.8)	0.5 (1.0)
Partial	3.4 (1.5)	2.9 (1.5)	0.4 (2.1)
Elaborate	2.9 (0.8)	1.9 (0.7)	1.0 (0.9)
Complete	2.6 (0.9)	2.2 (0.8)	0.3 (0.7)

4.2.2 Response errors

The average number of errors during the three training sessions was 2.1 (sd=1.7). An analysis of variance showed a significant effect of training sessions but no significant interaction between training sessions and feedback condition ($F < 1$). In Table 2 the average numbers of response errors in the pretest and the posttest are shown per experimental condition.

Table 2. Average number of response errors in the pretest and the posttest in the four conditions (with standard deviations in parentheses).

Condition	Pretest	Posttest	Pretest-Posttest
Control	2.3 (1.9)	1.8 (2.1)	0.5 (1.3)
Partial	2.5 (2.2)	1.9 (1.9)	0.5 (2.0)
Elaborate	2.9 (1.7)	0.4 (0.9)	2.5 (1.9)
Complete	2.4 (2.0)	2.1 (2.5)	0.3 (1.9)

Children made fewer response errors in the posttest than in the pretest ($F(1,62) = 19.11$; $p < 0.05$). A differential effect of condition on the decrease in response errors was found ($F(3,60) = 5.12$; $p < 0.05$). Post-hoc analysis revealed that children in the elaborate-feedback condition improved markedly more than those in the control, partial-feedback or the complete-feedback condition ($p < 0.05$).

The differences in scores for pretest and posttest errors were separately subjected to an analysis of variance with the pretest score as a covariate. There was a significant effect of the covariate ($F(1,59) = 18.43$; $p < 0.05$) in that the decrease in response errors was greater for the poor performers. This tendency was only found in the elaborate-feedback condition and the complete-feedback condition. There was a reliable effect of condition on the decrease in response errors, ($F(3,59) = 4.94$; $p < 0.05$). A posteriori Scheff contrasts showed that children in the elaborate-feedback condition improved markedly more than the others.

5 Discussion

The results clearly indicate that elaborate feedback has a positive effect on response accuracy. The improvement in response accuracy in the elaborate-feedback condition was greater than in the three other conditions. The advantage of elaborate feedback over feedback that mainly indicates whether a response is correct or not (as in the control condition and the partial feedback condition) may be caused by the fact that it gives the beginning readers the opportunity to detect errors and guides them to the correct response after an error has been made. That is, whenever an error is made, the goals of supplying feedback are to eliminate the wrong answer and to substitute correct information. These results comply with the notion that feedback on errors acts primarily as a correcting agent (Kulhavy, 1977). This finding is also in accordance with earlier research findings of Travers et al. (1964).

They studied the learning effects of various feedback strategies in teaching vocabulary to German children. Their results showed that children who were told that a response was wrong and who were then corrected did far better than children who received "Yes" or "No" following each response. Also, in more recent research (e.g., Terrell (1990); Kim & Phillips (1991)) it was found that students who were informed whether their answer was correct or incorrect scored lower in posttests than students who were provided with an explanation of the correct answer.

The results of the present study also showed that the learning effects found for the complete-feedback condition were poorer than those for the elaborate-feedback condition. This may be due to the fact that children receiving complete feedback whenever an error is made easily mix up the incorrect with the correct answer, partly owing to pro-active inhibition (Kulhavy, 1977); the delay between the presentation of the incorrect answer and the correct answer is very short and young children frequently show attention lapses in learning and memory tasks. The processing of the large amount of information which is presented in the complete-feedback condition may also be hindered by the short delay between the presentation of the feedback and the presentation of the next item. A learning situation in which the learner is allowed to control the timing of the presentation may be more effective.

Furthermore, the results showed that there was a tendency for the decrease in response errors to be greater for the poor performers in the elaborate-feedback condition and the complete-feedback condition. Apparently, poor performers are in need of more information than good performers; a finding also reported by McGowen & Clark (1985). For the development of computer-based reading programs using speech feedback this finding means that speech feedback should be incorporated in an adaptive way.

Children needed less time to respond correctly in the posttest than they did in the pretest. This is probably not only an indication of the improvement in skill in associating graphemes with phonemes but also an indication for the improvement of the level of skill in handling the mouse. Furthermore, these results are in agreement with the results of previous studies that showed that corrective feedback is primarily important to help a learner correct errors and has hardly any effects on initially correct responses (Kulhavy, 1977).

In summary, it is tentatively concluded that interactive reading programs for beginners should present information about the correctness of the pupil's answer in terms of right or wrong and an indication of the right answer when an error is made. In other words, the feedback should be focused on the correct response. Also, poor learners especially seem to be in need of corrective feedback. Thus, it may be necessary to implement feedback in an adaptive way: give elaborate feedback to poor performers and combinations of elaborate and partial feedback to good performers.

Acknowledgements

The research reported here was supported by the Netherlands Ministry of Education and Science.

References

Anderson, J.R., Kline, P.J. & Beasley, C.M. (1980) Complex learning processes. In: Snow, R., Frederico, P. & Montgue, W. (eds.) Aptitude, Learning, and Instruction. Hillsdale NY: Lawrence Erlbaum Associates Incorporation.

Anderson, R.C., Hiebert, E.H., Scott, J.A. & Wilkinson, J.A.G. (1985) Becoming a Nation of Readers. Washington, DC: National Institute of Education.

Andrews, G.R. & Debus, R.L. (1978) Persistence and the causal perception of failure: Modifying cognitive attributions. J. Ed. Psych., 70, 154–166.

Bouwhuis, D.G. (1993) Interactive instructional systems as dialogue systems. In: Verhoeven, L. (ed.) Training for literacy. Dordrecht: Foris Publications.

Calfee, R.C., Chapman, R. & Venezky, R. (1972) How a child needs to think to learn to read. In: Gregg, L. (ed.) Cognition in learning and Memory. New York: Wiley.

Carroll, J.B. (1976) Promoting language skills: The role of instruction. In: Klahr, D. (ed.) Cognition and Instruction. Hillsdale: Halsted Press.

Ehri, L.C., Deffner, N.D. & Wilce, L.S. (1984) Pictorial mnemonics for phonics. J. Ed. Psych., 76, 880–896.

Hudson, R.C. (1981) Feedback administered by a computer. Ph.D. thesis, West Virginia University.

Kim, J.-Y.L. & Phillips, T.L. (1991) The effectiveness of two forms of corrective feedback in diabetes education. J. Comp. Bas. Instr., 18, 14–18.

Kulhavy, R.W. (1977) Feedback in written instruction. Rev. Ed. Res., 47, 211–232.

Kulhavy, R.W. & Anderson, R.C. (1972) Delay-retention effect with multiple-choice tests. J. Ed. Psych., 63, 505–512.

Kulhavy, R.W. & Stock, W.A. (1989) Feedback in written instruction: The place of response certitude. Ed. Psych. Rev., 1, 279–308.

Kulhavy, R.W., White, M.T., Topp, B.W., Chan, A.L. & Adams, J. (1985) Feedback complexity and corrective efficiency. Cont. Ed. Psych., 10, 285–291.

Kulik, J.A. & Kulik, C.C. (1988) Timing of feedback and verbal learning. Rev. Ed. Res., 58, 79–97.

McGowen, J. & Clark, R.E. (1985) Instructional software features that support learning for students with widely different ability levels. Perf. Instr., 24, 4–17.

Roth, K.J. (1985) Conceptual Change and Student Processing of Science Texts. Paper presented at the annual meeting of the American Educational Research Association, Chicago.

Samuels, S.J. (1972) The effect of letter-name knowledge on learning to read. Am. Ed. Res. J., 1, 65–74.

Sassenrath, J. & Yonge, G.D. (1968) Delayed information feedback, feedback cues, retention set and delayed retention. J. Ed. Psych., 59, 69–73.

Sassenrath, J.M. (1975) Theory and results on feedback and retention. J. Ed. Psych., 67, 894–899.

Schimmel, B.J. (1988) Providing meaningful feedback in the courseware. In: Jonassen, D.H. (ed.) Instructional Designs for Microcomputer Courseware. Hillsdale NY: Lawrence Erlbaum Associates Incorporation.

Spaai, G.W.G. (forthcoming) The use of speech feedback in an interactive reading program for beginners. Doctoral dissertation, University of Technology Eindhoven.

Tait, K., Hartley, J.R. & Anderson, R.C. (1973) Feedback procedures in computer assisted arithmetic instruction. Brit. J. Ed. Psych., 43, 161–173.

Terrell, D.J. (1990) A comparison of two procedures for remediating errors during computer-based instruction. J. Comp. Bas. Instr., 17, 91–96.

Travers, R.M.W., van Wagenen, R.K., Haygood, D.H. & McCormick, M. (1964) Learning as a consequence of the learner's task involvement under different conditions of feedback. J. Ed. Psych., 55, 167–173.

Wentling, T.L. (1973) Mastery versus non-mastery instruction with varying test-item feedback treatments. J. Ed. Psych., 65, 50–58.

Relying on a Sophisticated Student Model to Derive Dialogue Strategies in an Intelligent Tutoring System

Violaine M. Prince

LIMSI/CNRS, P.O. Box 133, 91 403 Orsay cedex, France, e-mail: prince@limsi.fr

Abstract. In this paper we present a tutoring system relying on the properties of its natural language interface. Intended to check the linguistic expression of abstract concepts by means of natural language parsing, the system is based on student modelling for deriving its dialogue strategies. The paper presents the underlying hypothesis and focusses on dialogue strategies applied to the case of definition checking.

Keywords. Intelligent tutoring systems, student modelling, human-machine dialogues

1 Introduction

TEDDI[1] is a tutoring system using non-constrained natural language, not only as a communication medium between student and machine, but also as a knowledge representation system. TEDDI's purpose is to train and check concept acquisition by university-level students. This group is seldom addressed in the literature, which focusses mainly on children's knowledge acquisition. We think that university students may have difficulties in conceptual knowledge acquisition and, moreover, that these difficulties may be easier to solve for adults than for children. An automatic system could be used for the afore mentioned purpose with a good chance of success.

1.1 Concept acquisition: the status of expression

Concept acquisition has attracted interest in many investigations in CAL.[2] However, the methods used in these investigations were generally either problem-solving oriented or relied on discovery dialogues (Shute et al., 1989). Problem-solving is a very reliable method, but applies to only some aspects of scientific knowledge: what about more descriptive knowledge (e.g., definition knowledge, terminology, classification)? What about domains where problems do not exist (e.g., geography, zoology, history)? Shall we restrict tutoring systems to problem-solving domains only? An answer was given by discovery tutors who concentrated on non-problem-solving

[1] Acronym for: Tuteur d'Enseignement de Definitions Individualise, which means: Individualized Definition Teaching System.

[2] Computer-Aided Learning.

domains. But discovery tutors do not aim at coaching students as problem-solving techniques do, and coaching could be a useful role of tutors. Also, both methods seem to have been used for scientific knowledge acquisition, mainly by children: are they suitable for modelling for adult knowledge acquisition?

When dealing with adult difficulties in concept acquisition, a possible solution could be to rely on language in order to determine some of the cues of these difficulties. Adults, unlike children, are supposed to have certain linguistic skills, especially when they are of university level. That led us to the idea to try to analyse linguistic expressions of concept definition in order to make a first-degree check. The underlying hypothesis is simple: a deficient expression could be a good variable for measuring conceptual acquisition problems. This hypothesis was developed in psycholinguistics by Daniel (1991) and is discussed in Daniel et al. (1992). We have relied on it to build our system and until now we have had no indications that this assumption could be wrong. It is based on the hypothesis that verbal expression reflects cognitive organization and could thus be a complementary approach to student mental modelling (Anderson, 1983). To a certain extent it restricts the ambitions of tutoring systems: we have designed an automatic tutoring system as a 'tool for learning' (Lesgold, 1992), rather than as a substitute for a teacher. In this paper we would like to show that it can be useful and that it needs sophisticated modelling for both dialogue and students' representations.

2 The role of language in TEDDI

2.1 Concept definitions as constituents of the student's knowledge

Our work was based on empirical assumptions: we noticed that concepts which are not clearly defined in 'words' by adult students (i.e., students not having expression problems) are seldom clearly understood by them. Thus, linguistic rendering of concept definition could be a good indication of how well the student has organized his/her knowledge (Nicaud & Prince, 1990). The choice of the words and the way the definition is put seemed very important to us: they could reflect the ability to generalize, which is essential for concept acquisition (Barth, 1987). Generalization is defined as the ability to express, in terms of laws and/or regularities, knowledge upon which a cognitive action of categorization and classification has been undertaken (Winkels et al., 1988).

2.2 A dialogue for checking and improving definitions

We decided to use an intelligent tutoring system (ITS) as a device for checking a student's linguistic rendering of a previously learnt concept. The student was assumed to have been trained by means of traditional teaching. Our system acts a posteriori to training and is to be considered a testing system. The definition given by the student was to be a free output, to be produced at a remote moment from the moment of learning.

The *utterance* acting as the *definition statement* was to give us information on how the concept had been remembered (validity of the related concepts). Further investigation by means of a *Human-machine educational dialogue*, was to help us evaluate to what extent the concept had been understood: in definition expression, understanding is assumed to be reached when the expression meets the requirements of 'a good definition'. This evaluation, made at every move, was to direct the dialogue, the ultimate goal being to make the student improve and reach the 'ideal level' which the human professor considered satisfactory. This was to help us to complete the learning process (Brown et al., 1983). At the end of the *session*, *TEDDI's success goal* was reached if the definition statement and the dialogue continuation had proved that the student was successful; the definition statement may not have been satisfactory but the dialogue continuation had made the student reach the 'ideal level'. When a student showed no improvement after repeated testing, the system was stopped.

2.3 The emerging architectural modules: student's model and dialogue manager

The student's model is a key element of our system: with respect to the usual ITSs, domain knowledge is a classical component; reasoning is not a relevant aspect because definitions are rather static knowledge, and no inference is required. Interactive interface and evaluative function are merged within the same frame. Student modelling is strongly dependent on the student's natural language expression. Since natural language plays such an important part in TEDDI it has acquired the characteristics of a Human-machine dialogue system. We will briefly present the general architecture of the system and will discuss on the modules and models concerning student and dialogue modelling.

2.3.1 General architecture

TEDDI's architecture is an instantiation of a multi-expert natural language processing architecture developed by LIMSI's research team in NLP (natural language processing). This architecture, named CARAMEL[3] (Sabah, 1990a; Sabah, 1990b), has given birth to many applications, among which a Human-machine Information Seeking Dialogue System, STANDIA (Vilnat & Nicaud, 1992). TEDDI is an educational application of CARAMEL and this tends to prove that the latter is general-purpose architecture as far as NLP is concerned. Figure 1 shows TEDDI's architecture.

2.3.2 Student and dialogue modelling

In this paper we will concentrate on two issues: how to evaluate a student's definition statement and how to pursue dialogue with the student in the light of evaluation

[3] Acronym for: Comprehension Automatique de Recits, Apprentissage, Modelisation des Echanges Langagiers, which stands for: Automatic Stories Understanding, Learning and Linguistic Exchange Modelling.

results.

- As far as evaluating the student's definition statement is concerned: this is done with the aid of the following modules and models. The rectangles store knowledge. The ellipses indicate local 'expert' processes. Session models contain knowledge available for the session only. Long-term models are knowledge relevant for the application, available at every TEDDI session. Communication between processes passes through the supervisor, which is responsible for process triggering and planification.

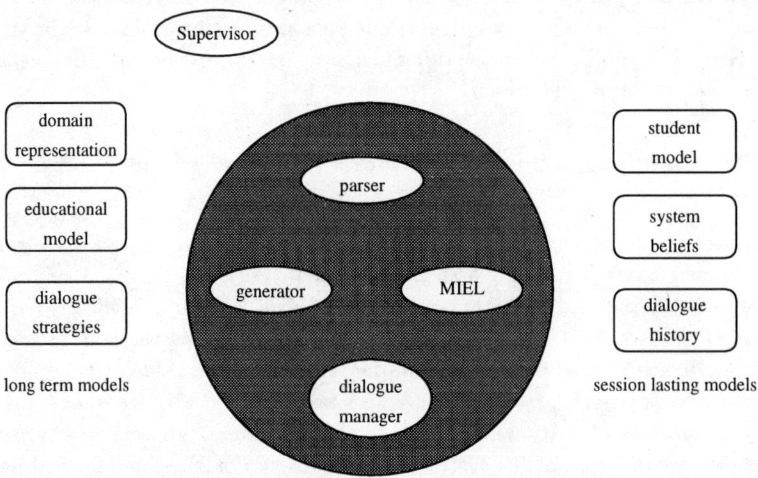

Fig. 1. TEDDI's architecture. The rectangles store knowledge. The ellipses indicate local 'expert' processes. Session models contain knowledge available for the session only. Long-term models contain knowledge relevant for the application, available at every TEDDI session. Communication between processes passes through the supervisor, which is responsible for process triggering and planification.

Domain representation: constituting the human teacher's expertise, domain knowledge is represented by means of reference conceptual graphs (Sowa, 1984), associated with a lattice of the concepts.

The MIEL module matches the student's definition's internal representation with domain representation and derives information from the corresponding results.[4] The student model is fed with the results of evaluation. It serves as a feedback source for further evaluations.

- As for pursuing dialogue: this is achieved with the aid of the following modules and models: The Dialogue Manager, which relies on system beliefs, Dialogue

[4] MIEL: Modelisation Inductive de l'Eleve selon son Langage. Stands for: Inductive Modelling of the Student according to his Language.

History and Student Model contents to pursue dialogue. Its strategies are stored in the dialogue strategies model and are dependent on the educational model.

2.3.3 Focussing on dialogue

Other contributions have given a detailed account of the process of answer evaluation and the technical aspects of knowledge matching (Prince, 1993), the level of generalization in the choice of words (Nicaud & Prince, 1991a) and the contents of the student model (Daniel et al., 1992). In this contribution we will focus on the dynamics of dialogue on the basis of the contents of the student model.

3 Educational dialogue conditions

3.1 When dialogue is necessary

Dialogue between TEDDI and a student is of course necessary if the answer is not correct. The system will then try to guide the student towards the correct answer. *Correcting strategies* will be discussed in section 4.2.1. Dialogue must also be pursued if the answer is correct but incomplete. All the examples given here come from a corpus and have been simulated (Nicaud & Prince, 1991b). We have chosen computer science as our field of research, because of the availability of students and the concept to be defined is 'sort'. During the experiments we discovered that some of the students who gave an unsatisfactory definition of the concept of 'sort' could not provide a general algorithm for a sort procedure.

Example: The concept to be defined is *sort*, the domain is *computer science.*
'*A sort is a classifying procedure*' is a correct but incomplete answer.

If the student has formulated part of the definition of the concept correctly, then the dialogue must continue with a *query for completion*, to be dealt with in section 4.2.1. A complete answer is not necessarily exhaustive. The expert determined the minimum required, visualized in the form of a *minimal reference graph*, which indicates the boundary between an incomplete and an acceptable graph.

This first step, rather common in CAL, seems to us to be insufficient. As pointed out before, the *ability to generalize* is the second property checked by TEDDI, along with the validity or the degree of completeness of the answer. This ability will only be tested in the case of valid and complete answers. The MIEL module gives an indication of the abstraction level of the answer. Two cues have been studied: abstraction level of words and abstraction level of texts.

3.1.1 Abstraction level of words used to refer to concepts

A proper abstraction level for words is given by the teacher. We have provided an algorithm which rates the *lexical abstraction level* of the student's answer (Nicaud & Prince, 1991a). When this level approaches too high a level of abstraction, the answer is too general and causes the system to ask for precision. Conversely, when the abstraction level drops too far below the correct level then the answer is too detailed which could denote an inability to generalize the scope of concepts. In order to reach its educational goal, the system has to trigger a generalization dialogue. Both *precision* and *generalization strategies* are dealt further with in section 4.2.1.

Example: The concept to be defined is *sort*, the domain is *computer science*. '*A sort is a classification of items according to a criterion.*' is a correct and complete answer. However, it is also too general.

3.1.2 Abstraction level of text

Some linguistic studies on the form of the definitions (Péry-Woodley, 1990) in our corpus (Nicaud & Prince, 1991b) have led us to the conclusion that linguistic style is in fact a good measure of what we have called the *cognitive style of the student* (Daniel, 1991; Daniel et al., 1992). Categories of students have been defined according to their style. These categories help the system develop the appropriate educational plan and feed the system beliefs on such a student.

3.2 Dialogue headlines

The Dialogue Manager controls the dialogue and is triggered when a session with a student begins. Dialogue is always launched as a query from the system like:

S: Please define the concept of 'sort' in computer science

a query that is supposed to be answered with:

U: *A sort is a classifying procedure*

The answer evaluation process is triggered, and if:

- the answer is not valid or
- the answer is incomplete or
- the answer is valid and complete but too general or
- the answer is valid and complete but too detailed or
- the answer is valid, complete and at the correct level of abstraction, but seems to be a learned definition.

Dialogue will continue, and the Dialogue Manager will be invoked to pursue dialogue according to the current state of its educational plan (recorded in the educational model), of the possible dialogue strategies (triggered by the current state of the student model), of its own opinion on the student's abilities. All these aspects will be discussed in the next section.

4 Managing dialogue

The Dialogue Manager relies on the idea of *cooperation* between an *educational model*, whose contents is designed according to the teacher's requirements, and a 'dialogue model', which takes into account the system's beliefs on the student (the local dialogue user model) and some dialogue strategies classically based on Grice's maxims. Models and Dialogue Manager properties like architectural components cannot be discussed here: they meet the requirements in Sabah (1990a). We shall adhere to those requirements in the following sections.

4.1 The Educational model

The educational model we have adopted is rather simple. It is composed of educational requirements, and educational plans. The importance of planning in Human-machine dialogues has been extensively discussed in Carberry (1988) and Pollack (1990). We will assume that a Human-machine dialogue within a CAL application meets the same planning requirements as general-purpose Human-machine dialogues.

Educational requirements: The criteria of these requirements are fixed by the teacher. They are parameters that different teachers of different domains can change at will.

1. The correct and satisfactory answer: a VALIDITY PLAN is required to be able to meet this requirement.
2. The satisfactory abstraction level: an ABSTRACTION PLAN is required to be able to meet this requirement.
3. A good level of understanding: the system may suspect that a definition which satisfies both requirements 1 and 2 may have been learned 'by heart'. The system will then use many strategies to check whether the definition is indeed understood. An UNDERSTANDING PLAN is required for this end.

Properties: Requirement 3 implies requirement 2, which in turn implies requirement 1.

Educational plans: As the requirements depend on one another, the corresponding plans depend on one another. UNDERSTANDING is launched if ABSTRACTION is satisfied and ABSTRACTION is launched if VALIDITY is satisfied.

Plan priorities are the other way round. Hence, VALIDITY is the first plan to be developed and dialogue must continue until the requirement is met. ABSTRACTION is then triggered from the moment the definitions are correct and, finally, UNDERSTANDING is realised. However, educational plans could be interrupted by dialogue necessities. Educational plans trigger dialogue strategies according to the content of the Student Model. Dialogue strategies are organized in plans, and because laws of conversation (in the Gricean approach to conversation) entertain the idea that conversation must be maintained at any cost, dialogue plans prevail over educational plans.

4.2 Dialogue strategies

Dialogue strategies are encapsulated in the system by means of rules which dictate the system's behaviour according to the contents of the student model and the opinions on the student. Dialogue strategies are composed of two major constituents: *educational strategies* and *conversational strategies*. The strategies of the first type are triggered by educational plans. Those of the second type belong to 'pure' dialogue planning.

4.2.1 Educational strategies

- Correcting strategies

Correcting strategies are triggered when graph matching has failed. The nature of the failure is analysed (in Nicaud & Prince (1990) we have determined a typology of errors) and questions will are then asked on the basis of the results obtained. For instance, if the concepts constituting the definition of the required concept are wrong, then the system will present them to the student and ask for reformulation.

- Query for completion: the validity plan

This strategy is triggered when the graph matching has successful and has led to a subset of the minimal reference graph and the answer has been labelled 'correct but incomplete'. The system will try to instantiate the missing relations in the answer graph.

Example: The concept to be defined is *sort*, the domain is *computer science.*

S1. *Please define 'sort'.*

U1. *A sort is a classifying procedure*
(is a correct but an incomplete answer.)

S2. *This is correct. What is the object of classification?*
(trying to instantiate the 'object' relation in the conceptual graph).

U2. *A set of data.*

S3. *This is correct. What is the mean of classification?*
(trying to instantiate the 'instrument' relation in the conceptual graph).

U3. *A criterion. For instance, alphabetic order.*
(minimal graph is reached.)

S4. *This is correct.*
end of VALIDITY PLAN
beginning of ABSTRACTION detection

...

Note: in this example the system's repetition of its sentence 'this is correct' is meant as an encouraging feature in the dialogue. The student may be troubled by the system's insistence. Thus, encouragement seems needed to preserve the student's 'good will'. The VALIDITY plan has been implemented in Lisp, after answer evaluation had been implemented and tested with the aid of the examples given in this paper.

- Abstraction level strategies: constituents of the abstraction plan
Abstraction level strategies are triggered when the result of the abstraction detection procedure is outside the range fixed by the teacher as the acceptable lexical abstraction level. Two types of strategies are triggered.

When the level of lexical abstraction is too high (conversely, the computed score is too low) then a *precision strategy* is triggered. For every concept node in the graph that is too general (i.e., too high in the lattice of concepts), a *request for precision* will be issued.

Example: The concept to be defined is *sort*, the domain is *computer science.*
S1. *Please define 'sort'.*
U1. *A sort is a classification of items according to a criterion.*
(is a correct answer and is also satisfactory in terms of completeness. Abstraction detection denotes a too important generality.)
S2. *Could you detail the items to be classified?*
(a question for precision on the object of classification)
U2. *elements of arrays, lists, files, whatever.*
(a well illustrated answer, this corrects the impression of generality. However, the system pursues for all concepts which have been termed too general).
S3. *What kind of criteria?*
U3. *Alphabetic order, upwards or downwards for integers.*
(same kind.
end of ABSTRACTION PLAN
beginning of UNDERSTANDING detection)

The *generalization strategy* is somewhat converse to the preceding one. It is triggered when the abstraction level is too low (conversely, the computed score is too high). Its aim is to guide the student towards an expression of his knowledge in terms of general laws.

Example: the 'sort' example.
...
U. *To sort is for instance to put in order a set of figures, either upwards or downwards.*
(correct and complete. Abstraction level too low. → generalization strategy of every concept node.)
S. *Have you a more general term in 'put in order'?*
U. *To classify.*
(correct level. Move to the next).
S. *Have you a more general term in the object of classification?*
U. *A set of data.*
...

The ABSTRACTION plan has been specified (using a proprietary specification language) but not yet implemented, although abstraction level detection has been implemented. It is currently in the implementation phase.

- Understanding strategies: an idea of the understanding plan

As we have said, the student may successfully pass the preceding tests. We believe that they are necessary for cheking his knowledge, but they are not sufficient: the student may have learnt definitions by heart and not by understanding. Hence, the system will develop a number of 'strategies' in order to investigate the extent of the student's understanding. These strategies have not yet been designed, but are being contemplated. Among the strategies that we are planning are the following:

- subconcepts investigation: a concept is defined by means of a combination of other concepts (e.g. the concept of 'sort' is defined as 'classification', as 'set of data', and so on). All major subconcepts (i.e., acting as 'object', 'subject', 'goal') will be checked by issuing a definition query to the student.
- relationship investigation: if the student has passed the preceding test, then questions will be asked about the roles played by the different items.

Example: pursuing the investigation into the sort concept.
(the student has not filled the 'slot' for 'agent'. However, his answer was correct and complete because the minimal reference graph allows this case to be discarded. In the 'understanding' plan the system tries to fill the empty slots.)

S. *What is the agent of the sort procedure?*

U. *The system.*
(the reference concept is 'processor'. However, the system accepts the word 'system' as a local synonym for processor).

4.2.2 Educational plans interruption: conversational strategies

As pointed out before, the system endeavours to pursue conversation throughout the session. Educational plans are interrupted when conversation is jeopardized. Two major cases have proved possible dangers for conversation: a *misunderstanding* or a *persistent failure*.

- Misunderstanding

Misunderstanding can occur on the part of the system or of the student.

System misunderstanding:

- Linguistic: misspelled words, unexpected forms.
- Thematic: no relation to the subject.

Student misunderstanding:

- about the *subject* of the system's question (level of language): the student is not able to fathom what he/she has been asked to do. (*unknown goal*)

- about the concept itself: the student is unable give a definition, because he/she doesn't know or understand the concept. (*unknown word*)

More general dialogue handling is addressed in these cases. We will adopt a goal formulation close to the one developed in Prince et al. (1991).

- Persistent failure

This happens when the first educational plan, VALIDITY, is not reached after some repeated queries. Persistent failure in an initial VALIDITY plan has more consequences than persistent failure after the UNDERSTANDING strategy has been triggered (e.g., in subconcepts definition): a student may know how to define a concept and be unable to define subconcepts. This inability does not necessarily express a disorganization in knowledge. A concept may be rather clear in one's mind although its defining subconcepts are sketchy. Further investigation prior to UNDERSTANDING planning is then carried out to clarify assumptions.

4.3 What is needed

The dialogue and educational strategies outlined above cannot perform the tasks described, i.e. the student's definition statement evaluation and the dialogue continuation, by themselves. Components are needed to launch these strategies: educational plans depend on the results of definition validity evaluation, which are stored in the Student Model. Conversational strategies depend on linguistic aspects of the dialogue, on the state of the student model and on the dialogue history. The elements needed, i.e. Student Model, Dialogue History and what we have called the system's belief, recorded in Figure 1, will be discussed in the next section.

5 The Student Model and system's beliefs

All the knowledge necessary for launching strategies, both educational and conversational, is found in two models, the student model and the system's belief model. Sections 5.1 and 5.2 will focus on the student model, section 5.3 will provide information on the system's belief. However, dialogue continuation relies upon a 'memory' of dialogue. Human-machine dialogue models generally contain a dialogue history. In section 5.4 we will present the outlines of such a model, which does not differ from traditional design in the domain of dialogues.

5.1 Contents of the Student Model

A Student Model is a session model, that is:

- it is *initialized* at the beginning of the session with the student, on the basis of the results of the evaluation of the first definition.

- It is *updated* whenever, during the dialogue, the system asks the student to define or redefine a particular concept or subconcept according to the system's plan.

The Student Model is composed of records, providing information at every update. Every record of the student model is named the *momentary student's cognitive profile* (Daniel et al., 1992). The momentary student's cognitive profile is computed with the aid of four procedures, whose results are the following:

1. An evaluation procedure, answering the following questions:
   - is the definition valid? (i.e., success of pattern matching)
   - is the definition complete? (i.e., the minimum graph has been reached necessary for the VALIDITY plan)
2. A lexical abstraction evaluation procedure, giving the score of the abstraction level of the words chosen.
3. A text abstraction evaluation procedure, classifying the definition according to a pattern whose results do or do not trigger strategies in the abstraction plan. Both 2 and 3 are necessary for the ABSTRACTION plan
4. A procedure suggesting some cognitive features, based on the form of the definition, to help dialogue continuation (mainly problems in continuation such as misunderstandings or requests to stop; defined in (Daniel, 1991)). Necessary for triggering dialogue strategies.

Both 1 and 2 have been completed and implemented whereas 3 and 4 are still being studied because we have obtained only partial results in psycholinguistic experiments and these results have to be implemented (implementation details in Péry-Woodley (1990); Daniel (1991)). We plan to pursue experiments (as explained in Daniel et al. (1992)) before fixing 3 and 4.

5.2 Evolution of the Student Model

The different records of the Student Model store information on his/her evolution during conversation. The lack of evolution, after a number of sessions, will make the system shut down. A possible alternative would be to provide an explanation, but we have not studied this possibility. Two important elements of evolution are to be studied: the spontaneous cognitive profile and the current cognitive profile.

The *spontaneous cognitive profile* (SCP) computed after the first definition, acting as initial value for the Student Model, is determined as:

PC0 $\leftarrow$ evaluation of first definition, lexical abstraction score of first definition, text abstraction class of first definition, cognitive features of first definition.

The *current cognitive profile* (CCP), during the session, is computed for a current definition, def_i, as follows:

Pfi ← evaluation of def_i lexical abstraction score of def_i, text abstraction class of def_i, cognitive features of def_i

with the assumption that if evaluation and lexical abstraction scores vary greatly from one statement to another, text abstraction class and cognitive features will not differ much. However, this assumption must still be verified.

What has been tested is:

- if evaluation stabilises with a failure of validity plan, then conversation will stop;
- if lexical abstraction score stabilises with a failure of abstraction plan then conversation will also stop, but with the presentation of a 'good abstraction level' definition.

Both are conversational closing strategies (discussed in section 4.2.2).

5.3 The system's beliefs

In our application the roles of both the system and the user are reversed from those when seeking information dialogues. Here, the system's goal has priority, and the student is supposed to be 'a willing and obedient' partner. This has led us to design a model of 'the system's beliefs on its own behaviour with the student'. This rather long formulation intends to describe an unusual model. The system's beliefs constitute a particular 'user model' when the student is viewed as a partner in a Human-machine dialogue. According to well-known techniques in user modelling (Allen & Perrault, 1980; Bunt, 1989), the user's intentions can be extracted from his/her uterrances. Our application, being education-oriented, considers user modelling a 'subtask' of student modelling, aimed at specific dialogue goals. Thus, the system's view of the student as a 'user' is particular and constitutes the system's prime goal; in that sense, *user's intentions* can be translated into '*user's preferential learning ways*'.

This model is fed with the results of the Student Model, in particular the two 'cognitive-modelling-oriented' functions, text abstraction class and cognitive features determination. Let us assume that a student, having been able to propose a correct definition for a concept, is unable to continue when the system investigates the 'subconcepts' involved in the definition of that given concept. After a number of attempts in which no correct answer is provided (persistent failure), the system triggers an *explanation goal*. Explanation could be given as an academic definition; however, the student's failure indicates that an academic formulation is not necessarily appropriate for comprehension. If the student's model purpose is indicate the adequate stage in the educational plan, the beliefs model gives information for the linguistic counterpart of the system, in designing response planning.

The system's beliefs model records three elements: what can the student understand (illustrated or general terminology, misunderstandings, etc.)?; what are the student's preferential ways of expressing things (inferred from the results of text abstraction class)?; what are the student's chances of improvement (inferred from both the dialogue history and the function determining cognitive features)? This model is ruled by pragmatic knowledge about education. For instance, it is useless for the system to use a very general language in explanation, or in issuing its queries, when the student has been interpreted as very 'concrete' in his formulations. While explaining, the system will suggest examples. This model is being studied, and we have not yet reached a point at which results could be given.

5.4 The Dialogue History

A history is necessary in order to be able to compute the results of the session with the student. It helps to know when a persistent failure appears; whether the student's values have changed in any of lexical abstraction procedures, text abstraction class determining; whether the dialogue is going round in circles and so on.

Viewed as a 'notebook' according to the definition in Vilnat (1989) and Vilnat & Nicaud (1992), the Dialogue History serves two purposes: it provides the Dialogue Manager (see Figure 1) with a record of linguistic events (and problems such as ellipses, anaphors, and so forth are dealt with by the linguistic part of the architecture); it provides a personal record of 'profile evolution' in the Student Model and problems such as educational plans and strategies are likely to be better specified or interrupted, depending on the history results. The history has been implemented as a set of records with pointers and has been specified according to the results described in Vilnat & Nicaud (1992).

6 Conclusion

TEDDI is a tutor for definition checking and associated academic knowledge acquisition, closely related to natural language processing. It is based on the idea that the linguistic expression of a concept definition, given by a person, is a good indication of how well the knowledge about that concept has been organised in that person's mind. We believe that this has to be checked first, before the person's problem-solving ability is evaluated. If the definition does not prove to be compatible with a standard provided by the human teacher, then TEDDI assumes a tutor's role, its goal being to coach the student towards an adequate knowledge representation.

The tutor's architecture is designed as a multi-expert system, controlled by a supervisor and possessing cooperating models. TEDDI's special property is to suggest a customised Student Model, which will help to derive the appropriate educational plans. This model is supported, on the dialogue side, by a system's beliefs model, which helps the Dialogue Manager to plan the system interventions in accordance with the student's preferential way of 'expressing knowledge'.

Part of the tutor, corresponding to the Student Model, has already been implemented. The NLP and dialogue aspects will be based on results already achieved in LIMSI mentioned in section 2. We will carry our empirical studies and will perform experiments in educational modelling and planification before undertaking the final computational implementation.

References

Allen, J. & Perrault, C.R. (1980) Analysing Intention in Utterances. Artificial Intelligence, 15, 148–178.

Anderson, J. (1983) The Architecture of Cognition. Harvard University Press.

Barth, B.M. (1987) L'apprentissage de l'abstraction. In: Actualités des Sciences humaines. Paris: Retz.

Brown, A.L., Bransford, J.D., Ferrara, R.A. & Campione, J.C. (1983) Learning, Remembering and Understanding. In: Handbook of Child Psychology: Cognitive Development, vol. 3. New-York: Wiley.

Bunt, H.C. (1989) Information Dialogues as communicative action in relation to partner modelling and information processing. In: Taylor, M.M., Néel, F. & Bouwhuis, D.G. (eds.) The Structure of Multimodal Dialogue. Amsterdam: Elsevier North-Holland.

Carberry, S. (1988) Modelling the user's plans and goals. Computational Linguistics, 14, 23–27.

Daniel, M.P. (1991) Modélisation cognitive de l'apprenant selon son expression langagière. M.Phil. thesis, Université Paris 11, DEA Sciences Cognitives.

Daniel, M.P., Nicaud, L., Prince, V. & Péry-Woodley, M.P. (1992) Apport du style linguistique à la modélisation cognitive de l'élève. Proceedings of ITS-92.

Lesgold, A. (1992) ITS as tools for learning. Invited speech at ITS 92, Montreal.

Nicaud, L. & Prince, V. (1990) TEDDI: An ITS for Definitions Learning. Proceedings of PRICAI'90, 877–882.

Nicaud, L. & Prince, V. (1991a) Modélisation du niveau d'abstraction d'un apprenant dans un tuteur contrôlant l'acquisition de définitions de concepts abstraits. Proceedings of the Conference 'Reconnaissance de Formes et Intelligence Artificielle' (RFIA91) Lyon: AFCET, 1161–1167.

Nicaud, L. & Prince, V. (1991b) Six corpus de définitions d'étudiants recueillis pour la mise en oeuve d'un tuteur intelligent avec une interface en langage naturel. Tech. rept. 91-6. IR LIMSI.

Péry-Woodley, M.P. (1990) Textual clues for user modeling in an ITS. M.Phil. thesis, University of Manchester, Cognitive Science.

Pollack, M.E. (1990) Plans as Complex Mental Attitudes. In: Cohen, P.R., Morgan, J. & Pollack, M.E. (eds.) Intentions in Communication. Cambridge, MA: MIT Press.

Prince, V. (1993) Evaluation de la réponse d'un apprenant en langage natural non restreint. In: Baron, M., Gras, R. & Nicaud, I.F. (eds.) Environnements Interactifs d'Apprentissage. Paris: Eyrolles.

Prince, V., Pernel, D. & Godin, C. (1991) Discourse model & dialogue history. Internal Paper PLUS (A Pragmatics Based Language Understanding System) ESPRIT P5254. EEC.

Sabah, G. (1990a) CARAMEL: A Computational Model of Natural Language Understanding using a Parallel Implementation. Proceedings of ECAI-90, 563–565.

Sabah, G. (1990b) CARAMEL: a flexible model for interaction between cognitive processes underlying natural language understanding. Proceedings of COLING-90, 446–448.

Shute, V.J., Glaser, R. & Raghavan, K. (1989) Inference and discovery in an explanatory laboratory. In: Ackerman, P.L., Sternberg, R.J. & Glaser, R. (eds.) Learning and individual differences. San Francisco: Freeman.

Sowa (1984) Conceptual structures: processing in mind and machine. Reading, Massachussetts: Addison-Wesley.

Vilnat, A. (1989) Relevant responses in man-machine conversation. In: Taylor, M.M., Néel, F. & Bouwhuis, D.G. (eds.) The Structure of Multimodal Dialogue. Amsterdam: North Holland.

Vilnat, A. & Nicaud, L. (1992) Un système de dialogue Homme-Machine: Standia. Proceedings of 'Séminaire Dialogue Inter-PRC CHM-LN'.

Winkels, R., Breuker, J. & Sandberg, J. (1988) Didactic Discourse in Intelligent Help Systems. Intelligent Tutoring Systems, 88, 279–285.

Part 3

Natural Dialogue and Interaction Theory

Dialogue Control Functions and Interaction Design

Harry C. Bunt

Institute for Language Technology and Artificial Intelligence ITK, P.O. Box 90153, 5000 LE Tilburg, The Netherlands, email: H.C.Bunt@kub.nl

Abstract. This paper is concerned with the design of interactive teaching systems from the point of view of dialogue theory. It is argued that *transparency* and *naturalness* are important qualities of a dialogue for the student, helping him to concentrate on the learning task (thanks to naturalness) and to understand his own performance (thanks to transparency). It is argued that these qualities are also important for system design, since they result in student communicative behaviour that is easier to understand.
A concise, non-technical description is provided of the framework of *Dynamic Interpretation Theory*, an approach to dialogue developed especially for information dialogues. On this approach, a dialogue is viewed as a sequence of complex elements of communicative behaviour, intended to change the dialogue context. The elements of communicative behaviour are analysed as simultaneously expressing a variety of 'dialogue acts'; dialogue acts being defined as the functional units used by the speaker to change the context. Based on a fairly detailed analysis of the notion of context which is relevant here, a system of communicative functions of dialogue acts is developed with a focus on 'dialogue control' functions, i.e. functions specific to the management of the interaction.
It is argued that the understanding and application of the notions of transparency and naturalness can benefit from using the concepts of Dynamic Interpretation Theory, and that these concepts are also of importance for the construction and maintenance of adequate student models by the system.

Keywords. Dialogue theory, dialogue act, dialogue control, context analysis, transparency, naturalness

1 Introduction

As interactive teaching systems are concerned with a particular form of systematic, goal-driven interaction, their design could benefit from what we know about the general principles and mechanisms governing natural goal-driven dialogue. We deliberately use the phrase 'natural dialogue' here, rather than 'natural *language* dialogue', since communication in natural settings is not purely linguistic in nature but multimodal; when speaking, people use paralinguistic devices such as laughs, coughs, and sighs, as well as intonation, and nonlinguistic means such as gestures, mimics, and direction of gaze in order to effectively perform the desired communicative functions. The use of these devices depends on properties of the communication situation, properties that range from technical conditions, such as the available media, to social characteristics. For example, in a telephone conversation the technical conditions rule out the effective use of gestures, mimics, and other visual cues; more socially determined is the phenomenon that in an information-seeking dialogue at an information desk one finds little use of laughs and shoulder clapping, compared to the situation of running into an old friend.

The interaction between a computerized teaching system and a student commonly bears some resemblance to telephone conversation in that the system has no visual channel for communication. It also has features in common with the natural information dialogue, in being matter-of-fact and lacking some of the 'social' and emotional aspects of other, less formal forms of interaction, and also in being driven by a well-defined goal which is intended to be reached effectively and economically.

In this contribution we discuss some of the central concepts of dialogue analysis according to a theoretical framework called *Dynamic Interpretation Theory*, developed especially to deal with information dialogues, with an eye to their potential importance in the design of interactive teaching systems.

2 Dialogue theory and teaching systems

One of the most important aspects of designing an interactive teaching system is designing the interaction, i.e. the *user interface*. A user interface is a gateway for two-way information traffic between user and system. We argue in this paper that it can be advantageous for both system and user to develop the user interface on the basis of well-founded general principles for systematic, goal-driven communication:

1. For the user, it can facilitate the development of a communication form that is transparent and natural to him;
2. For the system, it can support the construction and maintenance of adequate student models by the system.

We consider these advantages for each side of the user interface in turn.

2.1 The user side

2.1.1 Transparency

Concerning the advantages for the user, *transparency* of the user interface means that the user is offered a clear view of the system activities concerned with the teaching task. The student can thus understand the system's communicative behaviour in relation to aspects of the teaching and learning. Understanding the system's behaviour may be advantageous for two reasons:

1. It permits the student a view of how the system views the progression of the teaching/learning task; this may help the student to understand his learning performance.
2. It provides the student optimal information as to what kind of actions the system expects him to perform.

The first of these advantages concerns the educational task, which can be facilitated by not only the teacher (system) but also the student (user) having a model of the current state of the task, a model that may be more explicit and more accurate by seeing the system's model than it would otherwise be (notably, on the basis of mere introspection).

To appreciate the second advantage, we should bear in mind that the system's (and the student's) communicative behaviour is the result not only of the teaching/learning task to be accomplished, that is of the application of a *didactic strategy*, but also as the result of applying a *communicative strategy*. Didactic goals have to be turned into communicative goals and communicative effects have to be interpreted in terms of didactic effects, with the result that didactic and communicative planning and interpretation are intertwined; moreover, communicative events by themselves can trigger other communicative events, not directly relating to didactic goals. Transparency of the user interface allows the student to see what motivates the system's communicative actions, and thus to have an optimal understanding of what he is expected to do and why.

2.1.2 Naturalness

The notion of *naturalness* concerns a quality aspect of human-computer dialogue, particularly from the user's point of view. There are two sides to naturalness, relating to the system's and the user's communicative options. We will say that a dialogue has a high degree of naturalness if it has the following two properties.

1. The user's communicative options are natural to him in the sense that he is not put under obligations to perform communicative actions he would find unnecessary or irrelevant, nor does he have to observe restrictions forcing him to wriggle in order to achieve his goals.
2. The system's communicative behaviour is natural to the user: he is not required to explicitly devote effort to interpreting the system's behaviour; it comes to him as obvious.

Naturalness and transparency in a well-designed dialogue go hand in hand and enhance each other; nonetheless, they correspond to different aspects of the quality of a dialogue interface.

Transparency relates to the possibility to 'look through' the communicative behaviour; it deals with the quality of the coupling between communicative activities and the underlying teaching activities (activities such as assessing the correctness of a student response, selecting a test, diagnosing a student error, etc.). Naturalness, on the other hand, is a quality aspect of the dialogue design ensuring that the student is not required to devote specific effort to interpretation and generation of communicative actions; in a natural dialogue, the student can concentrate all his efforts on the learning task. In particular, he can communicate about his learning activities in what is for him the easiest, most natural way.

2.2 The system side

2.2.1 Student modelling

For an interactive teaching system to act sensibly and flexibly, taking the student's behaviour adequately into account, it must base its actions on a model of what the student knows (including any mistaken beliefs), what actions he performs well, etc. In relatively simple teaching systems, system actions are related *directly* to student behaviour rather than via an explicitly constructed student model (*'If student does X, then do Y'*); this relation incorporates implicit assumptions on what the student's behaviour signals about his current state of beliefs and competence, as well as about appropriate actions to perform, given that state.[1] The implicitness of these two kinds of assumption imposes two important limitations on such systems:

1. the system is unable to separately investigate or reason about the student's current state;
2. the system is not in position to derive its teaching actions from the application of a reasoned didactic strategy to the current state of the learning task.

More sophisticated teaching systems build up and maintain an explicit student model, often using the dynamics of this model and its comparison with an ideal student model to determine appropriate continuations of the interaction (see e.g. Sleeman (1984); Sleeman & Brown (1982); Kearsley (1987)) The quality of such systems clearly depends on their success in understanding student behaviour as a basis for constructing a student model. Since good understanding of student interactive behaviour is hardly possible without an analysis process based on knowledge of the general pcinciples for rational and purposeful communicative action, it follows that the system may benefit from principle-based dialogue design in important ways:

- A principle-based dialogue, as opposed to one that is 'engineered' in an *ad hoc* fashion, is more natural to the student as he is allowed to act according to the general principles for communicative action — which is precisely the natural thing to do.
  Increased naturalness of the student's behaviour is advantageous for the system, as it can rely in its analysis of student interactive behaviour on the application of well-tested generally valid principles. The communicative behaviour of the student in a dialogue with an *ad hoc* design is more difficult to interpret, since the student in this case will often have to act in unusual ways, not corresponding to well-established ways of signalling aspects of one's cognitive state. In sum, natural dialogue behaviour is easier to understand and allows for a more generic system design.
- The principles for rational, purposeful cooperative dialogue involve relations between communicative activity and the underlying noncommunicative goals and activities, in this case of the teaching/learning task. More specifically, the

[1] On this approach, often no clear distinction is made between teaching actions and communicative actions, although this distinction is crucial from the point of view of transparent user interface design.

use of particular communicative acts in order to signal the speaker's state of beliefs, disbeliefs, and other attitudes, is governed by general principles allowing the interpreter to reconstruct the relevant aspects of the speaker's cognitive state. These principles and their application to the specific kinds of communicative act, relevant in the interaction between student and interactive teaching system, form an essential part of the basis for constructing and maintaining articulate student models.

Having looked at both the user side and the system side of the advantages of designing the dialogue between the two according to general principles of rational, purposeful cooperative dialogue, we now turn to these principles and the conceptual framework of *Dynamic Interpretation Theory*, in which they are developed.

3 Dynamic Interpretation Theory

In Dynamic Interpretation Theory we view dialogues in an action perspective and communication as a way to bring about changes. Communication leads, first of all, to changes in what each participant knows about the other; we might call this changes in *cognitive context.* However, communication may also affect other aspects of the context besides the cognitive dimension. In the next subsection we briefly look at the various aspects of dialogue context in relation to potentially being affected by communicative activity.[2]

3.1 Dimensions of dialogue context

The term 'context' is used in many different ways in the literature about (linguistic) communicative behaviour, ranging from referring to the preceding text to referring to the goals of the underlying task. What is common to the various uses of the term 'context' is that they all refer to *factors, relevant to the understanding of communicative behaviour.* We believe that these factors can be grouped into five categories: the *linguistic, semantic, physical, social,* and *cognitive context.* Moreover, for each of these 'dimensions' of context we may fruitfully distinguish between *global* aspects, determined at the beginning of the dialogue and remaining constant throughout, and *local* aspects, whose values develop and change as the dialogue proceeds, and which have a momentary significance in determining the continuation of the dialogue. Some of the most important global and local aspects of these context dimensions are the following.

3.1.1 Linguistic context

With the term 'linguistic context' we refer to properties of the surrounding linguistic material (textual or spoken). 'Linguistic' should be taken in a very broad sense here,

[2] Much of the remainder of this section is material from Bunt (1994), and Bunt (1993), in a condensed and simplified form.

including prosodic properties and use of nonlinguistic sounds in the case of spoken interaction, and interpunction, use of italics, graphics, and other visual elements in the case of textual interaction.

Global aspects: what, if anything, the participants have said (or written) to each other on previous occasions; the language they speak;

Local aspects: the surrounding linguistic (textual or spoken) material; raw material as well as relevant properties, detected by its analysis.

3.1.2 Semantic context

The semantic context is formed by the underlying task and the task domain (the objects, properties and relations relevant to the task).

Global aspects: the underlying task as a whole, in particular its overall goal; global characteristics of the task domain;

Local aspects: specific facts in the domain of discourse; the current state of the underlying task.

3.1.3 Physical context

The physical dimension of dialogue context comprises the physical circumstances in which the interaction takes place.

Global aspects: place and time; the question of whether there is eye contact between the participants; the communicative channels that may be used; the presence or absence of third parties;

Local aspects: current availability of communicative channels and, in the case of communication at a distance or through electronic devices, the presence of the partner at the communicative device.

3.1.4 Social context

By 'social context' we mean the type of interactive situation and the roles of the participants in that situation, with their specific communicative rights and obligations.

Global aspects: the 'dialogue genre': the type of institutional setting in which the dialogue occurs, or the type of communicative event that the dialogue represents; the roles of each participant in the event or setting; the relative social status of the participants (employer and employee; teacher and pupil; shopkeeper and customer);

Local aspects: the communicative rights and obligations that each participant has at a given point in the dialogue, including the right or obligation to say something at a given moment, and the right or obligation to perform a communicative act with a specific form and function.

3.1.5 Cognitive context

The 'cognitive context' comprises the participants' beliefs, intentions, plans and other attitudes; their states of processing relating to perception, production, interpretation, evaluation, dispatch (such as carrying out an instruction or fulfilling a request), and their attentional states.

Global aspects: overall communicative goals of each participant; the question which participant, if any, has expert knowledge about the task;

Global aspects: overall communicative goals; the question which participant, if any, has expert knowledge about the underlying task;

Local aspects: current participants' beliefs, intentions, and other attitudes; plans for performing the underlying task and for continuing the communicative task; participants' states of processing; current attentional states; active discourse topics and their relative salience.

Communicative activity in itself cannot accomplish a change in physical circumstances, nor can it directly change the state of the underlying task and its domain of discourse. Directly, communicative actions can only change the linguistic context, the knowledge of an interpreter, i.e. the cognitive context, and local communicative rights and obligations, i.e. local social context. Indirectly, in principle every aspect of the context can be changed through the dialogue. However, some aspects are more readily changed than others. In general, the local aspects of each context dimension change much more readily than the global aspects.

3.2 Local context change

The first and most obvious contextual changes that communicative actions may bring about concern new information becoming available to the hearer, i.e. they change the local cognitive context. We will often speak of hearer *beliefs* rather than *information*, to avoid the connotation with factual truth. The beliefs that a hearer builds up on the basis of his interpretation of the speaker's communicative actions are, initially, always beliefs about the speaker; indirectly, they can relate to any of the context factors listed above. For factual questions and answers, the beliefs generated indirectly in the interpreter concern the underlying task and its domain of discourse, and are thus part of the *local semantic context.* For feedback utterances, the beliefs generated concern *only* the local cognitive context: beliefs about the speaker's processing of the other's previous utterances.

Secondly, a communicative act may create 'social obligations' for the hearer. For instance, when the speaker greets the hearer, he thereby puts a certain pressure on the hearer to respond with a return greeting. Similarly for introducing oneself, for apologizing, and for thanking, where utterances like *"Thank you"* create a pressure to say something like *"You're welcome"*; we refer to such pressures as *'reactive pressures'* (Bunt, 1991).[3] Resolving reactive pressures is one of the basic mechanisms in dialogue, besides acting on the basis of intentions. Creating and resolving reactive

[3] We think this term is more appropriate than other terms found in the literature, such

pressures are ways of changing the *local social context* of the dialogue. Taking turns in a dialogue is also a case of creating and resolving a kind of reactive pressure; when a speaker indicates that he considers his turn to be finished, for example, he puts pressure on his partner to take over.

Finally, and trivially, a communicative action changes the local linguistic context. This aspect of utterances is only rarely addressed explicitly in dialogue; it comes to the fore most clearly when there is uncertainty or disagreement about what one of the partners has contributed to the dialogue (*"Did you say 'Thursday'?"; "But you said... "*).

3.3 Dialogue acts

Communicative behaviour, according to Dynamic Interpretation Theory, consists of expressions of communicative actions, aimed at changing the context in specific ways. We introduce the concept termed *'dialogue act'* as the *functional units used by the speaker to change the context.* These functional units do not correspond to natural language utterances or other instances of communicative behaviour in a simple way, because utterances in general are *multifunctional*, as we will see below. The important point of the stipulation ... *used by speakers* is that we are not considering elementary update functions in a mathematical or computational sense, but update functions *that speakers try to perform* with their utterances. We therefore require every communicative function to correspond to features of communicative behaviour.

The most important aspects of a dialogue act are its *communicative function*, and its *semantic content.* In addition, a dialogue act is expressed through its *utterance form*, which determines the changes to the linguistic context that a dialogue act causes. The idea of the communicative function and semantic content is that the semantic content will have a particular significance in the new context, resulting from the performance of the dialogue act; the communicative function defines precisely what this significance is. The communicative function tells us how to update the context, given the semantic content. In other words, a communicative function is a particular context update function.

For instance, a dialogue act with the utterance form *"Does it rain?"*, the communicative function `yes/no question` and the proposition `it is raining` as semantic content, has the effect of adding the utterance *Does it rain?* to the linguistic con-

---

as communicative 'obligations' (Allwood, 1994); 'adjacency pairs' (Schegloff & Sacks, 1973), and 'preferred organization' (Levinson, 1983). 'Obligation' is slightly too strong, as the 'obligating' utterance does not really *oblige* the addressee to respond in the 'obligated' way. 'Adjacency pair' is also too strong, since the two elements of the pair do not really have to be adjacent, and in fact the second element does not necessarily have to appear at all. 'Preference organization' would seem to have the right kind of strength, but this term belongs to a structural framework of dialogue analysis, where the term 'preference' is not meant to have a cognitive interpretation (Levinson, 1983, p. 332-333). Our approach, by constrast, does have a strong cognitive orientation and considers reactive pressures to be an aspect of the local cognitive context.

text, and creating in the addressee (among other things) the belief that the speaker wants to know whether the proposition `it is raining` is true.

Using the term 'utterance' to refer to everything contributed (said, keyed, ...) by a speaker in one turn, an utterance may correspond to more than one dialogue act, and thus be multifunctional, for several reasons. First of all, an utterance may consist of several sentences or phrases that each express dialogue acts. So dialogue acts often relate to parts of utterances. Moreover, the expressions that carry functional meaning in terms of dialogue acts, typically carry more than one functional meaning simultaneously, due to the following factors.

1. Indirectness. A question like *"Do you know where John's office is?"* may function indirectly as a request to tell where John's office is.
2. Functional subsumption. Some dialogue act types are more specific than others. The promise *"I will come tonight"* is, besides a promise, also an informative statement.
3. Functional multidimensionality. Aspects of performing the underlying task are very often combined in one utterance with aspects of dialogue control.

As an example of functional multidimensionality, consider the utterance *"Thank you"*. Used in reaction to an answer, the utterance not only expresses gratitude but also offers feedback information, since it implicitly indicates that the answer was understood and, by default, accepted; depending on intonation, it may in addition have a turn management function.[4]

Goal-driven dialogues, like instruction dialogues and information-seeking dialogues, by their very nature find their motivation in an underlying task that the participants want to carry out and for which the dialogue is instrumental. Since cooperative communication is an activity with its own rules, rights and obligations, two kinds of elements are commonly found in cooperative goal-driven dialogues: communicative actions motivated by the underlying task, such as instructions, questions, and answers, and actions motivated by the communicative task, such as acknowledgements, attention signals, self-corrections, and turn taking signals. We call these actions *task-oriented dialogue acts* and *dialogue control acts*, respectively. Dialogue control acts, which include feedback acts as an important subclass, have a variety of functions in making communication smooth and succesful, and are largely responsible for the naturalness of a dialogue.

The action view on communication obviously owes much to speech act theory (Austin, 1962; Searle, 1969). We use the term 'dialogue acts' rather than 'speech acts', firstly in order to avoid the association with pure linguistic, in particular spoken forms of communicative behaviour; secondly in order to restrict ourselves to those types of communicative act relevant in *dialogue*; thirdly to avoid the frequent confusion between the use of the term as referring to a linguistic token ('locutionary act', in Austin's original terminology), or as referring to an abstract action denoted by the linguistic token ('illocutionary acts'), or as referring to both together. The dialogue act concept is not situated at the linguistic level of words and phrases, but

[4] On multifunctionality see also Allwood et al. (1990).

at the level of formal operations changing local aspects of the context. The idea to view communicative acts as context-changing operations has occasionally been suggested in the speech act literature (e.g., Gazdar (1981); Isard (1975)), but has not been worked out to the point of formalization. In Bunt (1989; 1990) a proposal has been formulated for formalizing task-oriented dialogue acts in information dialogues in terms of context changes, context construed as the pair of the cognitive states (consisting of intentions and strong and weak beliefs) of the two participants. In what follows we will focus on dialogue control acts ('DC acts', for short), which have received much less attention in the speech act literature and in earlier work in Dynamic Interpretation Theory.

3.4 Dialogue control acts and task-oriented dialogue acts

In terms of context change, we can make the distinction between task-oriented and dialogue control acts precise as follows. Every dialogue act, when interpreted by the addressee, changes the cognitive context; the difference between a task-oriented ('TO-') dialogue act and a DC act is that the former only causes further changes in the *semantic context*, whereas a dialogue control act may cause changes in the social or physical context, but does *not* affect the semantic context.

Note that the TO/DC-distinction is primarily one between classes of dialogue acts, not between communicative functions. Although there are indeed communicative functions specific for dialogue control purposes, a dialogue control act can also be formed by combining a communicative function, seemingly typical for a task-oriented dialogue act, such as `inform`, with a semantic content relating to some aspect of context other than the semantic dimension, as in *"I didn't hear you"*.

We will refer to all those dialogue acts, formed with a communicative function concerned with information-seeking and information-providing, as 'informative dialogue acts', and we call their communicative functions 'informative functions'. Depending on their semantic content, these acts are TO-acts or DC-acts.

Among the dialogue control acts, of particular interest are those that have communicative functions specific for dialogue control purposes. We call such functions *'dialogue control functions'* or *DC functions.*

3.5 Dialogue control functions

To identify a communicative function, we have two criteria that follow immediately from the definition of dialogue act:

- the function defines a specific way of changing the context, which is elementary in the sense that this context change cannot be obtained through a combination of dialogue acts with other communicative functions;[5]

[5] This aspect of the definition of a communicative function can be expressed in terms of the preconditions for appropriate use of a dialogue act with that function; see further Bunt (1989) and Beun (1989).

– specific features of communicative behaviour (notably linguistic or paralinguistic features of utterance forms) are used to refer to the context change defined by this communicative function;

This leads to the following clusters of DC functions in information dialogues, clusters being defined on the basis of similarity w.r.t. their associated utterance features or update operations, or both. Three major clusters of dialogue control functions are those concerned with *feedback, discourse structuring*, and *interaction management*. Each of these is subdivided into smaller clusters. For each cluster we provide a general description of the function and some characteristic utterance forms.

Feedback functions: Feedback is the phenomenon that a dialogue participant provides information about his processing of the partner's previous utterances. This includes information about perceptual processing (hearing, reading), about interpretation (direct or indirect), evaluation (agreement, disbelief, surprise,...), and dispatch (fulfillment of a request, carrying out a command,...), and possibly other aspects of local cognitive context.
Feedback is either 'positive' or 'negative' in the sense that negative feedback messages report difficulties in processing, whereas positive messages report successful porcessing.[6]
Feedback is realized through a large variety of specific linguistic, paralinguistic and nonlinguistic means. Positive feedback is for instance expressed linguistically by *"OK"* or *"Yes"*, paralinguistically by *"Mmm"*, *"Ah"* and the like, and nonlinguistically by nodding.

Discourse structuring functions: Dialogue acts with a discourse structuring function serve to indicate the speaker's view of the state of the dialogue (local linguistic context) and his plan for how to continue.
Utterance forms: expressions for (sub-)dialogue delimitation include *"OK then"*, *"Now then"*, *"Something else"*; devices for topic introduction like *"Now concerning John,... "*, *"As for John,... "*.

Interaction management functions:

Turn management functions: Dialogue acts with a turn management function put a pressure on the addressee to continue the dialogue, in the case of a `turn-giving` act; to allow the speaker to continue in the case of a `turn-keeping` act, and so on.
Turn-giving and turn-keeping functions are seldom expressed linguistically; paralinguistic means such as intonation are more commonly used for this purpose. In the case of human-computer interaction, common nonlinguistic devices are the use of the `RETURN` key and of cursor prompts or auditory prompts.

Time management functions: Direct communication, be it in spoken form or through a keyboard, is subject to conventions for how quickly one is supposed to continue the dialogue when one has the turn. This is especially

[6] See also Bego (1994) on this subject.

important when there is no visual feedback, as in a telephone conversation. Here, a prolongued silence creates uncertainty as to whether there is contact.

When a speaker needs more time before continuing the interaction than is conventionally allowed, for instance because something has to be looked up, he should therefore issue a warning or a request for patience (*"Just a moment"*), or use 'fillers'.

Contact management functions: These functions are meant to establish and to check contact; if they reach the partner and elicit a response, they thereby establish contact and thus change the local physical context.

A prototypical expression is here *"Hello?"*, for checking contact. *"Yes"* and other expressions of positive feedback can be used to confirm contact.

Own communication management functions:[7] These functions update the addressee's information about the speaker's ongoing speech production processes. Hesitations, self-corrections and apologies for (speech) errors are the main functions in this class. These acts typically do not call for any reaction from the partner. A persistent hesitation can, however, have the additional function of inviting the partner to take the turn.

Typical expressions of these functions are *"eh"*; "... *I mean*...".

Social obligations management functions: Subclasses within this class are functions concerned with introducing oneself; with greeting (welcome or farewell); with apologizing; and with thanking.

All functions in this class have two variants, an 'initiative' one and a 'reactive' one, borrowing terminology from the 'Geneva school' of discourse studies (e.g., Moeschler (1989)). The initiative variant creates a reactive pressure which can be resolved by the corresponding reactive act. The same expressions can often be used for either purpose (like *"Dag"* in Dutch, or *"God Dag"* in Danish).

Figure 1 represents this system of communicative functions.

3.6 Principles for the use of dialogue acts

Goal-driven communication is generally believed to be governed by general principles, such as those concerned with rational action, with ethical behaviour, or with cooperation (e.g., Grice (1975); Searle (1969); Allwood (1976; 1994); Bunt (1993)). These principles apply partly at the level of observable communicative behaviour, such as Grice's principle of manner. For the most part, however, these principles address a more abstract ('illocutionary') level, such as the Gricean principles of relevance, quality, and quantity. In the framework of Dynmaic Interpretation Theory, this more abstract level is the level of context change, and the various principles translate to context-based rules for the use of dialogue acts.

In Bunt (1993) we have discussed some of these principles. The 'Dialogue Act Licensing Principle' formulated there says, in essence:

[7] term borrowed from Allwood et al. (1992).

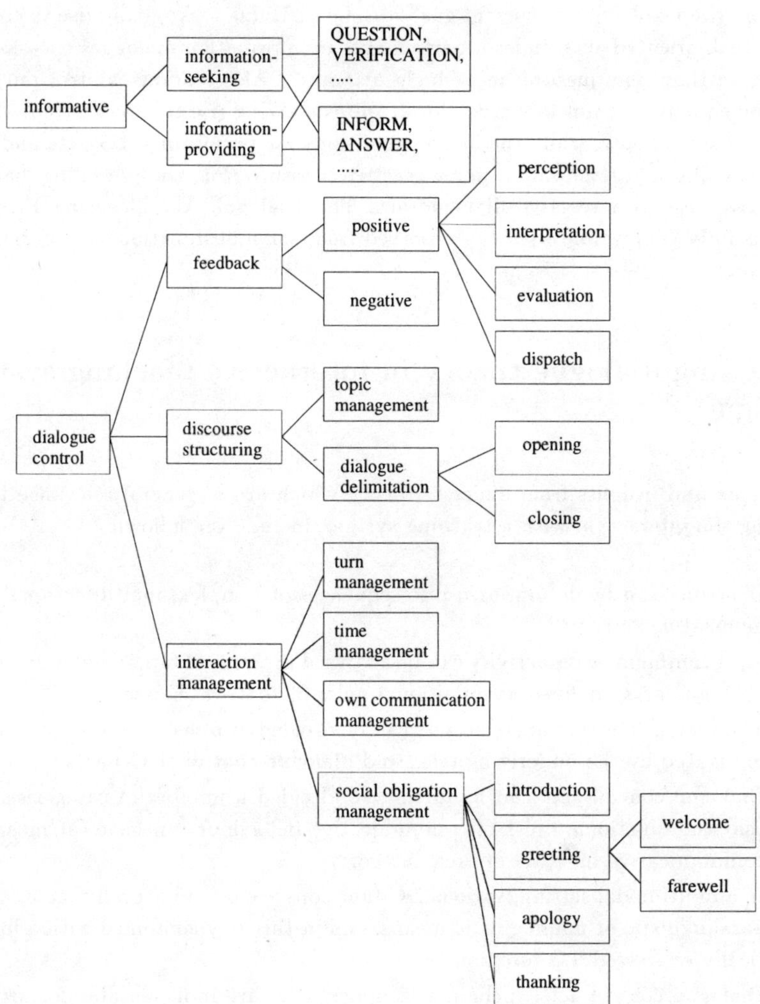

Fig. 1. Dialogue control functions.

Every dialogue act should either:

- contribute to achieving a current goal of the local semantic context (the underlying task);
- contribute to achieving a dialogue control purpose;
- relieve the speaker from an existing reactive pressure.

This principle can be seen as summarizing the reasons for performing a dialogue act. Note that the principle may allow various dialogue acts to be licensed: there may be more than one, equally current goal of the underlying task, giving rise to equally many task-oriented acts. Indeed, participants in information dialogues occasionally ask more than one question in a single utterance. Also, various control purposes may be equally relevant in a given local context, giving rise to alternative dialogue control acts. Finally, while the above conditions for performing TO-acts and DC-acts may obtain, at the same time a reactive pressure from the preceding dialogue may give rise to a reactive dialogue act. The Dialogue Act Licensing Principle is thus fully compatible with the observed frequent multifunctionality of dialogue utterances.

4 Using dialogue theory in interactive teaching system design

Concepts and insights from dialogue theory which are of general relevance to designing the interaction with a teaching system, include the following:[8]

- Dialogues can be decomposed into sequences of complex, multifunctional communicative activity;
- Such communicative activity can be analysed in terms of functional units, called 'dialogue acts', defined as intentional units of context change;
- The various kinds of dialogue acts can be divided into task-oriented (TO-) acts, motivated by the underlying task, and dialogue control (DC-) acts;
- Dialogue control acts can be further subdivided a number of categories, such that the functional units of communicative behaviour can have (at most) one communicative function in each category.
- In a multimodal setting, various DC-functions are often naturally realized with paralinguistic or nonlinguistic means, and in this way combined with a linguistically expressed TO-function;
- Dialogue control acts, including feedback acts, are indispensable for securing successful communication and, more generally, for making a dialogue natural.

Specific contributions from dialogue theory to the design of interactive teaching systems we believe to be in the following two areas:

1. The design of the system-student interaction in a way which is natural and transparent to the student;
2. The design of student models taking into account not only the student's position with respect to the learning task, but also his 'interactive state', i.e. his interactive goals and his assumptions about the ongoing interaction.

[8] See also Bouwhuis & Bunt (1994) for the use of concepts from language technology and dialogue theory in the domain of computer-assisted teaching of reading skills.

4.1 Transparency and naturalness

In the introduction, we have argued the importance of both the transparency and naturalness of the dialogue. Transparancy enables the student to understand how he is doing with respect to the learning task, and to understand how the system's communicative behaviour relates to that. To achieve transparency, it is essential to clearly distinguish TO-acts form DC-acts and to express TO-acts in such a way that it is clear to the student how the communicative goal of the dialogue act relates to a goal of the underlying teaching/learning task. A simple, effective instrument can be to *describe* this relation explicitly (see below).

Naturalness has two functional sources, corresponding to the two possible motivations of a dialogue act: a task-oriented goal or a dialogue control goal. The naturalness of a TO-act is determined by the rationality of the underlying task structure. An instruction dialogue, for example, where the user is instructed how to assemble a bicyle, would be most unnatural if after dealing with the attachment of one of the pedals, the dialogue would switch to the attachment of the front light and subsequently turn to the second pedal.

The naturalness of dialogue control acts, by contrast, is determined by conventions of cooperative communication. These conventions can be expressed as preconditions for the appropriate use of DC acts, these preconditions being primarily conditions on the local cognitive and social context, also taking global social and physical context properties into account (differences in global social context often corresponding with differences in style of communication.) Appropriate use of DC-acts often determines the feel of naturalness of a dialogue.

Finally, a third aspect of naturalness concerns the form, rather than the function of communicative behaviour. Every global social context has certain standard ways of expressing dialogue acts, and the behaviour is 'natural' only if it conforms to those standards. We will return to this issue below.

4.2 Student modelling

Using the concepts of Dynamic Interpretation Theory, student modelling has two sides: a task-oriented side and a dialogue control side. Interpretation of the student's communicative behaviour will, in all cases, provide information to the system about the student's communicative goals. This is 'simply' a matter of recognizing the preconditions of the dialogue acts expressed in the behaviour.

For TO-acts, having an underlying task-related motivation, the system should in addition derive the task-related aspects of the student's cognitive state. For instance, if the student gives an incorrect answer to a question, the system may infer that the student doesn't know how to perform the operations needed for finding the answer to the question. Further diagnosis may then be needed to determine the precise nature of the student's problem, possibly leading to new communicative goals.

For DC-acts, the situation is often different in the sense that a DC act by the student once being dealt with by the system is no longer of interest, and does not lead to persistent changes in the student model. This is for example the case with perception- or interpretation feedback (*"Did you say/mean Thursday?" "Yes."*). In other cases, however, the situation is very similar to that of TO-acts, for instance, if the student responds being unable to answer a certain question, the system may infer that the student doesn't know how to perform the operations needed for finding the answer to the question. Fine distinctions between types of DC-act, as made above in Figure 1, are essential here.

4.3 New forms of interaction

When new forms of human-computer interaction are designed, innovative features in user interfaces are almost invariably *innovative expressions of 'old' communicative functions.* Entirely new functions are hardly ever invented, and that's perhaps just as well, since these would not be easy to understand for untrained users. What does happen, of course, is that frequent users of a program label certain combinations of functions, for instance by programming a function key. Some examples of innovative 'computer forms' of dialogue control functions from the schema in Figure 1 are the following, where we indicate the location in Figure 1 by means of a dotted path.

- Prompts on the screen, like '>' or '$':
  dialogue-control.interaction-management.turn-management.
- Rectangle, gradually filling up:
  dialogue-control.interaction-management.time-management.
- Messages like `'MS-DOS>'` or `'This is the interactive YP System'`:
  dialogue-control.interaction-management.social-oblig-management.
- Graphics in email communication, like ':-)':
  dialogue-control.feedback.positive.evaluation.

The use of dialogue control communicative functions to enhance the transparency and naturalness of the dialogue is illustrated in the following fragment of an instructional dialogue:

`System:` Now what is the result of substituting this value?
`Student:` (*gives correct answer*)
`System:` OK. Next problem. Mr Jones has bought ...

In the first two sentences of its second turn, the system performs the following communicative functions:

1. Positive evaluative feedback on the preceding student response.
   (Implicitly also positive feedback concerning the system's processing of that response.)
2. Dialogue structuring. The second sentence makes clear that what follows is a new problem, not a continuation of the previous problem. As usual in dialogues that have a tight coupling with an underlying task, the dialogue structure often reflects the structure of the task (see Grosz & Sidner (1986)). This utterance therefore adds to the transparency of the dialogue.

3. Turn management. The first two sentences in this turn in no way elicit a response from the student; rather, it is understood that the system is going to continue the dialogue (turn keeping').

It is quite clear that the interaction in this example would be much less transparent and natural to the student if the system, in its second turn, would omit the first two sentences. If the system would immediately present the next problem, without any feedback or dialogue structuring, the student could at most guess that his previous answer is correct, and that the system present a new exercise, rather than elaborate on the previous one. The student would, however, face a great deal more uncertainty and potential confusion.

4.4 Concluding remarks

We hope to have shown that the use of concepts and insights from dialogue theory may be useful for designing the interaction with a teaching system. In particular, use of the 'dialogue act' concept as a local context-changing operation, combined with an articulate notion of local context and with an understanding of what drives a dialogue forward as expressed in the 'Dialogue Act Licensing Principle', may be helpful in

- designing a user interface which is natural and transparent to the student. This is not only in the interest of the student, but also in the interest of the system, as it supports student communicative behaviour that is easier to understand.
- supporting the construction and maintenance of a student model by the system.

References

Allwood, J. (1976) Communication as Action and Cooperation. Gothenborg monographs in Linguistics, 2. University of Göteborg: Department of Linguistics.

Allwood, J. (1994) Obligations and options in dialogue. THINK Quarterly, 3(1), 9–18.

Allwood, J., Nivre, J. & Ahlsén, E. (1990) Speech Management: On the Non-Written Life of Speech. Nordic Journal of Linguistics, 13, 1–48.

Allwood, J., Nivre, J. & Ahlsén, E. (1992) On the Semantics and Pragmatics of Linguistic Feedback. Journal of Semantics, 9(1), 1–26.

Austin, J.L. (1962) How to Do Things with Words. Oxford: Clarendon Press.

Bego, H. (1994) A context change model of feedback acts. In: Makkai, V. (ed.) The 1993 LACUS Yearbook (forthcoming).

Beun, R.J. (1989) Declarative questions in information dialogues. Ph.D. thesis, Tilburg University. Also available as ITK Research Report 13.

Bouwhuis, D.G. & Bunt, H.C. (1994) Interactive instructional systems as dialogue systems. Verhoeven, L. (ed.) Functional Literacy. Theoretical Issues and Educational Implications. Amsterdam: John Benjamins.

Bunt, H.C. (1989) Information Dialogues as communicative action in relation to partner modelling and information processing. In: Taylor, M.M., Néel, F. & Bouwhuis, D.G. (eds.) The Structure of Multimodal Dialogue. Amsterdam: Elsevier North-Holland.

Bunt, H.C. (1990) DIT – Dynamic Interpretation in Text and Dialogue. Kálmán, L. & Pólos, L. (eds.) Papers from the Second Symposium on Logic and Language. Budapest: Akademiai Kiadó.

Bunt, H.C. (1991) Dynamic interpretation and dialogue theory. Taylor, M.M., Néel, F. & Bouwhuis, D.G. (eds.) Proceedings of the second Venaco workshop on Multimodal Dialogue, Acquafredda di Maratea (forthcoming).

Bunt, H.C. (1993) Dialogue Management through context dynamics. In: Black, W.J. & Bunt, H.C. (eds.) Computational Pragmatics vol. 2, Abduction, Belief and Context. London: Pinter Publishers (forthcoming).

Bunt, H.C. (1994) Context and dialogue control. THINK Quarterly, 3(1), 19–31.

Gazdar, G. (1981) Speech act assignment. In: Joshi, A.K., Webber, B.L. & Sag, I.A. (eds.) Elements of Discourse Understanding. Cambridge (UK): Cambridge University Press, 64–83.

Grice, P. (1975) Logic and Conversation. In: Cole, P. & Morgan, J.L. (eds.) Syntax and Semantics: Speech Acts. Vol. 11. New York: Academic Press, 41–58.

Grosz, B.J. & Sidner, C.L. (1986) Attention, Intention and the Structure of Discourse. Computational Linguistics, 12(3), 175–204.

Isard, S. (1975) Changing the context. In: Keenan, E.L. (ed.) Formal semantics of natural language. Cambridge, UK: Cambridge University Press.

Kearsley, G.P. (ed.) (1987) Artificial Intelligence and Instruction; Applications and methods. Reading, Mass.: Addison-Wesley.

Levinson, S.C. (1983) Pragmatics. Cambridge: Cambridge University Press.

Moeschler, J. (1989) Modélisation du dialogue. Paris: Hermès.

Schegloff, E. & Sacks, H. (1973) Opening up Closings. Semiotica, 7(4), 289–327.

Searle, J.R. (1969) Speech Acts. Cambridge: Cambridge University Press.

Sleeman, D.H. (1984) UMFE: A user modelling front end subsystem. Heuristic Programming Project HPP-84-12. Department of Computer Science, Stanford University, Stanford, CA.

Sleeman, D.H. & Brown, J.S. (1982) Intelligent tutoring systems. New York: Academic Press.

The Role of Feedback in a Layered Model of Communication

David A. Waugh[1] and Martin M. Taylor[2]

[1] Andyne Computing Ltd.,552 Princess St., Kingston Ontario, Canada, K7L 1C7,
email: daw@andyne.on.ca
[2] DCIEM, Box 2000, North York, Ontario, Canada, M3M 3B9,
email: mmt@ben.dciem.dnd.ca

Abstract. The 'Layered Protocol' (LP) model of interaction has evolved over the last decade from its initial status as a design method for human computer interaction (Taylor et al., 1984) into a general theory of communication between any two 'intelligent' partners (Taylor, 1987; Taylor, 1988a; Taylor, 1988b; Taylor, 1989; Taylor & Waugh, 1992), and is now seen as an extension of a general theory of psychology called Perceptual Control Theory (e.g., Powers (1973)). Perceptual Control Theory is a general basis for psychology that has special relevance for people acting in a real, as opposed to a laboratory world. The layers in LP theory represent the transmission of *virtual messages* by Protocol Nodes (PNs) at different levels of abstraction. LP theory includes: a hierarchy of Protocol Nodes; all PNs have the same structure; communication proceeds simultaneously at many levels of abstraction from high-level goals down to muscular actions and back up from sensory mechanisms to high-level goals; each PN at any abstraction level has its own lexicon, syntax, semantics and pragmatics; feedback is integral to the functioning of each PN; progress of an interaction is a function of each dialogue separately and simultaneously at each PN; and communicative acts are determined by recursive belief states at each PN. This paper discusses how the provision of appropriate feedback is the most important requirement for designing successful, learnable human-computer interactions.

Keywords. Human-computer interaction, layered protocol theory, perceptual control theory, feedback, learning, dialogue

1 Introduction

Some issues must be addressed in any theory of interaction. We consider them in the context of three different, but related, theories: Norman's theory of action, which involves multiple levels of processing from goals to actions and back to the evaluation of the results in relation to the goals (Norman, 1986); Layered Protocol (LP) theory, a general theory of communication that involves multiple layers of abstraction, both for transmitting and receiving information (Taylor, 1987; Taylor, 1988a; Taylor, 1988b; Taylor, 1989; Taylor & Waugh, 1992); and Perceptual Control Theory (PCT), a theory of psychology about humans in a real world (Powers, 1973). The three theories evolved independently, but are all related. Each can be viewed as a theory of interaction, dealing with people acting purposefully in a variable world.

The word 'Action' implies a one way flow of activity from a person to the various artifacts encountered in the pursuit of a goal, but this is a misleading view. More properly, events in the world affect perception of the state of the world and the ongoing discrepancy between this state and the goal state generates actions that change the perception so as to reduce the discrepancy. The flow is a continuous feedback loop. Feedback from action through perception to action is how the variability of the world is detected and countered. The centrality of feedback in interaction is the focus of this paper.

We include Norman's rather than other theories of action (e.g., Miller, Galanter & Pribram (1960); Card, Moran & Newell (1983)), because it bears the closest resemblance to some of the key concepts embodied in LP theory. Powers' PCT is included because it offers a powerful, if often misunderstood, approach to explaining and predicting human performance in the world. LP theory can be seen as a specialized version of PCT adapted to modeling human communication in particular. This paper provides a brief description of Norman's theory of action, a description of the significant aspects of PCT, and a description of those aspects of LP theory that show in a layered model the importance of feedback and the ramifications of learning new interactions, such as new software packages.

1.1 Norman's Theory of Action

Norman (1984; 1985; 1986) has developed a cognitive model of activity for users of computer systems. This model was initially described as a progression of four stages a user proceeds through during any interaction, but has evolved to include seven stages, as sketched in Figure 1. The seven stages are:

1. establishing the goal,
2. forming the intention,
3. specifying the action sequence,
4. executing the action,
5. perceiving the system state,
6. interpreting the system state, and
7. evaluating the system state with respect to the goals.

Norman's model is based on the idea that people think in terms of goals and intentions, which are psychological variables, whereas a computer requires specific mechanistic actions to manipulate symbolic or physical variables. Between these concepts there is a large gap, which Norman calls the Gulf of Execution. Similarly, to evaluate whether various actions had the desired effect, the user must perceive the computer's display of the state of the various symbolic or physical variables and interpret them in terms of the original goal, a psychological variable. This distinction can be seen as a second large gap, which Norman calls the Gulf of Evaluation.

Each of the three stages on the execution side in Norman's model requires a translation from a more abstract to a less abstract description. This translation is

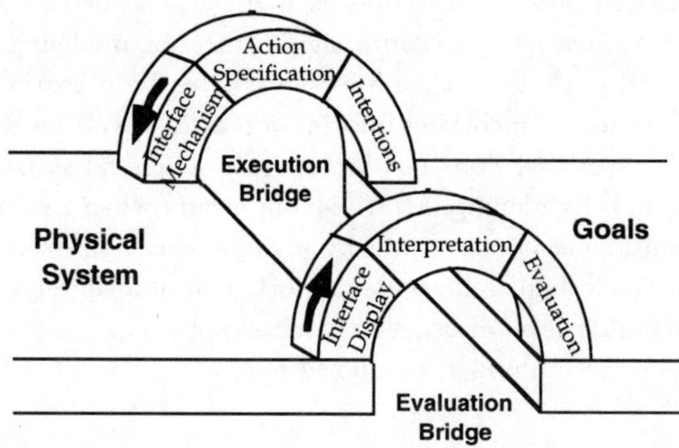

Fig. 1. Norman's stages of interaction. Adapted from (Norman, 1986).

not one to one but one to many, as any one goal may be represented as multiple intentions. Each intention, in turn, can be achieved by multiple actions. Each action can be a complex action, requiring multiple complex motor functions. The machine interprets each of the user's actions, calculates the effect on the system state, and displays the result for the user to perceive on the evaluation side of Norman's model, through the available sensory mechanisms. Perceptions are transformed into a more abstract form that the user can interpret. Interpretations are then evaluated against the original goals. Each level of transformation is a many to fewer operation, implying a reduction of information as the interpretation proceeds through the levels of abstraction. The effect of each intention is evaluated to determine what level of success has been achieved. Norman describes the role of ongoing *feedback* as being central to this evaluation process.

1.2 Layered Protocol theory (LP) and Norman's model

LP theory is a theory of communication between cooperative partners.[1] LP theory, like Norman's, is based around the concept of multiple levels of abstraction, both for the transmission and for the reception of information. LP theory, like Norman's, is based around the concept of using feedback to evaluate the approach to a goal, which in the case of LP is communicative.

Norman's model, however, implies some things that LP denies. In particular, it implies a sequential and discrete model of action within each stage where one in-

[1] Cooperation in dialogue implies commitment from each partner. It has been argued that it is impossible for natural communication to occur with a machine partner because a machine cannot make a commitment (Winograd & Flores, 1986). We however, view commitment by a machine partner as an attribute of interface design that is the responsibility of the designer. The designer's task is to create an interface that gives the effect of a cooperative partner, while making explicit the obvious restrictions such a limited partner may bring to the interaction.

tention must complete before another begins, whereas LP is inherently parallel and continuous. It also implies that each stage must be complete before the next stage is begun, which has particular significance for modeling the reception of information. LP theory asserts the importance of 'early interpretation' which allows for the immediate use of incoming information at all levels on a continual basis.

Norman's model does not incorporate a central construct of LP theory: multiplexing and diviplexing. Multiplexing occurs when two or more higher level layers are simultaneously supported by a single common lower layer. Diviplexing occurs when a single higher layer is supported by multiple lower layers. To recreate the original higher-level messages, the receiving partner must demultiplex a multiplexed message or recombine a diviplexed one.

1.3 Perceptual Control Theory (PCT)

PCT asserts that behaviour is the control of perception. This is quite a different perspective on human psychology than the traditional views that behaviour is a response to stimuli, or that actions are cognitively planned. PCT asserts that all behaviour is purposeful, the purpose being to bring perceptions to desired states, and that the purpose is internal, not externally driven. The concept of 'perception' in PCT is not restricted to low level sensory mechanisms, but includes all states a living organism can detect and affect, regardless of the level of abstraction.

Like Norman's model and LP, PCT is based on a hierarchy of abstractions. Discrepancies between goal states and actual states (called 'error') are detected at all levels of abstraction. High-level error gives rise to high-level actions that determine lower-level goals. These lower level goals are compared with corresponding lower-level perceptions to drive lower-level actions, and so on down to motor functions and sensory inputs. This process of error correction is done concurrently and continuously at all levels of abstraction.

The term Elementary Control System (ECS) is given to a unit that produces from its sensory input a perceptual signal that it compares to a reference level, to give an error signal from which it generates output signals (see Figure 2). A hierarchy of ECSs is formed by connecting the perceptual signal from possibly many lower ECSs to the sensory input of a higher level ECS. The amplified error signal that forms the output from a higher ECS is connected to the reference level input for possibly many lower ECSs. Each output from a higher ECS connected to the reference input of a lower ECS has an associated polarity which determines whether the error in the higher ECS leads to an output of the same or the reverse sign. Within the hierarchy, connections can be from any ECS to any other, provided no cycles are formed in which a perception or action depends on itself.

Each ECS, whatever its level in the hierarchy, is said to be controlling for a particular level (its reference level) of a specific perception. If the incoming perception does not match the required reference level, the error is transformed into an output appropriate to bring the perception closer to the reference signal. The effect of the output must be to change the percept so as to reduce the error. A loop with this property is said to demonstrate negative feedback, and is required for the stable control of perception. The correct polarities of the various links are either built-in by evolution or are learned in response to interactions with the world.

A central tenet of PCT is that the system operates with continuous as opposed to discrete signals. This single concept of continuity separates PCT from other control theories of interaction, in particular TOTE (Miller et al., 1960), which imply that the result of an action is evaluated after each discrete action is finished.

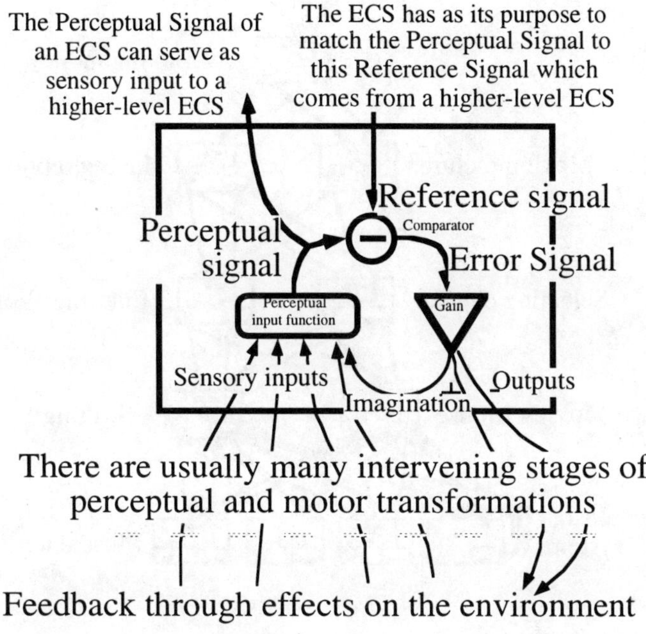

Fig. 2. The basic elements of an Elementary Control System (ECS). An 'imagination' loop, which is conceived to include some aspect of a world model, permits the ECS to assess what might happen if it were to act in the world.

An example of multiple parallel distinct perceptions at different levels in PCT would be the perception of the flexing of finger muscles to hit the correct keys on a keyboard, the perception of typing the correct set of words to create a desired phrase, the perception of forming an adequate set of phrases to complete an argument, the perception of structuring together a set of arguments to form a report, the perception that a report is being written to satisfy a deadline, the perception of meeting a deadline to retain a job, the perception of retaining a job to earn money, etc. Part of a similar example is shown in Figure 3. Each of these perceptions must be controlled simultaneously if the desired results are to be obtained.

Controlling for a perception does not always mean that the reference level will be met. The world may not be so kind as to permit it and two references in ECSs at the same level may be impossible to satisfy simultaneously (e.g., you can't eat your cake and have it, too). Rather, controlling for a perception implies that resources will be devoted to reducing the error as far as possible in the ECS that controls the perception. Each ECS seeks minimal error, but the actions of other ECSs sometimes frustrate that goal. Because of the continuous nature of each ECS, the goals being pursued by an individual are changing continuously at most levels of the hierarchy, in response to disturbances in the world that affect perceptions at all levels.

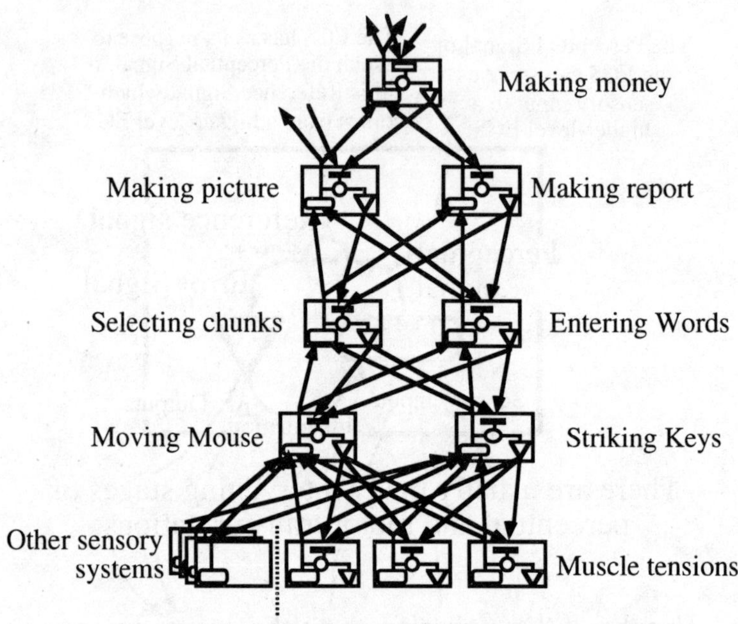

Fig. 3. Some Elementary Control Systems arranged in a hierarchy, showing what is 'done' in order to 'do' something else.

In particular, when an individual encounters and uses artifacts in the environment, the various goals in the hierarchy are modified not only by the encounter itself, but during the encounter. We change our goals as we learn what possibilities and limitations are embodied in the design of a particular artifact. Norman also makes this point with respect to the evolution of goals from interaction with artifacts, with particular reference to his ideas about cognitive artifacts (Norman, 1991). Engel and Haakma (1993) make the same point in quite a different way, within the LP framework. They call it *E-feedback* (for 'Expectation feedback'), by which the artifact signals to the user its capabilities, and assists the user in developing the partner models that allow for effective communication.

2 Communication

What does it mean to *communicate* with an inanimate object such as a screwdriver? This at first seems odd even to ponder, but it makes sense if we regard communication and interaction as varying on a scale from reactive to proactive. A screwdriver simply reacts, with no internal goals or reference levels, although its design imposes some definite intrinsic limitations. A human partner can be totally proactive, in which case communication proceeds with the two independent partners attempting to achieve separate distinct goals, which might even conflict.

Interaction with a human partner is based on belief. One partner attempts to cause the other's beliefs to change until they correspond to a desired belief state. What one wants to believe about the partner's beliefs is analogous to the PCT reference level (to Norman, a psychological variable; we call it the *Primal Message*) and what one does believe about the partner's beliefs is analogous to the PCT percept. The difference is analogous to the PCT error, and the message is the PCT action output that is used to reduce the error.

In LP, communication in its general form assumes that the two partners are intelligent, which by our definition implies three independences:

– independence of design,
– independence of sensing mechanism, and
– independence of action.

Independence of design means that the processes for generating and interpreting communication are not identical in both partners; independence of sensing mechanism means that neither partner can be certain of what the other is actually sensing; independence of action means that neither partner is certain as to all of what the other partner is doing at any given moment. Given these conditions, neither partner can guarantee the reception of a particular message by the other, regardless of the amount of redundancy used to encode it. In contrast, in machine communication using network protocols (Tanenbaum, 1981), the decoding process of one machine is an exact inverse of the encoding process of the other machine, which means that any level of error in the communication link can be corrected if the message is encoded with sufficient redundancy and delay. Two intelligent entities attempting to communicate cannot rely on redundancy and must resort to feedback to ensure the correct reception of a message.

2.1 Feedback

Feedback in communication is used to indicate either that a message has been correctly received or that a problem exists. If a problem exists, the originator can either attempt to correct the message or retract the original goal to communicate that message. The timing of feedback plays a crucial role with respect to the stability of any interaction. If feedback is delayed, has too strong an influence on the forward channel, or changes too rapidly, it can cause the connection to become unstable. The output comes to depend on the characteristics of the feedback connection, which, taken to an extreme, can lead to a situation in which none of the original information gets through. This problem can be avoided if the attempt to resolve a possible error is distributed over multiple levels of abstraction, each having successively longer periods (Taylor, 1989). Some lower level errors are allowed to pass uncorrected to higher levels, but the imperfect lower-level interpretation is done quickly. Most corrections of the remaining errors can be made at a higher level of abstraction, slowly but more stably.

Interaction between two partners proceeds with neither partner devoting conscious effort to the simultaneous maintenance of multiple levels of abstraction. The two partners focus on the interaction at some particular level of abstraction. The level of abstraction in focus is a function of the goals of the partners and the similarity between the partners' communicative abilities. If the two partners are old friends (or enemies) who share a great deal of experience and previous communication, they can communicate with very little effort, taking advantage of accurate mutual models to enhance operations at the lower levels, as in the example in Figure 4.

Partner Models
in fiction

Professor Moriarty, "The Napoleon of Crime," visits Sherlock Holmes, the two having never previously met...

Moriarty: You evidently don't know me.
Holmes: On the contrary, I think it is fairly evident that I do. Pray take a chair. I can spare you five minutes if you have anything to say.
M: All that I have to say has already crossed your mind.
H: Then possibly my answer has crossed yours.
M: You stand fast?
H: Absolutely!

(A. Conan Doyle: *The Final Problem*)

Fig. 4. If two partners have good models of each other, much can be communicated in few words.

At the other extreme, two partners who have never communicated before can do no better than to use protocols based on common cultural models, assuming they are from the same cultural background. The worst case would be two partners who do not speak the same language, between whom a dialogue often becomes a task of exploration to find the correct word, aided by the use of culture-independent gesture.

Using the terminology of Winograd and Flores (1986), it is only when a communicative breakdown occurs that one needs to be aware of multiple levels. A breakdown in communication may occur at any of the levels of abstraction in use during a dialogue. When the breakdown occurs at a level different from the one currently in focus (Grosz & Sidner, 1986), both partners must synchronize the shift in attention to effect an efficient repair. If the listener responds with "What did you say?", it does no good for the talker to repeat a word, if what the listener wants to know is how that piece of the argument fitted with what went before. A similar effect can be observed in non-communicative behaviour, which also occurs at many levels of abstraction, only one of which is normally thought of as what one is 'doing' at any moment. Which level that is (e.g., pressing a doorbell, getting into a house, visiting a friend, trying to arrange a loan) depends on a variety of factors, prominent among which is the current ease of attaining the desired result (Vallacher & Wegner, 1987).

In the area of Human Computer Interaction (HCI), improved interfaces may be designed if the designer has explicit awareness of multiple levels of communication. A designer can attempt to anticipate breakdowns at each of the levels that could be used in an interaction. Appropriate feedback requires that the correct level be identified and that the nature of the breakdown in the level also be identified.

2.2 LP and General Protocol Grammar

To understand feedback as it is used in LP theory, we must examine the structure of a protocol. Each transmitting protocol transforms 'virtual messages' at a higher level of abstraction into virtual messages at a lower level of abstraction. The messages are virtual because they have no physical or tangible properties, yet they exist. Each virtual message is transformed through successively less abstract layers until an actual physical message is sent, such as a sound wave. The recipient of a virtual message reconstructs it by transforming the physical messages into higher level, more abstract messages.

The transformation of messages in LP theory from higher to lower levels of abstraction implies some form of encoding of the higher level messages. This 'encoding' is not a simple invertible mapping like the coding that occurs in encryption, but a transformation of a kind that depends largely on the beliefs the originator and recipient hold about each other's beliefs and intentions. 'Coder' is the term we give to the process in a protocol that performs the necessary transformation from higher to lower abstraction level. The recipient of the message has a corresponding 'Decoder' process.

To ensure correct reception, the protocol relies on feedback from the recipient to the originator of the message. To generate the feedback, the recipient has a coder process, and to interpret it, the originator has a decoder. Finally, a third component of each protocol, the 'Model', supports both Coder and Decoder. The triad of coder, decoder and model form the basic structural unit of LP, the Protocol Node (PN).

An analogy can be made between a Protocol Node in LP and an Elementary Control System in PCT, as shown in Figure 5. The coder corresponds to the output function, the decoder to the perceptual input function and, possibly most significant, the model to the comparator.

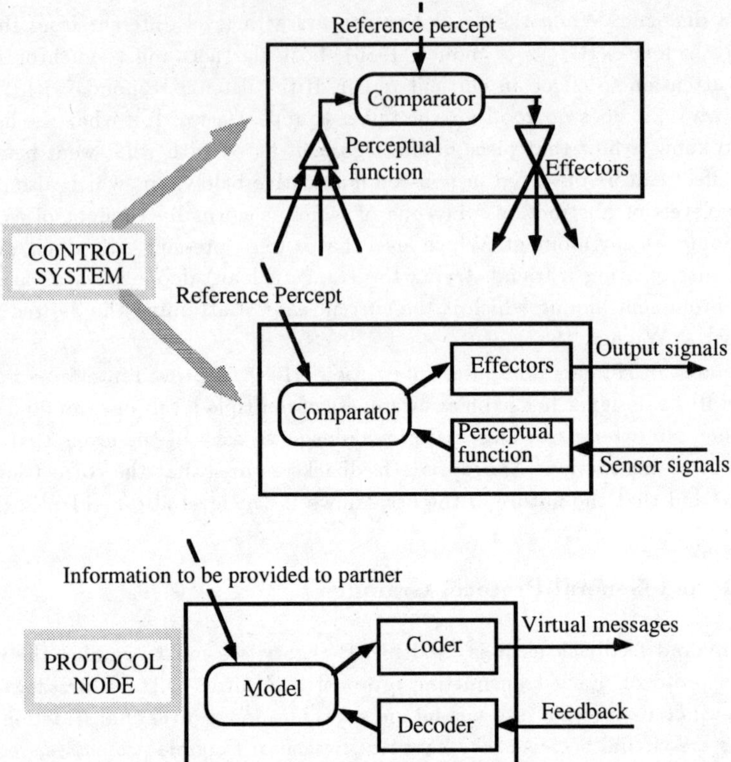

Fig. 5. The analogy between an Elementary (or Structured) Control System and a Transmitting Protocol Node. The two representations of a control system are functionally identical, the lower one being rotated to show its relation with a protocol node.

2.2.1 Protocol loops

It is natural to extend the hierarchy of Elementary Control Systems (ECSs) in PCT or the Protocol Node in LP theory to include a mirror image of the hierarchies representing the elements in the world corresponding to the controlled percepts or beliefs. If we do so in LP, we find a series of virtual circuits connecting the corresponding elements in each partner. These virtual circuits, suggested in Figure 6, represent all of the concurrent dialogues during any interaction between two partners.

In LP terms, the Protocol Node at one end of any loop is either a transmitting or a receiving Protocol Node. The virtual circuit between a transmitting and the corresponding receiving node forms what is known as a protocol loop. Sometimes we ignore its loop function and treat it as a support channel for higher level messages.

A dialogue using this protocol loop begins when the transmitting node in one partner is requested to transmit a message. The receiving node in the partner attempts to receive this message, providing feedback as necessary. The course of each dialogue in each protocol loop has the appearance of a series of exchanges between the partners, which we model using a General Protocol Grammar.

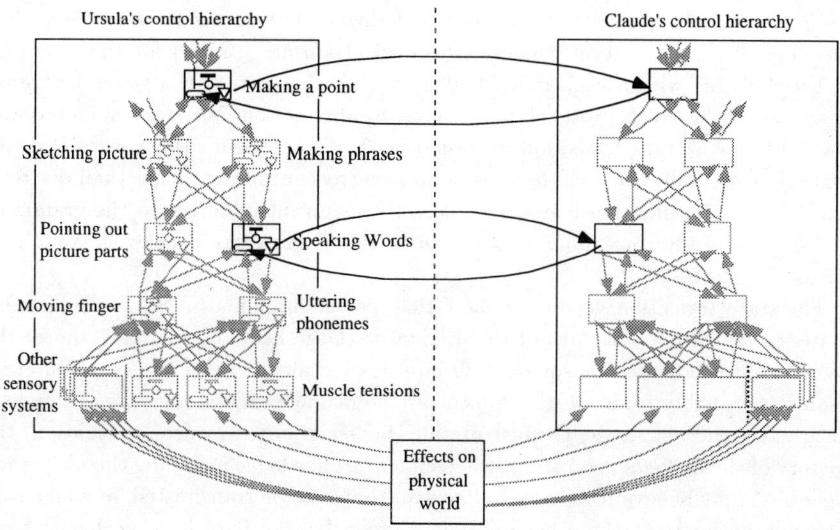

Fig. 6. A control hierarchy in one partner and the corresponding control hierarchy in the other partner. Here, User and Computer could be substituted for Ursula and Claude respectively. A loop is formed between the matching nodes in each partner.

2.2.2 General Protocol Grammar

Many kinds of feedback can occur within a protocol, depending on the current status of the dialogue within the protocol as modeled by each partner. It has been argued that a grammar to model conversation is impossible due to the unbounded number of different situations that must be taken into account (e.g., Good (1989)). These arguments tend to be based on two problems that do not arise within LP. First, the arguments refer to global descriptions of the dialogue, whereas LP considers a set of distinct levels. Secondly, they depend on the pragmatic situation of the dialogue partners which can only be seen by each partner individually.

We agree that a global grammar of dialogue is impossible, partly because it depends on the interactions among layers, which depend greatly on the mutual modelling performed by the partners, and largely because such a grammar must take an 'absolutist' standpoint, providing a description that could, in principle, be determined by a non-participant in the dialogue — a 'third party'. We think such an absolutist view cannot be found, and hence no global dialogue grammar is possible. The General Protocol Grammar of LP is a local grammar that models the succession of views taken by one of the participants on the progress of a message within a single protocol and is thus not vulnerable to arguments such as those of Good.

Our grammar is not intended to represent all possible communicative acts and the rules for their composition and interpretation, but rather is a mechanism to model the kinds of belief transitions during the dialogue that occurs for a single virtual message. We use the term 'General Protocol Grammar' (GPG) for the grammar of the dialogue within each individual protocol. The grammar is general because it applies within each protocol at any level of abstraction. We start by describing the GPG as a state transition grammar with discrete transitions from state to state, but we really view the process of dialogue as continuous rather than discrete. The discrete formulation is easier to describe as an introduction to the grammar. Discussions of the continuous version can be found elsewhere (Taylor & Waugh, in Press).

The state transition version of the GPG, shown simplified in Figure 7, includes states in which it is the turn of the originator (O, indicated by circles) and of the recipient (R, indicated by squares). O initiates a dialogue by acting on an internal request (probably from a higher protocol) to encode a virtual message. To encode accurately and efficiently, O must use any beliefs about the current situation, the history of the dialogue, and about the recipient's knowledge including the recipient's beliefs. O may believe R already to know all that is to be transmitted, in which case O sends nothing. At the other extreme, O may believe R to have no background knowledge, which means that O must teach R the necessary material before R can correctly receive the current virtual message.

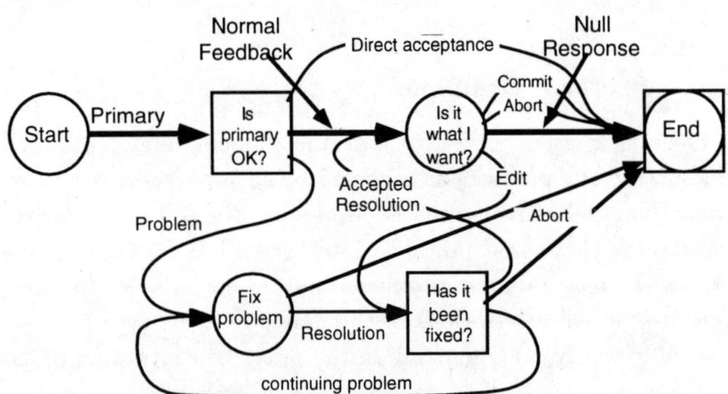

Fig. 7. A sketch of the General Protocol Grammar, showing the major arcs. Circles represent stages at which the originator of the primary message must do something; squares represent stages at which the recipient of the primary must do something.

Once O has determined an initial encoding of the virtual message, O transmits what is known as the 'Primary Message'. The primary represents a first attempt by

O to communicate the virtual message. It causes a transition from "Start" to "Is primary OK?", at which point it is the turn of R to do something. R determines if what is received is likely to be what O intended R to receive and sends an appropriate message as feedback.

The form of the feedback from R to O depends on how R assesses the situation with respect to the correctness of the message transmission and of O's probable beliefs about it. Each arc in the GPG can be instantiated in multiple forms. If R believes the message to be OK, R uses the Normal Feedback arc, but how R instantiates it can vary. If R believes the message received to be correct and that O believes R to have received the message correctly, then R sends a null feedback message (i.e., does nothing). If R believes the message reception to be OK, but that O may doubt the correctness of the received message, R uses informative feedback to verify the reception of the message. Similarly, if R believes that the message received and interpreted is correct, but that O misstated it, R may use feedback to correct O. However it is instantiated, the Normal Feedback arc effects a transition to "Is it what I want?", at which point the Originator may choose to modify what was sent initially, based on the feedback obtained from R.

R may use arcs in the grammar other than 'Normal Feedback'. An arc commonly used is the one labelled 'Problem' in Figure 7. This arc is taken by R if the Primary Message did not seem to be plausibly correct, because of an erroneous reception by R or an ambiguous initial attempt by O.

The beliefs of the two partners may differ about the current state of the dialogue. O could believe the message to have been correctly received and interpreted by R, resulting in a perceived current state of "Is it what I want?", whereas R might at the same time believe the message to be erroneous and the current state to be "Fix problem?". O would have misinterpreted R's instantiation of the 'Problem' arc as being 'Normal Feedback'.

Each partner must model not only what is happening in the dialogue, but also the view taken by the partner, which includes the partner's self view. This recursive nature of partner models could, in principle, go to infinite depth, but we believe for practical purposes it only goes three levels deep (from a different point of view, so does Beun (1991)).

A problem with the state transition representation is that each of the beliefs held by either partner may not be certain, either in belief or in disbelief. These issues are discussed in depth in Taylor and Waugh (in press). Here it is only necessary to point out that these beliefs change continuously throughout the transmission of messages and they change concurrently at all protocol levels. The discrete GPG is a useful tool for examining what the partners might be doing and for designing interfaces, but the continuous change of beliefs is more accurate and must be considered in dealing with multi-layer interactions.

3 Learning

Many issues face a user learning a new software package, even on a familiar computer platform. We assume the user needs the computer and the package to accomplish some task. As a subtask, the user must learn enough of the software's abilities to understand how to address the main task. What is learnable might include everything about the computer system, but for the sake of simplicity, we assume the user already understands enough about the system to view the learning subtask as restricted to the particulars of the software package itself. The user brings some previous experiences of other software packages on this platform to the task, and that knowledge will bias some expectations of how the new one works. This bias may either help or hinder the progress of the user, depending on how closely the software package matches other packages for the same platform. For example, the Macintosh has an explicit set of interface design guidelines allow the user to use the same low-level protocols on many packages. The user can begin communication with a new software package at a level higher than with the first few packages encountered on the same platform.

One theory of learning to interact with a new software package assumes that the learner needs an adequate conceptual model (Norman, 1986; Riley, 1986). In the absence of effective high-level protocols, such a model may be necessary, but when effective feedback is available, the need for initial clarity and understanding of the conceptual model might be relaxed. Rapid feedback at the appropriate level of abstraction could allow a user to explore and to see the effects of each exploratory move. Active exploration is often more effective than passive observation or instruction in allowing a learner to develop an effective conceptual model of a complex system (Carroll, 1990). So, even if no conceptual model is explicitly presented to a user, one may be formed rapidly through the proper use of feedback.

Learning by exploring is likely to increase the user's retention (Carroll, 1990). In PCT terms, the user is developing an effective subhierarchy of ECSs with percepts, references, and output connections appropriate to the task. This is good if the conceptual model so developed is correct, bad if it is wrong. Adequate user modelling may allow the system to monitor the user's construction process. In effect, the system and the user would engage in an interactive process to construct and verify the model. Even if the user is provided beforehand with an explicit conceptual model, it must be tested, using feedback in situations relevant to the main task. In particular, the various partial tasks a user attempts must use operations that relate to the conceptual model and to the mechanisms afforded by that model. This process is inherently interactive.

Most interfaces provide consistent results to consistent actions, at least at the lower levels of abstraction. At these levels the user does not have to pay much attention to feedback, because of the predictability of the system's response. The user can concentrate on any protocol (or intention in Norman's terms) that is not passing its messages easily. The system may provide unexpected responses, because it has not been designed to recognize the user's intention. More interestingly, the user may not be exactly sure of what the intention is. This latter case is especially true during learning by exploration; "*lets see what happens if I do this...*" The intention to learn something is well formed, but not only is the expectation as to the system's response not well formed, it may not exist at all.

4 Conclusion

We have tried to provide a conceptual sketch of the Layered Protocol Theory of interaction between intelligent partners. LP theory is concerned with modeling the process, as opposed to the content, of communication between two partners. We compare it with two other layered approaches to human interactions with the world, Norman's action theory and Powers' Perceptual Control Theory. Regardless of which of the three layered models described in this paper is chosen to model and design interaction, feedback plays a crucial role. Feedback is the central mechanism that ensures efficient communication between any two partners, regardless of their level of sophistication. A good conceptual model is crucial to many forms of learning and understanding. Using the feedback possible at many levels of abstraction, a user can develop such a conceptual model through exploration, perhaps more readily than through reading a manual or the instruction of a teacher.

References

Beun, R.J. (1991) Moves in Dialogue. Presented at the second Venaco workshop on The Structure of Multimodal Dialogue, Aquafredda di Maratea, Italy, September 1991.

Card, S.K., Moran, T. & Newell, A. (1983) The psychology of human-computer interaction. Hillsdale, NJ: Lawrence Erlbaum Associates.

Carroll, J.M. (1990) The Nurnberg Funnel. Cambridge, MA: The MIT Press.

Engel, F.L. & Haakma, R. (1993) Expectation and feedback in user-system communication. International Journal of Man-Machine Studies, 39, 427–452.

Good, D.A. (1989) The viability of conversational grammars. In: Taylor, M.M., Néel, F. & Bouwhuis, D.G. (eds.) The Structure of Multimodal Dialogue. Amsterdam: Elsevier North-Holland.

Grosz, B.J. & Sidner, C.L. (1986) Attention, Intention and the Structure of Discourse. Computational Linguistics, 12(3), 175–204.

Miller, G.A., Galanter, E. & Pribram, K. (1960) Plans and the Structure of Behavior. New York: Henry Holt.

Norman, D.A. (1984) Stages and levels in human-machine interaction. International Journal of Man-Machine Studies, 21, 365–375.

Norman, D.A. (1985) Four stages of user activities. Shackel, B. (ed.) INTERACT '84: First conference on human-computer interaction. Amsterdam: North-Holland.

Norman, D.A. (1986) Cognitive engineering. In: Norman, D.A. & Draper, S.W. (eds.) User centered system design: New perspectives in human-computer interaction. Hillsdale, NJ: Lawrence Erlbaum Associates.

Norman, D.A. (1991) Cognitive artifacts. In: Carroll, J.M. (ed.) Designing interaction — Psychology at the Human Computer Interface. Cambridge, UK: Cambridge University Press.

Powers, W.T. (1973) Behavior — the control of perception. Chicago: Aldine.

Riley, M.S. (1986) User Understanding. In: Norman, D.A. & Draper, S.W. (eds.) User centered system design: New perspectives in human-computer interaction. Hillsdale, NJ: Lawrence Erlbaum Associates.

Tanenbaum, A.S. (1981) Network protocols. Computing Surveys, 13, 453–489.

Taylor, M.M. (1987) Layered protocols in voice interaction with computers. In: Information management and decision making in advanced airborne weapons systems, AGARD Aeromedical panel CP-414. Neuilly sur Seine: AGARD.

Taylor, M.M. (1988a) Layered Protocols for computer-human dialogue. I: Principles. International Journal of Man-Machine Studies, 28, 175–218.

Taylor, M.M. (1988b) Layered Protocols for computer-human dialogue. II: Some practical issues. International Journal of Man-Machine Studies, 28, 219–257.

Taylor, M.M. (1989) Response timing in Layered Protocols: a cybernetic view of natural dialogue. In: Taylor, M.M., Néel, F. & Bouwhuis, D.G. (eds.) The Structure of Multimodal Dialogue. Amsterdam: Elsevier North-Holland.

Taylor, M.M. & Waugh, D.A. (1992) Principles for integrating Voice I/O in a complex interface. AGARD Avionics Panel Symposium CP-521: Advanced Aircraft Interfaces: the machine side of the man-machine interface, Madrid, Spain. Neuilly sur Seine: AGARD.

Taylor, M.M. & Waugh, D.A. (in press) Dialogue analysis using Layered Protocols. Presented at the Esprit Pragmatics in Language Understanding Systems workshop, Sorrento, 1991.

Taylor, M.M., McCann, C.A. & Tuori, M.I. (1984) The Interactive Spatial Information System. DCIEM report 84-R-22. Defence and Civil Institute of Environmental Medicine, Downsview, Canada.

Vallacher, R.R. & Wegner, D.M. (1987) What do people think they're doing? Action identification and human behavior. Psychological Review, 94, 3–15.

Winograd, T. & Flores, C.F. (1986) Understanding computers and cognition: A new foundation for design. Norwood, NJ: Ablex.

Communicative Action and Feedback

Joakim Nivre

Department of Linguistics, University of Göteborg, Renströmsparken, S-41298 Göteborg, Sweden, email: joakim@ling.gu.se

Abstract. The concept of *feedback* is potentially relevant to the understanding of any sort of goal-directed behavior or action. In this paper, the general cybernetic notion of feedback is applied to the domain of *communicative action*. An attempt is made to define the information space for feedback in communication by distinguishing a set of *feedback dimensions* and a set of *constraints* relating these dimensions to each other. It is argued that these dimensions, as well as the constraints relating them, can be derived from the general concept of feedback combined with a certain analysis of communicative action. In addition, a formal model of the space of feedback information is presented. Finally, implications for the design of dialogue systems are briefly discussed.

Keywords. Feedback, communicative action, dialogue systems

1 Introduction

The concept of *feedback* originates in cybernetics (Wiener, 1948; Ashby, 1956), where it refers to the processes by which an agent receives information about the consequences of her own actions, information which is used by the agent in guiding her further actions in order to achieve her goals. Since communication involves goal-directed action, several people have argued that the concept of feedback should be relevant for the study of communication in one way or the other.[1] As an example of this, Jens Allwood has in a series of papers developed a notion of *linguistic feedback*, which refers to the intentional use of special linguistic mechanisms (expressions such as 'yes' and 'no', mechanisms such as repetition and reformulation, etc.) in order to give the interlocutor information about whether and how a preceding utterance has been perceived, understood and reacted to attitudinally (Allwood, 1988a; Allwood, 1988b; Allwood et al., 1992).

In the present paper, I am not interested in this restrictive notion of feedback in communication. Instead, I want to combine the general cybernetic notion of feedback with a certain analysis of communicative action in order to study the general information space for feedback in communication. Starting from the analysis of communicative action, I will distinguish a set of *feedback dimensions* and a set of *constraints*, which give rise to a structured space of feedback information. Although the main purpose of the paper is theoretical, towards the end I will try to say something about the way in which this is relevant to the design of dialogue systems and other systems involving user modelling.

[1] For an overview of some of this work, see Allwood (1988a; 1988b) and references herein.

2 Communicative action

As a point of departure for the discussion of feedback in communication, I will present a simple analysis of *communicative action*.[2] The analysis is meant to be compatible with most mainstream approaches to communicative action and I hope that most of the things I shall have to say in this section will be fairly uncontroversial.

2.1 Evocative goals

First of all, I assume that the primary goal of a communicative act performed by an agent a (the *sender*) is to evoke a certain cognitive state s in another agent b (the *receiver*). The term 'cognitive state' should be taken in a fairly broad sense. It may refer to a belief about the world, a belief about the sender's belief about the world, an intention to perform a certain action, a certain emotion or attitude, etc. The goal to evoke such a state in another agent I will call the *evocative goal* of a communicative act.

For example, suppose that in a certain situation I utter the sentence 'shut the door' intending to get my addressee to shut a particular door. In this case, my evocative goal is to get the addressee to form the intention to shut the door. In a similar fashion, if I nod my head in response to a question as to whether I am hungry, thereby intending my addressee to believe that I am hungry, then my evocative goal is to get my addressee to believe that I am hungry (at the relevant point in time).

2.2 Signalling goals

Evocative goals are not by themselves sufficient to characterize communicative acts. Such acts typically also involve the goal to make the evocative goal manifest to the receiver. In the following, I will call this the *signalling goal* of a communicative act.[3]

The signalling goal is instrumental in relation to the evocative goal, i.e., it is (partly) by making the evocative goal manifest to the receiver that the sender can hope to achieve the evocative goal (Grice, 1957; Grice, 1969). However, the sender need not be explicitly aware of the signalling goal as such. It is rather a precondition for the achievement of the evocative goal which may but need not be focused by the sender.

Returning to the earlier examples, we may note that when I utter the sentence 'shut the door' with the goal of getting my addressee to form the intention to shut a particular door, I mean to achieve this goal (partly) by getting my adressee to

[2] In the (partly stipulative) usage adopted here, the term 'communicative action' is a mass noun referring to the intentional activity involved in communication, and the term 'communicative act' (see below) is a count noun denoting discrete instances of such activity.

[3] The term 'signalling' is borrowed from Allwood's (1976) analysis of communicative sender activity.

realize that I want her to react in this way (although I may not be fully aware of this at the time of the utterance). Similarly, when I nod my head in response to a question as to whether I am hungry, thereby intending to induce a belief in my addressee to the effect that I am hungry, a precondition for the achievement of this goal is normally that I get my addressee to believe that I want her to believe that I am hungry.[4]

2.3 Utterance goals

In addition to the evocative goal and the signalling goal, a communicative act normally also involves an instance of perceptible behavior and the goal that this instance of behavior should be perceived in a certain way by the receiver (i.e., that it should be perceived by the receiver as an instance of a certain *type*). A goal of the latter kind I call the *utterance goal* of a communicative act.

The utterance goal is instrumentally related to the signalling goal in a way which is similar to the relation between the signalling goal and the evocative goal. The achievement of the utterance goal (i.e., an identification by the receiver of the sender's behavior as belonging to the intended type) is normally a prerequisite for the achievement of the signalling goal (which in its turn is a prerequisite for the achievement of the evocative goal). Again, it is important to note that the utterance goal need not always correspond to a conscious intention on the part of the sender.

For instance, when I utter the sentence 'shut the door', intending my addressee to believe that I intend her to shut the door, I attempt to achieve this goal (partly) by producing an acoustic signal which my addressee should perceive as an instance of the English sentence type 'shut the door', although I may not be consciously aware of this at the time of the utterance. Similarly, if I nod my head as an affirmative answer to a *yes/no*-question, it is essential for the success of my communicative act that my addressee perceives my head movement as an instance of the (conventional) gesture type 'head nod' (and not as, say, a nervous tic).

2.4 Hierarchies of goals and acts

Let us summarize the analysis of communicative action sketched so far. I have claimed that a communicative act with sender a and receiver b is connected with (at least) the following three goals:

1. The *evocative goal* to evoke a certain cognitive state s in b.
2. The *signalling goal* to get b to believe that a intends to evoke s in b.

[4] Some theorists have suggested that it is not sufficient that I intend my addressee to believe that I intend her to believe that I am hungry. I must also intend her to believe that I intend her to believe that I intend her to believe that I am hungry (see, e.g., Strawson (1964)). Others have suggested that I must intend it to be *mutually* believed that I intend her to believe that I am hungry (see, e.g., Schiffer (1972)). I will not go into these vexed and complex issues here. I will assume that the present characterization of communicative acts provide at least necessary if not sufficient conditions.

3. The *utterance goal* to get b to believe that a produces an instance of behavior belonging to a certain type t.

Moreover, I have claimed that these goals are instrumentally related in the following way:

- Achieving the utterance goal is a way for a to achieve the signalling goal.
- Achieving the signalling goal is a way for a to achieve the evocative goal.

This means that if the communicative act is altogether successful (in the sense that the ultimate goal of evoking s in b is achieved) then, first of all, a successfully performs the act of getting b to believe that a produces an instance of behavior of type t;[5] let us call this a successful *utterance act*. Secondly, the successful utterance act *causally generates* a successful *signalling act*, i.e., the act of getting b to believe that a intends b to believe that a intends to evoke s in b.[6] Thirdly and finally, the successful signalling act causally generates a successful *evocative act*, i.e., the act of getting b to believe that a intends to evoke s in b *causally generates* the act of evoking s in b. In the fully successful case we thus have a *hierarchy of acts*, where each higher act is *causally generated* by the next lower act.[7]

For example, if I succeed in getting my addressee to form the intention to shut a particular door by uttering a token of the sentence 'shut the door', then (normally) this implies

- that I successfully perform the utterance act of getting my addressee to believe that I have produced a token of the sentence 'shut the door',
- that the successful utterance act causally generates the signalling act of getting my addressee to believe that I intend her to intend to shut the door, and
- that the successful signalling act in its turn causally generates the evocative act of getting my addressee to form the intention to shut the door.

In the same way, if I succeed in getting my addressee to believe that I am hungry by nodding my head in response to her question as to whether I am hungry, then this successful evocative act is causally generated by the (successful) signalling act of getting my addressee to believe that I intend her to believe that I am hungry, which in its turn is causally generated by the (successful) utterance act of getting my addressee to believe that I have produced a token of the gesture type 'head nod'.

---

[5] This belief need not be fully conscious on the part of b, just like a's intention to evoke this belief need not be fully conscious on the part of a.

[6] For the notion of *causal generation*, see Goldman (1970); see also Pollack (1990). Roughly speaking, to say that an act x causally generates another act y is to say that the result of y is caused by the result of x (given appropriate background conditions).

[7] It should be pointed out that it is a controversial issue in the philosophy of action whether there are several *acts* involved here, or a single act with several possible *act descriptions*. The former position is taken by Goldman (1970), whereas Anscombe (1981) and Davidson (1982) are proponents of the second view. For a similar controversy in the theory of *speech acts*, see Allwood's (1977) discussion of Austin (1962) and Searle (1969).

However, communicative acts are not always fully successful. For all kinds of action, we must distinguish between the *attempt* to perform an act—which depends only on the presence of the right kind of intention (or goal)—and the *successful performance* of the act in question—which also requires that the intention gets realized (that the goal is actually achieved).[8] It is because of the (potential) discrepancy between attempts and successful performances that *feedback* is essential to all kinds of action, communicative action being no exception.

3 Feedback in communication

A *cybernetic agent* is an agent that receives *feedback information* about the consequences of her own actions and uses this information to determine her further actions in order to achieve her goals. Assuming that communicative agents can be regarded as cybernetic agents, I will now try to characterize the type of feedback information that is relevant in relation to communicative acts.

3.1 Dimensions of feedback information

According to the analysis outlined above, a communicative act is normally connected with at least three different goals on the part of the sender: the *evocative goal*, the *signalling goal*, and the *utterance goal*. Since each of these goals may or may not be achieved as a result of the sender's activity, information about their outcome constitutes relevant feedback information for the sender as a cybernetic agent. I will say that the issue of whether such a goal is achieved defines a *feedback dimension* in relation to the communicative act in question. For a communicative act involving a sender a, a receiver b, a cognitive state s, and a behavior type t, we then have the following three feedback dimensions:

1. The *evocative dimension*, defined by the issue of whether b enters state s.
2. The *signalling dimension*, defined by the issue of whether b comes to believe that a intends to evoke s in b.
3. The *utterance dimension*, defined by the issue of whether b perceives a's behavior as an instance of type t.

Given this notion of feedback dimension, we can define the notion of *feedback information* (in relation to a given communicative act) as that information which is available to the sender about the currently relevant feedback dimensions. For each of these dimensions, the information available may fall into three categories, which I will call *positive*, *negative*, and *neutral*, respectively:

Positive: The information entails that the relevant goal is achieved.

[8] As a further complication, we sometimes speak of acts being performed unintentionally, i.e., with the right kind of result but without the characteristic intention. I will largely ignore this complication in what follows, and discuss only cases where the characteristic intention is in fact present.

Negative: The information entails that the relevant goal is *not* achieved.

Neutral: The information is inconclusive (i.e., it entails neither that the relevant goal is achieved nor that it is not achieved).

For example, suppose that I utter the sentence "shut the door" with the evocative goal of getting my addressee to form the intention to open a particular door. If my addressee responds by shutting the door, this will normally entail that she has perceived my utterance as a token of the sentence "shut the door", that she has taken this as evidence that I intended her to shut the door, and that she has in fact formed this intention. In other words, her act of opening the door will be a source of positive feedback with respect to all three feedback dimensions discussed above. If, on the other hand, she responds by asking me which door I mean, then the feedback information is presumably positive with respect to the utterance dimension (since she has correctly perceived the sentence "shut the door"), but negative with respect to the two other dimensions (since she has not yet understood my precise communicative intention let alone formed an intention to shut the door).[9]

However, we must also remember that the sender's goals are not all of equal standing, but are ordered in a hierarchy where the achievement of a lower goal is a precondition for the achievement of every higher goal. This means that positive feedback on the highest possible dimension in the hierarchy—in this case the evocative dimension—will normally have the highest priority. Only if the feedback on a higher dimension is negative or neutral will feedback on lower dimensions become relevant.

For instance, as long as I get my addressee to shut the door for me, I am normally not interested in whether my utterance goal and signalling goal have been achieved properly. By contrast, if my addressee reponds by asking me which door I mean and it is clear that the evocative goal has not been fully achieved, then it becomes important to know at which level in the hierarchy there is positive feedback information, i.e., how far my original goals have been achieved, because this will influence my further actions in order to achieve the original evocative goal.

3.2 Constraints on feedback information

Three feedback dimensions (evocative, signalling, utterance) and three information categories (positive, negative, neutral) together yield a total space of feedback information with 3^3 possible cases. However, since the feedback dimensions are not independent of each other but hierarchically ordered, there are important *constraints* on the information space, and the real number of possibilities is normally smaller than 3^3.

First of all, if the feedback is *negative* on some dimension d, then it is normally *negative* on every dimension *higher* than d (where the evocative dimension is higher than the signalling dimension, which is higher than the utterance dimension). For

[9] It is important to note that feedback information, in the sense intended here, is independent of whether the addressee (or any other agent) *intends* to convey the information. I will return to this issue in section 3.3 below.

example, if I try to get my addressee to form the intention to open a particular door by uttering the sentence "shut the door" and if the information available to me entails that my addressee has not perceived my utterance as a token of the sentence "shut the door", then I can normally conclude that I have not succeeded in getting her to believe that I intend her to intend to open the door in question. And from this I can normally also infer that I have not succeeded in getting her to form the intention to open the door either.

The above constraint relates negative feedback on lower dimensions to negative feedback on higher dimensions. However, there is also an opposite constraint that relates positive feedback on higher dimensions to positive feedback on lower dimensions. In other words, if the feedback is *positive* on some dimension d, then it is normally *positive* on every dimension lower than d. For example, if I nod my head in response to a question as to whether I am hungry, thereby intending to get my addressee to believe that I am hungry, and if the feedback information entails that my evocative goal has been achieved, then this normally implies that the signalling goal and the utterance goal have been achieved as well.

The space of feedback information can be given a precise mathematical model using notions from situation theory (Barwise, 1989; Cooper et al., 1990; Nivre, 1992). More precisely, the space of feedback information forms a *constraint infon algebra* in the sense of Barwise and Etchemendy (1990). This model is given in the appendix to this paper.

3.3 Veridical versus intentional feedback

As indicated in an earlier footnote, the notion of feedback information discussed in this paper refers to the information that is available to a communicative agent about the outcome of her goals, regardless of whether this information is intentionally conveyed by another agent. We may call this *veridical* feedback to stress the fact that we are concerned with veridical information about the outcome of a communicative act.

However, it is an important fact about human communication that communicative acts themselves may be used to give feedback information. In other words, the evocative goal of a communicative act may simply be to convey information to the interlocutor about the outcome of a previous communicative act. Allwood's theory of linguistic feedback referred to in the introduction is concerned precisely with communicative acts of this kind, a phenomenon that we may call *intentional* feedback.[10]

I believe that the notions of veridical and intentional feedback will both prove useful in the study of communicative action and it is clear that they have important interrelations. For example, intentional feedback is one of the most important sources of veridical feedback. Nevertheless, it is important to keep the two notions

[10] The distinction between veridical and intentional feedback is related to the meaning-theoretic distinction between veridical and intentional meaning. For an account of the latter distinction, see Nivre (1992).

apart for several reasons. First of all, intentional feedback is by no means the only source of veridical feedback in communication. (For instance, the puzzled look on my addressee's face may tell me that she has not perceived my utterance correctly, even if she does not intend to convey this information.) Secondly, there may be a discrepancy between intentional and veridical feedback information because an agent giving (intentional) feedback may be mistaken or may intentionally be trying to mislead her interlocutor. Thus, while intentional feedback is certainly a phenomenon worth studying for its own sake, it cannot replace the notion of veridical feedback in a model of the way communicative action is guided by feedback in the cybernetic sense.

4 Implications for dialogue systems

The analysis of communicative action and feedback outlined in this paper has important implications for computational models of dialogue. In building a sophisticated dialogue system for natural language, we must take into account the fact that communication crucially involves goal-directed action supported by feedback.[11]

On the one hand, this means that if a system attempts to perform a communicative act by producing, say, a declarative sentence intended as a statement with propositional content p, then it cannot be directly assumed that, as a result, the user will come to believe that p. This can only be established (if at all) by interpreting the feedback information available in the user's subsequent contributions to the dialogue (or in any other possible input from the user to the system). If the feedback information is positive on the evocative dimension, then the system can assume that the evocative goal has been achieved and proceed accordingly. If not, the system must consider the information available with respect to other feedback dimensions and take appropriate actions in order to achieve the evocative goal (or eventually give it up completely).

On the other hand, it means that the system must attempt to give unambiguous feedback on the user's contributions, since the user can be expected to behave as a cybernetic agent using this feedback to assess the outcome of her goals in the dialogue. In this way, the notion of feedback can be seen to play a crucial role in the process of interpretation as well as in the planning of system acts.

In order to make effective use of the notion of feedback in dialogue systems, we need to give a formally precise account of this notion. While such an account lies outside the scope of this paper, it is hoped that the situation-theoretic model of feedback spaces given in the appendix can provide a first step in this direction.

5 Conclusion

In this paper, I have outlined an analysis of feedback in communication, based on the general cybernetic notion of feedback combined with a certain analysis of

[11] On a more general level, this holds for any kind of system involving action and its effect on other agents.

communicative action. I have argued that this analysis has a role to play in computational models of dialogue, and I have provided a first step towards a formalization by giving a situation-theoretic model of the space of feedback information in communication.

Appendix: A model of feedback information

The space of feedback information with respect to a given communicative act can be conveniently modelled using the situation-theoretic notion of an *infon algebra*, developed by Barwise and Etchemendy (1990).

An infon algebra $I = \langle Sit, I, \Rightarrow, \models \rangle$ consists of a non-empty collection Sit of objects called *situations*, a distributive lattice $\langle I, \Rightarrow \rangle$ with $\mathbf{0}$ and $\mathbf{1}$ (with domain I of objects called *infons*), together with a relation $\models$ on $Sit \times I$ satisfying the following conditions for all $s \in Sit$ and all $\sigma, \tau \in I$:

1. If $s \models \sigma$ and $\sigma \Rightarrow \tau$ then $s \models \tau$.
2. $s \not\models \mathbf{0}$ and $s \models \mathbf{1}$.
3. If Σ is any finite set of infons, then $s \models \widehat{\Sigma}$ if and only if $s \models \sigma$ for each $\sigma \in \Sigma$.
4. If Σ is any finite set of infons, then $s \models \vee\Sigma$ if and only if $s \models \sigma$ for some $\sigma \in \Sigma$.

The relation $s \models \sigma$ is read: s supports σ, or σ provides (veridical) information about s.

In order to model the space of feedback information in relation to a given communicative act, we may for instance take the set I of infons to be the following set:

$$\{utt(pos), utt(neg), sign(pos), sign(neg), evoc(pos), evoc(neg)\}$$

Intuitively, if $s \models utt(pos)$ then s is a situation containing positive feedback information with respect to the the utterance dimension; if $s \models evoc(neg)$, then s contains negative information on the evocative dimension, etc. In order to obtain the constraint relation $\Rightarrow$ for this model, we simply take the reflexive and transitive closure of the following relation in I:

$$\{\langle utt(neg), sign(neg)\rangle, \langle sign(neg), evoc(neg)\rangle,$$
$$\langle evoc(pos), sign(pos)\rangle, \langle sign(pos), utt(pos)\rangle\}$$

Acknowledgements

I wish to thank Jens Allwood, Robbert-Jan Beun and an anonymous reviewer for helpful comments and criticisms on previous versions of this paper.

References

Allwood, J. (1976) Communication as Action and Cooperation. Gothenborg monographs in Linguistics, 2. University of Göteborg: Department of Linguistics.

Allwood, J. (1977) A Critical Look at Speech Act Theory. In: Dahl, Ö. (ed.) Logic, Pragmatics and Grammar. University of Göteborg: Department of Linguistics.

Allwood, J. (ed.) (1988a) Feedback in Adult Language Acquisition. Final Report II. Ecology of Adult Language Acquisition (ESF), Strasbourg and Göteborg.

Allwood, J. (1988b) Om det svenska systemet för språklig återkoppling. In: Linell, P., Adelsvärd, V. & Gustavsson, L. (eds.) Svenskans beskrivning 16. University of Linköping: Department of Communication Studies.

Allwood, J., Nivre, J. & Ahlsén, E. (1992) On the Semantics and Pragmatics of Linguistic Feedback. Journal of Semantics, 9(1), 1–26.

Anscombe, M. (1981) Metaphysics and the Philosophy of Mind. Collected Philosophical Papers, volume II. Minneapolis: University of Minnesota Press.

Ashby, W.R. (1956) An Introduction to Cybernetics. London and New York: Methuen.

Austin, J.L. (1962) How to Do Things with Words. Oxford: Clarendon Press.

Barwise, J. (1989) The Situation in Logic. Stanford: CSLI Publications. CSLI Lecture Notes no. 17.

Barwise, J. & Etchemendy, J. (1990) Information, Infons and Inference.

Cooper, R., Mukai, K. & Perry, J. (eds.) (1990) Situation Theory and Its Applications, volume 1. CSLI Lecture Notes 22. Stanford: CSLI Publications.

Davidson, D. (1982) Essays on Actions and Events. Oxford: Clarendon Press.

Goldman, A.I. (1970) A Theory of Human Action. Princeton, NJ: Princeton University Press.

Grice, H.P. (1957) Meaning. Philosophical Review, 66, 377–388.

Grice, H.P. (1969) Utterer's Meaning and Intentions. Philosophical Review, 78, 147–177.

Nivre, J. (1992) Situations, Meaning and Communication: A Situation Theoretic Approach to Meaning in Language and Communication. Gothenburg Monographs in Linguistics, 11. University of Göteborg, Department of Linguistics.

Pollack, M.E. (1990) Plans as Complex Mental Attitudes. In: Cohen, P.R., Morgan, J. & Pollack, M.E. (eds.) Intentions in Communication. Cambridge, MA: MIT Press.

Schiffer, S.R. (1972) Meaning. Oxford: Clarendon Press.

Searle, J.R. (1969) Speech Acts. Cambridge: Cambridge University Press.

Strawson, P.F. (1964) Intention and Convention in Speech Acts. Philosophical Review, 73, 439–460.

Wiener, N. (1948) Cybernetics or Control and Communication in the Animal and the Machine. Cambridge, MA: MIT Press.

Reasons for Management in Spoken Dialogue

Jens Allwood

Dept. of linguistics, University of Göteborg, Renströmsparken, S-412 98 Göteborg, Sweden, email: jens@ling.gu.se

Abstract. This paper characterizes and exemplifies management in dialogue. *Own communication management* (choice and change directed) is distinguished from *interactive communication management* (sequences, turn management and feedback). An attempt is then made to motivate and explain the existence of various types of interactive management in dialogue. The suggested explanations involve a combination of general rational and ethical factors with more specific factors related to particular types of management.

Keywords. Communication management, feedback, turn management, sequential management, cohesion, context, ethics, rationality, interaction

1 Purpose

A point of departure for this paper is that a number of different phenomena in spoken dialogue (like self correction, hesitation, feedback, and turntaking) exist primarily in order to enable management of dialogue. The term *management* has been chosen instead of the related terms *regulation* and *control* because it is less authoritarian and machine-like and allows, but does not require, intentional control. The purpose of the paper is to briefly describe and initiate an explanation of some of these types of management.

2 Background

My account will presuppose a framework for the description of spoken interaction, (Allwood, 1984; Allwood, 1992), where language and communication, in general, but especially spoken language, are seen as aspects of underlying social activities for which they serve a mainly instrumental role. Communication is taken to be an essential instrument of activity coordination in a given natural and social environment. Spoken communication is constituted by utterances (more generally by contributions) from speakers in specific activity roles to listeners in other activity roles, for example, a lawyer talking to a client or a sales clerk talking to a customer, etc. Each role is described in terms of the duties, privileges and competence requirements which go with the role. The actual properties of the communicative interaction are seen as being codetermined by many different factors including the following:

- The physical, biological, psychological and social background of the communicators
- The activity at hand with a certain purpose, particular roles and available resources
- The social, cultural and natural environment (including linguistic and communicative conventions pertaining to environment, activity and individual background).

Since the requirements on both communication per se and on the activities underlying the communication are very varied and complex, management becomes necessary to ensure efficiency, flexibility and quality of both activity and communication.

3 Management in spoken dialogue

In order to get a better understanding of the kind of management which is required, let us now take a look at some features of spoken dialogue. In the descriptive framework presupposed here, an utterance can be subdivided into

- *management* related parts and
- *main message* related parts.

Both main message and management features have a backward orientation with regard to preceding discourse as well as a forward orientation with regard to coming discourse. To illustrate consider the following example, where '?' signifies rising intonation:

A (ice cream salesman): ice cream?
B (customer): yes vanilla eh no chocolate

The salesman's utterance *ice cream*, said with a questioning intonation, could, for example, simultaneously express an intended offer and a desire for information about the hoped-for customer's intentions. The utterance with this message would also normally be intended to evoke the prospective customer's perception, understanding and, in the case at hand, positive reaction to the message. Except for the rising intonation, the management features in A's utterance are largely implicit. A relies on the main message and the obvious role and activity expectations generated by the physical, social and artifactual attributes of his location (his ice cream stand and ice cream salesman uniform) to put sufficient interactive pressure on B (Bunt, 1993). The rising intonation of his utterance would, however, be counted as a management related feature with an interactive function.

The need for management is strengthened by the fact that contributions (utterances) in a dialogue normally are connected with both sender directed and receiver directed obligations (Allwood, 1976). The sender has responsibility for his contribution in the sense that he in many contexts is

– supposed to be sincere,
– supposed to have reasons/motives for his utterance, and
– supposed (not) to make contributions that (do not) take the receiver into cognitive and ethical consideration.

(The choice of a negative or positive formulation here depends on how strong a version of the 'golden rule' you subscribe to.) I refer to these as the *sender obligations of sincerity, grounding* and *consideration*, respectively.

When a contribution has been made, it normally generates two receiver directed obligations. The first is that the receiver should consider the sender and evaluate whether he is willing and able to continue the contact and to perceive and understand the message. He should also evaluate whether and how he is willing and able to respond to the main evocative intention of the preceding contribution. The second obligation is that he or she should act in accordance with the result of the evaluation, which should mean some form of response to the sender. We can call these the *receiver obligations of consideration (evaluation)* and *response*. Efforts to satisfy and manage both sender and receiver obligations are an important part of what creates cohesion and dynamics in dialogue.

Let us now return to the customer B, who upon noticing the salesman A becomes connected with A and his utterance through the (receiver) obligation of consideration.

He will therefore, more or less consciously, evaluate and decide whether he is able (and willing) to continue contact, to perceive and understand what A is doing and saying and whether and how he should respond, in the event that he is able and willing to continue contact. He could, for example, *do nothing* and just *watch*, or say *"pardon"* if he can't hear, say *"what is ice cream"* if he is learning English, *"shut up"* if he wants to be insulting, *"no thanks"* if he wants to break contact in a fairly polite way, etc. In the example given he says *"yes vanilla eh no chocolate"*, which, in the framework mentioned above, could be given the following analysis:

The word *"yes "* would be classed as a positive feedback giver, with a clear interactive communicative management function (IACM) (Allwood et al., 1992), which affirms part of, or all of the evocative intentions of the preceding utterance. How much is affirmed depends on how the utterance following the *"yes"* continues. In this case, the *"yes"*, in combination with the lack of relevant counter evidence in the rest of the utterance, affirms contact, perception, understanding and positive reaction to the salesman's offer of service. Since the offer is related to ice cream, the next word *"vanilla"* which, in fact, refers to a type of ice cream turns the positive reaction into an acceptance of the offer and a specification of the type of service wanted (i.e., a sort of request). The next words *"eh no "* are related to what, in the framework mentioned on page 2, is called own communication management (OCM) (Allwood et al., 1990). The word *"eh"* functions to express hesitation and choice and the word *"no"* to express cancellation and change. The word *"chocolate"*, finally, gives a new main message specification to replace vanilla which has been cancelled. We thus have two main kinds of management in spoken interaction:

1. Own communication management (OCM) and
2. Interactive communication management (IACM).

OCM provides mechanisms which allow a speaker to manage his/her own communication with regard to processing, choice (including hesitation, etc.) and change (including cancellation). IACM provides mechanisms which allow a speaker (and to some extent a listener) to structure the flow of interaction in the following respects:

- Sequencing (with regard to subactivities, topics, speech acts, etc.)
- Turntaking (with regard to yielding, holding, giving, taking and assignment of turns)
- Feedback (with regard to contact, perception, understanding and reactions to evocative intentions)
- Rhythm and spatial positioning.

Together OCM and IACM are therefore essential to make speech and gestures efficient and flexible instruments for sharing of information under different conditions pertaining to activity and interpersonal relations.

4 The role of context

In discussing the role of context for communicative management functions and other communicative functions, we can, as is common practice, distinguish a *type* level and an *occurrence* (or token) level. On the occurrence level, the meaning (including what here somewhat vaguely is called function) of all contributions to communication depends on context.

Thus, let us contrast the child's utterance in the following dialogue with the salesman's in the preceding one:

A (parent, returning home): do you know what I have in the bag
B (child): ice cream?

In both cases, the utterance is *"ice cream"* with rising intonation, but we can easily imagine that the utterance could have different functions in the two contexts. In the case of the ice cream salesman, it expresses willingness to perform service and desire for information concerning whether this service is wanted. In the case of the child, it might merely express a guess on the part of the child. As has already been stressed, this difference in the functional role of the utterance can most easily be explained by the differences in speaker role, activity and preceding utterance that exist between the two cases.

Besides giving a relatively full context dependent account of functioning on the occurrence level, we can also give an a-contextual type level account which is a more abstract partial account relying only on the utterance itself. In this case, we might, for example, say that an utterance of *"ice cream"* with rising intonation can be used to express a wish for some type of information related to ice cream which is connected with an intention to evoke this information. A type level analysis need not, however, be completely a-contextual. It can be related to context in an abstract way. For example, the word *"I"* can be said to always pick out the contextually given currently relevant communicator (or thinker).

Like other communicative functions, management functions on their occurrence level are, thus, contextually determined. For example, depending on context a *"no"* can be used to negate if it follows an affirmative statement or to confirm if it follows a negative statement. Compare the status of B s utterance in the following two cases.

A: it is raining
B: no it isn't (denial)

A: it isn't raining
B: no it isn't (confirmation)

"No" can also be used in other functions, e.g. as a cancellation device for own communication management, as we saw in the example discussed above.

5 Another look at management

5.1 General

On a general level, reasons for the existence of management functions in communication have to do with ensuring an optimal functioning both of communication per se and communication as an instrument for underlying activities. This means that management mechanisms must be able to influence both communication features per se and the various background factors, which, in section 2 above, were said to co-determine the properties of communication. I will here restrict myself to a few remarks which become relevant when communication is seen as a species of motivated rational action and interaction. Given this perspective, the main reasons for communicative management are to ensure the rationality and ethicalness of communication.

Departing from the four factors which according to the present framework are thought to mainly influence activity based features of communication, we can distinguish four general areas which require management both from a rational and an ethical point of view.

1. Purpose; purpose relevance (functional)
2. Role; role relevance
3. Artefacts and management; artefactual attunement
4. Social and natural environment; environmental attunement

From a rational point of view, it should be possible to manage communication in such a way that it both achieves its basic purpose - sharing of information - and the purpose of the underlying activity in which the communication is being used. There must, therefore, be devices that ensure perception and understanding (feedback). It must also be possible to manage it in such a way that it can serve a useful purpose in coordinated activities, i.e., there must be ways of managing the distribution of the communication roles of sending and receiving information (turntaking) and there must be ways of dividing the communication in parts so that it best serves the needs of the underlying activity (sequencing). There must further be ways to manage communicative requirements of a specific role in the activity and there must be ways to manage communication so that it best fits with the artificial and natural environment of the activity.

From an ethical point of view, it must be possible to manage communication in such a way that the following goals are maximized (Allwood, 1976), and for a slightly different perspective (Grice, 1975):

- Freedom of communication
- Avoidance of pain and possibility to seek pleasure
- Correctness of information

To a degree which varies with culture and activity, there will be norms for achieving these goals. Often they are norms of communicative politeness used, for example, to manage turntaking or to guide ways of reporting one's reactions to another person's communicative contributions. The goals and the specific norms will form the motivation for different idioms of politeness and can be used as the basis for positive and negative sanctions of interlocutors against each other.

5.2 Interactive communicative management functions

Below, I will now take another look at interactive communicative management functions and attempt to say a little more about their raison d'etre. I will consider three types:

1. sequences
2. turn management
3. feedback

5.2.1 Sequences

Most complex activities can be subdivided in different ways. Such divisions can be made both with respect to an activity holistically (including communication) and more specifically with regard to its communicative aspects (Schegloff & Sacks, 1973). For example, it is often possible to divide an activity into subactivities or topics which in turn can be subdivided into sequences of communicative acts or into sequences of premises and conclusions.

Such units frequently are not merely an analytical tool for a researcher but also have psychological and social reality for the participants in the activity. Thus, they are often connected with mechanisms for:

- initiation (opening, entering an activity, a subactivity or a topic)

- maintenance (maintaining a subactivity or topic)
- changing (changing a subactivity or topic)
- ending (closing an activity, a subactivity or a topic)

From what has already been said, the motivation for mechanisms of this type should be fairly clear. In order to achieve the goals of most activities, a decomposition of the activity as a whole into component subactivities will be necessary on logical, physical and functional grounds. Everything cannot be done simultaneously, rather a sequence of partial results which fit into each other is required. Even if in most cases such divisions can be functionally motivated, a subdivision may in some cases be the result of a historically given custom which is no longer clearly functionally motivated. Thus, we add the motivation of historical convention to that of functional necessity. Another special case which is interesting are the reasons for why communicative interactions are divided into distinct utterances (or turns) and characteristic combinations of these (Sacks, 1975). The basic reason is perhaps that human beings are not rigidly integrated parts of a collective information processing system, but distributed and fairly autonomous information processing agents who have a need for flexible information coordination. However, since there is also a need for a certain rigidity and predictability, this leads to the building up of communicative obligations in relation to certain evocative communicative intentions in certain contexts. For example, you should try to answer questions or you should try to respond to greetings. This, in turn, leads to the existence of fairly stable combinations of speech acts (adjacency pairs) such as greeting-greeting, question-relevant answer, etc.

5.2.2 Management of turns

In the present framework, a turn is defined as a speaker's right to the floor. (This definition is slightly different from the classical one given in (Sacks et al., 1974)). Turns differ from utterances since one can have the turn without uttering anything. One can also utter something without having the turn, for example to give feedback to a current speaker. Norms regulating the right to the floor are connected with such things as who may speak, about what topic, at what time, how long and in what manner. Activities can vary from allowing simultaneous talk with few restrictions as to topic, time, duration and manner to distribution of turns administered by a specially designated turn assigner, e.g. a chairman who might impose clear restrictions on topic, time and manner.

Turn management is carried out through a number of subfunctions (for an early description (Duncan, 1974)), whose verbal and nonverbal expression is often standardized in a way which may also vary with activity and culture. Some of these are:

- means for assigning turns
- means for accepting the turn
- means for taking the turn (interrupting)
- means for maintaining (keeping) the turn

– means for yielding the turn

If we reflect on the reasons and motivations for why there might exist ways of managing the distribution of turns, I would like to point to two types of motivation.

1. Physical-psychological constraints: there are physical and physiological constraints on human information processing ability. We cannot both send and receive a large number of simultaneous messages. Even sending or receiving two simultaneous messages causes problems. It is also the case that several simultaneous messages may interfere with each other and lessen the probability that any one of them reaches its destination.
2. Requirements of motivated, rational and cooperative communication and need of conventions to support these requirements.

Given the already mentioned physical and physiological constraints on communication, and given rational constraints having to do with communicating efficiently in some activity and ethical constraints (for example, allowing everyone a just chance to both send and receive information) which are relevant for many types of interaction, a system for managing turns is clearly motivated. Since, however, the constraints already mentioned (physical, rational and ethical) still leave many degrees of freedom for how this system should be managed, we may empirically observe that systems of conventions bound to particular cultures and activities have developed. For example, in Swedish and other western cultures, it is much harder to interrupt someone (take the turn) in a formal meeting than it is in an informal meeting.

5.2.3 Feedback

Another aspect of interactive communication management concerns means to ascertain whether your interlocutor is able and willing to continue, perceive, understand and how he reacts to the main evocative intentions of your message. The set of verbal and bodily means which allow interlocutors, in a minimally obtrusive way, to both elicit and give information about these basic communicative functions has been called the linguistic feedback system (Allwood et al., 1992). As is the case with the systems of turn management, the conventions involved in systems for managing feedback with regard to contact, perception, understanding and main evocative intention vary with culture and activity. So, for example, in informal conversation auditive feedback seems to be more important in Swedish and Japanese conversations than in conversations in the Rio de la Plata area of South America, where visual feedback is more important. An example of activity influence can, for example, be seen in the way a simultaneous *"mm"* (as an indicator of contact, perception/understanding and possibly acceptance) occurs in informal conversation but not in public lectures (in Swedish culture).

If we turn to the reasons and motivations for management of communicative feedback, it seems plausible that contact, perception and understanding are a sine qua non of one-way communication while two-way communication also requires reactions to evocative intentions. Without feedback, in this sense, and ways of managing it, no communicative activity or system of communication can ever hope to aspire to such properties as robustness, relevance, adequacy and flexibility.

Feedback systems can also be related to another fairly basic type of management in communication, namely, the need for ways of managing (repairing, correcting) other interlocutor's contributions with regard to correctness, relevance, etc. Such reactions to other interlocutors can be seen as a kind of elaborated feedback governed by various types of normative considerations.

As for the reasons for this type of feedback, one might say that it exists in order to provide interlocutors with the means to impose normative constraints (e.g. ethical or rational) on each other.

6 Concluding remarks

In this paper I have outlined a few components of a framework for describing and explaining communicative interaction (Allwood, 1976; Allwood, 1984; Allwood, 1992) in which management of the ongoing dialogue plays a central role. To put my claims in a nutshell, I have argued that management is necessary to ensure optimal on-line organization of communication under changeable circumstances in the service of an underlying activity, where both communication per se and the underlying activity are under certain rational and ethical constraints.

The systematic verbal and bodily means for management which exist in spoken dialogue serve to uphold physical, physiological, functional (rational) and ethical requirements on communication.

They also give interlocutors flexibility so that they can handle 'on-line' any unforeseen changing circumstances. This, in turn, has the consequence that normal (spoken) dialogue is a remarkably robust system of communication.

Acknowledgements

I want to thank Elisabeth Ahlsén and an anonymous reviewer for comments on the paper.

References

Allwood, J. (1976) Communication as Action and Cooperation. Gothenborg monographs in Linguistics, 2. University of Göteborg: Department of Linguistics.

Allwood, J. (1984) Relevance in Spoken Interaction. Bäckman & Kjellmer (eds.) Papers on Language and Literature. Acta Universitatis Gothenburgensis, 18–35.

Allwood, J. (1992) On Dialogue Cohesion. Gothenburg Papers in Theoretical Linguistics, 65.

Allwood, J., Nivre, J. & Ahlsén, E. (1990) Speech Management: On the Non-Written Life of Speech. Nordic Journal of Linguistics, 13, 1–48.

Allwood, J., Nivre, J. & Ahlsén, E. (1992) On the Semantics and Pragmatics of Linguistic Feedback. Journal of Semantics, 9(1), 1–26.

Bunt, H.C. (1993) Dialogue Management through context dynamics. In: Black, W.J. & Bunt, H.C. (eds.) Computational Pragmatics vol. 2, Abduction, Belief and Context. London: Pinter Publishers (forthcoming).

Duncan, S. (1974) Some Signals and Rules for Taking Speaker Turns in Conversations. Weitz, S. (ed.) Nonverbal Communication. New York: Oxford University Press, 298–311.

Grice, P. (1975) Logic and Conversation. In: Cole, P. & Morgan, J.L. (eds.) Syntax and Semantics: Speech Acts. Vol. 11. New York: Academic Press, 41–58.

Sacks, H. (1975) Everyone has to lie. Sanches, M. & Blount, B. (eds.) Sociocultural Dimensions of Language Use. New York: Academic Press, 57–80.

Sacks, H., Schegloff, E. & Jefferson, G. (1974) A Simplest Systematics for the Organization of Turn-taking in Conversation. Language, 50(4), 696–735.

Schegloff, E. & Sacks, H. (1973) Opening up Closings. Semiotica, 7(4), 289–327.

Context Change and Communicative Feedback

Harry Bego

Institute for Language Technology and Artificial Intelligence ITK, P.O. Box 90153, 5000 LE Tilburg, The Netherlands, email: H.Bego@kub.nl

Abstract. Speakers need to perceive the effects of their utterances to be able to plan continuations. Evidence of effects is sent as *feedback acts.* Focusing on illocutionary and perlocutionary levels of communication, we see that feedback acts differ from other communicative acts that are caused by static properties of the context model in that they are triggered by context *change.* We propose a few principles of feedback implication, which are needed to be able to generate and interpret feedback at the right functional level of communication.

Keywords. Pragmatics, language understanding, dialogue systems

1 Introduction

In communication, where many actions aim at information transfer, feedback refers to utterances which function as signals of properties of interpretive processing. Feedback signals can originate at various levels of analysis, and types of feedback associated with *contact, perception, understanding* and *evaluation* have been recognised in linguistic literature (the 'basic communicative functions' in Allwood et al. (1992)). It is likely that as many types of feedback exist as there are cognitive and interactional subprocesses in a communicative system. A major point made in the present paper is that a pragmatic level of *perlocutionary feedback* should be recognised as associated with the propositional attitudes of *belief* and *intention*, and that two related subtypes of feedback exist. Secondly, implicative relations exist between feedback types at different levels, which should be exploited in both interpretation and generation. Several interesting principles concern implications between positive and negative epistemic and intentional feedback acts.

As argued in Bego (1992), certain types of feedback can perhaps fruitfully be viewed as resulting as *side effects* of updates of the information state connected with an interpretive subprocess. Focusing on pragmatic interpretation, we can say that feedback acts differ from normal communicative acts, which are triggered by *static* properties of the *context model*, in that they are caused by context *change*, an idea which derives from Heritage's (Heritage, 1984) analysis of 'change-of-state tokens'. Expressed in speech act theoretical terms this entails that feedback acts have *dynamic preconditions.* In terms of a communicative system it means that feedback is triggered by a dialogue control process when interpretive rules are fired, such as rules deriving communicative function from expression type, or rules determining whether information is consistent.[1] Whether this triggering of feedback conditions leads to utterances depends on perceived needs on the part of the previous speaker, and on principles derived from the hierarchy of feedback types, as we will see below.

The *relevance* of the concept of communicative feedback derives first of all from the view of language as goal-oriented behaviour which is behind speech act theoretical and plan-based approaches to dialogue, but more in particular from the fact that large-scale dialogue planning is in fact not well possible; hence what we need is a notion of local and *reactive* dialogue planning and execution, a type of process of which feedback is an essential ingredient. In reactive planning, agents acting on an environment need to perceive the effects of their actions to be able to plan continuations. Direct or indirect signs of effects can be used. We can maintain a 'receiver-defined' view of *feedback* as those data an agent *uses* as feedback. This holds for communication as well, in which another agent is part of the environment. A hearer recognising the needs of a speaker may also *send* data as feedback.[2] An integration of both sides is the essence of full communicative feedback. When receivers use precisely those signals as feedback that responding agents send, we can speak of a 'conventional' feedback system.

Before we can set out to associate interpretion and generation of acts of feedback with a context-change theory of speech acts, we must take a brief look at conversational and cognitivist bases for a theory of feedback, for in the study of feedback generation and interpretation these two fields meet. In fact we will obtain backing from cognitive science for the 'peripheral' part of the feedback typology. At the 'central' level, we relate types of feedback to basic attitude operators, and to principles of cognitive/behavioural organisation perhaps best described as 'knowledge sources'.

2 Feedback as a communicative category

Linguistic feedback has recently been identified as a class of dialogue management functions (Allwood et al., 1992).[3] Dialogue management functions enable continuation of conversation by other means than those usually explained in a speech act theoretical (i.e., essentially Gricean) way. While the latter perspective focuses on the information transfer properties of communication and prescribes what standards such transfer should meet, dialogue management functionality concentrates on procedural and meta-level aspects of communication. Such aspects are the establishment or suspension of contact, opening, resumption and closing of exchanges, how to take, keep or give turns, but also when and how to send messages on processing of previous conversation and on mental states and state changes. Many dialogue

---

[1] In fact, it will mean that a monitoring process records the triggering conditions and passes them to the context model, as we shall see below.

[2] We will use 'sender' and 'receiver' to refer to the agent giving or receiving feedback.

[3] We will use 'dialogue management' in a general sense, including utterances regulating conversation as a conventionally structured event and feedback. To my knowledge Allwood et al. were the first to clearly relate feedback to a layered model of communication.

management functions are perhaps best viewed as performed from the meta-level and triggered by a process *monitoring* the effects of communicative action.

Often, however, a 'conversational' linguistic approach to dialogue management phenomena is taken which is syntactic in spirit, e.g. in terms of combinatorial concepts such as *adjacency* and *exchange structure* (e.g., Schegloff (1968), Clark and Shaefer (1989)). In such a view no distinction is made between functionality for management of dialogue as a conventionally structured event and signals on cognitive process.

Heritage (1984) was probably the first linguist to take a non-syntactic point of view and to associate certain utterances with cognitive processing. Heritage saw what we here call linguistic feedback as signals of mental processing. The following is a part of a telephone conversation that will indicate the sort of acts involved:[4]

A1: [Asks B whether a certain person is on board an incoming flight]
B1: "Nee, dat is niet na te gaan, omdat passagierslijsten die blijven in New York en die zijn geheim" *("No, I can't check that, because passenger lists stay in New York and they are classified.")*
A2: "O" *("Oh")*
B2: "Dus het is nooit te checken" *("So it can never be checked")*
A3: "Goed" *("Good")*
B3: "Ja?" *("Yes?")*
A4: "Ja, bedankt hoor" *("Yes, thanks")*

Several utterances in this conversation pertain to mental processing or to the dialogue itself, rather than to the domain of conversation (flight arrivals). From a cognitive perspective such acts as "O" in A2 function as mental state change signals reporting that new information is being processed and recorded. This is what Heritage referred to as 'change-of-state tokens' and what we are here calling feedback. Utterances A3, B3 and A4 are dialogue control acts, aimed at procedural organisation of the dialogue itself as an event. "Goed" in A3 accepts and closes a previous exchange, although it is ambiguous as to the extent of the exchange accepted; hence B3: "Ja?" is a prompt for continuation and A4 more clearly initiates the closing of the dialogue as a whole.

State change signals such as A2 are not feedback in themselves, however. In essence, they are mere signals of processing. They are feedback acts (or rather, they *function* as feedback to a receiver) only if the state change occurred because of communication rather than mere observation, or retrieval from memory.[5] In the following example of the use of Heritage's change-of-state token "Oh" the new information state resulted from observation and memory (from Heritage; A saw somebody wearing a teeshirt):

[4] From a corpus of Dutch telephone dialogues collected by the Institute for Perception Research/IPO, Eindhoven. English translations are given in italics.

[5] Only if the state change was not caused by input from 'cognitive peripherals', so to speak. But note that observation of *symbolic* behaviour *is* communicative in this sense. We will discuss this issue further below.

A: "Oh, that teeshirt reminded me... [tells story] " (2)

"Oh" is here a signal of ongoing processing (observation, memory access and retrieval) and, more importantly, it is sent as a signal of floor taking, i.e. it is dialogue control in a specific sense.[6] The feedback concept should be restricted to communicative acts triggered by changes resulting from communication, and it must not be stretched to cover what is in fact control (such as turn taking signals). We should therefore not consider this use of "Oh" as feedback. On the other hand, we must be careful not to define a reaction as feedback if it was triggered by change resulting *directly* from communication, for then we run the risk of having to call any response to any communicative act feedback. Let us briefly clarify this with the following example:

A: "Please close the door" (3)
B: [closes the door]

If B closes the door upon A's request to do so, the true response, the closing itself, is not feedback. It implies positive feedback at all communicative levels, but it is not in itself a token of any type of 'feedback act', and it is not *sent by B as such.* On the other hand, responding by "OK" upon such a request *is* feedback in that it signals *acceptance*, the acquiring of the right mental state property (an intention: hence we will call this 'positive intentional feedback' below). All actions performed as 'true responses' imply feedback and are in a sense communicatively *stronger* than feedback. For instance, the answer "yes" to a yes/no-question is such a true response.

Explicit feedback utterances become important especially when the true response is not immediately observable, as is the case with belief states after assertions, or with the response to a request.[7] Neither 'Gricean' pragmatics nor its descendant, speech act theory, clearly give reasons for such responses to an assertion (if there is no relevant indirect interpretation).

To gain a clearer picture of feedback generation and interpretation, and in particular to be able to assess ordering and implicitness principles, we will next examine the organisation of the process of communication and will relate types of feedback to it.

2.1 Types of feedback

Layered models of language production and interpretation have recently been considered in explanations of dialogue management phenomena. According to Allwood et al. (1992) we can associate types of feedback with the four 'basic communicative functions': *contact maintenance, perception understanding* and *attitudinal reactions* such as acceptance and rejection. At every level feedback is elicited and given.

[6] Note that here, as in feedback, we should distinguish the *prime cause* of the utterance (a state change) and its *use* (here floor taking), controlled by the 'dialogue management process'.

[7] Thus contradicting the opinion that primarily negative feedback is important.

Clark (1993) defines similar levels of interaction at which interlocutors invite and send evidence of success or failure, i.e. levels of 'vocalisation and attention', 'presentation and identification', 'meaning and understanding'. Clark (pers. com.) indeed defines a fourth level of 'proposal and consideration' that is similar to Allwood's level of attitudinal reactions.

Of course a layered organisation of 'basic communicative functions' can in part be related to models of cognitive organisation and process from cognitive science as Fodor (1983) has done. We have already used Fodor's terminology above in distinguishing *peripheral* and *central* processes. If we want to adhere closely to existing views of the make-up of the linguistic system and base the feedback types on it, we should recognise roughly the following subprocesses and data: sensory input, phoneme recognition, lexical, syntactic and referential analysis, semantic representation and pragmatic understanding.

The lowest levels of processing, i.e. sensory, phonemic and perhaps the syntactic levels, are determined by physical system properties. The higher levels are characterised by truly cognitive properties: attitude operators and knowledge sources guiding communicative behaviour.

Furthermore, the pragmatic level of analysis can (and should, if we hold on to speech act theory) be subdivided into illocutionary and perlocutionary levels.[8] The level concerning 'other attitudinal reactions' (Allwood) and 'proposal and consideration' (Clark) is in fact the level of perlocutions. The main subdimensions of the illocutionary and perlocutionary levels are the propositional attitudes of *belief* and *intention*. Illocutionary understanding, i.e. recognition of speech acts, uses speech act rules (direct and 'conventionally' indirect). The perlocutionary level uses general principles of rationality and cooperation, such as the rule of 'belief transfer', and common-sense knowledge, e.g. about domain activities stated as planning operators, to determine what is in fact being said and what goals are involved.

At every process level feedback is needed. We will focus on the illocutionary and perlocutionary levels here. Feedback at the illocutionary level is left implicit most of the time. We will see two explicit examples in the next section. Feedback at the perlocutionary level, however, is the most important type, and is very often given explicitly at its main subdimensions, *belief* and *intention*. We will term the illocutionary and perlocutionary types of feedback 'context-change feedback' below.

2.2 Dimensions of context-change feedback

The illocutionary level of interpretation is the lowest epistemic/intentional level of analysis if we take a speech act theoretical perspective. It is here that propositional attitudes interface with lower levels of interpretation (semantic, syntactic, surface properties), in a manner governed by conventions. Attitudes can be viewed as attached to surface features, which leads to the inclusion of such features in the definitions (e.g., Beun (1989)). If this illocutionary level of speech acts as packages

---

[8] In fact the existence of acts of illocutionary feedback can provide an empirical basis for speech act theory.

of attitudes attached to surface features and semantic content is indeed a distinguishable level of interpretation, we may find feedback acts associated with it. We of course find utterances like B1 in (5), which may be conceived of as giving explicit negative feedback at the illocutionary level:

A1: "You drive" (5)
B1: "Is that a question?"

The following occurrence of "Oh" in B2 is a rare example of positive illocutionary feedback, but this is obvious only if we realise that A2 "I don't know" explicitly states the sincerity precondition of A1 (dialogue taken from Hirst et al. (1993)):

A1: "Do you know who's going to that meeting?"
B1: "Who?"
A2: "I don't know"
B2: "Oh. Probably Mrs McOwen and probably Mrs Cadry and some of the teachers"

"Oh" here signals a belief change concerning the precondition stated in A2, after which A1 is re-interpreted as a question. Part of the illocutionary level is a computation of speaker and hearer effects upon recognition of preconditions (as e.g. proposed by Bunt (1989)). This level consists of rules which realise for a hearer that he knows that the preconditions of the recognised communicative act hold, and that the speaker knows that the hearer knows this (and, ideally, that this is mutually known).

More truly 'perlocutionary' are changes brought about as the effect of the principle of *belief transfer*, a rule that states that if A believes that B believes that P holds, then, in the absence of evidence to the contrary, A comes to believe P herself. We have already seen an example in dialogue (1), where A2 signals belief change upon the information in B1.

The upper level of feedback, then, is first of all associated with state changes that affect belief and intention. The *extent* of a belief change can be reported as a 'news value' measure (a term coined by Heritage; equivalent to 'surprise' in Allwood's article, related to uses of 'expectancy' elsewhere). The extent of change with respect to intentions can be reported as a value on an 'intentionality' or 'desirability' scale.

It seems reasonable to assume a default ordering of feedback types that derives from a hierarchical ordering of interpretive processes, as argued in Bego (1992).[9] A general principle of course is that:

1. explicit positive feedback on higher interpretive levels implies positive feedback at lower levels.

[9] cf. Edmondson (1981) who uses such an ordering to explain the optionality of uptakers. The ordering is justifiable inasmuch as a sequential (time) order exists on the stages of analysis, which is a research issue in psycholinguistics. We will return to the issue of implied feedback below.

Positive feedback at the intentional level, for instance, implies positive feedback on all other levels of processing. The converse does not hold: negative feedback at some level usually means 'no feedback' at higher levels, except perhaps for 'contact'. Consider e.g. the belief level: negative belief feedback does not give feedback at the intentional level. But there are two more implications that are often exploited:

2. explicit negative feedback at some level entails positive feedback at lower levels;
3. explicit positive feedback at some level may entail negative feedback at higher levels.

For example, according to the second rule, if I ask what entity you refer to, thus giving negative semantic/reference feedback, this will mean that I have been able to syntactically analyse your utterance. But with the third rule (which is the converse of the second), if I repeat your utterance, giving positive perceptive feedback, I may imply that I have problems in further processing it. This is probably a major function of *repetitions.*

Figure 1 visualises some of the implications of explicit feedback acts at a certain level, according to the first and second rules. An instance of a feedback act at some level is drawn as a bullet.

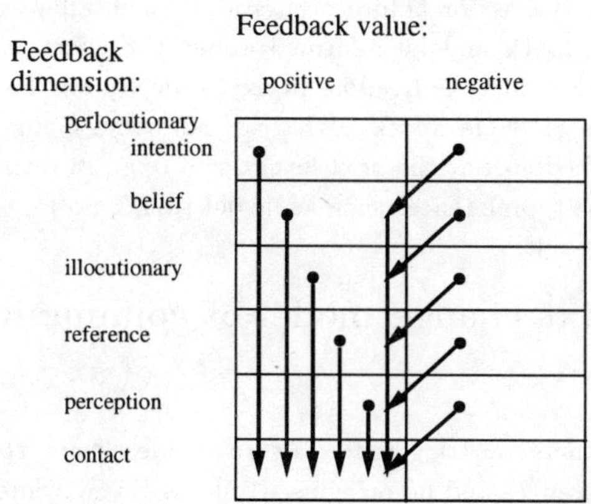

Fig. 1. Implications of explicit feedback.

We have next placed a few utterances typical of perlocutionary belief and intentional feedback in Figure 2, with their implications, but we have now included an implication of rule 3.

Thus at the perlocutionary level, according to the third rule, positive belief feedback can imply negative intentional feedback, since positive intentional feedback could have been given, but was not. The following principles can be proposed to guide the expression and interpretation of feedback:

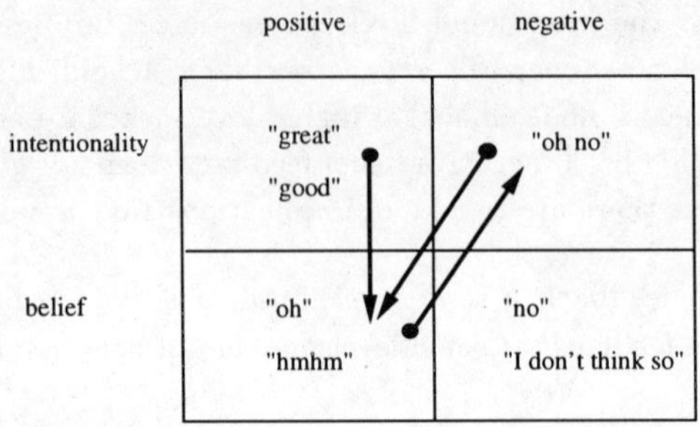

Fig. 2. Perlocutionary feedback with implications.

- positive feedback should be maximal, i.e. given at the highest level at which success is achieved;
- negative feedback should be minimal, i.e. given at the lowest level at which a negative result occurs;
- implied feedback should be left implicit.

It is these three rules which obviate the need for a feedback sender to signal at every level whether success or failure occurs and which allow a feedback receiver to interpret the feedback and be informed about the effects achieved. But they are not absolute rules: there is freedom in exploiting them. There is an option of giving positive or negative feedback in that we can avoid giving negative feedback by giving positive feedback at the next level down (e.g., in response to additional, culturally determined, preferences such as 'avoid saying no').

3 The context change model of communicative feedback

Although feedback acts are triggered as a sort of side effects, they have to be processed (lead to utterances and be recognised) like ordinary communicative acts (so that we can e.g. have feedback on feedback). In this sense they must be treated like other dialogue management functions, which work on data in the context model. Feedback is triggered by the process monitoring interpretive rule-firing and is channelled to the context model, which leads to communicative acts in the normal way.[10]

Figure 3 schematically represents the context-change view of feedback generation.[11] A13a and A13b are contexts, i.e. sets of beliefs and intentions, B12 and A13

[10] Note that complex communicative acts have to be *composed* from communicative functions and that expression principles as stated above must determine feedback explicitness.

[11] In this and the following figures solid arrows, labeled 'B...' or 'A...', represent utter-

are utterances. The wavy arrows represent the context changes caused by an incoming utterance (the control process realising the change by applying interpretive rules is not shown).

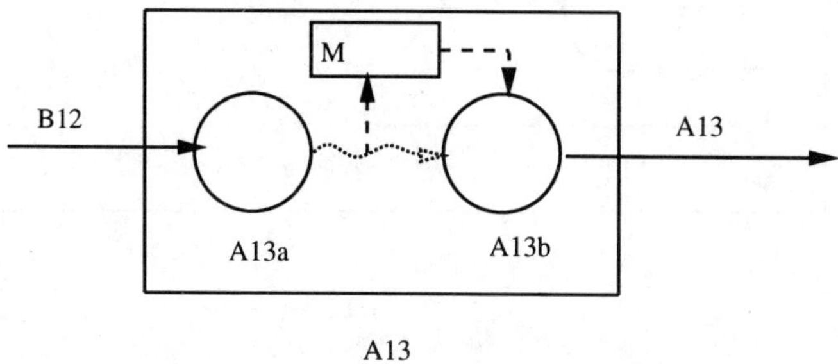

Fig. 3. Feedback signals generated in response to B12, monitored and reported to context model A13b.

In this process-oriented representation the process labeled 'M' monitors the triggering of rules for recognition of communicative acts and inference rules such as 'belief transfer' (see below). Context A13b gives rise to communicative feedback, in that a feedback act may now be triggered (but it may still remain implicit, depending on expression principles and perceived receiver needs). Feedback is thus generated in two stages, i.e. feedback triggering from monitored state change and feedback sending based on perceived receiver needs. Note that this is feedback in the *sender-defined sense.*[12]

At the same time the representation tells us nothing about feedback interpretation. A receiver-defined notion of feedback focuses on data that the receiver uses to evaluate effects; it needs feedback analysis rules like the ones proposed above, which derive this information from an incoming utterance. The schematic representation has to be extended to incorporate such interpretative functionality. In particular, we have to represent the receiver context in a slightly more complex way. In Figure 4 the feedback-analysis process labeled 'F' analyses the incoming utterance B12 as a feedback act (dotted output) and a 'main message' (Allwood's term, blank line).

A12b is the A context saved from the previous turn. Note that the feedback data is interpreted in a different context than the main message![13]

---

ances, where 'A13' refers to utterance 13 by speaker A. Circles represent states (contexts), gray wavy arrows represent state changes, straight dotted arrows represent feedback dataflow. Small boxes are procedures, a large box labeled 'A' represents the part of the process belonging to one agent A. Main processes such as inferential mechanisms are not included.

[12] Although we should distinguish two stages: a. the side-effect, i.e. the monitoring of changing context, and b. the decision to report it. The latter decision marks feedback as sender-defined in the indicated sense, in that the receiver's needs are recognised.

[13] Here we see that context change feedback concerns the *establishment of givenness.* In

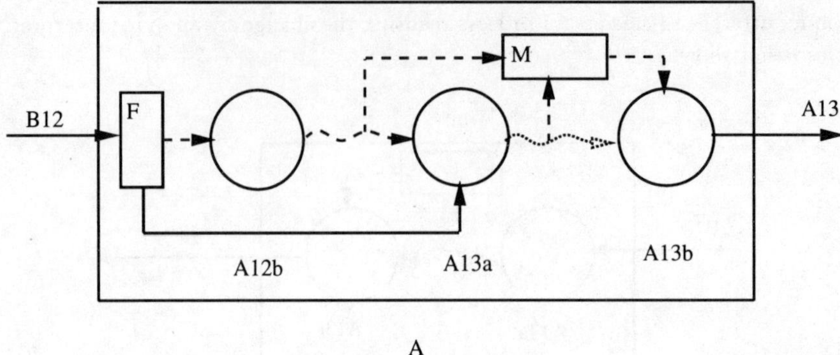

Fig. 4. Feedback interpretation added to figure 3. A12b is the context before utterance B12.

We can now in principle generate feedback on interpretation of feedback (the incoming dotted line in M). Note that if only the feedback is responded to, A13a is the final context at this point. Note also that the representation is too simple in that process F has to *test* A12b to be able to analyse B12 as feedback and main message.

4 Conclusion

The context change model can shed some light on particular utterances that have often been analysed in conversational terms. For example, principles for interpretation and expression of feedback utterances can be derived from the ordering of communicative function levels, although these are no more than default orderings. Interesting from the present perspective is the ordering of the subprocesses of illocutionary and perlocutionary analysis.

Perlocutionary feedback needs further attention in the light of remarks by Allwood et al. about the context sensitivity of functions of feedback-expressions, that next to news value and desirability depend as well on the *mood* and *polarity* of the preceding communicative act.

Acknowledgements

This research was carried out within the framework of the research program 'Human-Computer Communication using natural language' (MMC). The MMC Program is sponsored by Senter, Digital Equipment B.V., SUN Microsystems Nederland B.V., and AND Software.

---

this paradoxical statement lies the link between feedback and the notion of shared belief. In fact, feedback is the *control* of shared belief.

References

Allwood, J., Nivre, J. & Ahlsén, E. (1992) On the Semantics and Pragmatics of Linguistic Feedback. Journal of Semantics, 9(1), 1–26.

Bego, H. (1992) Communicative Acts and Rule Systems. MMC Semiannual report. Tilburg University.

Beun, R.J. (1989) Declarative questions in information dialogues. Ph.D. thesis, Tilburg University. Also available as ITK Research Report 13.

Bunt, H.C. (1989) Information Dialogues as communicative action in relation to partner modelling and information processing. In: Taylor, M.M., Néel, F. & Bouwhuis, D.G. (eds.) The Structure of Multimodal Dialogue. Amsterdam: Elsevier North-Holland.

Clark, H.H. (1993) Managing Troubles in Speaking. Shirai, K. (ed.) Proceedings of the International Symposium on Spoken Dialogue, Tokyo.

Clark, H.H. & Schaefer, E.F. (1989) Contributing to Discourse. Cognitive Science, 13, 259–294.

Edmondson, W. (1981) Spoken Discourse: A model for analysis. London: Longman.

Fodor, J. (1983) The modularity of mind. MIT Press.

Heritage, J. (1984) A change of state token. In: Atkinson, J.M. & Heritage, J. (eds.) Structures of Social Action. CUP, Cambridge.

Hirst, G., McRoy, S., Heeman, P., Edmonds, P. & Horton, D. (1993) Repairing Conversational Misunderstandings. Shirai, K. (ed.) Proceedings of the International Symposium on Spoken Dialogue, Tokyo.

Schegloff, E.A. (1968) Sequencing in Conversational Openings. American Anthropologist, 70, 1075–1095.

The Design of Interacting Agents

David M. Connah

Institute for Perception Research/IPO, P.O. Box 513, 5600 MB Eindhoven, The Netherlands

Abstract. It is generally recognised that the human-machine interface is crucial to the design of complex products. Agents are one way in which robust and flexible interfaces can be created. In this paper some of the principles guiding the design of selected agents are discussed with particular emphasis on the design of systems of interacting agents.

Keywords. Situated agents, behaviour, interactivity, societies of agents, feedback

1 Introduction

Interfaces come in varying degrees of complexity ranging from that of the mechanical alarm clock (or even simpler devices) on the one hand to the computer interface on the other, with machines like the video recorder somewhere in between. In dealing with such systems the designer naturally tries to find ways of specifying the interface which cover all its possible states and transitions so that he can then use formal methods to ensure that it will work as he intends. In the more complex cases this may not be possible, making the design of a reliable interface difficult.

At one level the interface actually consists of electromechanical or electronic components such as knobs, keyboards, displays and so on, but there is always a level of interaction which transcends this and which is to do with getting the apparatus to satisfy one's goals for it. Sometimes this level of interaction can be very content-dependent, for example in the case of the computer or of apparatus supporting a multi-media application. Here, ideally, we want the user to feel that he or she is interacting in a very direct way with whatever constitutes the application. One framework which is designed to make this more plausible consists of a series of agents in the interface which are designed to ease the potentially complex nature of the communication between user and machine.

In the course of work on the design of groups of interacting agents, we[1] have been concerned with trying to deal with examples of systems whose behaviour was not easily predictable. The reason for this unpredictability is the non-linear nature of the interaction between agents. We have developed some software and, more importantly, a way of working, specifically intended for such systems. What we have

[1] The work described in this paper was done by a team at Philips Research Laboratories, Redhill, England. The team has included at various times, apart from myself, Peter Wavish, Mike Graham, Martin Shiels and Steve Hickman.

learned from this work is that it is perfectly possible to construct systems like this incrementally. The system behaviour then either emerges from, or is constructed from, the interaction between individual behaviours (Wavish, 1991).

In this paper I will describe the technology we have used in designing systems of interacting agents and illustrate points of interest by reference to a demonstration system we have built. The method of working which I wish to advocate is bottom-up rather than top-down and furthermore does not proceed from specification to implementation to testing (as is usually advocated) but rather goes through (a potentially endless) cycle of implementation, simulation, correction/refinement, simulation, etc.

These working practices are, perhaps, controversial and in order to justify them it will be necessary to sketch at least part of the theory that underlies them. The body of the paper is therefore arranged in four sections. The next section gives an outline of the more important theoretical ideas on which this approach is based. The third section describes software which has been developed to support those theoretical ideas and section 4 is concerned with the way in which an application is developed using this theory and these software tools. The application of the technology to interface design is discussed briefly in section 5.

2 Theory

Whereas most attempts to design intelligent agents emphasise the centrality of knowledge, our approach stresses the notion of behaviour. Before I go any further, I want to indicate what I mean by 'behaviour'. Behaviour is what we observe when we watch other people or animals going about their normal everyday activities. We can extend the notion to objects. Objects are also capable of exhibiting behaviour: balls roll ('rolling' behaviour), stones fall ('falling' behaviour) but objects also exhibit more passive kinds of behaviour including, in the limit, having an existence ('existing' behaviour). Events are changes in behaviour. If a ball is falling, bounces, and then rises, there is an event (a 'bounce') as the falling behaviour changes to rising behaviour.

2.1 Situated behaviour

At the heart of the method advocated here is the notion of situation. By this I mean that the actions of an agent are always taken in some very specific context; the action it is appropriate for one agent to take is in most cases dependent on the moment-to-moment activities of other agents (and of physical events in the world) and *its* actions, in turn, form part of *their* situation. For this reason, the interaction between agents is non-linear and hence unpredictable in detail. A further consequence of this view is that the actions of one agent are only *intelligible* to another if the situation is also perceived by the second agent. Apparent cooperation between agents can be based on mutual intelligibility of this kind and on the consequent interleaving of actions (Hickmann & Shiels, 1990). Suchman discusses the whole question of situated action at some length in Suchmann (1987).

The non-linearity of agent behaviour, particularly in complex environments, may give rise to doubts about our ability to deal with such situations, but there is, fortunately, a redeeming feature; most complex environments (including the real world) are not random, or malign. There is a structure of which the agent can take advantage and which massively reduces the cognitive load imposed upon it (Agre, 1985); much of the apparent cognitive effort is rendered unnecessary for one reason or another. A simple example is given by Simon in his parable of the ant (Simon, 1981).

There is another way of thinking of situated behaviour. Imagine a loop of activity which is threaded through the agent and the world; events in the world, the perceptions of the agent, the actions of the agent and the effect of these actions on the world all go to make up this loop and hence couple the agent closely to the rest of the world. There are very many of these loops which together determine the interactions between the agent and the rest of the world and the survival of the agent requires that they are dynamically stable. Thus any perturbation in the loop must induce compensating behaviour in some other part of the loop. It is in this sense that an agent's actions can be said to be situated. This notion of interaction *via* a threaded loop applies also to the social behaviour of agents. Social structures are maintained, and stability in an interaction achieved, by situated social action. This model emphasises the fact that we cannot simply think of the agent acting on the world. The actions of the agent and the behaviour of its environment are *co-determined.*

The world is not a place in which all the knowledge that is required for the solution to a problem is available or derivable, and the task of the agent is not simply one of information processing and reasoning. Only a small fraction of all the behaviour and events in the world are relevant to any agent and the successful agent (in an evolutionary sense) is the one that has developed strategies to cope with these relevant bits. For the most part these are not information processing or problem solving strategies, but appropriate ways of reacting to events; the agent's relationship with the rest of the world is one of coping with ongoing events which never terminate and which do not normally require a 'solution' as such. The process of filtering out relevant events and coping with them by situated behaviour is what allows relatively simple biological agents to exist and prosper in our complex world and the process must be closely tailored to the needs of the agent. In the biological case tailoring is achieved by evolution, supplemented in some cases by cultural and individual learning. In the case of artificial agents it is the designer who must provide these strategies perhaps with the aid of machine learning. Of course an agent may reason, but it is important to realise that this is only one strategy, and in any case reasoning may well emerge from more fundamental behaviour (Chapman & Agre, 1986).

2.2 The social behaviour of agents

Although one can think of applications where an agent acts in isolation, the majority of cases, and particularly those falling under the rubric of this workshop, involve cooperation between agents. Even in cases of apparent isolation (e.g., a Mars rover) the behaviour of the agent will have been learned or given to it, and its concepts will have been acquired, in a multi-agent society. Without that society its actions would have no purpose and it would not have formulated the concepts which appear to drive it. In other words, the science of autonomous agents is, in an important sense, a social science. This idea of a society of agents is an extension of the idea of situated agents where account is taken of the fact that the agent is not merely situated in the physical world, but specifically in a society. The fullest expression of this idea is to be seen in Coulter (1979), for example, in which the thesis that mind itself is a social construct is proposed. (See also Ryle (1962) for an earlier account of the non-objectivity of mind.)

Social agents of this kind exhibit behaviour which is complementary to the behaviour of other agents and to the behaviour of objects in their surroundings. By this I mean, for example, that one gesture will elicit another, that handing something to someone is complemented by their acceptance of the object and that questions (usually) receive answers. This means that it makes little sense to design agents in isolation; agents must be designed to function as members of a group which will in turn give meaning to their behaviour as individuals. This point is illustrated specifically in section 4. The social view of agents also allows, indeed even requires, one to take a different view of the intensionality of agents and of their goals from that usually taken. The usual view treats beliefs, plans and goals as objectively real and builds on these objects a logic for their manipulation and exploitation. There are many examples of this: Cohen & Levesque (1987), Fagin & Halpern (1985) and Konolige (1986) are some of the best known workers in the field of beliefs, and the planning literature is full of references to goals, plans, means-ends analysis and so on. The social viewpoint, on the other hand, treats such concepts as being ascribed to an agent by an observer. The role of the observer thus becomes very important. The ascriptions are part of the way an observing agent tries to structure its view of the world and not (at least not always or usually) part of the explicit state of the observed agent. A belief, for example, is not an explicit sentence or state in an agent but a disposition to behave in a certain way in particular situations. Of course it is possible to verbalise plans, goals and beliefs, but even then they may not fulfil the role assigned to them in most AI literature. Plans, for example, as Suchmann (1987) puts it, are just one resource for action amongst many. Except in the simplest cases, they cannot be a list of actions to be undertaken sequentially in order to achieve a pre-determined goal.

2.3 The importance of time

It has been observed by many workers, including Allen (1984) and Allen & Hayes (1985), that time is important in considering the behaviour of agents. In fact, it is rather surprising that anyone could think of designing systems of agents (for example groups of cooperating expert systems) in which time does not have a central role. Shoham (1985) has discussed the requirements, as he sees them, for a theory of time and change and has evaluated some temporal theories against these criteria. However, the way in which time has been treated is not altogether satisfactory. It tends to be viewed purely as something that can be reasoned about and so, in Allen's calculus for example, one can state and deduce things about the simultaneity, sequence or inclusion of events. Whilst this is clearly important in some applications, it does not seem to be sufficiently radical. Lavignon and Shoham have, more recently, developed a theory of temporal automata in which time has a more central role (Lavignon & Shoham, 1990). Time is as fundamental as space to the operation of an agent and should be built into the heart of any system used for designing agents.

All behaviour takes place in time and requires a finite time for its execution. Furthermore the time available for an action is one of the constraints determining the nature of the action. There is, however, another reason for being interested in how time is represented in agent systems: understanding (and, indeed, reasoning) are spread out in time in the real world. Let us contrast two extremes. In one case everything is known, all the facts are simultaneously available and a choice of action has to be made. In the other, the situation unfolds dynamically, new information arrives and the state of the agent continually changes. In the latter case, action occurs when the constraints which govern that action are satisfied; it is not a decision making process but a case of situated action. Further, to be realistic, one requires not a single strand of events and behaviour but a high degree of *concurrency* in the operation of the agent. It is this possibility of concurrency which, in large part, lends richness to the behaviour of agents.

There are several other theoretical issues which have not been dealt with here including emergence and learning. A start has been made on trying to understand and control emergent behaviour (Wavish, 1991), but we have not yet made any serious attempt to introduce machine learning into our agents although this is an important topic.

In this section, I have emphasized the importance of situated, social and temporal behaviour in the design of agents. In the next section, I describe a software tool which allows for the easy expression of the situated and temporal aspect of agents. The question of achieving the right perspective, particularly with respect to the intensional and social aspects of the agent, remains the direct responsibility of the designer.

3 A language for the design of agents

Over the past few years we have developed a language which is particularly appropriate for the design of the kind of agents outlined in the previous section. We need a language in which we can express any kind of behaviour, the interdependence of behaviours and the temporal relationship between them. In addition we need help in understanding the non-linear effects of agent interaction.

The first version of this language was called ABLE — Agent Behaviour LanguagE. The fundamental constructs in this language were referred to as 'behaviours' because they represent instances of what we have been calling behaviour throughout this paper. These constructs include *atomic behaviours* which do no more than establish the existence of the behaviour in question, *simple behaviours* which define a dependency relationship, *licences* and *schemas* which control the creation or the destruction of behaviours and *worlds* which encapsulate bodies of behaviour which we wish to group together (usually because they occur in the same time frame). The language resembles a production rule system but the direct incorporation of time in the rules (or in our terminology, licences or schemas) gives a very different flavour to it and results in a quite different form of operation. Some licences, for example, are:[2]

hungry(Agent) & food(Food) → eat(Agent, Food)

The capital letters signify variables and this licence simply means that if an agent is hungry and there is food about the agent will eat it.

What happens when the agent eats the food?

eat(Agent, Food)/60.0 → {no(Food), no(hungry(Agent)) }

This licence corresponds to the observation that if the agent eats the food, after one minute the food has gone and the agent is no longer hungry; time has entered into the description of behaviour. A time annotation such as this one on the left-hand side indicates that the annotated behaviour has to have been in existence for that length of time before the term as a whole is satisfied. A time annotation on the right-hand side expresses the *duration* of the behaviour annotated.

Every symbolic behaviour in an agent must be grounded by reference to the world in which the agent exists. At the bottom level, that is to say at the point at which the agent is directly interfaced to the world, this grounding is achieved by using C to link RTA behaviours to behaviours in the world. Thus the connection to the world is effected by C modules controlling such things as sensors, actuators and graphics. This layer is crucial in that it allows agents to be situated in the world.[3]

This first version of the language was interpreted, and an early description of it is given in Wavish & Connah (1990). The result of running the interpreter on an ABLE text was a simulation over time of the behaviour of the system described by the text. The ability to simulate the behaviour of systems directly is precisely what was needed to help us understand non-linear behaviour. This language was satisfactory in most ways except that interpretation was very slow and that it consumed quite large amounts of memory. These limitations were serious for two reasons. In the first place, slow interpretation made the development of demonstrations or applications very difficult. As will be seen later, the natural method of working with

[2] These examples are taken from Graham & Wavish (1991).

[3] It could, of course, be implemented in other languages, but C is both portable and convenient.

this kind of language is iterative and many iterations may be required before a satisfactory result is achieved. Slow interpretation made this method unacceptable. In the second place, we wanted to be able to develop viable solutions to realistic problems which might involve large numbers of licences (productions) running on quite modest machinery. This also meant that speed and space were at a premium.

In order to overcome this problem another version of the language was developed called Real Time ABLE (usually referred to as RTA). There is not space here to describe RTA in detail. Suffice it to say here that it is a compiled language which allows the saving of much storage space and much greater speed in execution.

4 Designing groups of interacting agents

With the aid of RTA and the theoretical orientation outlined at the beginning of the paper we are in a position to design groups of interacting agents. I will illustrate this process with examples suggested by a demonstration program (Wavish, 1991). This program is in the nature of a game or entertainment based on the idea of a sheep dog rounding up sheep and driving them into a pen (cf., the British TV programme 'One Man and his Dog'). The demonstration is a simulation of a system containing seven agents: a sheep dog, five sheep and a shepherd. The shepherd is rather passive and although his existence is important his behaviour can safely be ignored for our purposes here. The idea is that the dog (either by itself or with the help of the player) should round up the sheep and drive them towards the shepherd who usually stands at the entrance to the pen. For this to happen both the sheep and the dog must, in some simple way, be able to perceive each other. As far as the dog is concerned, its surroundings are notionally divided into eight sectors centred on the dog itself. It has a rudimentary 'vision' system which informs it of which octants contain sheep. (This is all; it doesn't know how many sheep or how far away they are). The sheep on the other hand are 'aware' of the presence of the dog when it gets too close for comfort. Most of this part of the demonstration together with some anti-collision algorithms and all of the graphics are written in C. Given this rather basic perceptual ability, what behaviour should we write down in the form of licences that will cause the dog to round up the sheep and herd them towards the pen?[4]

Let us first consider the sheep:

perceive_dog_nearby(sheep) → run_away(sheep)

(any sheep near the dog move away and then stop)

run(dog)

(the dog runs in a straight line and any sheep in the path of the dog scatter)

[4] These fragments of RTA are for illustration only. It is not suggested that they are exactly what one would write in the real application. They would also, of course, have to be supported by many other licences to achieve their intended effect.

no(see_sheep_on_left(dog)) → turn_left(dog)

(the dog circles round to the left)

no(see_sheep_on_right(dog)) → turn_right(dog)

(but it could equally well circle round the other way — this behaviour will never co-exist with the previous one)

circle_left(dog) & see_shepherd_in_front(dog) → circle_right(dog)
circle_right(dog) & see_shepherd_in_front(dog) → circle_left(dog)

(by changing from one direction to the other the dog drives the sheep towards the shepherd).

We are now making some progress which would be readily visible in the sequence of simulations that we would make. In fact it turns out that fundamentally only four behaviours are required. They are as follows:

1. If the dog is circling right and there are no sheep in the dog's front-right octant, it will turn right until sheep appear in that octant, (Similarly if it is circling left).
2. If, at any time, the shepherd appears in one of the dog's three front octants, it must reverse its direction of travel.
3. If the dog approaches a sheep too closely, the sheep must move (run) away from the dog.
4. Sheep must avoid colliding with each other.

The result of these four behaviours is that the sheep are compressed into a flock and that the dog weaves to-and-fro behind the flock, driving it towards the shepherd.

What points are illustrated by this fragment of the demonstration?

1. The behaviour of the agents is situated. This is inherent in the structure of a licence. The situation is described on the left-hand side of the licence and appropriate behaviour is brought into existence by the right-hand side of the licence. Time is an integral part of the description of the situation and of the duration of the resulting behaviour.
2. The four behaviours described are (indeed have to be) present concurrently. It makes no sense to think in terms of priorities or sequences for these behaviours; any or all of them must be triggered in the appropriate situation.
3. When watching the demonstration it is natural to view it and describe it in terms of words or phrases such as 'flock', 'rounding up', 'herding the flock' and so on. None of these concepts is explicitly represented in the RTA text but they are ascribed by the observer to the behaviours of agents in the system.
4. Similarly, the dog has no explicit goal. It is natural to think of the dog as rounding up the sheep and driving them towards the shepherd but in fact the behaviour of the dog (in this fragment) is limited to the two behaviours described above which make no mention of these concepts and no mention of an explicit goal.

5. The flocking and herding of the sheep is not achieved solely by the dog's behaviour as one might assume but requires the complementary behaviour of the sheep. It is, in this sense, a kind of social behaviour in which all the agents (dog and five sheep) trigger behaviour in each other leading to stable behaviour of the social group as a whole.
6. The stability mentioned in 5 is important. The overall behaviour of the group is not predictable in detail (although it is deterministic) and different starting positions of the agents lead to sequences which, in detail, are completely different. However, over a wide range of parameters, the behaviour at the level of the flock (and this indeed is what leads us to *ascribe* the term 'flock') is extremely stable and robust in the sense that it can be deliberately disrupted (e.g., the player can pick up and move the dog or any or all of the sheep) and will fairly rapidly return to the stable flocking and driving behaviour. This combination of stability with lack of any detailed predictability is characteristic of a chaotic system and we might speculate that 'flock' is the name we give to an attractor in such a system. We have not as yet pursued this idea any further. The applicability of chaos theory to agents has been discussed in Kiss (1991).

5 Situated feedback

In the major part of this paper I have been concerned to show how situated agents interact with each other in general terms and I have put forward theoretical and practical suggestions for implementing this kind of interaction. In this section I want to speculate on how they can be used to implement particularly natural forms of feedback.

Feedback is an aspect of dialogue that has received much attention during the workshop. It can take many forms but I would like to concentrate on three types of feedback that are particularly appropriate to the situated agent approach and to illustrate them by reference to a simple agent-based program. This basic program has been implemented but the extensions demonstrating feedback have not, although there seem to be no major obstacles to making such an implementation.[5]

Chapman (1989), by way of replying to a problem envisaged by Ginsberg (1989), demonstrated the way in which a situated agent making use of visual markers (Ullman, 1984) could copy a pile of child's bricks which spelled out a word by means of letters on their front faces. One could imagine that making such a copy might form part of a spelling tutorial for a small child although the exact nature of the task is not important in the present context. Chapman's copy was made without resort to planning or to any internal representation of the problem or the world. The world that I am describing, with the copy partially completed, is shown in Figure 1.

[5] In saying this, I am referring to the RTA program. The graphics required may or may not be easy depending in part on the platform chosen but the task is quite feasible. It is, in any event, outside the scope of this paper.

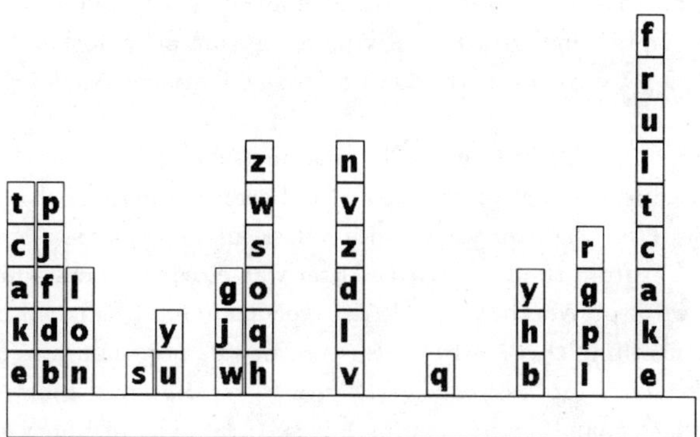

Fig. 1. Chapman's blocks world

An extension to this idea, which I have implemented, is one in which the original is not built once and for all but is maintained in the face of destructive changes in the world. The agent in the program is invisible; the copy seems to grow or to undergo correction without any obvious agency. If the agent were to be made visible, at least three types of feedback could be used to assist someone trying to make such a copy.

The agent in the program is always performing some sub-task. These sub-tasks include checking the correctness of the copy, looking for a block in order to continue building the copy or, perhaps, searching for the position of the copy if it has been moved or substantially changed. These activities are identifiable with certain behaviours in the program and thus it would be possible to associate with them appropriate movements on the part of the agent. These movements of the head, eyes or hand would serve to indicate the current focus of attention of the agent and thus help naturally to direct the attention of the student to an appropriate task or problem area. It would also be possible for the agent to make simple gestures, like pointing, to help the user. Thus the first feedback mode is one concerned with this communication of the *focus of attention*. Notice that it is made possible because of the fact that using markers to mark points in the agent's visual field preserves for the agent the spatial relationships present in the world. In the conventional AI solution to blocks world problems, although a simple 'ON' relationship is retained, other spatial relationships are not. Indeed to try to retain them would cause serious problems for such an approach.

The second kind of feedback concerns those moments when it might be appropriate for the agent to express some simple *emotion*, e.g. when the copy was complete or had just been successfully restored or when a block was found during a search. Frustration might be occasioned by the copy continually being damaged and so on. Encouragement to the user could be given in a similar way. These emotional responses could take the form of an expression on the face of the agent (a smile or a puzzled look) or possibly simple sounds such as clapping, saying "yes" or "no" or making a sound expressing irritation. Giving agents simple emotional responses has been investigated by workers in the Oz project at Carnegie-Mellon (Bates et al., 1992).

The third type of feedback would be by *demonstration*, in which the agent would simply intervene and do part of the task if it became apparent that the user was having difficulty. That the user was in difficulties might be obvious either from the time being taken or from the fact that the user was moving blocks which were inappropriate. The work of Wood et al., (1978) (see also Good, this volume) discusses strategies for controlling this kind of intervention so as to maximise learning.

These three feedback modes, *focus of attention, emotion* and *demonstration* have in common the fact that they are completely natural. The ordinary user might be unaware that he or she was in fact receiving feedback on their performance and thus would not feel inclined to reject it. The feeling would simply be that the user and the agent were *cooperating* in a game or in a joint task; a cooperation which was enabled and maintained by physical activities in the world (Hickmann & Shiels, 1990). Furthermore it would be particularly easy to implement in a situated agent because of the fact that such an agent can react quickly and directly to the current situation and does not have to reason about, or plan, its own actions. In addition RTA treats these different kinds of behaviour uniformly and it is thus trivial to integrate simple emotional or attitudinal behaviour with either observations of the user's actions or with its own physical behaviour.

6 Conclusion

In this paper I have attempted to show that systems of interacting agents can be designed by a method which has situated behaviour, time and social behaviour as its foundation. The description of the method of working given in section 4 was oversimplified, but it serves to illustrate the incremental nature of the process and the important role that simulation plays in it. In designing agents of this kind, account must be taken of their social dimension and groups of agents should be designed together rather than individually. The resulting designs are very different from top down designs but they have the advantage that they are often surprisingly robust and can be implemented so efficiently that very large systems can be contemplated with the resources currently at our disposal. Feedback to the student of a particularly natural kind can be easily implemented because spatial and temporal location are an integral part of the agent's situation and because emotional aspects of the agent's behaviour can easily be integrated with its perceptions and actions.

Acknowledgments

The ideas put forward in this paper were evolved during many discussions with other members of the team involved in the project. I would particularly like to acknowledge the work of Peter Wavish in developing the RTA software and in writing one of the demonstrators which I used for illustrative purposes in this paper. I would also like to thank Peter Wavish and Mike Graham for their helpful criticism of earlier drafts of the paper.

References

Agre, P.E. (1985) Routines. MIT AI Memo 828.

Allen, J.F. (1984) Towards a general theory of Action and Time. Artificial Intelligence, 23, 123–154.

Allen, J.F. & Hayes, P.J. (1985) A Common-Sense Theory of Time. Proceedings of IJCAI 1985, 528–531.

Bates, J., Loyall, A.B. & Reilly, W.S. (1992) An Architecture for Action, Emotion, and Social Behavior. Proceedings of the 4th. European Workshop on Modelling an Autonomous Agent in a Multi-Agent World. Amsterdam: Elsevier North-Holland.

Chapman, D. (1989) Penguins Can Make Cake. AI Magazine, 45–50.

Chapman, D. & Agre, P.E. (1986) Abstract Reasoning as Emergent from Concrete Activity. Georgeff & Lansky (eds.) Workshop on Reasoning about Actions and Plans. Timberline, Oregon: Morgan Kaufmann.

Cohen, P.R. & Levesque, H.J. (1987) Persistence, Intention, and Commitment. SRI International Technical Note 415.

Coulter, J. (1979) The Social Construction of Mind: Studies in Ethnomethodology & Linguistic Philosophy. Macmillan Press.

Fagin, R. & Halpern, J.Y. (1985) Belief, Awareness, and Limited Reasoning: Preliminary Report. IJCAI 85, 491–501. Morgan Kaufmann.

Ginsberg, M.L. (1989) Universal Planning: An (Almost) Universally Bad Idea. AI Magazine, 40–44.

Graham, M. & Wavish, P.R. (1991) Simulating and Implementing Agents and Multiple Agent Systems. Moskilde (ed.) Proceedings of the 1991 European Simulation Multi-Conference.

Hickmann, S.J. & Shiels, M.A. (1990) Situated Action as a Basis for Cooperation. Proceedings of the 2nd. European Workshop on Modelling an Autonomous Agent in a Multi-Agent World. Amsterdam: Elsevier North-Holland.

Kiss, G. (1991) From Animals to Animats. MIT Press.

Konolige, K. (1986) A Deduction model of Belief. London: Pitman and Morgan Kaufmann.

Lavignon, J.F. & Shoham, Y. (1990) Temporal Automata. Tech. rept. STAN-CS-90-1325. Stanford University, Computer Science Department.

Ryle, G. (1962) The Concept of Mind. London: Hutchinson.

Shoham, Y. (1985) Ten Requirements for a Theory of Change. New Generation Computing, 3, 467–477. Ohmsha Ltd. and Springer-Verlag.

Simon, H.A. (1981) The Sciences of the Artificial. Cambridge, MA: MIT Press.

Suchmann, Lucy A. (1987) Plans and Situated Actions: the problems of human-machine communication. Cambridge: Cambridge University Press.

Ullman, S. (1984) Visual Routines. Cognition, 18, 97–159.

Wavish, P.R. (1991) Exploiting Emergent Behaviour in Multi-Agent Systems. Demazeau, Y. & Werner, E. (eds.) Proceedings of the 3rd. European Workshop on Modelling an Autonomous Agent in a Multi-Agent World. Kaiserslautern, 5-7 August 1991. Amsterdam: Elsevier North-Holland.

Wavish, P.R. & Connah, D.M. (1990) Representing Multi-Agent Worlds in ABLE. Technical Note 2964. Philips Research Laboratories, Redhill, England.

Wood, D.J., Wood, H.A. & Middleton, D.J. (1978) An Experimental Evaluation of Four Teaching Strategies. International Journal of Behavioural Development, 1(2), 131–147.

Method for Dialogue Protocol Analysis

Maddy D. Brouwer-Janse

Institute for Perception Research/IPO, P.O. Box 513, 5600 MB Eindhoven, The Netherlands, email: brouwerm@prl.philips.nl

Abstract. Guidelines for analyzing dialogues that people generate when they are involved in a problem-solving situation are presented. A coding system for verbal data analysis is presented that consists of different levels of data observation and that can account for the diversity of human problem-solving behaviour, learning effects, and development.

Keywords. Problem solving, thinking aloud, protocol analysis, verbal reports

1 Introduction

Thinking-aloud protocols obtained in human problem-solving studies provide insight in the structure and the content of a particular type of dialogue. The partners in these dialogues are the problem-solving person and the experimenter or interviewer. The role of the experimenter may vary from silent observer to active collaborator. These problem-solving dialogues are generated in many different situations, for example, to study problem-solving behaviour, to compare different levels of human expertise, to elicit knowledge from humans for intelligent system support, to induce a user-centered approach to system development, to acquire data for training tools, intelligent assistants and help systems, and to evaluate the effect of a tutor.

This paper presents guidelines for analyzing the dialogues that people generate when they are involved in a problem-solving situation. A model for data analysis is presented that consists of different levels of data observation and that uses a coding instrument that accounts for the diversity of human problem-solving behaviour, learning effects, and development. This model is based on experience in verbal protocol analysis of different studies in academic and industrial settings. The subjects are system users. The stimuli are problem-solving tasks at different levels of complexity presented by these systems. The conditions are determined by the environments in which these systems are used. The response data consist of user behaviour collected as verbal reports.

First an overview will be given of different types of verbal data and the way they are collected. In the second part of this paper the model for verbal data analysis will be presented and examples of its use will be given.

2 Collection of verbal protocol data

Verbal protocols are collected as data in formal problem solving studies and in applied research. These formal problem solving studies usually address the distinctions between novices and experts in a specified domain, for example, physics, computer programming, or chess. The applied research areas are knowledge-based system design (knowledge acquisition) and user-centered system design. Verbal protocol data used for application purposes are usually generated by an amalgam of methods that originate from research on the cognitive processes involved in human problem solving, i.e. the use of

- spontaneous thinking-aloud verbal protocols,
- interactive interview protocols, and
- retrospective reports.

To generate *thinking-aloud verbal protocols*, people are asked to think aloud while solving problems. It is assumed that people's contemporaneous verbalizations about what they are thinking is as close as we can get to their actual underlying thinking processes. Interactions between experimenter and participant are as limited as possible, verbalizations are spontaneous, and the use of cues and probes is not allowed (Ericsson & Simon, 1984). The purpose of the thinking-aloud method is to study observable problem-solving behaviour on a controlled task in a controlled environment making minimal assumptions about the underlying competence of the problem solvers.

To generate *interactive interview protocols*, people are placed in the position of a scientist exploring unfamiliar or novel problems and inventing ways for solving them. The verbal protocols are the result of the interaction between experimenter and participant. The purpose of the interactive method is to infer the underlying problem-solving competence by trying to elicit maximum problem-solving performance. These experiments are, however, not controlled; experimenter probes may vary with each individual participant and results are not reproducible. Thinking-aloud verbal protocols and interactive interview protocols are concurrent verbal reports, i.e. the cognitive processes while completing the task are not modified by these verbal reports.

Another type of verbal protocol is the *retrospective report*, i.e. a durable memory trace of the information heeded while completing the task. To generate retrospective reports people are asked immediately after completion of the task to tell what they did. Serious caveats for the reliability of retrospective data are

- the desire of experimenters to ask participants to verbalize their motives and reasons, which may not be available directly or even at all from memory, and
- the inability to avoid participants' tendencies to fill in information that they cannot remember but 'must' have thought.

In addition to their blending and unproper usage, the limitations of these methods for system development are manifold. First, the behaviour of a user solving a problem in a relevant domain is observed at a given point in time. The implicit assumptions are

- that human problem solving behaviour does not change over a period of time,
- that users will always solve the same problem in the same way, and
- that there is basically one best approach to the solution of a problem.

Second, the process of designing the content, number and order of cues and questions is heavily biased towards the interviewer's expectations about the problem and its domain, and the available development or prototyping tools. Third, the end-users of the system have to adapt their problem-solving behaviour to the model extracted from the original test person(s) as interpreted by the system designer.

Furthermore, using systems induces changes in human knowledge and expertise as an ongoing process. These changes occur at the observable level of performance and at the inferred level of competence. They can be produced by means of:

- problem solving — achieving new knowledge by way of thinking things out in a specific situation;
- learning — improving general cognitive capacities under outside influences, i.e. by example, by being told or by doing;
- creativity — generation of new representations of the world.

Models for describing and predicting user's behaviour have to account for these changes. Hence, to conduct problem-solving studies of users of professional and consumer products, procedures and protocol coding instruments have to be developed that take these changes into account. These instruments will be discussed in the next session.

3 Model for data analysis

The procedure for protocol generation may comprise three phases. First, participants are asked to think-out loud while solving the problem. This phase can be followed by an interactive interview and a retrospective report in which participants tell what they did in their own words. For example, a problem-solving session may consist of a period of thinking-aloud until the participant indicates that the problem is solved or finished. Then the session continues with prompts and cues for other possibilities until depletion, followed by a debriefing in which the participant provides a description of the problem in domain-specific terminology.

The model for data analysis is organized into two levels. Level I includes the preprocessing of the 'raw' verbal data into codeable propositions and episodes. This phase consists of producing a written transcript of all the verbal output, including temporal information, repetition and stress. If available and needed, video observations are included to support the verbal data. Level I provides a global analysis of and insight into the overall approach of the participant(s). Level II, the encoding phase, consists of determining coding categories *a priori* and having human judges make the coding assessments. Each level comprises a number of steps.

The importance of these steps and the level of detail depend on the objectives of the intended study. Examples of such objectives are:

- initial exploration of acceptability of system concepts by end-users;
- in-depth analysis of how professionals go about their actual professional tasks;
- identifying the peculiarities of system characteristics that cause user problems and frustrations;
- determining when, where, and how to provide user feedback, user assistance and user guidance;
- showing system designers the results and effects of their product concepts.

3.1 Level I: pre-processing

The analysis in level I consists of 7 steps. These steps require an extensive effort, depending on the complexity and duration of the task, the number of participants and focus of interest.

1. *Description of problem.* Immediately after the task is finished, ask the participants to describe the problem in their own words, using their domain terminology and interpretation. This record provides retrospective information about the task, its content and knowledge of domain-specific terminology. This is the only phase in the protocol analysis process in which retrospective data are used.
2. *Verbatim transcript of data.* Transcribe the verbal output that is recorded on audiotape or videotape. Pauses, expressions with emotional content (for example, "ah", "hhehe", "shoot", "hmmm"), broken words, mumbles, half sentences, and experimenter prompts are included in the raw transcript.
3. *List of propositions.* Edit the raw protocol into an ordered list of problem-relevant propositions. Verbal propositions are defined as simple sentences occurring in the context of connected discourse.
4. *Protocol episodes.* Divide the edited protocol into episodes to address contextual factors. That is, verbal propositions whose function when tested in isolation is not clear are disambiguated in the context of the episode in which they occur. The boundaries of the episodes are determined by a combination of semantic and syntactic criteria. For example, summarizing statements, e.g. "Here, I am okay", indicate the end of an episode, and a transition statement, e.g. "So, now I can...", the beginning of the next. Transitions between episodes are also indicated by exclamations, e.g. "okay!, forget it!", "so, well!". In nearly all cases, transitions between episodes are marked by pauses of several seconds followed by changes in inflection.
5. *Proofread the episoded protocol.* Ask the participant to
   - proofread the episoded protocol against the tape to clarify technical expressions and 'mumbles' and
   - check the episode boundaries within the domain context.

   This step is especially useful for complex technical problems to clarify domain-specific concepts and terminology. If the number of participants is too high, a sample of participants can be used.

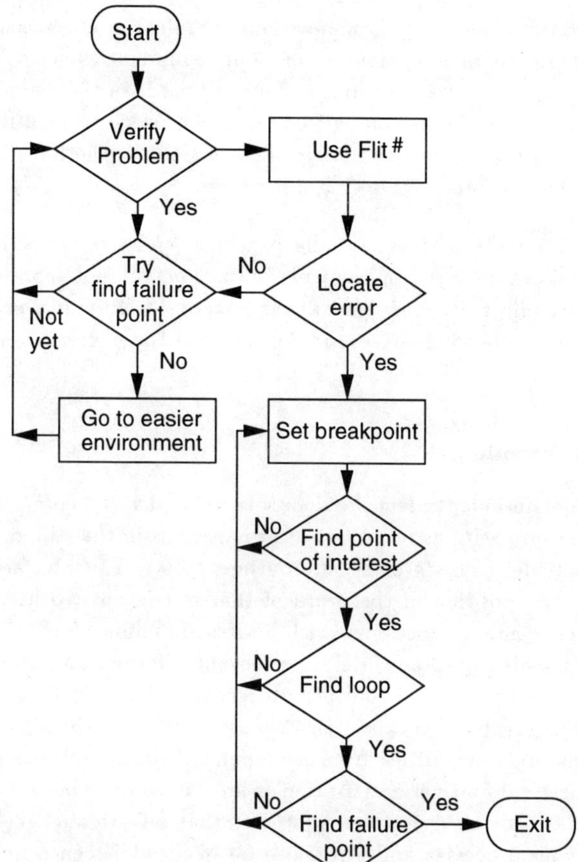

Fig. 1. Flow diagram of episode content. Expert software engineer debugging a program. The original protocol, from a 150-minute session, was 16784 words long with 1943 propositions divided into 55 episodes (Brouwer-Janse & Reeves, 1986). Passages from one state to another are represented by arrows. It is not always clear from the protocol what justification the subject used.

6. *Summarize episodes.* Make short summary statements of the content of each episode. These summaries represent the interpretation of the problem-solving process in the domain context. They contain the procedures used by the participants; the knowledge about 'what' is done, not about 'how' and 'why' it is done. In other words, they represent knowledge states and procedures.
7. *Flow diagram of problem-solving process.* Represent the knowledge states and procedures as flow diagrams. These flow diagrams of the episode contents show

the overall picture of the problem-solving process, i.e. the major activities and their relations. It does not show how long certain processes take, how many back-ups there are, or how many errors and redundancies occur. They can be used, for example, to make scripts and story boards of the overall process for follow-up studies, to make comparisons between users, to identify conceptual problems or to find patterns of usage. Figure 1 shows the flow diagram of an expert software engineer debugging a program.

Information about the problem solving processes and strategies that are available to users and are deployed in particular situations are not represented in flow diagrams. For this information analyses at the level of the individual protocol propositions are necessary. These analyses are described in the next section at the Level II of the model.

3.2 Level II: encoding

A theoretical domain-independent problem-solving model (Brouwer-Janse, 1983) is used to code the propositions or groups of propositions in the edited and episoded protocol. This model consists of 24 subroutines (SRs). The SRs are used to label every verbal proposition in the protocol that is relevant to the problem. The SRs represent elementary processes which address functions such as list given information, list possible questions, delete irrelevant information. At a second level of analysis the problem solving routines are grouped into eight strategies. These strategies address functions such as: use of means-end algorithms to acquire data, extract patterns and regularities from accumulated data, and generate and test hypotheses. These subroutines and strategies are shown in Table 1.

This model has been used in different studies that investigated the development of problem-solving processes and strategies between adolescence and adulthood, and between experts and non-experts (Pitt, 1983; Brouwer-Janse & Pitt, 1983). In these studies the SRs and strategies were used to code over 200 verbal protocols for determining qualitative and quantitative differences. The groupings of SRs into strategies is based on experimental results; they occurred together over and over again in subjects' protocols. The type of problem, its complexity in relation to the person's expertise, and the underlying concepts determine the pattern of strategies used by the problem solver. For example, Table 2 shows the proportional use of strategies by novices and experts solving a simple and complex problem (Brouwer-Janse & Pitt, 1986). The proportional use of strategies was calculated as the number of different subroutines expressed at least once within each strategy.

Different problem concepts elicit different patterns of strategy use. These different patterns and the possibilities of using the coding instrument at different levels of detail will be illustrated with three examples from the following domains: evaluating professional software, designing analogue circuits and debugging software programs.

Table 1. Strategies and consisting subroutines.

Strategy	Subroutine	Subroutine Description	Strategy Description
Selection	SR6 SR9 SR13 SR19	List Relevant Information Select Relevant Question(s) Identify Available Algorithms Organize and Compile Data	Process of selecting the most appropriate information, specifying the crucial question to address, deliberate choosing of the algorithm, and a selective reorganization and compiling of the data.
Evaluation	SR2 SR4 SR5 SR15	List Assumptions Select Evaluative Criteria Assign Priorities Edit Algorithm	Continuous evaluation process, monitoring and reappraising the total problem-solving process as well as its constituents.
Hypothesizing	SR7 SR8 SR20 SR21	Formulate Hypotheses Define Predictions Match Data to Predictions Determine Truth Value Predictions	The generation of an if-then hypothesis and its corresponding predictions, and the confirmation and disconfirmation of predictions.
General Problem Solver (GPS)	SR10 SR11 SR12	Define Initial State Define Goal State Identify Data Needed	Use of means-end algorithm to achieve consecutive subgoals.
Pattern Extraction	SR22 SR23	Extract Patterns from Data Summarize Relevant Patterns	Identification of relevant patterns, symmetries, regularities, analogies in the assembled data.
Condition	SR1 SR3 SR14	List Given Information List Possible Questions Select Rule, Method or Algorithm	Compiling the necessary conditions for the execution of a program; e.g., directly available information, a question to address and a rule to apply.
Act	SR16 SR17 SR18	Execute Program Identify Feedback Tag New Information	Execution of a program and recording of the results.
Conclusion	SR24	Output Conclusions	Outcome or result of the problemsolving process reached after deliberation and often including a summing-up of the preceding.

Table 2. Use of strategies (Level II).

	Simple Problem		Complex Problem	
Strategy	Novice	Expert	Novice	Expert
Selection	.29	.31	.61	.86
Evaluation	.13	.18	.26	.61
Hypothesizing	.00	.02	.06	.34
GPS	.03	.06	.21	.75
Pattern Extraction	.08	.00	.75	.69
Condition	.43	.53	.66	.68
Act	.84	.82	.86	1.00
Conclusion	.89	.86	.69	1.00

3.3 Example 1: Statistical-software evaluation problem

The problem in this example concerns the evaluation of software for linear modeling. The problem solver was an expert statistician and a frequent user of the previous versions of the software. The new version is extended with an intelligent help system. The task consists of plotting a simple graph with the new software. The propositions in the protocol are encoded in chunks at the strategy level (Table 3). The dominant strategies are: General Problem Solver (GPS), Act and Evaluation. This pattern of strategy usage differs from that of the following two examples.

Table 3. Use of strategies at the proposition level (Level I, step 3).

Propositions	Strategy
Could it be that we first have to make a calculation before we can make a raw plot?	Selection
Activity D1. Back to the main menu.	GPS
Response variable T. A bracketed list A, B, E. Prior knowledge? No, then we'll get advice.	Act
Still problems. Let's try yes. I don't understand it, what is subset one? Data validation when no advice is given. What did I do with that?	Evaluation
But, I do want to make a graph.	GPS
I am being protected against myself. It is absurd. Compare to X. Two commands and I can make every graph I want.	Evaluation
...task unsuccessful.	Act

3.4 Example 2: Design problem

In this study, an expert in analog-circuit design addresses an optimization problem. The purpose of the study was to investigate how professional circuit designers go about their tasks. The results of the study were used for the design of a CAD tool for analogue circuit designers. Chunks of strategies found in the episode coding were used for representing goal-plan building blocks and for developing modes for the tool's user interface (Colgan & Brouwer-Janse, 1990). This protocol was analyzed at the level of episodes, i.e. Level I, step 4. The episodes with the assigned strategies (Level II) are shown in Table 4. The episode summaries (Level I, step 6) represent the first 60 minutes of the protocol (length 7800 words). The dominant strategies used in the episodes are: Selection, Evaluation, Hypothesizing, and General Problem solver (GPS).

Table 4. Use of strategies at the episode-summary level (Level I, step 6 and level II).

Episode (#propositions)	Episode Summary	Strategy
1(4)	Description of problem in general, limitations of technology and constraints	Selection
2(29)	Description of specifications for designing the circuit	GPS
3(2)	Identifies alternatives to meet the specs	Selection
4(16)	Inventory of possible characteristics of a FET	Hypothesizing
5(56)	Explanation of equations for the FET characteristics	Evaluation
6(47)	Prediction of possible solutions for a FET	Hypothesizing

3.5 Example 3: Debugging software programs

In this study an expert software engineer, the designer of a linking system, diagnoses a problem with this system submitted via a user bug report (Brouwer-Janse & Reeves, 1986). The protocol was coded at the proposition level. Table 5 shows the use of strategies in the protocol, that is, the frequency distribution for subroutines grouped as strategies. This use of strategies shows that the searching process is directed by Pattern Extraction, broken down into subsequent subgoals, General Problem Solver, and evaluated continuously, Evaluation. This pattern of strategy usage, which differs from that of Examples 1 and 2, illustrates that conceptually different problems generate different patterns in strategy usage.

Table 5. Distribution of strategy use calculated as frequency of constituting subroutines (Level II).

Strategy	Mean Usage
Selection	5.50
Evaluation	15.50
Hypothesizing	7.25
GPS	11.66
Pattern Extraction	25.00
Condition	32.33
Act	7.33
Conclusion	2.00

4 Discussion

Analyzing dialogues between humans or between humans and systems requires discipline. This type of research is extremely tedious and time-consuming. Methods that are developed and carefully tested in research laboratory and that are suitable for use under the constraints and conditions of system development are hard to find. The problem is at least twofold.

First, systematic data collection and obtaining results that can be generalized and that have descriptive and predictive power requires carefully designed experimentation. This is nearly impossible to accomplish in environments in which the development of systems and/or applications, such as educational systems, are at the core of the activities. It is not possible, because of available time, available subjects (or users), project constraints, availability and situation of practitioners, pressures caused by the development of new technologies, and so on. At best, a few case studies can be conducted.

Second, a model-based manageable analytic instrument that has been tested for its suitability is needed. Unfortunately, developing such an analytic instrument or coding system with a taxonomy that is appropriate for each dialogue domain requires also an enormous investment in research and experimentation. In this paper a general problem-solving model was used as the coding instrument. This model has been tested in different controlled problem-solving studies, with over 200 subjects, at different levels of age and experience, and with different problem concepts and levels of complexity. The model was used in case studies in applied environments to provide descriptions at different levels of abstraction of human problem-solving behaviour.

The results from these case studies provide knowledge about the structure of the dialogue they conduct and about the communication process while they are engaged in complex tasks. First, the pre-processing and encoding procedures provide structure for the interpretation process of verbal data obtained in user studies and evaluations. If an appropriate experimental design is used, quantitative and qualitative data can be obtained and results could be generalized to other products and systems. Second, the domain-independent coding instrument can account for differences in development and experience, i.e. changes in performance induced by using systems over a period of time. Differences between novice, casual and expert users or between first-time users and seasoned users are issues that crop up in most design processes; they underlie, for example, the requirements for help system levels, intelligent assistance, usability, ease of learning. Third, different classes of problems induce different patterns of strategy use. The ability to match problem solving patterns and task concepts reduces the product design space. To acquire this type of classification schemes, more data obtained from controlled problem solving studies are needed. Fourth, the coding instrument can be used at different levels of detail: episode, individual or chunks of propositions. The objectives of the observation determine the level of detail and consequently the amount of effort involved. Fifth, a formal description tool, such as the episode flow diagrams for describing actual user behaviour can be used to reveal the discrepancy between what users really do and what system designers think users should do. These flow diagrams can also be used to identify the conceptual problems users have with a system. Finally, dialogue data obtained in controlled problem-solving settings are amenable to generalization and comparisons and provide the basis for conducting and interpreting case studies in applied environments.

References

Brouwer-Janse, M.D. (1983) The concept of equilibrium in cognitive development. Ph.D. thesis, University of Minnesota, Minnesota.

Brouwer-Janse, M.D. & Pitt, R.B. (1983) Problem solving in adolescence and adulthood: Equilibrium concepts. Society for Research in child Development Biennial Meeting.

Brouwer-Janse, M.D. & Pitt, R.B. (1986) Knowledge acquisition; methodological issues and problem-solving profiles. Proceedings of the Seventh European Conference on Aritificial Intelligence, 120–127.

Brouwer-Janse, M.D. & Reeves, J. (1986) Extracting problem-solving knowledge from experts: a case study. Sperry Technical Memorandum. Sperry Technical Symposium.

Colgan, L. & Brouwer-Janse, M.D. (1990) An analysis of the circuit design process for a complex engineering application. Interact '90, 253–257.

Ericsson, K.A. & Simon, H.A. (1984) Protocol analysis; Verbal reports as data. Cambridge, UK: MIT Press.

Pitt, R.B. (1983) Development of a general problem-solving schema in adolescence and early adulthood. Journal of Experimental Psychology, 112(4), 547–584.

Part 4

Feedback and Control in Human-Machine Communication

Natural Dialogue in Modes other than Natural Language

Robert J.K. Jacob

Department of Electrical Engineering and Computer Science, Tufts University, Medford, Mass. 02155, USA, email: jacob@cs.tufts.edu

Abstract. Each command or transaction in a modern graphical user interface exists as a nearly independent utterance, unconnected to previous and future ones from the same user. This is unlike real human communication, where each utterance draws on previous ones for its meaning. While some natural language human-computer interfaces attempt to include such characteristics of human dialogue, they have been notably absent from graphical user interfaces. Our goal is to connect these properties of human dialogue to direct manipulation or graphical styles of user-computer interaction. This chapter describes our approach to incorporating some of the properties of natural dialogue (such as conversational flow, discourse, focus) into 'other' (that is, not natural language) modes of human-computer communication. It also describes our research on building a natural user-computer dialogue based on a user's eye movements. That work shows that starting from natural, rather than trained, eye movements results in a more natural dialogue with the user.

Keywords. Human-computer interaction, interaction techniques, dialogue, discourse, direct manipulation, graphical user interface, eye movements

1 Introduction

In a direct manipulation or graphical interface, each command or brief transaction exists as a nearly independent utterance, unconnected to previous and future ones from the same user. Real human communication rarely consists of such individual, unconnected utterances, but rather each utterance can draw on previous ones for its meaning. It may do so implicitly, embodied in a conversational focus, state, or mode, or explicitly (e.g., 'Do the same sorting operation you did before, but on these new data').

Our goal is to connect these properties of human dialogue to direct manipulation or graphical interaction styles. While some natural language human-computer interfaces attempt to exploit these characteristics of human dialogue, they have been notably absent from graphical interfaces. Some of the properties of dialogue seem tightly connected to natural language and hence may not apply to a graphical interface, but some reflect deeper structure of human discourse than can usefully be applied to other modes of communication, such as graphics, pointing, dragging, gesturing, looking, and form fill-in. Natural dialogue is by no means restricted to natural language. Most research on the processes needed to conduct such dialogues has concentrated on natural language, but some of them can be applied to any human-computer dialogue conducted in any language. A direct manipulation dialogue is conducted in a rich graphical language using powerful and natural input and output modalities. The user's side of the dialogue may consist almost entirely of pointing, gesturing, and pressing buttons, and the computer's side, of animated pictorial analogues of real-world objects. A dialogue in such a language could nevertheless exhibit useful dialogue properties, such as following focus.

2 Direct manipulation

Direct manipulation graphical interfaces provide many significant advantages in human-computer communication (Shneiderman, 1983). They exploit the high bandwidth of the human visual system through the use of graphics to communicate information. They provide inter-referential input-output, which allows the user to communicate back to the computer in the same graphical mode by referring to objects on display. A direct manipulation user interface typically presents its user a set of objects on a display and a standard repertoire of manipulations that can be performed on any of them. This means that the user has no command language to remember beyond the standard set of manipulations and few cognitive changes of mode. The displayed objects are active in the sense that they are affected by each command issued. Whenever the user requests output, the objects shown in the resulting display on the screen are acceptable inputs to subsequent commands. They provide a continuous, implicit reminder of the available objects and their states. Output is thus not a fixed, passive display, but a collection of dynamic, manipulable objects, each usable as an input to subsequent commands. A typical user command or input is synthesized from objects already on display, the outputs of previous commands.

Recent work has carried the user's illusion of manipulating real objects still further. By coupling a the motion of the user's head to changes in the images presented on a head-mounted display, the illusion of being surrounded by a world of computer-generated images or a virtual environment is created. Hand-mounted sensors allow the user to interact with these images as if they were real objects located in space surrounding him or her (Foley, 1987). Much of the advantage of such interfaces derives from the fact that the user seems to operate directly *on* the objects in the computer rather than carrying on a dialogue *about* them. Instead of using a command language to describe operations on objects, the user 'manipulates' objects visible to him or her.

In cognitive terms, the properties of direct manipulation interfaces can be decomposed into direct engagement and reduced semantic distance (Hutchins et al., 1986). Direct engagement is the sense of manipulating objects directly on a screen rather than conversing *about* them. 'There is a feeling of involvement directly with a world of objects rather than of communicating with an intermediary. The interactions are much like interacting with objects in the physical world. Actions apply to the objects, observations are made directly upon those objects, and the interface and the computer become invisible.' (Hutchins et al., 1986) The other property is a reduction of cognitive distance, the mental effort needed to translate from the input actions and output representations to the operations and objects in the problem domain itself. Using a display screen, the visual images chosen to depict the objects of the problem or application domain should be easy for the user to translate to and from that domain. Conversely, for input, the actions required to effect a command should be closely related to the meaning of the command in the problem domain. Research suggests that these two factors each contribute separably and additively to the higher performance observed with direct manipulation interfaces (Ballas et al., 1992).

Direct manipulation interfaces are thought to be 'modeless', in contrast to other interface styles. Modes or states refer to the varying interpretation of a user's input. In each mode, an interface may give different meanings to the same input operations. In a modeless interface, the system is always in the same mode, and inputs always have the same interpretation. Direct manipulation user interfaces appear to be modeless, because many objects are visible on the screen, and at any time the user can apply any of a standard set of commands to any object. In fact, this view ignores the input operation of designating the object of interest. That operation sets the mode. For example, moving the cursor to lie over an object *is* the command to cause a mode change, because once it is moved, the range of acceptable inputs is reduced and the meaning of each of those inputs is determined. The benefits of 'modelessness' come from the fact that the mode is always clearly visible (as the location of a cursor in this example), and it has an obvious representation (simply the echo of the same cursor location just used to enter the mode change command) (Jacob, 1986).

Direct manipulation interfaces, including those set within virtual environments, then, provide a rich and powerful style of interaction, well tuned to both the perceptual and the cognitive characteristics of the user. However, these advantages come to an abrupt end when considering interaction over more than a single transaction. In a typical direct manipulation interface, every user operation is an isolated one-shot transaction with the computer, unconnected to previous or future interactions. Perhaps the goal of 'modeless' operation has been carried too far.

3 A framework for human-computer dialogue

Human-computer interface design is typically decomposed into the semantic, syntactic, and lexical levels (Foley et al., 1990):

- The semantic level describes the functions performed by the system. This corresponds to a description of the functional requirements of the system, but it does not address how the user will invoke the functions. The semantic level defines 'meanings', rather than 'forms' or 'sequences', which are left to the lower levels. It provides the high-level model or abstraction of the functions of the system.
- The syntactic level describes the sequences of inputs and outputs necessary to invoke the functions described. That is, it gives the rules by which which

sequences of words ('tokens') in the language are formed into proper (but not necessarily semantically meaningful) sentences. The design of the syntactic level describes the sequence of the logical input, output, and semantic operations, but not their internal details. A logical input or output operation is an input or output token. Its internal structure is described at the lexical level, while the syntactic describes when the user may enter it and what will happen next if he or she does (for an input token) or when the system will produce it (for an output token).

- The lexical level determines how the inputs and outputs are actually formed from primitive hardware operations or lexemes. It represents the binding of hardware actions to the hardware-independent tokens of the input and output languages. While tokens are the smallest units of meaning with respect to the syntax of the dialogue, lexemes are the actual hardware input and output operations that comprise the tokens.

Extending the linguistic analogy, we add a higher level to the interface design, above the semantic level:

- The discourse level is concerned with the flow of the human-computer dialogue over the course of more than one transaction. The semantic, syntactic, and lexical levels are concerned with a single user-computer transaction or brief interaction. The discourse level introduces elements that relate one transaction to another, such as dialogue focus.

We hope to bring some of the higher-level dialogue properties of natural language to the direct manipulation interaction style by adding the discourse level to the interface design. Previous work on graphical interaction techniques has been restricted to single transactions and single modes. Dialogue includes phenomena that happen over a series of transactions and integrates actions that occur in several modes. For example, a precise meaning can often be gleaned by combining imprecise actions in several modes, each of which would be ambiguous in isolation. We thus attempt to broaden the notion of interaction techniques in these two dimensions (multiple transactions and multiple modes). The rest of this paper describes, first, our ideas about how these areas can be melded and, second, our results results to date in obtaining single-transaction natural human-computer communication using eye movements as input.

4 Natural dialogue in a direct manipulation interface

We will begin with simple examples that allow movement from the utterly isolated-command-at-a-time situation in current graphical user interfaces. First, the notion of a single, prominently highlighted currently selected object (CSO), to which commands are applied, can be viewed as one simple step along these lines. It was incorporated into the first desktop interface, the Xerox Star, and nearly all subsequent direct manipulation interfaces. A further simple example would be for the computer to know where the user is looking and interpret his or her command in the light of that information. We will describe our current work in that area below. More interesting cases involve examining the recent history of the user's behaviour — what objects he has referred to, looked at, and manipulated over a longer time scale. We will describe our embryonic work in that area.

One useful property of dialogue that can be applied to a graphical interface is focus (Grosz, 1978). The graphical user interface could keep a history of the user's current focus, tracking brief digressions, meta-conversations, major topic shifts, and other changes in focus. Unlike a linguistic interface, the graphical interface would use inputs from a combination of graphical or manipulative modes to determine focus. Pointing and dragging of displayed objects, user gestures and gazes as well as the objects of explicit queries or commands all provide input to determine and track focus (Perez & Sibert, 1993). Moreover, focus would not be maintained as a single object, but rather a history of the course of the user-computer dialogue. It is necessary to track excursions or digressions in the dialogue so focus can be restored as necessary. In addition, it is helpful to track focus by categories. This allows the user to refer to 'the ship' even though the current focus is another object. In that case, the recent history of focus would be searched to find a ship of the appropriate category. Finally, focus is not necessarily a concrete object; it may be a class or category of objects ('all blue ships') or a more abstract entity ('the previous command').

As a simple example of the use of such focus information, the user might give a command (verb) without specifying its object, and the interface would supply the object based on the user's current focus. A more sophisticated approach would deduce the object of the command based on the recent history of the user's focus, rather than its single latest manifestation. The nature of the command might constrain the possible objects. For example, 'display hull speed' might apply only to ships. If the current focus were not such a ship, the interface would backtrack through recent focus objects to find the last applicable ship and use it as the inferred object of the command. Further, a 'retrieve data' command might indicate a shift from a digression back to the main dialogue, hence the appropriate object of this command would be not the current (digression) focus but the previous (main dialogue) focus.

Another use of focus is not based on supplying data to complete explicit commands, but rather passively deducing the user's current area of interest. The computer could, unasked, simply provide more detail about such an area. If the system had limited resources for obtaining data, it might even use this information to deploy its resources preferentially. For example, it might concentrate its display rendering computations in a particular area of the display or concentrate scarce communication bandwidth on the data that lie in that area. Extending outward from the computer itself, it might even order a change in the targeting of its external measuring instruments or sensors to the area of interest or initiate background tasks to collect additional data in that area.

Human dialogue often combines inputs from several modes. Deixis often involves a pointing gesture that does not precisely specify its object; the listener deduces the correct object from the context of the dialogue and, possibly, from integrating information from the hand gesture, the direction of the user's head, tone of his or her voice, and the like (Hill & Hollan, 1991). A user could, similarly, give a command and point in a general direction to indicate its object. The interface would disambiguate the pointing gesture based on the recent history of its dialogue with the user and, possibly, by combining other information about the user from physical sensors. An imprecise pointing gesture in the general direction of a displayed region of a map could be combined with the knowledge that the user's recent commands within that region referred principally to one of three specific locations (say, river R, island I, and hill H) within the region and the knowledge that the user had previously been looking primarily at islands displayed all over the map. By combining these three imprecise inputs, the interface could narrow the choice down so that (in this example) island I is the most likely object of the user's new command.

This example combined inputs in several modes and interaction history to disambiguate an imprecise pointing gesture. The same approach applies in the absence of a pointing gesture. The user might simply ask for 'that' without pointing. Recent history and focus plus physical information about the user may still be adequate to disambiguate the referent of 'that'.

The problem is usefully constrained if the user asks for 'the aircraft carrier' rather than simply 'that'. History, focus, and other information may then be combined with the restriction that aircraft carriers are the only pertinent objects to search for the last-referenced aircraft carrier (rather than the last-focused object in general) and thereby determine unambiguously the correct object of the user's command.

Another quite different use of dialogue in a graphical interface is to maintain a history of what the user has or has not processed. As a crude example, when new and urgent information appears on the display, it may be necessary to alert the user with a tone or a mandatory confirmation — but only if he or she has not already seen or acknowledged the information. Otherwise, in a critical situation warning tones may be sounding continually, often for information the user has processed, and the user will thus begin to ignore (or disable) the tones or become used to performing the mandatory confirmation action automatically. More generally, knowing whether the user has seen a particular object recently can often be helpful in providing the context in which to interpret the next action or command. Some cognitive user models attempt to keep track of what the user knows or does not know at any point in time in a dialogue. The present approach relies instead on explicit physical user actions (pointing to an object, seeing it, querying it) to determine what the user is aware of. This is somewhat more crude, but gives quite positive indication of knowledge the user does *not* have. Specifically, with this physically-based approach the interface can determine positively that the user has *not* seen something or has not seen it in a given time period. It can also determine that he or she *has* seen it, but it cannot be positive that he or she understood or remembered it.

5 Natural eye movement

This section reports our work to date on using eye movements as a medium for human-computer communication, in single isolated transactions (Jacob, 1990; Jacob, 1991; Jacob, 1993). This work differs from much other work on eye movements for input in that it emphasizes the use of natural eye movements rather than trained ones. Our approach has been, wherever possible, to obtain information from the *natural* movements of the user's eye while viewing a display, rather than requiring the user to make specific *trained* eye movements to actuate the system. To date, we have implemented only single transactions, that is, the human-computer interface has no longer-term dialogue or discourse properties. We are currently proceeding toward these longer-term properties, by beginning with the methods outlined in the previous section.

We began this work because HCI technology is currently stronger in the computer-to-user direction than user-to-computer, hence today's user-computer dialogues are typically one-sided, with the bandwidth from the computer to the user far greater than that from user to computer. Using the movements of a user's eyes as input to the computer can provide an additional high-bandwidth channel for obtaining data from the user conveniently and rapidly. Our focus has not been on technology for measuring a user's eye movements, but rather on developing appropriate interaction techniques that incorporate eye movements into the user-computer dialogue in a convenient and natural way. We thus begin by studying the known characteristics of natural eye movements and then attempt to design dialogues based on these characteristics.

6 Classes of eye movement-based interaction

In eye movements as with other areas of user interface design, it is helpful to draw analogies that use people's already-existing skills for operating in the natural environment and then apply them to communicating with a computer. One of the reasons for the success of direct manipulation interfaces is that they draw on analogies to existing human skills (pointing, grabbing, moving objects in physical space), rather than trained behaviours; and virtual environment offer the promise of usefully exploiting people's existing physical navigation and manipulation abilities. These notions are more difficult to extend to eye movement-based interaction, since few objects in the real world respond to people's eye movements (except for other people). In describing eye movement-based human-computer interaction we can draw two distinctions, one in the nature of the user's eye movements and the other, in the nature of the responses. Each of these could be viewed as *natural* (that is, based on a corresponding real-world analogy) or *unnatural* (no real world counterpart):

User's eye movements: Within the world created by an eye movement-based interface, users could move their eyes to scan the scene, just as they would a real world scene, unaffected by the presence of eye tracking equipment (i.e., *natural* eye movement). The alternative is to instruct users of the eye movement-based interface to move their eyes in particular ways, not necessarily those they would have employed if left to their own devices, in order to actuate the system (i.e., *unnatural* or learned eye movements).

Nature of the response: Objects could respond to a user's eye movements in a natural way, that is, the object responds to the user's looking in the same way real objects do. As noted, there is a limited domain from which to draw such analogies in the real world. The alternative is unnatural response, where objects respond in ways not experienced in the real world.

This suggests a range of four possible styles of eye movement-based interaction:

Natural eye movement/Natural response: This area is a difficult one, because it draws on a limited and subtle domain, principally how people respond to other people's gaze. Starker and Bolt provide an excellent example of this mode, drawing on the analogy of a tour guide or host who estimates the visitor's interests by his or her gazes (Starker & Bolt, 1990).

Natural eye movement/Un-natural response: In the work described below, we try to use natural (not trained) eye movements as input, but we provide responses unlike those in the real world. This is a compromise between full analogy to the real world and an entirely artificial interface. We present a display and allow the user to observe it with his or her normal scanning mechanisms, but such scans then induce responses from the computer not normally exhibited by real world objects.

Un-natural eye movement/Un-natural response: Most previous eye movement-based systems have used learned ('unnatural') eye movements for operation and thus, of necessity, unnatural responses. Much of that work has been aimed at disabled or hands-busy applications, where the cost of learning the required eye movements ('stare at this icon to activate the device') is repaid by the acquisition of an otherwise impossible new ability. However, we believe that the real benefits of eye movement interaction for the majority of users will be in its naturalness, fluidity, low cognitive load, and almost unconscious operation; these benefits are attenuated if unnatural, and thus quite conscious, eye movements are required.

Un-natural eye movement/Natural response: The remaining category created by this taxonomy is anomalous and not seen in practice.

7 Interaction techniques based on natural eye movements

In order to work toward natural eye movement-based interaction, we began by studying the nature of human eye movements and attempted to develop interaction techniques around their characteristics. To see an object clearly, it is necessary to move the eyeball so that the object appears on the fovea, a small area at the center of the retina. Because of this, a person's eye position provides a rather good indication (to within the one-degree width of the fovea) of what specific portion of the scene before him of her is being examined. The most common way of moving the eyes is a sudden, ballistic, and nearly instantaneous saccade. It is typically followed by a fixation, a 200–600 ms. period of relative stability during which an object can be viewed. During a fixation, however, the eye still makes small, jittery motions, generally covering less than one degree. Smooth eye motions, less sudden than saccades, occur only in response to a moving object in the visual field. Other eye movements, such as nystagmus, vergence, and torsional rotation are relatively insignificant in a user-computer dialogue.

The overall picture of eye movements for a user sitting in front of a computer is a collection of steady (but slightly jittery) fixations connected by sudden, rapid saccades. The eyes are rarely entirely still. They move during a fixation, and they seldom remain in one fixation for long. Compared to the slow and deliberate way people operate a mouse or other manual input device, eye movements careen madly about the screen. During a fixation, a user generally thinks he or she is looking steadily at a single object — he or she is not consciously aware of the small, jittery motions. This suggests that the human-computer dialogue should be constructed so that it, too, ignores those motions, since, ultimately, it should correspond to what the user *thinks* he or she is doing, rather than what the eye muscles are actually doing. The most naive approach to using eye position as an input might be to use it as a direct substitute for a mouse: changes in the user's line of gaze would directly cause the mouse cursor to move. This turns out to be an unworkable (and annoying) design for two main reasons. The first is in the eye itself, the jerky way it moves and the fact that it rarely sits still, even when its owner thinks he or she is looking steadily at a single object; and the second is the instability of available eye tracking hardware.

Moreover, people are not accustomed to operating devices just by moving their eyes in the natural world. They expect to be able to look at an item without having the look 'mean' something. Normal visual perception requires that the eyes move about, scanning the scene before them. It is not desirable for each such move to initiate a computer command. At first, it is empowering simply to look at what you want and have it happen. Before long, though, it becomes like the Midas Touch. Everywhere you look, another command is activated; you cannot look anywhere without issuing a command. The challenge in building a natural eye movement interface is to avoid this Midas Touch problem. Ideally, a natural interface should act on the user's eye input when he wants it to and let him just look around when that's what he wants, but the two cases are impossible to distinguish in general. Instead, we investigate interaction techniques that address this problem in specific cases.

Finally, our goal is to provide interactions that are faster, more convenient, and more natural than competing alternatives such as gesture, key presses, and other conventional input media. This is in contrast to much previous work using eye movements as an input medium, which has focused on constrained situations such as disabled users or users whose hands are otherwise occupied (e.g., pilots). Since the other input media are typically unavailable to such users, any practical eye movement interface is an improvement; and requiring careful, deliberate, slow, or trained eye movements from the user is still workable. We seek to satisfy a more rigorous standard of comparison: the user's hands are available for input, but our eye movement-based interaction technique should be faster or more natural than using the hands.

8 Feedback

In an eye movement-based user-computer dialogue an interesting question arises with respect to feedback, which is an important component of any dialogue: Should the system provide a screen cursor that follows the user's eye position (as is done for mice and other conventional devices)? This would provide feedback at the lexical level, as does the mouse cursor or the echoing of keyboard characters.

However, if the eye tracker were perfect, the image of such a cursor would occupy a precisely stationary position on the user's retina. An image that is artificially fixed on the retina (every time the eye moves, the target immediately moves precisely the same amount) will appear to fade from view after a few seconds (Pritchard, 1961). The large and small motions the eye normally makes prevent this fading from occurring outside the laboratory, and few eye trackers can track small, high-frequency motions rapidly or precisely enough for this to be a problem, but it does illustrate the subtlety of the design issues.

A more immediate problem is that an eye-following cursor will tend to move around and thus attract the user's attention. Yet it is perhaps the *least* informative aspect of the display (since it tells you where you are already looking). Further, if there is any systematic calibration error, the cursor will be slightly offset from where the user is actually looking, causing the user's eye to be drawn to the cursor, which will further displace the cursor, creating a positive feedback loop. This is indeed a practical problem, and we often observe it.

Finally, if the calibration and response speed of the eye tracker were perfect, feedback would not be necessary, since a person knows exactly where he or she is looking (unlike the situation with a mouse cursor, which helps one visualize the relationship between mouse positions and points on the screen).

9 Experience with interaction techniques

An interaction technique is a way of using a physical input device to perform a generic task in a human-computer dialogue (Foley et al., 1990). It is an abstraction of some common class of interactive task, for example, choosing one of several objects shown on a display screen. We have developed natural eye movement-based interaction techniques for performing some basic operations in direct manipulation systems, such as selecting and moving objects.

Selecting an object among several displayed on the screen is customarily done with a mouse, by pointing at the object and then pressing a button. With the eye tracker, there is no natural counterpart of the button press. We reject using a blink for a signal because it detracts from our goal of natural interaction by requiring the user to think about when to blink. We examined two alternatives. In one, the user looks at the desired object then presses a button on a keypad to indicate that the looked-at object is his choice. In the second, the user must continue to look at the object for a dwell time, after which it is selected without further operations. In practice, however, the dwell time approach — with a short dwell time — is preferable in meeting our goal of natural interaction. While a long dwell time does ensure that an inadvertent selection will not be made by simply 'looking around' on the display, we found it unpleasant to use, probably because it does not exploit natural eye movements (people do not normally fixate one spot for that long). Short dwell time selection requires that it be possible trivially to undo the selection of a wrong object. For example, if selecting an object causes a display of information about that object to appear and the information display can be changed instantaneously, then the effect of selecting wrong objects is immediately undone as long as the user eventually reaches the right one. This approach, using a 150–250 ms dwell time gives excellent results. The lag between eye movement and system response (required to reach the dwell time) is hardly detectable to the user, yet long enough to accumulate sufficient data for our fixation recognition and processing. The subjective feeling is of a highly responsive system, almost as though the system is executing the user's intentions before he expresses them. For situations where selecting an object is more difficult to undo, button confirmation is used.

For moving an object on a display, we segregated the two functions usually performed by the mouse — selecting an object to be manipulated and performing the manipulation. We experimented with using eye position for the selection task and hand input for the move itself. The eye selection is made as described above; then, the user grabs the mouse, presses a button, drags the mouse in the direction the object is to be moved, and releases the button. We also experimented with using the eye to select *and* drag the object and a pushbutton to pick it up and put it down. With that approach, the user selects the object, then presses a button; while the button is depressed, the object drags along with the definite fixations (not raw movements) of the user's eye. The effect is that the object actually jumps to each fixation after about 100 ms and then remains steadily there — despite actual eye jitter — until the next fixation. At first, we thought the second method would be unnatural and difficult to use, because eye movements would be better for selecting an object than picking it up and dragging it around. This was not borne out. While the eye-to-select/mouse-to-drag method worked well, the user was quickly spoiled by the eye-only method. Once you begin to expect the system to know where you are looking, the mouse-to-drag operation seems awkward and slow. After looking at the desired object and pressing the 'pick up' button, the natural thing to do is to look at where you are planning to move the object. At this point, you feel, 'I'm looking right at the destination I want, why do I now have to go get the mouse to drag the object over here?' With eye movements processed to suppress jitter and respond only to recognized fixations, the motion of the dragging object is reasonably smooth and predictable and yet appears subjectively instantaneous. It works best when the destination of the move is a recognizable feature on the screen rather than an arbitrary blank spot. If that is a problem, it can be solved by temporarily displaying a grid pattern during dragging.

Another interaction technique was developed for a scrolling window of text, in which not all of the material to be displayed can fit. We present arrows below the last line of the text and above the first line, indicating that there is additional material not shown. If the user looks at an arrow, the text itself starts to scroll. However, the text never scrolls when the user is actually reading it (rather than looking at the arrow). The assumption is that, as soon as the text starts scrolling, the user's eye will be drawn to the moving display and away from the arrow, which will stop the scrolling. The user can thus read down to end of the window, then, after he or she finishes reading the last line, look slightly below it, at the arrow, in order to retrieve the next part of the text.

Since pop-up menus inherently assume a button, we experimented with an eye-operated pull-down menu. If the user looks at the header of a pull-down menu for a brief dwell time, the body of the menu will appear on the screen. Next, he or she can look at the items shown on the menu. After a brief look at an item (100 ms), it will be highlighted, but its command will not yet be executed. This allows the user time to examine the different items on the menu. If the user looks at one item for a much longer time (1 s) or presses a button at any time, the highlighted item will be executed and the menu erased. As with the long dwell time object selection, here, too, the button is more convenient than the long dwell time for executing a menu command. This is because the dwell time necessary before executing a command must be kept quite high, at least noticeably longer than the time required to read an unfamiliar item. This is longer than people normally fixate on one spot, so selecting such an item requires an unnatural sort of 'stare'. Pulling the menu down and selecting an item to be highlighted can both be done effectively with short dwell times.

Another appropriate use of eye movements is to designate the active window in a window system. Current systems use an explicit mouse command to designate the active window. Instead, we use eye position — the active window is simply the one the user is looking at. A delay is built into the system, so that user can look briefly at other windows without changing the listener window designation. Fine cursor motions within a window are still handled with the mouse, which gives an appropriate partition of tasks between eye tracker and mouse, analogous to that between speech and mouse used by Schmandt, Ackerman, and Hindus (1990).

Acknowledgments

I want to thank my colleagues in the Dialogue Research Program at NRL for helpful debates and discussions on these issues. I thank Robert Carter, Connie Heitmeyer, Preston Mullen, and Linda Sibert for much help on the eye movement work reported herein, and Linda Sibert for fruitful collaboration on all of this research. This work was sponsored by the Office of Naval Research.

References

Ballas, J.A., Heitmeyer, C.L. & Perez, M.A. (1992) Evaluating Two Aspects of Direct Manipulation in Advanced Cockpits. Proceedings ACM CHI'92 Human Factors in Computing Systems Conference. Addison-Wesley/ACM Press, 127–134.

Foley, J.D. (1987) Interfaces for Advanced Computing. Scientific American, 257(4), 127–135.

Foley, J.D., van Dam, A., Feiner, S.K. & Hughes, J.F. (1990) Computer Graphics: Principles and Practice. Reading, Mass: Addison-Wesley.

Grosz, B.J. (1978) Discourse. In: Walker, D.E. (ed.) Understanding Spoken Language. New York: Elsevier North-Holland, 229–284.

Hill, W.C. & Hollan, J.D. (1991) Deixis and the Future of Visualization Excellence. Proceedings IEEE Visualization'91 Conference. IEEE Computer Society Press, 314–319.

Hutchins, E.L., Hollan, J.D. & Norman, D.A. (1986) Direct Manipulation Interfaces. In: Norman, D.A. & Draper, S.W. (eds.) User Centered System Design: New Perspectives on Human-computer Interaction. Hillsdale, NJ: Lawrence Erlbaum, 87–124.

Jacob, R.J.K. (1986) A Specification Language for Direct Manipulation User Interfaces. ACM Transactions on Graphics, 5(4), 283–317. Special Issue on User Interface Software.

Jacob, R.J.K. (1990) What You Look At is What You Get: Eye Movement-Based Interaction Techniques. Proceedings ACM CHI'90 Human Factors in Computing Systems Conference. Addison-Wesley/ACM Press, 11–18.

Jacob, R.J.K. (1991) The Use of Eye Movements in Human-Computer Interaction Techniques: What You Look At is What You Get. ACM Transactions on Information Systems, 9(3), 152–169.

Jacob, R.J.K. (1993) Eye Movement-Based Human-Computer Interaction Techniques: Toward Non-Command Interfaces. In: Hartson, H.R. & Hix, D. (eds.) Advances in Human-Computer Interaction, Vol. 4. Norwood, NJ: Ablex Publishing Co., 151–190.

Perez, M.A. & Sibert, J.L. (1993) Focus in Graphical User Interfaces. Proceedings ACM International Workshop on Intelligent User Interfaces. Orlando, Fla: Addison-Wesley/ACM Press.

Pritchard, R.M. (1961) Stabilized Images on the Retina. Scientific American, 204, 72–78.

Schmandt, C., Ackerman, M.S. & Hindus, D. (1990) Augmenting a Window System with Speech Input. IEEE Computer, 23(8), 50–56.

Shneiderman, B. (1983) Direct Manipulation: A Step Beyond Programming Languages. IEEE Computer, 16(8), 57–69.

Starker, I. & Bolt, R.A. (1990) A Gaze-Responsive Self-Disclosing Display. Proceedings ACM CHI'90 Human Factors in Computing Systems Conference. Addison-Wesley/ACM Press, 3–9.

Coherence and Portrayal in Human-Computer Interface Design

Thomas Erickson

User Experience Architect's Office, Apple Computer, MS 301-3UE, 1 Infinite Loop, Cupertino, CA 95014, USA, email: thomas@apple.com

Abstract. Feedback can play two important roles in future human-computer interfaces: coherence and portrayal. Coherence has to do with human-computer dialogues that have many stages; it is what provides continuity across the different stages of the dialogue. Portrayal has to do with the model that the system presents to its users. Portrayal is important because it affects the user's experience with the system: how the user interprets the system's behaviour, how the user diagnoses errors, how the user conceives of the system. The chapter begins with an analysis visual feedback, discusses some two problems that are likely to be common in future application programs, and gives an example that illustrates the use of feedback to address these problems.

Keywords. Visual feedback, user interface, dialogue, conversation, mental models, interface design, interaction design, coherence, portrayal

1 Introduction

A decade ago life was simple for the interface designer. Personal computers, at least those used by ordinary people, were relatively straightforward. They ran one and only one application program at a time. The program was passive: the user specified an action and the computer did it. Most interactions consisted of a series of unconnected action-response pairs: the computer made no attempt to keep track of what the user had done. Human-computer interaction occurred through a few input and output channels: the user typed or used a mouse; the computer displayed text or graphics, or beeped.

Today things have changed. A user can run multiple application programs at once, switching between them at will. Programs are no longer passive: they may carry out tasks without direct supervision by their users; they may interrupt their users to request information or to deliver results. Human-computer interaction is much more complex: not only may the user be communicating with several of the programs that are running simultaneously, but some of those programs may be initiating the communication. Finally, there are many more channels through which humans and computers can interact: the user can type, use a mouse, use a stylus to write or gesture, and speak; the computer can display text, graphics, synthesize speech, and play complex sounds and animations. All of these factors impose new demands on the human-computer interface.

What should interfaces of the future look like? How should they support the increased complexities of human-computer interaction? As desktop computers begin to offer voice recognition and speech synthesis capabilities, conversation becomes an increasingly popular candidate for the interface of the future. Certainly human conversation has many attractive properties. Multiple people can participate in a conversation, taking turns, interjecting comments, requesting clarification, and asking questions, all in a remarkably easy and graceful interaction. And best of all, people already know how to converse.

Unfortunately, turning computers into conversants is a difficult challenge. Consider some of the fundamental ways in which human-human conversations and human-computer dialogues differ: The object of a human-computer dialogue is for the human to specify an action for the computer to do; the object of human-human conversation is usually to accomplish more abstract ends such as imparting information or altering beliefs. Second, human-human conversations occur principally through the medium of speech, which consists of a serial stream of transitory input used to construct and maintain a largely mental model; in contrast, human-computer dialogues are mediated by an external, visible representation, which can display information in parallel, and which persists over time. Third, a human-human conversation is a two way process in which the participants jointly construct a shared model (e.g., Clark & Brennan (1991)). In contrast, a human-computer dialogue is primarily a one way process which results, at best, in the user understanding the computer's model of the situation. In no real sense can the computer be said to participate in constructing a model, or even to adjust its model to approximate that of the user. Related to this point is that participants in a human-human conversation are intelligent, whereas the computer is so lacking in intelligence about both the process and content of the dialogue that even the term 'stupid' is a misnomer. When a human-human conversation breaks down, human participants are typically aware of the misunderstanding and take steps to repair the breakdown; when a human-computer dialogue fails, the computer is typically oblivious; it is only in a few well-defined situations — anticipated by designers — that the computer can detect the misunderstanding and repair the breakdown.

The basic difficulty is this: Because human-human conversations occur through the transitory medium of speech, which produces no lasting, external representation, considerable intelligence and continuous interaction and feedback between conversants is required to effectively maintain the mental model of what is occurring. Computers are far from having the requisite intelligence to do this. Instead, I believe that the most promising approach is to use one of the strengths of computers — their ability to produce a persistent visual representation — to instantiate some of the more general properties of human conversations.

With this approach in mind, I begin by presenting an analysis of the types and roles of visual feedback used in today's graphic user interfaces. I suggest that two uses of feedback, supporting coherence in multi-stage dialogues and providing system portrayals, have important roles to play in making future human-computer interfaces more conversational. Next, I describe a commercial program with sophisticated functionality that illustrates two problems that I believe will be common in future application programs. Finally, I give an example of an interface design that illustrates the use of feedback to address these problems.

2 Types of feedback in human-computer interaction

In this section, I analyze some of the ways in which feedback is used in the Macintosh graphical user interface (Apple Computer, 1992). The goal is to provide some categories and language for talking about the use of feedback in future graphical user interfaces. I focus mainly on temporal properties of feedback; other chapters in this volume (Wroblewski et al., this volume; de Vet, this volume; Jacob, this volume) discuss other aspects of feedback in human-computer interaction.

In interface design the term 'feedback' typically refers to providing information relevant to the interaction in which the user is currently involved (note that 'feedback' is used in a more restricted sense by conversational theorists). Feedback can be presented in a multitude of ways. It may be visual, auditory, or tactile; it may be either ephemeral or relatively persistent. Feedback may use multiple attributes of the modality in which it is represented — thus, visual feedback may involve the use of text, graphics, colour, or animation; and of course, feedback need not be confined to a single modality. Examples of feedback in graphic user interfaces range from simple beeps, to dialogue boxes, to animated pointers.

2.1 Types of feedback

Feedback can be divided into three types based on its temporal relation to the user's activity: synchronous feedback, background feedback and completion feedback. As I describe these types of feedback, I'll provide examples by referring to the feedback that occurs during a single operation: copying a folder that contains many files by selecting its icon and dragging it to a window on another volume (Figure 1).

2.1.1 Synchronous feedback

Synchronous feedback is closely coupled with the user's physical actions; in most cases, it is important that there be no perceptible time lag in the coupling between the user's actions and the feedback. For example, the Macintosh usually displays a pointer that moves in synchrony with the mouse. On the Macintosh, synchronous feedback is the default state: at virtually any time, a user's physical interactions with the system ought to — in some way — be mirrored by the interface.

When a user copies a folder, several kinds of synchronous feedback occur: the pointer is shown moving to the to-be-copied folder in synchrony with the user's movements, the folder icon turns black when the user clicks on it to select it, and the outline of the folder is displayed as it is dragged to the new window, again in synchrony with the user's movements of the mouse (Figure 1a).

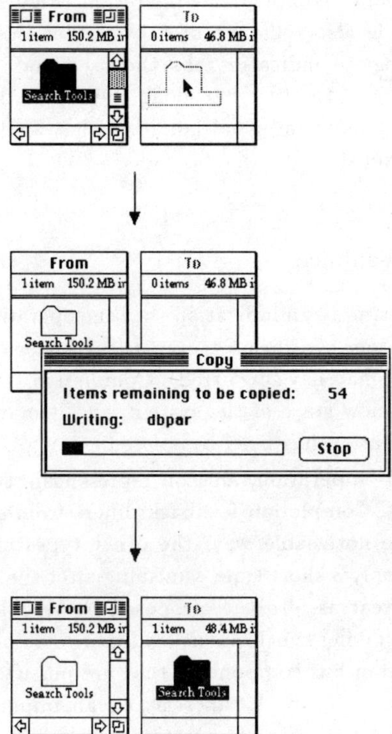

Fig. 1. Types of feedback that occur while copying a folder on the Macintosh. Feedback can be divided into three types according to its temporal relationship to the activity of the user and the system: a) synchronous feedback occurs in synchrony with the user's actions; b) background feedback occurs after the user has completed specification of the action but while the computer is carrying out the action; c) completion feedback occurs when the system finishes the action.

2.1.2 Background feedback

Background feedback is provided after the user specifies the action, but before the system completes the action: it represents the activity of the system as distinct from that of the user. Its basic purpose is to let the user know that the system is carrying out the specified action. Originally, when the Macintosh was single-tasking, the user could do nothing else during this period; now the user can initiate other actions. It is important that background feedback be provided whenever an operation takes longer than about half a second.

In the folder copying example, after the user drags the folder to the new window and releases the mouse button, it may take the system some time to copy the contents of the folder: in this case, the system puts up a progress indicator to assure the user that the system has not crashed, and to allow some estimate as to how long the system will take to complete the operation (Figure 1b). The background feedback in this example also tells the user two other things: the presence of a stop button in the progress indicator tells the user that the operation may be interrupted; the presence of the title bar along the top of the indicator tells those who understand the Macintosh's visual language that another operation may be started before this one finishes.

2.1.3 Completion feedback

Completion feedback is simply an indication that the operation has been completed or at least that the system can do no more (in the latter case it may need more information, or an error may have occurred). Completion feedback fulfills two purposes: it represents the new state of the system, and it may be used to notify the user that a lengthy operation has been completed.

In the case of the copy operation, an icon representing the newly copied folder is displayed (Figure 1c). Completion feedback differs from synchronous and background feedback in one noticeable way: the other types of feedback are usually ephemeral — they last only a short time, vanishing after the operation is completed (although the idea of wear as feedback proposed by Wroblewski, et al. (this volume), can be viewed as giving synchronous feedback some persistent components). Completion feedback often has components that are persistent. The persistence of components of completion feedback can serve as an important way of reflecting what has been achieved by a series of operations.

2.2 Roles for feedback

2.2.1 Operational support

The typical role of feedback is to support the operation the user is currently performing. Moving the cursor in synchrony with the mouse enables the use of the mouse to become an automatic process; providing background feedback provides assurance that the system has not crashed, and often provides some indication of how much longer it will take; the completion feedback, of course, alerts the user that the operation has finished, and often provides a new representation on which the user may perform direct manipulation. The use of feedback for these purposes is essential in allowing users to gracefully complete operations. Ideally, skillful use of feedback permits users to automatically perform operations without thinking about the details of what they are doing. For example, it is very natural to say "Now click on the OK button"; only the rawest novice needs to be told "Use the mouse to position the pointer on the screen over the OK button on the screen and then press the button on the mouse." It is synchronous feedback that permits the user to meld the physical operations of moving and clicking the mouse with clicking the OK button on the screen.

2.2.2 Maintaining coherence during extended dialogues

A second role for feedback is to create coherence across the stages of extended dialogues. An extended dialogue is a series of operations all aimed at accomplishing a particular, high-level goal. Examples of extended dialogues include retrieving a useful set of records from a database, changing the layout of a document, and reading and managing electronic mail. However, today computers have almost no awareness of extended dialogues: the fact that one user-action follows another has no relevance; the system typically does not recognize that the user may have a goal that goes beyond completion of the current operation.

A limited example of supporting coherence in extended dialogues is the way the Macintosh deals with some error conditions. For example, suppose a user tries to empty the trash (this is graphical user interface parlance for deleting files) when the trash contains a running application as well as other files. The first stage in the dialogue is when the user chooses the 'Empty Trash' command. In response, the system displays a standard dialogue box that tells the user how many files will be deleted and asks for confirmation. Once the user provides confirmation, the system will attempt to delete the files and will discover that one of the files is a running application that we will call X. Since deleting a running application is likely to be a mistake, the system initiates a new stage of the dialogue: it displays a dialogue box that explains that the trash contains a running application called X that it cannot delete, and gives the user the choice of stopping or continuing (deleting the other files). The key point here is that the system is still aware of what the user did in the previous stage of the dialogue, and gives the user the option of deleting the other items in the trash and thus accomplishing as much of the original goal as possible. While this seems like a sensible response, unworthy of special remark, the fact is that today's systems would be more likely to abort the entire operation. In general, today's systems do not recognize higher level goals, and do not support incremental progress towards them.

2.2.3 Feedback as portrayal

As computing systems begin to manifest increasingly complex functionality, it is becoming increasingly important that users receive feedback that allows them to build up a mental model of the system. That is, rather than just supporting the current operation, feedback can work in a global way, helping the user understand not only the state of the current operation, but the structure of the application program, and the ways in which the program accomplishes actions. I call this portrayal.

An example of portrayal can be found in the use of background feedback in an electronic mail and bulletin board program called AppleLink. After a user launches AppleLink and enters the password, it accesses a modem and connects to a remote, mainframe computer. Since it takes several seconds to make this connection, AppleLink displays a connection storyboard showing the stages in connecting to the remote computer (Figure 2 illustrates two states of the connection storyboard).

The connection storyboard plays two roles. First, it plays an operational role, showing the user that the program is doing something and indicating approximately how far along the system is. Second, the storyboard also provides a portrayal by depicting a simple model of the system and the connection process (although the model could be improved, as it contains some frivolous and obscure elements). By watching the connection storyboard, users can learn that the system is working over a phone line, that it is connecting to a different computer, that it is using the password the user entered to gain access to the other computer, and so on. None of this is immediately useful information. However if something goes wrong — there is trouble with the phone system, or the mainframe is down — the user has a better chance of understanding the problem.

2.3 Summary

This section has presented an analysis of feedback according to how it temporally relates to the activities of the user and the system. It identified three types: synchronous feedback, background feedback, and completion feedback. Feedback can play at least three roles in human-computer interaction: First, it can be used for to support the user in smoothly completing the current operation. Second, feedback can be used to add coherence to a human-computer dialogue by recognizing that users have higher level goals, and supporting extended dialogues by preserving information across the stages of the dialogue. Finally, feedback can assist the user in forming appropriate mental models of the overall structure of the system and its processes: portrayal.

3 Two design problems

DowQuest (Dow Jones & Company, 1989) is a commercially available, on-line system with sophisticated functionality. It provides access to the full text of the last 6 to 12 months of over 350 news sources, and permits users to retrieve articles via pseudo natural language and an information retrieval technique called relevance feedback (Stanfill & Kahle, 1986). Relevance feedback means that users instruct the system on how to improve its search criteria by showing it examples of what is wanted. Relevance feedback allows users to say, in essence, 'find more like that one.'

While the version of DowQuest described here does not have a state-of-the-art interface, it has two characteristics of interest to us: it is based on the assumption that its users will interact with it through multi-stage dialogues; it appears to possess some degree of intelligence. These characteristics are relevant because they seem likely to be true of many future computer systems and applications, and because they both give rise to usage problems.

3.1 How DowQuest works

Let us examine the process of retrieving information in DowQuest.

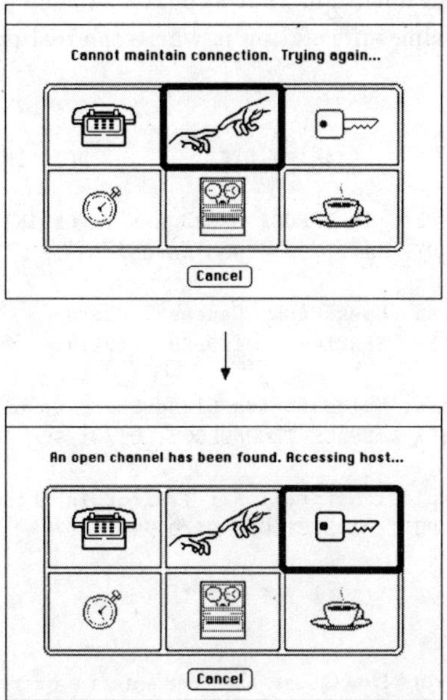

Fig. 2. Two phases of the AppleLink connection storyboard. Notice that the storyboard is fulfilling two separate purposes: it is showing the user that something is happening, and it is providing a model of the relevant parts of the system.

3.1.1 The natural language query

The user begins by entering a query describing the desired information in natural language. As the user's manual says, DowQuest "lets you describe your topic using everyday English. You don't have to be an expert researcher or learn complicated commands." For example, the user might enter: "Tell me about the eruption of the Alaskan volcano". However, DowQuest does not really understand natural language; instead it uses only the lower frequency words of the query in conjunction with statistical retrieval algorithms. In the example shown, the system eliminates the words 'tell', 'me', 'about', 'the', and 'of' and uses the other, lower frequency words — 'eruption', 'Alaskan' and 'volcano' — to search the database.

3.1.2 The starter retrieval list

In response to the initial query the system returns a list of titles called the 'Starter List' (Figure 3 shows the Starter List for the 'Alaskan volcano' query). The list is ordered by relevance, with the first article being most relevant, and so on; 'relevance' is defined by a complex statistical algorithm based on a variety of features of which the user has no knowledge. While this list of articles may contain some relevant items, it also usually contains items that appear — to the user — to be irrelevant. The next stage of retrieving information is where the real power of DowQuest lies.

```
DOWQUEST                 STARTER LIST          HEADLINE PAGE 1 OF 4

  1 OCS: BILL SEEKS TO IMPOSE BROAD LIMITS ON INTERIOR . . .
    INSIDE ENERGY, 11/27/98  (935 words)

  2 Alaska Volcano Spews Ash, Causes Tremors
    DOW JONES NEWS SERVICE , 01/09/90  (241)

  3 Air Transport: Volcanic Ash Cloud Shuts Down All Four . . .
    AVIATION WEEK & SPACE TECHNOLOGY, 01/01/90  (742)

  4 Volcanic Explosions Stall Air Traffic in Anchorage
    WASHINGTON POST: A SECTION, 01/04/90  (679)

                              * * * * *
```

Fig. 3. In stage 1 of querying DowQuest, the user enters a query and the system returns a list of titles of the 'most relevant' articles. The Starter List shown here is in response to the query, "Tell me about the eruption of the Alaskan volcano".

3.1.3 Relevance feedback retrieval

In stage 2 of the retrieval process the user employs relevance feedback to refine the query. A simple command language is used to tell the system which articles in the starter list are good examples of what is wanted. The user may either specify an entire article or may display an article and specify paragraphs within it (in the 'Alaskan volcano' example, the user might enter "search 2, 3, 4"). The system takes the full text of the selected articles and chooses a limited number of the most informative words for use in the new version of the query. It then returns a new list of the 'most relevant' items (Figure 4). This second, relevance feedback retrieval stage may be repeated as many times as desired. Because the real power of DowQuest lies in its ability to do relevance feedback, it is in the user's best interest to perform this stage of the query process at least once, and preferably a couple of times.

3.2 Problems encountered by DowQuest users

Users encountered difficulties due to two general problems: failure to support multi-stage dialogues, and unrealistic expectations of intelligence.

```
DOWQUEST              SECOND SEARCH        HEADLINE PAGE 1 OF 4

   1 Air Transport: Volcanic Ash Cloud Shuts Down All Four . . .
     AVIATION WEEK & SPACE TECHNOLOGY, 01/01/90  (742 words)

   2 Alaska Volcano Spews Ash, Causes Tremors
     DOW JONES NEWS SERVICE , 01/09/90  (241)

   3 Volcanic Explosions Stall Air Traffic in Anchorage
     WASHINGTON POST: A SECTION, 01/04/90  (679)

   4 Alaska's Redoubt Volcano Gushes Ash, Possibly Lava
     DOW JONES NEWS SERVICE , 01/03/90  (364)

                              * * * * *
```

Fig. 4. In stage 2 of querying DowQuest, the user instructs the database to find more articles 'like' 2, 3 and 4, of Figure 3, and the system returns a new set of relevant articles. Note that the first three, 'most relevant' articles shown here are those that were used as examples (an article is most 'like' itself); the fourth article is a new item.

3.2.1 Multi-stage dialogue support

One problem with DowQuest was that although users had to go through two stages of dialogue before getting the benefits of the system's power, the only support provided for extended dialogues was to display the number of iterations the user had gone through. In general, the system erased commands after they were executed, and provided no feedback on which articles had been accessed. Thus, users had to rely on their memories or, more typically, jotted notes, for information such as the text of the original query; which articles had been opened and read; which articles had been sent to the printer; which articles or paragraphs had been used as examples in relevance feedback; which titles in the retrieval list had shown up in previous iterations of the search; and so on. This missing information made the search process cumbersome.

3.2.2 Misleading expectations of intelligence

Although no explicit attempt was made to portray DowQuest as intelligent, new users of DowQuest generally expected it to exhibit intelligent behaviour. One reason for this is that DowQuest's behaviour implied intelligence. It appeared that DowQuest could understand English; the fact that DowQuest dropped words out of the search query and used a weighted keyword search was never made explicit in the interface. It appeared that DowQuest could be given examples of what was wanted, and could retrieve articles that were like those examples; the fact that this was an entirely statistical process was not made clear to the users. It appeared that DowQuest could order a list of articles in terms of their relevance; the fact that DowQuest's definition of relevance was very different from its user's definition was not evident. Finally, the fact that some users knew that DowQuest ran on a supercomputer may have contributed to the expectations of intelligence.

Users' expectations of intelligent behaviour were usually not met. For example, one user typed in a question about 'Ocean Technologies' (a maker of optical disk drives) and got back a list of stories about pollution control technologies (for controlling pollution produced by off-shore oil rigs). He responded by concluding that the system was no good, and never tried it again. While such a reaction is perfectly appropriate in the case of conventional applications — a spreadsheet that adds incorrectly should be rejected — it prevented the user from proceeding to a point where he could have benefited from the system's power.

3.2.3 Interactions between the problems

It is interesting that in spite of such disappointments, many users continued to act as if DowQuest was intelligent; in fact, assumptions of intelligence were used to generate reasons for the program's behaviour in extended dialogues. For example, one study revealed an interesting problem in the second stage of a DowQuest query (Meier et al., 1990). Users would ask the system to retrieve more articles 'like that one'. In response, the system would display a new list of articles ordered by relevance. Typically, the list would begin with the article that had been used as the example for relevance feedback. While computer scientists will be unsurprised to find that a document is most relevant to itself, ordinary users lacked this insight. Instead, some users assumed that the only reason for the system to display something they had already seen was that there was nothing else that was relevant. Thus, some users never looked at the rest of list. This behaviour is in accord with Grice's (1975) conversational postulates, where a conversational partner is expected to provide new information if it is possessed; this reasoning fails when one of the 'conversants' is utterly lacking in intelligence.

3.3 Summary

While DowQuest does not have a state-of-the-art user interface, it is a useful example because it has two properties that will be common in future applications and computing systems. Its users need to interact with it through multi-stage dialogues, and it appears to understand natural language and to possess other capabilities that seem intelligent. As we have seen, both of these characteristics can give rise to problems.

4 Using feedback for portrayal and coherence

In this section I describe elements of a new interface design for a system with DowQuest-like functionality that illustrate the use of feedback for portrayal and coherence.

4.1 Coherence: Support for extended dialogues

There is no single method for using feedback to support coherence. In general, the approach is to make use of completion feedback which persists over the many stages of extended human-computer dialogues. The example that follows shows five stages in a dialogue in which someone is retrieving documents; it is based on a prototype system known as Rosebud that uses agents called Reporters to conduct searches of databases distributed across a network (see Erickson and Salomon (1991) and Kahle, et al. (1992) for more information). Note that the interface described below provided feedback by using colour and other subtle graphic effects that are not easily reproducible in black and white figures; where necessary, these effects have been transformed to make them visible (e.g., colour to italic text).

4.1.1 Results of the initial search

The dialogue begins with the user entering some initial search terms and specifying databases for the system to search (this stage of the dialogue is not shown). After the user presses the Search Now button, the dialogue box in Figure 5 appears. In the top pane, the system lists the initial set of documents it has found. These items are all displayed in a special highlight colour (represented here by italic text), that indicates that this is new information that the user has not previously seen. In the next to the last pane, the system retains the search terms previously entered ('Motorola Lawsuit')

At this point, the user can scroll through the Results List in the top pane, looking at the document titles to see whether any seem relevant. In the second stage of the dialogue, the user will select one of the retrieved documents.

4.1.2 Selecting a document

At this stage in the dialogue, the user has selected the second item in the Results List by clicking on it (see Figure 6). That item is highlighted, and a 'preview' of its contents is shown in the second pane in the window. Note that the original search terms are still visible in the lower part of the window, and the retrieved documents are still shown in the new information highlight colour. Completion feedback which persists across turns is being used to provide coherence.

At this point the user reads the preview, and decides that this is a good example of the information being sought. The third stage of the dialogue involves a diversion from the main goal of retrieving information: having discovered a relevant document, the user wants to make sure that it is saved to his system.

4.1.3 Saving the document

The user has asked the system to save the document to his computer by pressing the 'Save' button (see Figure 7). The system does so, and marks the document icon with an 'S' as a persistent indicator that it has been saved.

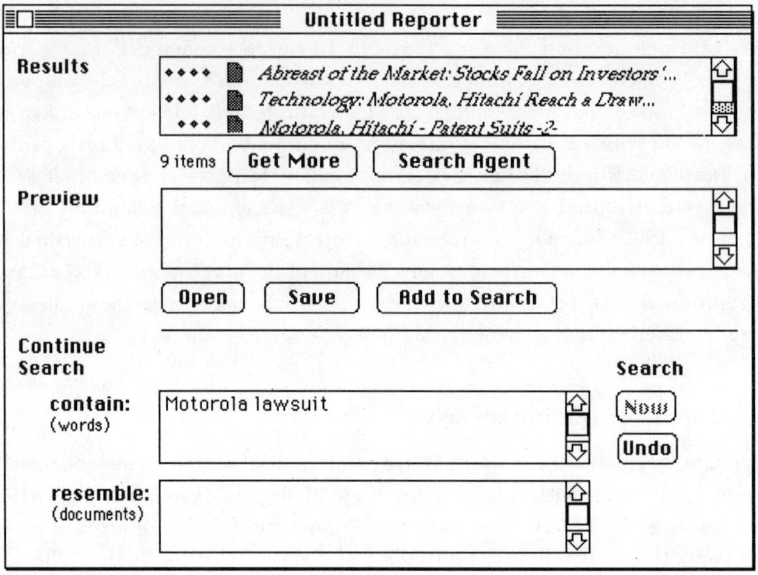

Fig. 5. The dialogue box after the user has entered the initial query ('Motorola Lawsuit') and pressed the Search Now button.

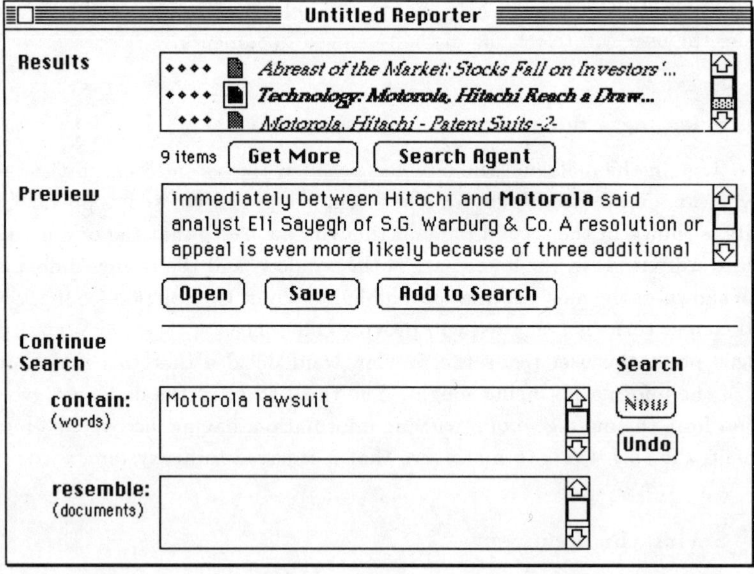

Fig. 6. The dialogue after the user has selected the second document.

Now the user returns to his original course of action: retrieving information. In the next stage of the dialogue the user instructs the system to use the selected document as an example of what to retrieve.

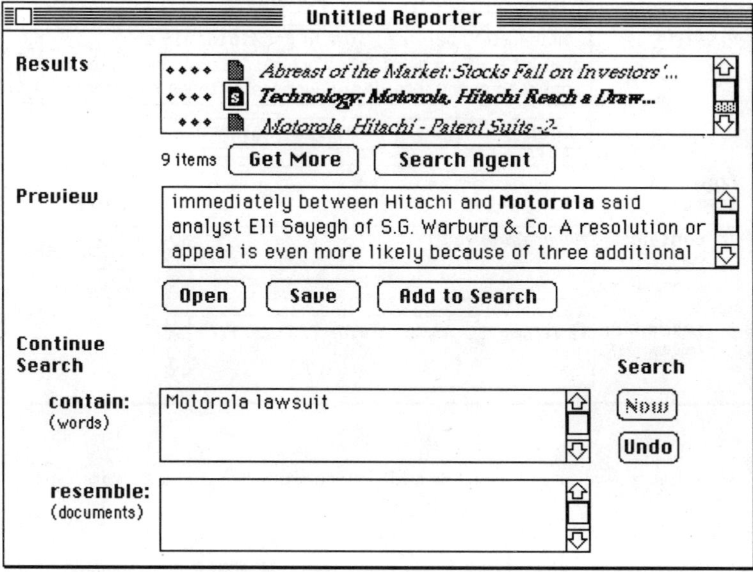

Fig. 7. The dialogue after the user has saved the selected document to the local system by pressing 'Save'.

4.1.4 Specifying the example document for relevance feedback

The user has just clicked on the Add to Search button (telling the system that the second document is a good example of what is wanted; see Figure 8). At this point, the document icon and title showed up in the bottom pane of the window; the document title and icon are displayed in the new information highlight colour (as indicated by the italic typeface). The goal is to help the user distinguish between information that was entered previously (and that has determined the current set of results), and information that applies to future stages of the dialogue (e.g., when the next iteration of the search is carried out). The Search Now button is also highlighted with this colour because pressing it will make use of the new information.

4.1.5 Initiating the relevance feedback stage of the search

The user has pressed the Search Now button, and the system has carried out a search using the new information (see Figure 9). The new results appear in the

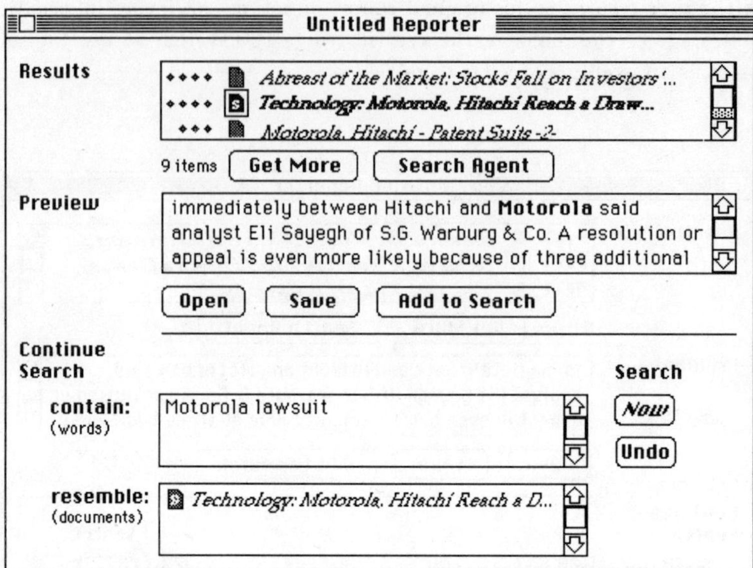

Fig. 8. The dialogue after the user has added document 2 as a search criterion).

top pane. Documents that have not been retrieved before are shown in the new information highlight colour (indicated here by italic text); documents that had been brought back by previous searches are no longer highlighted. Similarly, the Search Now button has reverted to its ordinary colour. Highlighting new items shows the user that new items have indeed been found, and directs the attention to the most relevant portion of the results.

Notice that persistent completion feedback has built up over the course of this extended dialogue. Looking at the dialogue box the user can see what the query is ('Motorola Lawsuit'), which documents were used as examples for relevance feedback ('Technology: Motorola Hitachi Reach a Draw'), which documents have been saved, which documents are new information, and which documents have been seen in previous stages of the search.

4.2 Portrayal: Controlling expectations of intelligence

Having looked at ways of using feedback to support coherence over five stages of an extended dialogue, let's turn to the problem of controlling expectations of intelligence. There are two complementary approaches. First, designers need to avoid creating unrealistic expectations to the extent possible. This is difficult because, as systems take on increasingly sophisticated and complex functionality, the easiest means of explaining the functionality is through analogy to intelligent behaviour.

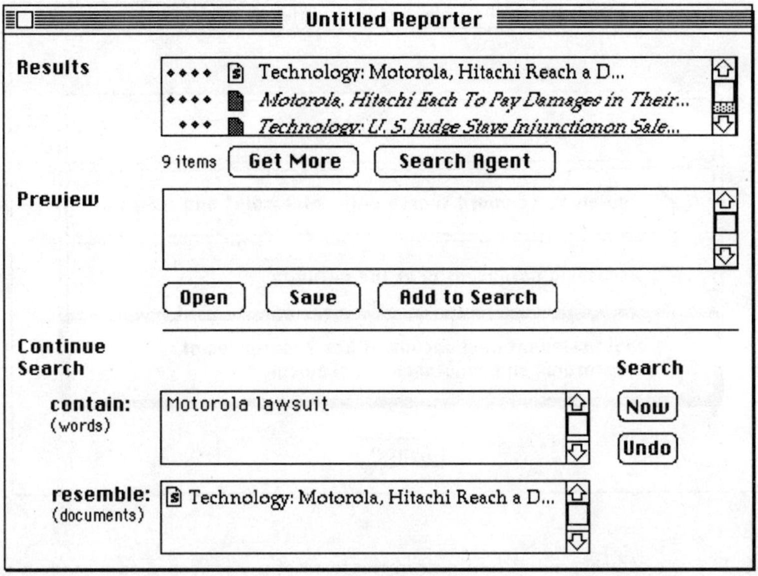

Fig. 9. The dialogue after search using relevance feedback; notice that the system uses the new information colour — here shown in italic typeface — to highlight the new information returned by the system, thus distinguishing it from information returned by previous iterations of this search.

But as we have seen in the case of DowQuest, unrealistic expectations can lead the user astray.

A more positive approach to the problem is to use background feedback to portray what the program is actually doing. A storyboard could be used to reveal the mechanism that underlies information retrieval (see Figure 10). In this case, the storyboard explicitly tells the user that it is dropping out common words like 'Tell', 'me', 'about' and only using keywords to search; and it also provides an explanation of why a particular document was retrieved. Using background feedback in this way does two things: it lessens the chance that users will assume the system is intelligent, and it gives the user a chance at understanding why the system did not produce the anticipated results, and thus provides the option for users to appropriately adjust their strategies. Because the user and the system really do not have a shared model of what is happening, it is essential that feedback be used to portray the system as accurately as possible.

5 Conclusion

In human-human conversations, parties to the conversation establish a common ground, a shared set of mutually understood terms, concepts, and referents. As the

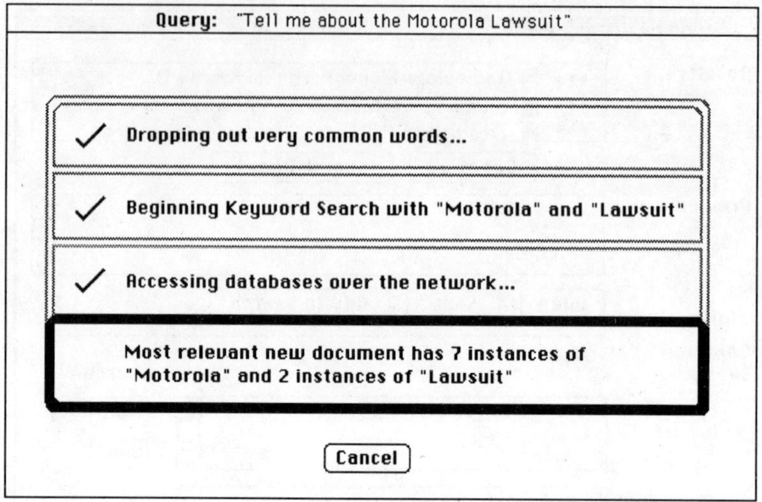

Fig. 10. The use of background feedback in the form of a storyboard to provide a model of the the underlying retrieval mechanism.

conversation proceeds, both parties repeatedly refer to the common ground, thus mutually reminding one another about it, and gradually extending and refining it. While this works well in human-human conversations, the verbal establishment and maintenance of common ground is likely to be beyond the capabilities of computers for quite some time.

In the absence of such intelligence, a valuable course to pursue is to use feedback to represent the common ground of the human-computer 'conversation'. In this chapter we have looked at the use of visual feedback to provide coherence and portrayal in the dialogue between human and computer. We looked at the use of completion feedback to provide coherence over five stages of an extended dialogue. It was used to indicate selected items, the state of retrieved documents (saved to the user's disk or not), and to distinguish between new and old information. In general, completion feedback was used to build up a persistent, explicit model of what had happened. Similarly, background feedback was used to lower expectations of intelligent behaviour by explicitly portraying the basically mechanical processes of the program. Portrayal is important because, in the absence of an explicit model, the user may make unwarranted assumptions about the system's intelligence, and misinterpret the system's responses. Even as feedback is used to provide the human computer dialogue with coherence closer to that of a human conversation, feedback must also be used to make it clear that the dialogue is being carried out between a human and a non-intelligent system.

Feedback is a vast topic, and I have touched on only a few of the more important points. I see two important directions for further research. First, we need a better understanding of how visual feedback can be used to support human-computer interaction. One important line of research is the study of design conversations. A variety of investigators (e.g., Tang (1989); Minneman & Bly (1991); Lee (this volume)) are examining conversations among members of design teams; such conversations occur in parallel with the use of visual and other physical representations and reveal interesting interactions between conversation and persistent visual feedback. Understanding the ways in which people use physical representations to help support design conversations is likely to yield insights into ways of improving visual feedback in graphic user interfaces. A second direction for investigation is the use of sound as feedback. Sound has great potential for enhancing portrayal through both synchronous feedback (e.g., Gaver (1989)) and background feedback (e.g., Gaver et al. (1991); Cohen (1993)), but has not yet received sufficient attention.

Acknowledgments

Gitta Salomon was a co-designer of the Rosebud interface described in this chapter. Other people who contributed to the design and subsequent implementation of Rosebud are: Charlie Bedard, David Casseres, Steve Cisler, Ruth Ritter, Eric Roth, Kevin Tiene, and Janet Vratny. My ideas on conversation and feedback have benefited from discussions with Susan Brennan, Jonathan Cohen, Gitta Salomon, and Yin Yin Wong. Jonathan Cohen and an anonymous reviewer provided helpful suggestions on earlier drafts of this chapter.

References

Apple Computer, Inc. (1992) Macintosh Human Interface Guidelines. Reading, MA: Addison-Wesley.

Clark, H.H. & Brennan, S.E. (1991) Grounding in Communication. In: Resnick, L.B., Levine, J. & Teasley, S.D. (eds.) Perspectives on Socially Shared Cognition. Washington, DC: APA.

Cohen, J. (1993) Monitoring Background Activities. First International Conference on Auditory Display, Santa Fé, New Mexico.

Dow Jones & Company, Inc. (1989) Dow Jones News/Retrieval User's Guide.

Erickson, T. & Salomon, G. (1991) Designing a Desktop Information System: Observations and Issues. Human Factors in Computing Systems: the Proceedings of the CHI'91. ACM Press.

Gaver, W.W. (1989) The Sonic Finder: An Interface that Uses Auditory Icons. Journal of Human-Computer Interaction, 4(1).

Gaver, W.W., O'Shea, T. & Smith, R.B. (1991) Effective Sounds in Complex Systems: The ARKola Simulation. Human Factors in Computing Systems: the Proceedings of CHI'91. ACM Press.

Grice, P. (1975) Logic and Conversation. In: Cole, P. & Morgan, J.L. (eds.) Syntax and Semantics: Speech Acts. Vol. 11. New York: Academic Press, 41–58.

Kahle, B., Morris, H., Goldman, J., Erickson, T. & Curran, J. (1992) Interfaces for Distributed Systems of Information Servers. Proceedings of the American Society for Information Science.

Meier, E., Minjarez, F., Page, P., Robertson, M. & Roggenstroh, E. (1990) Personal communication.

Minneman, S.L. & Bly, S.A. (1991) Managing a Trois: A Study of a Multi-User Drawing Tool in Distributed Design Work. Human Factors in Computing Systems: CHI'91 Conference Proceedings, 217–223.

Stanfill, C. & Kahle, B. (1986) Parallel Free-text Search on the Connection Machine System. Communications of the ACM, 29(12), 1229–1239.

Tang, J.C. (1989) Listing, Drawing, and Gesturing in Design: A Study of the Use of Shared Workspaces by Design Teams. Ph.D. thesis, Stanford University. (Also available as a Xerox PARC Technical Report, SSL-89-3, April 1989).

Feedback Issues in Consumer Appliances

John H.M. de Vet

Institute for Perception Research/IPO, P.O.Box 513, 5600 MB Eindhoven, The Netherlands, email: devet@prl.philips.nl

Abstract. This paper discusses feedback issues for consumer appliances in general and hi-fi audio sets in particular. Two case studies are presented which were set up as empirical evaluations of hi-fi audio sets. The usability problems with the sets are discussed in relation to the different feedback techniques employed. For the analysis of audio equipment we will distinguish three types of feedback: status feedback, corrective feedback and guidance. It is shown how, in an iterative user-centred design process, feedback improvements alone can lead to better user interfaces.

Keywords. User interface design, feedback analysis, usability, reactive systems, empirical evaluation, consumer products

1 Introduction

Modern consumer appliances — from washers to audio and video equipment — are becoming increasingly complex, turning into special-purpose computers, although the computer is carefully camouflaged. They use an *atomic* interaction style: commands are based on special-purpose buttons of various sorts, from plain push buttons to multi-position switches. Part of the interaction style is continuous, since controls such as sliders and rotaries allow analogue input. Atomic or continuous systems are *reactive*, because they require fast, per-action feedback (Thimbleby, 1990). The interaction styles have not changed much. New interfaces have mostly been shaped by new features and design cosmetics: fancier buttons and bigger displays. Functionality has been increased by adding more buttons and providing multiple functions per button through mode-switches, shift-buttons, and button time-outs.

Without sacrificing important functions, the operation of audio sets has been simplified along three lines. First, simplicity can be suggested cosmetically by hiding secondary functionality — such as amplifier controls, like balance, bass and treble, tape recording level adjustment and tuner preset programming — behind flaps. Flaps can be considered the physical equivalent of menus in computer interfaces. This accommodates novices and experts, but does not simplify the operation for those who want to use secondary functions. Second, the user actions needed to perform certain tasks can be reduced by control intelligence, by using clever system defaults and by automating functions. But this may introduce autonomous system behaviour and reduce the predictability of user actions. For example, the automatic programming of tuner presets requires scanning of wavebands, sometimes more than once and takes up minutes to complete. Once the procedure has been started, the old preset settings cannot be restored. Other functions require interaction between different components to sequence the underlying system actions. For example, making an automatic tape recording of a CD-program might mean winding the tape to the target position, pausing the CD at start position, starting the tape recorder, while simultaneously starting the CD. Third, 'common' buttons can be moved from the components to a central control panel and used for 'generic' functions, similar functions common to all (or most) components. The best known example of this option is the remote control device that comes with the audio system. However, this option does not work well if the components are heterogeneous.

One of the key elements in the operation of audio systems is the *transparency of control*. Given the physical limitations of displays and buttons for audio products, how can we make their operation transparent to the user and their functionality self-explanatory? The user of an audio product starts off with a model of the product that is based on experience with similar products. In order to support the building of an appropriate model, operations should be based on skills, concepts and conventions that ordinary users possess. However, audio products are usually designed for a broad target group, which often shows a big variety in skills and expertise. What may be transparent to some users, remains a mystery to others. How then can we design transparent interfaces for these products?

The basic assumption of 'situated' user interface design is that any designed system cannot be understood apart from the situations in which it is used (Suchmann, 1987). "Even small details can have substantial effects on the usefulness of a system, and such details emerge from the situation of use, and hence can neither be predicted outside of that context nor meaningfully abstracted from it." (Carroll, 1990, p. 322). Therefore, in order to improve the user interface, potential users must be enabled to somehow experience future-use situations. This requires the simulation of situations where customers can gain hands-on experience with a design or design solution on the basis of mock-ups, simulations, prototypes or actual products (Ehn, 1988).

This paper presents the results of the empirical evaluation of two hi-fi audio sets which were used as a starting point for a redesign of the next generation of audio sets. Many of the problems encountered by users during the operation of the sets can be explained in terms of flaws in the feedback. The kind of feedback techniques used in audio equipment will therefore be discussed first. Then the experimental set-up will be described. The usability problems will be presented in relation to the different feedback techniques employed. Finally, we will discuss the feedback improvements which solved some of the problems, and which were tested with a simulation of an audio set in a separate experiment.

2 Two audio sets

The two hi-fi audio sets used in the case studies consisted of a tuner, amplifier, CD-player and double cassette deck. However, they differed greatly in terms of the control concept and the types of feedback.

2.1 Set A

The first set, set A, differed from conventional audio sets because of its 'generic control' concept, which means that different components of the set were controlled by the same set of buttons. Generic control is commonly used in control panels of professional systems to reduce the number of buttons. The generic control and the addition of some automatic functions were expected to simplify the operation considerably. Most of the information from the set to the user was provided via a single, big display which was part of the control panel. In addition, two-coloured LEDs were added to the main buttons to indicate status (red) and 'activatability' (green). The latter type of feedback indicates whether the button can be pressed (green LED on) or not (green LED off), and is aimed at guiding the user towards appropriate buttons.

2.2 Set B

The second set, set B, was an audio set with conventional controls and a display on each component. However, some advanced system intelligence had been built in. For instance, if you listened to the tuner and pressed the Play button on the CD-player, the amplifier would automatically switch to the CD-player. Set B offered more functionality than set A did. Although these extra functions were not explored in the experiment, they undoubtedly were potential distracters during the execution of 'basic' tasks.

3 Feedback dimensions

In user interface design, feedback is defined as any response from the system to the user. Feedback can be described and analysed in respect of many dimensions, such as *type, content* and *form.* The type (the why) refers to the purpose of the feedback in the interaction. The content (the what) refers to the meaning of the feedback, whereas the form (the how) refers to the specific phrasing, representation or appearance of the message.

3.1 Feedback type

For the analysis of audio equipment we can distinguish three types of feedback: status feedback, corrective feedback and guidance.

Status feedback provides information on the current status of the set. For instance, the display of the CD-player shows the track that is being played, the time that has elapsed or is still remaining, and the tracks that remain to be played. The tuner provides information on the waveband, frequency and the preset number of the radio station that has been tuned. The dual, autoreverse cassette deck provides information on the selected deck, the current tape side, the play-direction and the tape counter. Proper feedback of the status of the set is crucially important during its operation. If nothing goes wrong, status feedback is all that users need to know that they are on the right track. The other two types of feedback are aimed at bringing them back on track (corrective feedback) and keeping them on track (guidance), respectively.

Corrective feedback consists of responses to activating functions (i.e., pressing buttons) that are currently disabled. They respond to user actions that are not allowed or are meaningless in the current situation. From a formal linguistics perspective, corrective feedback is a response to a user action embodying failed presuppositions, i.e. a user action for which a precondition has not been fulfilled, or, to put it differently, a user action triggered by an incorrect assumption the user has over the status of the system. When the interaction is viewed as a game, corrective feedback can be interpreted as a response to an 'ungrammatical' move of the user. For example, if the CD-player is started but no disc has been inserted, the message 'NO DISC' is shown. Set A has a semi-automatic tape recording function whereby a special time-out on the Record button helps to prevent erroneous recordings: if that button is released too soon, the message 'HOLD TO REC' notifies the user of the existence of the safety time-out. The CD-player of set B shows the message 'PRESETS ACTIVE' when inappropriate buttons have been pressed during the customization of certain default system settings. Textual corrective feedback messages often have the form of a negation of the failed presupposition — such as 'NO X', where X is the presupposition like 'disc is loaded'- or of a proposition of the current system state — like 'Y ACTIVE', where Y is the current state. Warning sounds are examples of auditory corrective feedback.

Guidance provides information which guides the user through a series of actions by showing what can be done next. They respond to correct user actions with the intention to avoid incorrect follow-up actions. So instead of feedback, guidance is a form of 'feed forward'. A button label is a simple example of guidance. Each button in set A contains a (green) LED to indicate that the button can be activated. The message 'HOLD TO START' guides the user of set A to hold down the button until the function that automatically stores the strongest radio stations as tuner presets has been activated. A prompt is another form of guidance. For example, with set B, a known frequency can be tuned after pressing a button that generates the message 'ENTER FREQUENCY'. Textual guidance messages often have the form of an imperative — like 'ENTER X' or 'HOLD TO Z'. Other guidance messages in set B have the general structure A X-Y-Z, shown when button A has just been pressed and to indicate that it can only be followed by X, Y or Z to form a valid command.

In addition, a single feedback message can combine different types of feedback. For example, if the Program button on the CD-player of set B is pressed while a CD is playing, the message 'GO TO STOP' indicates that CD-programming can only be done when the CD is stopped. This message combines corrective feedback, since it has been triggered by an inappropriate action, with guidance, since it explains what can be done about it.

Some properties of feedback types

Status feedback is continuous, persistent and constantly updated by system events. Corrective feedback and guidance are more transient and triggered by user actions. In the audio sets evaluated in the case studies, status feedback is used extensively but not always effectively. Corrective feedback is used occasionally to address a few well-known usability problems. Guidance is hardly used at all.

3.2 Feedback form

Three characteristics of feedback form important for our analysis are: timing, duration and modality.

Timing and duration People are very sensitive to delays between activating a function and receiving feedback. A problem with transient messages is attention: important information may not be noticed. Flashing may be used to draw the user's attention, or to indicate that some information is only temporary and not yet definite. A problem directly related to timing is *unintentional* feedback, where responses of the system happen to coincide with user actions, but are irrelevant to those actions. As the delay between user action and system feedback increases, the chances of unintentional feedback grow (e.g., by performing the action a second time[1]), because people expect response. But in general, unintentional feedback is hard to avoid. The timing and duration of the feedback can provide important cues during the operation of the set, but can cause misunderstandings when done poorly.

Modality In audio equipment we can identify three different feedback modalities: visual feedback, auditory feedback and tactile feedback. Increasing emphasis is placed on the visual feedback provided via large displays. Other forms of visual feedback are given by special indicators such as status LEDs, peak level meters, the position of switches and rotaries, the spinning wheels of a cassette and the amount of tape on a cassette wheel.

The primary form of auditory feedback in audio equipment is the presence or absence of the audio source itself. This is very clearly the case when selecting a tuner preset or playing a CD or cassette. Scanning the radio frequency band generates a typical alteration of noise bursts and radio sounds, although modern

[1] We have seen examples with opening the CD-tray of set A, where the Open/Close button was pressed twice before the tray opened and immediately closed again.

tuners tend to suppress the noise. Speech feedback is another form of auditory feedback which can be employed. Non-speech audio feedback, sometimes called functional sound, can be used as confirmation sounds (e.g., signalling the depression of touch-sensitive buttons), or as warning signals. Finally, there are 'undesigned' forms of auditory feedback which are caused by mechanical by-sounds, like the opening of CD-trays, the winding of a cassette, the spinning of a CD-disc or the clicking of the tape head mechanism at the start of a tape recording.

Tactile feedback is present in the texture of a button surface, the feel of a switch, the pressure on a depressed button and the definite mass slowness or clicks of a turning rotary. Compared to the old 'mechanical' audio products, the tactile feedback in contemporary 'digital' audio sets has, unfortunately, diminished over the years.

4 Two case studies

4.1 Method

Two case studies were set up for the empirical evaluation of hi-fi audio sets. We invited pairs of subjects to perform tasks with the set and to discuss problems. The evaluations involved 12 subjects (6 pairs) for set A and 14 subjects (7 pairs) for set B. None of the subjects had previous experience with the audio set used. Since they discover the potential and functionality of the set together, this technique is called 'co-discovery' (Comstock, 1983, p. 503). The sessions were video-taped and each videotape was analysed in detail. This technique provides insight into the usability problems with the set. Furthermore, the discussion between the subjects allows us — researchers and designers — to interpret their actions better. Pairs of subjects tend to act more freely than individual subjects do in an evaluation setting, or when they are confronted with developers. In addition, this technique gives us valuable information on the perceived quality and potential of the sets, based on 'first impressions' and outward appearance of the sets. The main drawback is that it provides merely qualitative data. Quantitative data can be obtained by measuring number of errors or task completion times, but this is complicated by the fact that subject pairs are involved. On the other hand, the usability problems are so evident that the lack of quantification is not so harmful.

4.2 Tasks

The intention in the experiments was to simulate the initial-use phase (learning phase) which usually starts in a shop when potential customers are attracted to an audio set and start to play with it. Once they decide to buy the set, the learning continues during and after the installation at home. In order to streamline the 'playing around' phase, we devised representative tasks. These had to be executed without a manual, references or instructions. Example tasks were: tuning to an FM radio station, programming a tuner preset, programming three favourite CD-tracks and recording a CD-program on to a cassette.

5 Usability problems: Feedback implications

A wide range of different usability problems was found in the experiments. People operating an audio set often do not know: where they are in the interaction, whether the intended result has been achieved, how to escape an unintended situation, and whether all preconditions for an action have been fulfilled.

Many of these problems can be explained in terms of limitations of the feedback. The problems will be discussed in relation to the different feedback techniques employed and illustrated with examples from the case studies. Some problems are shown to be due to specific design choices of the sets, while others seem to apply to audio equipment in general.

5.1 The recording problem

Traditional hi-fi audio sets can be viewed as 'a stack of boxes'. In order to combine components (boxes) of different manufacturers, most of the controls are component-related. This makes parallel tasks possible: you can listen to the radio while programming your favourite CD and rewinding a cassette. But when two components have to interact during a complex task, some of these separate actions need to be sequenced. For example, tape recording with a conventional set requires the user first to check the recording level, then to set the start positions of source (player) and recorder, to start the recorder and finally to start the source.

The strict implementation of generic control in set A prohibits any form of parallelism. Since only one component can be active at any time, all actions need to be sequenced. This poses particular problems for tape recording. The proper action sequence is:

1. set the start position of the cassette,
2. select the source to be recorded from,
3. set the start position of the source, and
4. hold down the Record button for at least two seconds.

This sequence of actions automatically starts playback of the source and recording onto tape with automatic control of the recording level. Most subjects who worked with set A pressed the Record button only briefly (i.e., a slip in action 4), or pressed it while the tape recorder was the active source (i.e., skipping action 2). Unfortunately, feedback on the Record button was only issued when an unprotected cassette was loaded in the tape recorder and the tape recorder was not the active source (i.e., after actions 1 and 2 had been successfully executed). These were precisely the preconditions for enabling the Record button, but the feedback was clearly insufficient to help first-time users.

Most subjects had problems selecting the source with set B, which was complicated by the explicit separation of the listening and recording source (see below). In both cases, odd as it may seem, very few subjects easily made the step from operating individual audio components to operating abstractions like source and destination. Providing proper status feedback on active source and guidance on the Record function in every state are essential.

5.2 The separation of listening and recording source: WYHIWYR

In audio sets the tape deck is different from most other components. All components are sources that can be listened to. But a tape deck, or its modern embodiments such as DAT, DCC or Mini Disc, can also be a destination since it can record. In conventional amplifiers/receivers a source-selection dial is used to switch to the sources and a special Tape Monitor button is used to listen to the tape deck or to check what will be recorded on it, thereby overriding the source-selection dial. The tape deck in set A cannot be monitored during a recording; only the source can be checked. Set B distinguishes between listening source and recording source. It offers the possibility to record from one source while listening to another and allows multiple recorders in one set. This separation between listening source and recording source breaks with the conventional rule that might be called 'What You Hear Is What You Record' (WYHIWYR). This applies to sets with a Tape Monitor button: in the case of a recording that button only differentiates between the original (input) sound and the recorded (output) sound. The WYHIWYR principle also applies to set A, but does not hold for set B.

The separation between listening and recording source caused problems, because subjects were not sure what was being recorded. The dominance of auditory feedback, i.e. what was heard, was significant. It overshadowed the visual feedback for the recording source on the amplifier. For this particular problem, it is hard to imagine that someone would want start a recording without checking the recording source, except for 'timed' recordings (e.g., recording a radio program on a time you are not able to listen to the radio). A solution would be to always *start* recording from the listening source, faithful to WYHIWYR and allowing the listening source to be *changed* during the recording without affecting the recording.

It was found to be a recurrent problem that people often misinterpreted, or simply did not notice, important, visual feedback. Visual feedback has to be explicitly recognized and interpreted. Looking at modern audio equipment one is led/tempted to believe that 'user are glued to the display'. It seems rather incongruous to offer primary feedback via *visual* displays in *audio* products. This problem only gets bigger when we take the normal home situation into account: the physical location of displays in sets placed in a corner and/or with poor lighting make them rarely easily visible and the viewing distance make displays unusable for remote control operation.

5.3 Problems with modes

A system, whether a computer or non-computer device, has modes if the effect of a given user action is not always the same (Johnson, 1990). According to this informal definition, any audio set is moded. For example, the source-selection buttons of set A introduce modes (CD-mode, tuner mode, etc.), since the active source determines the function of the generic buttons. The same is true for the source-selection buttons on the remote control of both audio sets. Entering a track number on the CD-player of both sets can have two effects: it selects that track for direct playback (i.e., in normal mode), or it adds that track to the CD-program (i.e., in program mode).

The Record button of set A starts a recording (i.e., in normal mode), but renders a mute when pressed during a recording (i.e., in record mode).

In general, there are four basic problems with modes:

- how to *discover* that modes even do exist,
- how to *recognize* the active mode,
- how to *select* a particular mode, and
- how to *exit* a mode.

Discovery Modes as distinguished by the system designer are not likely to be the modes as perceived by the user. First, the user must discover that modes actually do exist, i.e. that pressing a certain button has a different effect depending on previous actions.

Recognition During the remote operation of set B most subjects had difficulty determining what the active source was. In set A, the central display showed the active source. In addition, a red LED indicated that a button was active. But the Program button, which introduced an important mode, lacked this status feedback, which complicated the programming task. Status feedback should make it clear what the active mode is.

Selection In set A, a green LED indicated that a button could be activated, thus guiding the user towards active buttons. Unfortunately, the colour distinction was unclear to the subjects. They took the guidance for status feedback. In fact, colour coding is a simple language and must be learned before any benefits are obtained by the user. Apart from the green LEDs and the button labels, no other guidance was provided to support mode selections in set A.

Exit Neither set provided a clear, unambiguous way to exit a mode. Sometimes the button that induced a change between modes reversed the modes when pressed again (mode toggle). Sometimes the Stop button exited the current mode and sometimes the button that entered the mode stepped through several states before exiting it. We observed several escape methods by users of both sets, varying from pressing the button again, to opening and closing the CD-tray, to switching the whole set off and on! There should be a consistent convention to exit from any mode and appropriate guidance should support this.

5.4 Button time-outs as mode switches to add functionality

There are several ways to extend the functionality without increasing the number of buttons. One way is to add modes with an explicit mode selector. Examples of explicit mode selectors are Shift and Caps-Lock keys in keyboards and function-prefix (or second-function) keys in pocket calculators. Another way to add functionality is to use button time-outs. (The time-out is like the opposite of the double-click in WIMP interfaces, which also extends the functionality in the time space.) For example, a time-out on the numeric buttons of both sets makes it possible to enter a two-digit number without having to confirm it with a special button. (Note that this, so called 'time-out window', convention is optimised for two-digit numbers. Other remote controls distinguish between a short and a long press for the first digit, taking it either as units or tens, respectively. This convention is optimised for one-digit numbers.) The Tune buttons of both sets can be used for both manual and automatic tuning by pressing them briefly (short press) or holding them down (long press), respectively. In some car radios, pressing a preset button selects the tuner preset, whereas holding down a preset button will program the current station (frequency) under that button.

Although short time-out durations may turn number entry into a 'game of skill', we have found that the problem is not the use of a time-out itself, but the lack of feedback (and in particular guidance) *that* a time-out button is being pressed. For two-digit number entry, the bar shown after the first digit (e.g., '1–') is static, but could be flashing to indicate the focus position. The idea is that flashing information is temporary, not yet fixed. In contrast, the visual feedback of the Tune buttons of both sets seems sufficient, since the frequency is counting up or down for both manual and automatic tuning. However, the auditory feedback only comes in *after* the button has been released to avoid noise bursts when searching between two stations.

5.5 Button time-outs as a safety measure

In computer interfaces, critical actions are usually performed after an explicit confirmation (e.g., the 'OK-Cancel' dialog box) has been given. In audio equipment, button time-outs are also used as a *safety measure* to prevent an unintended request of a function. An example is the automatic recording function of set A. Pressing the Record button results in the message 'RECORD FRONT' (or 'RECORD BACK') and holding it down until after a time-out produces the message 'CD → TAPE2' (if CD was the active source). Both messages provide status feedback. The time-out prevents unintended recordings. Releasing the Record button too soon results in the message 'HOLD TO REC', which is corrective feedback. All subjects who worked with set A released the button too soon, but then misinterpreted the last message or even missed it altogether. The proper function was discovered only after holding down the button accidentally.

In this case, the type of feedback can be changed only by changing the *timing* of the message: start with the message 'HOLD TO RECORD' as guidance, followed by the status information 'CD → TAPE2 FRONT' after the time-out. Changing the modality from visual to speech feedback resolves the attention problem, as was shown in a third experiment (see feedback improvements below). Curious enough, the same guidance is provided for the 'safety' time-out on the Automemory button on the tuner, which automatically stores the strongest radio stations as tuner presets.

6 Feedback improvements

In the previous section some strengths and weaknesses of feedback in relation to the usability problems with the audio sets have been discussed. It is clear that there is much room for feedback improvement. The evaluation of set A revealed that it was not always clear which component was operated by the generic buttons. No distinction was made between the two-coloured LEDs, both being (mis)taken for status feedback. Another problem was what the current function of each generic button was. The mapping of the controls from tape deck to CD-player is easy, but mapping them to the tuner is rather far-fetched ("*what does fast-forward mean for a tuner?*").

6.1 Experiment: the simulation of an audio set with extended feedback

We implemented some feedback improvements in a simulation of audio set A and tested it in a co-discovery experiment with 10 subjects (5 pairs). The simulation consisted of a PC, equipped with a touch-screen monitor and a sound-sample card and connected to an audio set. The PC and the audio set were hidden behind a curtain except for the monitor and the loudspeakers. The simulation had the same functionality as set A but the feedback was extended: one version with extended visual feedback, one version with speech feedback added and one version with non-speech audio feedback added. The subjects were not told what the differences between the three versions were. In this particular experiment, order and practice effects were not completely controlled for, due to the small number of pairs: 3 pairs worked with the speech version *after* the visual version, 2 pairs worked with the speech version *before* the visual version.

6.2 Soft keys improve the transparency of control

The two-coloured LEDs were removed in the simulation. For the generic buttons, so-called 'soft keys' were added, i.e. explicit labels that change dynamically with the buttons' functions. It was our aim to compare the effectiveness of these different forms of feedback.

The soft keys provided instant guidance in operating the generic controls of the simulation and successfully replaced the two-coloured LEDs. This guidance is particularly helpful when the set's components are heterogeneous: mapping the controls becomes easier. This was shown for the tuner functions and the programming functions. Hence, the soft keys improve the self-explanation of the generic control concept. Even greater flexibility can be obtained with touchscreen-based menu controls which have been built into high-end audio/video equipment.

6.3 Corrective speech feedback shortens the learning process

From the evaluation of set A it was also found that the visual feedback from the central display was often misinterpreted, or simply went unnoticed. Speech has certain advantages over visual feedback; it offers more bandwidth (thus allows more detail), draws attention, is transient, and does not clutter up the display.

On the other hand, since speech feedback cannot be ignored, it may be obtrusive. In the experiment we tested three versions of a simulation of set A. It turned out that, once subjects had worked with the speech version, the tasks with the other versions were performed faster. For example, it was very hard to communicate the time-out of the Record button visually (textually), but it was immediately picked up after the message was heard. Also, corrective feedback during the programming task was more successfully communicated via speech than via text.

The use of speech feedback in audio equipment is a controversial topic. People sometimes voice criticism of speech feedback as being obtrusive in combination with audio equipment. About half of the subjects still objected to it after they had worked with the simulation. Others were enthusiastic, as one subject who said: "Look, if such a voice was *in* the appliance, that would be ideal. I would love it: 'Do you want to make a tape recording? Press that button'." It can be concluded that the explanatory capacity of speech can be used to notify the user of an 'incorrect' operation and thus reduce usability problems. Speech was always used in addition to, never instead of, the visual feedback. Users must have the possibility to switch off speech feedback.

7 Discussion

In this section the feedback issues discussed in this paper are put in the broader perspective of other workshop contributions. One of the main differences is that our feedback analysis is specifically targeted at consumer appliances, which differ from professional computer systems or applications mainly by their input and output devices, and therefore the kind of interfaces. With limited displays, for instance, the steps in the user-system dialogue are smaller as the information has to be provided piece-meal. Computer screens offer greater expressive capabilities for all types of visual feedback, especially guidance. This is particularly benificial for consumers who expect to use their appliances without any training. Modern TV-sets and other TV-related appliances, like video recorders and CD-I players, already apply on-screen display for various menu-control procedures for all but the most basic functions to guide the user through very elaborate features with a relatively few control conventions.

Erickson (this volume) mentions two roles that feedback can play. The usual role is to 'support the user in smoothly completing the current operation'. The second role, termed portrayal, is to 'support the creation of a mental model of the structure and activities of the system.' In our feedback categorization the temporal aspect has been mentioned as an important parameter. Erickson distinguishes three feedback types 'based on it's relation to the user's activity: synchronous feedback, background feedback and terminal feedback.' All three types can be considered a sub-classification of status feedback in our terminology, in this case differentiated by time (duration) as experienced by the user. Erickson's example of copying a folder on the Macintosh illustrates the use of these types of status feedback, which are partly made possible by the graphic capabilities of the computer screen. Due to the reactive nature of consumer appliances most feedback is synchronous feedback since it occurs in sync with the user's actions. Erickson's 'feedback as portrayal' becomes important at the system level as consumer appliances are becoming increasingly complex. Portrayal may also be beneficial for complex (semi-)automatic functions, such as automatic tuner programming, which is analogous to Erickson's example of the AppleLink 'connection storyboard'. Although the graphic capabilities of computer workstations outperform those of the most advanced consumer appliances, portrayal has strong potential in the auditory domain as exemplified by Erickson's 'background disc humming' anecdote.

Wroblewski et al. (this volume) argue that conversationally delivered feedback, and more specifically 'guidance' or what they call 'advice', is a matter of last resort and they introduce three loosely related feedback techniques, called advertisement, proxies and wear. The techniques are applied to information processing (c.q., problem solving) applications, basically by showing different and multiple properties of 'objects' in the application domain simultaneously. The work is said to be based on the 'situated' design approach (Schön, 1982) focusing more on 'opportunities provided by the context of use' rather than 'a complete encompassing model of task and user'. If we apply these techniques, two observations can be made. The first is that in the consumer-appliances domain the notions of 'tasks' and 'user models' are probably even more vague than in the information-processing domain. The second observation is that advertisement is a form of guidance, and proxies and wear are enriched forms of status feedback. It is assumed that showing more information on objects of interest, from different perspectives increases the understanding of the domain. A potential problem is that too much status feedback might distract the consumer from the task at hand (e.g., display pollution), requiring careful interaction design trade-offs to be made. The results reported by Wroblewski et al. at least seem promising for other domains.

8 Conclusion

The usability problems with two hi-fi audio sets were discussed in relation to the different feedback techniques employed. Three types of feedback seemed to be relevant: status feedback, corrective feedback and guidance. In the audio sets we analysed, status feedback ('to show users that they are on the right track') was used extensively, but not always effectively. Corrective feedback ('to bring users back on track') was used occasionally to cover a few well-known usability problems. The most impoverished type of feedback was guidance ('to keep users on track'). It was sparsely used in both sets. Both corrective feedback and guidance were extended in a simulation of one of the sets. The use of speech for corrective feedback appears to shorten the learning phase with the audio set.

An audio set should be designed to support exploratory learning. In the initial-use phase people constantly try to make sense of the effects of their actions (Carroll,

1990). Successful operation critically depends on the quality of the feedback. This can be improved when the set provides corrective feedback in response to inappropriate user actions and guidance to reveal appropriate user actions whenever these seem helpful.

Much work still needs to be done in the design of audio equipment in order to make them interesting and inviting on the one hand and easy-to-use on the other. The design of user interfaces is an iterative process (Gould & Lewis, 1983). The usability problems we have observed do not necessarily demand totally different interaction styles or control concepts. Many problems can be solved with feedback improvements alone, as summarized by the following examples:

- appropriate status feedback reduces mode recognition problems;
- corrective speech feedback shortens the learning process;
- corrective feedback can explain the proper use of 'inactive' buttons;
- corrective feedback and guidance help explain button time-outs;
- corrective feedback can be 'guiding' in its phrasing;
- clear button labels guide users towards appropriate buttons;
- dynamic button labels (soft keys) improve self-explanation;
- guidance reduces mode-exit problems;
- a single convention may eliminate mode-exit problems.

Based on modern display and speech technology, feedback messages can be improved considerably.

The analysis of the usability problems with audio sets was based primarily on empirical results. The problems can be considered typical for the given tasks and with that restriction the results give an indication of the frequency of occurrence and thus the severity of these problems, and consequently the relative importance of solving them. Other tasks might have highlighted other problems. We are currently developing an analysis tool, in a grammar formalism, to see how well usability (feedback) problems can be predicted and how consistency of operation (and consistency as to type, content and form of the feedback) can be guaranteed.

Acknowledgements

I would like to thank Tedde van Gelderen, Kees van Deemter, Reinder Haakma, Joyce Westerink, Maddy Brouwer-Janse and Anthony Creed for their constructive feedback, that is 'corrective feedback' and 'guidance' mixed with some 'status feedback', on earlier drafts of this paper.

References

Carroll, John M. (1990) Infinite detail and emulation in an ontologically minimized HCI. Proceeding CHI'90, Seattle, WA, 321–327.

Comstock, Elisabeth M. (1983) Customer installability of computer systems. Proceedings Human Factors Society – 27th Annual Meeting, 1, Norfolk, VA, 501–504.

Ehn, Pelle (1988) Work-oriented Design of Computer Artifacts. Falköping, Sweden: Arbetslivscentrum/Almquist & Wiksell International.

Gould, John D. & Lewis, Clayton H. (1983) Design for usability: key principles and what designers think. Proceedings CHI'83, Boston, 50–53.

Johnson, Jeff (1990) Modes in non-computer devices. IJMMS, 32, 423–438.

Schön, Donald (1982) The Reflective Practitioner. New York: Basic Books.

Suchmann, Lucy A. (1987) Plans and Situated Actions: the problems of human-machine communication. Cambridge: Cambridge University Press.

Thimbleby, Harold (1990) User Interface Design. ACM Press Frontier Series. New York: ACM Press.

Advertisements, Proxies, and Wear: Three Methods for Feedback in Interactive Systems

David A. Wroblewski[1], Timothy P. McCandless[1] and William C. Hill[2]

[1] U S West Advanced Technologies, 4001 Discovery Drive, Boulder, CO 80303, USA, email: davew@uswest.com and mccand@uswest.com
[2] Bell Communications Research, 445 South Street, Morristown, NJ 07962, USA, email: willhill@bellcore.com

Abstract. We consider conversationally delivered advice to be a method of last resort and search for methods of delivery less difficult for users to assimilate. Three alternative methods for presenting advice are discussed, namely, advertising, advertising by proxy, and wear. These techniques have several strengths. First, they draw users further into the problem at hand rather than distracting them with advice-interpretation and advice-following tasks, or with the added burden of participation in a conversation with a automated advisor. Second, they reveal emergent properties of the user's work-materials, many of which do not merit a full-fledged conversation, but which are useful for guiding the user's work. Finally, they present topics in parallel, leaving the user the choice of which issues will be followed up, and in what sequence.

Keywords. Computer based advising, graphical user interfaces, informational physics, professional work, reflective practitioner

1 Introduction

Our research (Hill, 1989; Hill, 1992; Hill & Miller, 1988) has led us to believe that delivering guidance to the user conversationally is a method of last resort. Unfortunately, few alternatives have been explored to date. Our goal is to articulate a spectrum of techniques for delivering user guidance and to understand the strengths and weaknesses of each point along the spectrum.

There are several reasons for looking for alternatives to conversationally delivered advice. First, some guidance is 'small', that is, it is worth informing the user but only if it can be done in a nonintrusive manner. Guidance of this type takes the form of noncritical reminders, or broader contextual information, such as properties of the users interaction history that have emerged over long periods of time. An ideal system would present such information peripherally, to be investigated and assimilated at the user's initiative.

Second, we believe conversational delivery of advice requires an accurate and complete model of the user and the user's task in order to be effective, and such models are extremely difficult to build. Two problems recur: the models are brittle, and the models do not accurately reflect the activities of the user. In practice, building complete and accurate models of users engaged in the kinds of complex activities that require advising is prohibitively expensive, even though incomplete models (e.g., incompletely covering a subset of the user activity) are sometimes available. An ideal system would incorporate such incomplete knowledge about the task and user and would deliver the computed guidance accordingly.

Finally, engaging the users in a conversation in order to provide guidance has the undesirable effect of distracting them from the problem-at-hand and, paradoxically, introducing a new problem to be handled, that is, participation in an advisory dialogue and all the conversational repair and contextual interpretation of the advice that such a conversation necessarily entails. In Wizard of Oz studies we have seen such advisory dialogues followed effectively and efficiently only about half the time, and even optimistic assumptions about automated advisory performance in real situations would fall short of this (Hill, 1989; Hill, 1992; Hill & Miller, 1988). In an ideal system, the delivery of guidance would further engage the user in the problem-at-hand, rather than to distract them or present them with equally difficult problems to solve.

The remainder of this paper presents three methods of delivering computed guidance. They are alternatives to conversational delivery, other points on a spectrum of techniques that system designers must select among based on the strengths of each technique and the context of use in which the human-computer system resides.

2 Method 1: Advertisement

The first method of guidance we wish to consider is embodied by a system called DETENTE.[1] DETENTE is an object-oriented application architecture that allows programs to track work that remains to be done and to deliver that information to the user without resorting to conversation.

A DETENTE application defines some of its objects as *resources* — objects that will appear to the user as the work materials of the work being performed in the application, such as items in an electronic form, paragraphs in a text editor, or messages in an email system. This is done by making those objects an instance of the class `resource`. Any resource object may be asked to generate *recommendation* objects. A recommendation describes a piece of work that remains to be done to the work materials, in this case the resource object that generated the recommendation. Recommendations are placed on an *agenda* and managed via the *task maintenance protocol*, a set of messages that can pass between resources, recommendations, and agendas, that allow for the retraction of recommendations when the state of the work materials change. The result is that a DETENTE application maintains a list of recommendations for work that remains to be done, and these recommendations are created and destroyed as appropriate with minimal user intervention.[2]

---

[1] Which stands for 'DETENTE Exists To Express New Tasks Effectively.'

[2] This is a highly abbreviated description of the DETENTE architecture. See Wroblewski et al. (1991) for a more complete description.

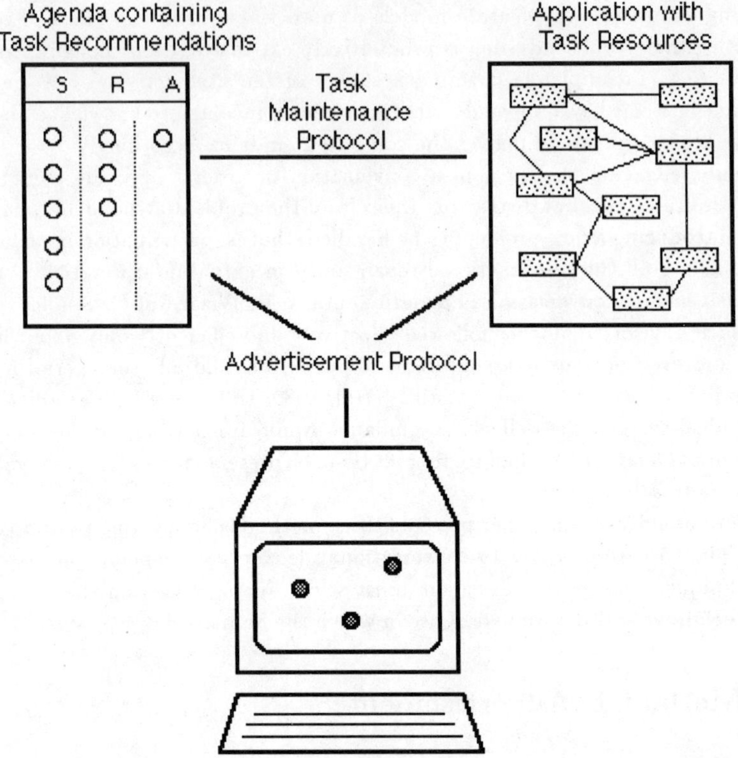

Fig. 1. Via the *task maintenance protocol*, application elements known as resources can suggest user activity; via the *advertisement protocol*, those recommendations are made apparent to the user.

Once a set of recommendations has been generated, the program must make the recommendations apparent to the user. DETENTE capitalizes on the notion of *advertising* to accomplish this. Advertising means *drawing the user's attention to the work materials that bear more work.* In many cases, it is sufficient to make the user aware of the general qualities of the work to be done, if not the specifics of the problem.[3]

Advertising is accomplished through the *advertisement protocol.* This is a set of messages between a view (in the Smalltalk model-view-controller sense of 'view') and an agenda. The protocol consists of two stages. First, when recommendations become *active*, the agenda sends an `Advertise` message to each view of the data. This can have various effects, or no effect at all, depending on the contents of

[3] Advertising is related to and inspired by the notion of an affordance, an object whose interactional possibilities are apparent from its form (Norman, 1988).

the view, although typically, when a view receives an `Advertise` message, it will attempt to find a screen representation of some participating resource and augment its appearance. When the recommendation is taken off the agenda (via the task maintenance protocol) the agenda sends each view the complementary `UnAdvertise` message. In this way, the display and the agenda are synchronized.

The advertising protocol does not dictate how advertising is done, it merely takes responsibility for mediating the process. The specific technique used to augment the view to account for a new recommendation is application-dependent. Indeed, there are many ways of doing this in common use today, such as putting the graphic in reverse video, blinking it, using a special color or font, moving the item to a special position in the view, producing some audible signal, or a combination of these things.

2.1 An example of advertising

Here is a simplistic example of the advertising in a hypothetical word processing application that uses scrolling windows for large documents. Suppose that after a text has been resident in the text buffer, a spell checking program runs over the text and notes apparently misspelled words. The resources in the program are buffers, lines, and words. The agenda is filled with recommendations concerning the presence of an apparently misspelled word at a certain position in the document. DETENTE must now mediate the advertising of these recommendations.

The screen consists of two views: the first displays the actual text and the second displays a scroll bar (essentially, an alternative graphic representation of the document.) When a new recommendation is added to the agenda, both views are notified via the `Advertise` message. The text display locates the word and inverts its video. The scroll bar view places a tic mark at the appropriate position in a contrasting color to indicate the presence of a possible misspelling at that relative position in the document.[4] If the word is corrected, the recommendation is retracted and both views are sent an `UnAdvertise` message to update the displays. After several recommendations are on the agenda, the user's screen would appear as shown in Figure 2.

2.2 Advantages of advertising

Advertising task recommendations has several strengths as a method for computing and delivering guidance. First, advertising is inherently parallel and passive: any number of task recommendations may be advertised simultaneously, and the user retains control of the order in which issues are explored.

Second, advertising helps reveal the emergent structure of the user's task, without imposing predefined procedures for work. Recommendations in a DETENTE

[4] This technique in its most general form is called attribute-mapped scroll bars, and is discussed in more detail in the Wear section of this paper. See Wroblewski et al. (1990) for more details.

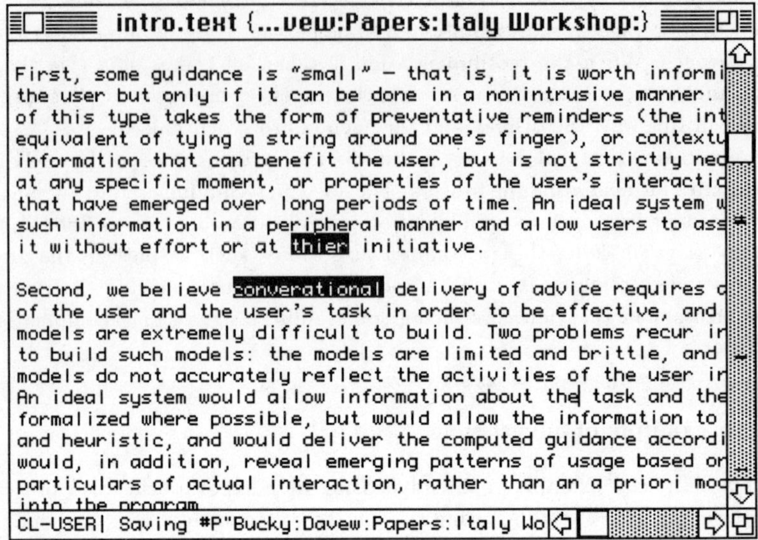

intro.text {...vew:Papers:Italy Workshop:}
First, some guidance is "small" – that is, it is worth informi
the user but only if it can be done in a nonintrusive manner.
of this type takes the form of preventative reminders (the in
equivalent of tying a string around one's finger), or context
information that can benefit the user, but is not strictly ne
at any specific moment, or properties of the user's interacti
that have emerged over long periods of time. An ideal system w
such information in a peripheral manner and allow users to as
it without effort or at thier initiative.
Second, we believe converational delivery of advice requires
of the user and the user's task in order to be effective, and
models are extremely difficult to build. Two problems recur i
to build such models: the models are limited and brittle, and
models do not accurately reflect the activities of the user i
An ideal system would allow information about the task and th
formalized where possible, but would allow the information to
and heuristic, and would deliver the computed guidance accordi
would, in addition, reveal emerging patterns of usage based o
particulars of actual interaction, rather than an a priori mo
CL-USER| Saving #P"Bucky:Davew:Papers:Italy Wo

Fig. 2. The text display and the scroll bar form two views of the same data. Inverting a word indicates that it may be misspelled (reflecting the presence of a recommendation on the agenda). A tic mark in the scroll bar has exactly the same meaning. Both displays are managed via the `Advertise/Unadvertise` messages in the Advertisement Protocol.

application are generated by the *local processing* of individual elements of the artifact being built. By collecting the recommendations on an agenda and advertising them, larger patterns of work to be done become apparent to the user without inference by the system, and those patterns change in response to change in user's work. There is no attempt to coordinate an internal model with the work being done.

Third, advertising draws users further into the problem-at-hand, rather than forcing the users into conversation and advice interpretation. It does this by using the work materials as arranged by the previous work of the user to 'articulate' the recommendations. This has the effect of making the materials themselves seem intelligent.

3 Method 2: Advertisement by Proxy

DETENTE does not implicitly know what resources appear in what views of the application, and therefore sends the `Advertise/UnAdvertise` messages to all known views of the data. Sometimes a view may only show objects *related* to the resources involved in a recommendation, but not the resources that are the subjects of the recommendation. In this case, the recommendation may be advertised through a *proxy*, i.e. a logically related resource. Some examples of relationships that could be used to compute proxyhood are: containment, data dependency, and super-component.

The algorithm for displaying a new advertisement, given a task recommendation with resources and proxies is simply to find the proxy nearest the original task resource and use it for advertising; the search must account for circularities in proxyhood and provide a depth limit to terminate the search.

3.1 Examples of advertising by proxy

Imagine that the hypothetical word processing program introduced in the last section partitions documents into objects representing paragraphs (many word processing programs do this) as well as objects representing sections, footnotes, and so on. Each section object knows what sections or paragraphs it contains, and each object knows its containing object. Additionally, suppose the program supports an 'outline' mode in which only the titles of the sections are visible. Without the use of proxies, only misspellings in the words of the section headings would be visible in outline mode, but recommendations within the text of each section would be hidden along with the text itself.

The addition of proxies can address this problem. One approach would be to allow paragraphs to designate their containing section object as a proxy. Thus, in outline mode, the section heading might be displayed in red as a proxy advertisement for some recommendation for its contained objects. Or it might become increasingly 'bright' as the number of recommendations it contained increased.

Another example of proxy display would allow an outline-format display of section headings to display search hits arrayed across the entire document, as in SuperBook (Egan et al., 1989). In this way, the results of a search are posed as one or more recommendations whose semantics are 'Investigate search hit at position xyz.' The distribution of search hits within the various sections of the document are apparent, which is useful information.

As a final example of advertising through proxies, forms-based interfaces (such as MacInTax (Softview, 1989)) that allow users to work on several forms concurrently (and move between them via a menu) could use the names of the forms on the menu as proxies for advertisements within each form. By looking at the menu, the users can see which forms demand the most attention, and adjust their work accordingly.

3.2 Advantages and disadvantages of advertising by proxy

Advertising by proxy solves one problem in a simplistic formulation of DETENTE, that of indirectly referring to materials that bear further work. In real systems this is important, since the objects that comprise the work materials may be numerous and complexly related, thus it is unlikely that they will all be visible at the same time.

On the other hand, advertising by proxy introduces ambiguity into advertising, and thus some of the problems of reference and reference resolution inherent in the conversational delivery of guidance. The user must now determine whether a augmented item on the screen represents a recommendation about it or some object that is logically related to it. Indiscriminate use of proxy advertising could render the whole advertising paradigm ineffective. We do not yet have enough experience with DETENTE to articulate a foolproof set of rules to limit advertising by proxy; future work should remedy this. In the meantime, we believe that practice with these techniques will not suffer from the in-principle worst cases, and rules of thumb will emerge.

4 Method 3: Edit Wear and Read Wear

Some information can guide user activity, yet is never so critically important that it warrants interrupting the user. An example of this kind of information is wear. In the physical world, use leaves wear on objects, and that wear can guide users. For instance, highly worn reference books often fall open to commonly used spots. The basic idea presented in this section is to record on computational objects (e.g., documents, spreadsheets, menus, images, email) the events that comprise their use, and then, on future occasions, when the objects are used again, display graphical abstractions of the accrued histories as parts of the objects themselves (Hill et al., 1992).

Two document processing applications resulted from considerations of this basic idea: Edit Wear and Read Wear. By modifying a document editor, these applications arrange for every edit and every episode of reading to leave wear on the document. In the case of Edit Wear, this means to graphically portray the document's authorship history by modifying the document's screen representation. In the case of Read Wear, it means to graphically portray the document's readership history.

4.1 Examples of wear

Using attribute-mapped scroll bars (Wroblewski et al., 1990), wear appears to users as marks mapped onto document scroll bars in positions relative to line positions. The length of the mark depicts the magnitude of the wear or other wear qualities. Attribute-mapped scroll bars can be used in a variety of ways.

Figure 3 shows five examples of what users see. Scroll bar (a) is a normal scroll bar unadorned with wear. Bar (b) shows a snapshot of edit wear on a document. The width of individual wear marks is proportional to the largest magnitude of edits per line. The fact that some sections have been edited more than others is visible and it is easy to get to those sections by clicking on them. Bar (c) is the same document at a later stage, with two categories of wear in right and left vertical bar bands. Edit wear displayed in (b) has been compressed into the left band. A second category of edit wear is displayed in the right band. Groups of edits in the second category of edit wear are visible along with a smattering of small edits. Bar (d) shows total read wear on a source code file. Bar (e) shows the same read wear

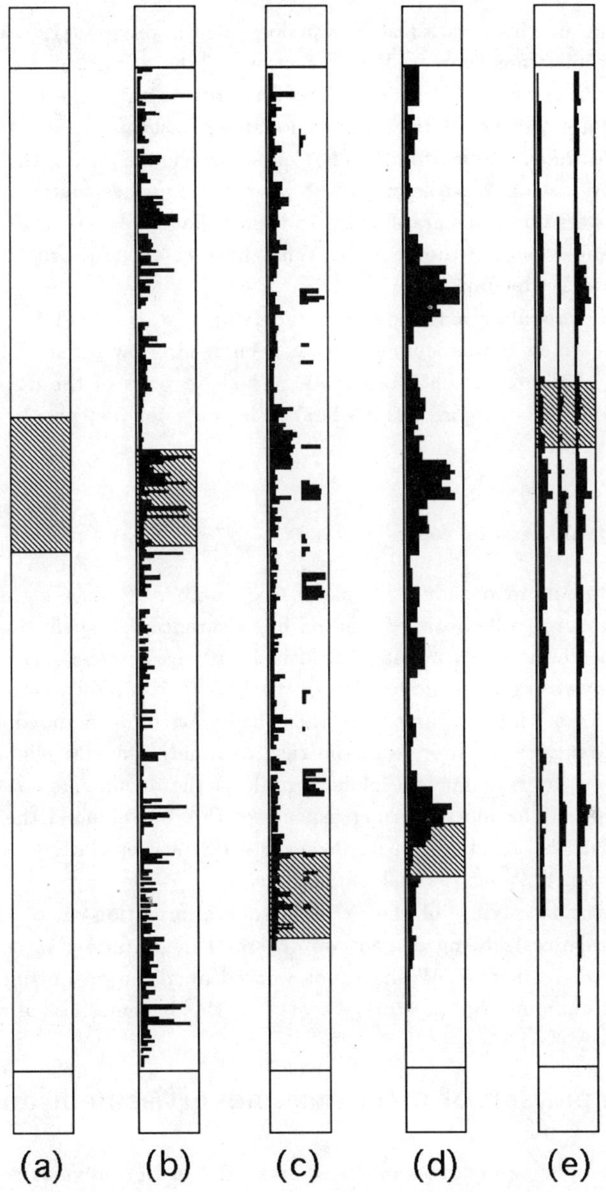

Fig. 3. Scroll bar (a) shows no wear. Scroll bars (b)-(e) show examples of one or more categories of wear displayed simultaneously.

as in (d) but now partitioned into three bands according to its three constituent categories.[5]

By displaying an edit-by-edit history of a document in progress, Edit Wear graphically answers questions such as: Which sections of the document are most stable (i.e., changing the slowest)? Which sections are most unstable (i.e., current editing hot-spots)? What are the relative ages of document sections? How often have sections of the document been edited? What edits were made during the last editing session? In the case of co-authorship, edit wear distinguishes contributions by author, and answers questions graphically and immediately: Who wrote what? Who edited what and when did they edit it? What have co-authors written and edited since I last saw the document?

Similarly, by providing a line-by-line readership history, Read Wear addresses questions concerning how documents have been read: How often and how much have sections of the document been read? Which sections of the document have been read by various categories of readers? Who were the last people to read this section, and when?

4.2 The advantages of wear

Read wear and edit wear should be useful in a number of areas, e.g. co-authored reports, large source-code libraries, and on-line reference document sets. Wear can show very long term trends in usage intuitively. It reveals emergent properties of use without any strong prior model of usage to drive it; it is purely empirical. It can be presented for a whole document at once (using attribute mapped scroll bars.) It does not disengage the user from the task at hand, and may slightly enhance user engagement by revealing the global profile of the documents construction or usage. And one of the most pleasing aspects of this technique is that document wear appears in the exact screen position on which a user clicks to scroll to the document section that has that self-same wear.

On the downside, saving all the extra history information on a per-line basis results in storage costs being one to two orders of magnitude greater than without edit wear or read wear. We have not worked at all on optimizing storage or compression techniques, but as storage costs fall, this becomes less of an issue.

5 A comparison of utterance, advertisement and wear

The following table summarizes material presented in the previous sections. The criteria used for comparison are:

[5] (Hill et al., 1992) details the algorithms used for calculating and displaying wear in ZMACS, a variant of EMACS. Note that the algorithms only approximate actual user time spent reading, since this cannot be measured directly without very sophisticated methods such as eye-trackers; instead, the algorithms use the duration that each line of text is visible while the user is active as an approximation.

Reflects emergent behaviour In other words, does this technique make evident patterns of usage based on the particulars of past interaction, or does it presuppose a model of the work being carried out by the human-computer system in order to provide guidance?

User problems introduced. Every technique for delivering guidance to users adds some new burden to the user. What new tasks are introduced because of the delivery vehicle?

Effect on user engagement. Does the technique tend to draw the user further into the problem-at-hand, distance him from it, or have no effect?

Presentation of topics. Are topics presented to the use serially or in parallel?

Table 1. A comparison of utterance, advertisement, and wear as vehicles for delivering guidance to users.

	Utterance	**Advertisement**	**Wear**
Reflects emergent behavior	Slightly and indirectly	Displays patterns of work remaining	Displays patterns of authorship and usage over time
User problems introduced	Referent resolution, Conversational repair and response, Advice interpretation	Advertisement interpretation	Wear interpretation
Effect on user engagement	Less engaged	More engaged	Slightly more engaged
Presentation of topics	Serial	Parallel	Parallel

6 Related work

All of the techniques discussed in this paper emerged from discussions around the problems we encountered building advice-offering user assistance software, and our subsequent search for advising and delivery paradigms without the practical problems of full-blown, conversational advising. At that time we began to consider some of the ideas of Donald Schön (Schön, 1982), specifically, his theory of professional practice as reflection-in-action.

Opposing the analytical view that professional activity consists in instrumental problem-solving made rigorous by the application of scientific theory and technique (Schön, 1982, p. 21). Schön proposes a reflection-in-action analysis of professional work:

> *When the practitioner tries to solve the problem he has set, he seeks both to understand the situation and to change it... Through the unintended effects of action, the situation talks back. The practitioner, reflecting on this back-talk, may find new meaning in the situation which leads him to a new*

> *reframing. Thus he judges a problem-setting by the quality and direction of the reflective conversation to which it leads.* (Schön, 1982, pp. 134–135)

Here, Schön emphasizes problem-*setting* over problem-*solving*. For Schön,

> *problem setting is a process in which, interactively, we name the things to which we will attend and frame the context in which we will attend them.* (Schön, 1982, p. 40),

Problem-setting precedes problem-solving. Considering interfaces for professional work in the light of Schöns analytical point of view, we might add and paraphrase:

> *Interfaces permit and encourage certain problem-settings and should be judged by the quality and direction of the reflective conversations that result from the problem-settings they engender.*

Often, interfaces presume an implicit immutable problem-setting and concentrate on supporting problem-solving within the resulting constrained framework. Interfaces often do notsupport the fuzzy work of problem-setting which, according to Schön, is the hallmark of professional work. What Schön terms the *perceptual emergence of the unnamed and unframed* is a critical aspect of supporting professional problem-solving in computation. For, unless an interface displays perceptual groupings that have yet to be named and framed in Schön's sense, all phenomena are already labelled and classified and creative problem-setting is constrained.

Another notion from Schön of importance to the design of these techniques is his concept of the *action present:*

> *A practitioners reflection-in-action may not be very rapid. It is bounded by the action present, the zone of time in which action can still make a difference to the situation... The action-present may stretch over minutes, hours, days, or even weeks or months depending on the pace of activity and the situational boundaries that are characteristic of the practice.* (Schön, 1982, p. 62)

As a result of our desire to embed prior activity information in the action present, the techniques of advertising and wear make patterns of past use apparent during all phases of editing and reading, rather than as an after-the-fact summary to be consulted in some other context. They allow the implicit structure of user activity to *emerge* from the accumulated particulars of actual interaction.

7 Summary

In this paper, we have made the case that a range of techniques exists for delivering guidance to users of interactive computer systems, and that conversational delivery using utterances as the unit of information exchange is a method of last resort, because of the demands it places on users and the difficulty with which such systems are implemented.

As alternatives, we have looked at two variants on the notion of *advertising*, either directly or through proxies. As embodied in the DETENTE system architecture, advertising can be an effective method for delivering guidance when that guidance is mainly concerned with what work materials bear further work. In addition, we have explored the notion of *wear* as a method of answering many questions implicit in the construction and consumption of electronic documents, questions that are central to the social context in which documents are created and used. All the techniques presented here use emergent properties of the user interaction to guide user work rather than presuppose a strong model of the user and/or the user's task, and all the techniques presented here appear to the user as smart materials rather than coaches, tutors, advisors, or assistants.

References

Egan, D.E., Remde, J.R., Gomez, L.M., Landauer, T.K., Eberhardt, J. & Lochbaum, C.C. (1989) Formative Design-Evaluation of SuperBook. ACM Transactions on Information Systems, 7(1), 30–57.

Hill, W.C. (1989) How Some Advice Fails. 1989 ACM Conference on Human Factors in Computing, Austin, Texas, 85–90.

Hill, W.C. (1992) A Wizard of Oz Study of Advice Giving and Following. HCI Journal.

Hill, W.C. & Miller, J.R. (1988) Justified Advice: A Semi-Naturalistic Study of Advisory Strategies. ACM Conference on Human Factors in Computer Systems, Washington, DC, 185–190.

Hill, W.C., Hollan, J.D., Wroblewski, D.A. & McCandless, T.P. (1992) Edit Wear and Read Wear. ACM CHI'92 Proceedings, 3–9.

Norman, D. (1988) The Psychology of Everyday Things. New York: Basic Books.

Schön, Donald (1982) The Reflective Practitioner. New York: Basic Books.

Softview, Inc. (1989) MacInTax software.

Wroblewski, D., McCandless, T. & Hill, W.C. (1991) DETENTE: Practical Support for Practical Action. 1991 ACM Conference on Human Factors in Computing Systems. New Orleans: Addison-Wesley, 195–202.

Wroblewski, D.A., Hill, W.C. & McCandless, T.P. (1990) Attribute-Mapped Scroll Bars. US Patent Applications. Serial Number 07/523,117, filed May 14, 1990, Serial Number 07/626,130 filed December 11, 1990.

Author Index[1]

[1] This index was generated with TExtract

Subject Index[1]

[1] This index was generated with TExtract

NATO ASI Series F

Including Special Programmes on Sensory Systems for Robotic Control (ROB) and on Advanced Educational Technology (AET)

Vol. 1: Issues in Acoustic Signal - Image Processing and Recognition. Edited by C. H. Chen. VIII, 333 pages. 1983. *(out of print)*

Vol. 2: Image Sequence Processing and Dynamic Scene Analysis. Edited by T. S. Huang. IX, 749 pages. 1983.

Vol. 3: Electronic Systems Effectiveness and Life Cycle Costing. Edited by J. K. Skwirzynski. XVII, 732 pages. 1983. *(out of print)*

Vol. 4: Pictorial Data Analysis. Edited by R. M. Haralick. VIII, 468 pages. 1983.

Vol. 5: International Calibration Study of Traffic Conflict Techniques. Edited by E. Asmussen. VII, 229 pages. 1984.

Vol. 6: Information Technology and the Computer Network. Edited by K. G. Beauchamp. VIII, 271 pages. 1984.

Vol. 7: High-Speed Computation. Edited by J. S. Kowalik. IX, 441 pages. 1984.

Vol. 8: Program Transformation and Programming Environments. Report on a Workshop directed by F. L. Bauer and H. Remus. Edited by P. Pepper. XIV, 378 pages. 1984.

Vol. 9: Computer Aided Analysis and Optimization of Mechanical System Dynamics. Edited by E. J. Haug. XXII, 700 pages. 1984. *(out of print)*

Vol. 10: Simulation and Model-Based Methodologies: An Integrative View. Edited by T. I. Ören, B. P. Zeigler, M. S. Elzas. XIII, 651 pages. 1984.

Vol. 11: Robotics and Artificial Intelligence. Edited by M. Brady, L. A. Gerhardt, H. F. Davidson. XVII, 693 pages. 1984.

Vol. 12: Combinatorial Algorithms on Words. Edited by A. Apostolico, Z. Galil. VIII, 361 pages. 1985.

Vol. 13: Logics and Models of Concurrent Systems. Edited by K. R. Apt. VIII, 498 pages. 1985.

Vol. 14: Control Flow and Data Flow: Concepts of Distributed Programming. Edited by M. Broy. VIII, 525 pages. 1985. *Reprinted as Springer Study Edition 1986.*

Vol. 15: Computational Mathematical Programming. Edited by K. Schittkowski. VIII, 451 pages. 1985.

Vol. 16: New Systems and Architectures for Automatic Speech Recognition and Synthesis. Edited by R. De Mori, C.Y. Suen. XIII, 630 pages. 1985. *(out of print)*

Vol. 17: Fundamental Algorithms for Computer Graphics. Edited by R. A. Earnshaw. XVI, 1042 pages. 1985. *Reprinted as Springer Study Edition 1991.*

Vol. 18: Computer Architectures for Spatially Distributed Data. Edited by H. Freeman and G. G. Pieroni. VIII, 391 pages. 1985. *(out of print)*

Vol. 19: Pictorial Information Systems in Medicine. Edited by K. H. Höhne. XII, 525 pages. 1986.

Vol. 20: Disordered Systems and Biological Organization. Edited by E. Bienenstock, F. Fogelman Soulié, G. Weisbuch. XXI, 405 pages.1986

Vol. 21: Intelligent Decision Support in Process Environments. Edited by E. Hollnagel, G. Mancini, D. D. Woods. XV, 524 pages. 1986.

Vol. 22: Software System Design Methods. The Challenge of Advanced Computing Technology. Edited by J. K. Skwirzynski. XIII, 747 pages. 1986. *(out of print)*

Vol. 23: Designing Computer-Based Learning Materials. Edited by H. Weinstock and A. Bork. IX, 285 pages. 1986. *(out of print)*

Vol. 24: Database Machines. Modern Trends and Applications. Edited by A. K. Sood and A. H. Qureshi. VIII, 570 pages. 1986.

NATO ASI Series F

Including Special Programmes on Sensory Systems for Robotic Control (ROB) and on Advanced Educational Technology (AET)

Vol. 25: Pyramidal Systems for Computer Vision. Edited by V. Cantoni and S. Levialdi. VIII, 392 pages. 1986. *(ROB)*

Vol. 26: Modelling and Analysis in Arms Control. Edited by R. Avenhaus, R. K. Huber and J. D. Kettelle. VIII, 488 pages. 1986. *(out of print)*

Vol. 27: Computer Aided Optimal Design: Structural and Mechanical Systems. Edited by C. A. Mota Soares. XIII, 1029 pages. 1987.

Vol. 28: Distributed Operating Systems. Theory und Practice. Edited by Y. Paker, J.-P. Banatre and M. Bozyiğit. X, 379 pages. 1987.

Vol. 29: Languages for Sensor-Based Control in Robotics. Edited by U. Rembold and K. Hörmann. IX, 625 pages. 1987. *(ROB)*

Vol. 30: Pattern Recognition Theory and Applications. Edited by P. A. Devijver and J. Kittler. XI, 543 pages. 1987.

Vol. 31: Decision Support Systems: Theory and Application. Edited by C. W. Holsapple and A. B. Whinston. X, 500 pages. 1987.

Vol. 32: Information Systems: Failure Analysis. Edited by J. A. Wise and A. Debons. XV, 338 pages. 1987.

Vol. 33: Machine Intelligence and Knowledge Engineering for Robotic Applications. Edited by A. K. C. Wong and A. Pugh. XIV, 486 pages. 1987. *(ROB)*

Vol. 34: Modelling, Robustness and Sensitivity Reduction in Control Systems. Edited by R.F. Curtain. IX, 492 pages. 1987.

Vol. 35: Expert Judgment and Expert Systems. Edited by J. L. Mumpower, L. D. Phillips, O. Renn and V. R. R. Uppuluri. VIII, 361 pages. 1987.

Vol. 36: Logic of Programming and Calculi of Discrete Design. Edited by M. Broy. VII, 415 pages. 1987.

Vol. 37: Dynamics of Infinite Dimensional Systems. Edited by S.-N. Chow and J. K. Hale. IX. 514 pages. 1987.

Vol. 38: Flow Control of Congested Networks. Edited by A. R. Odoni, L. Bianco and G. Szegö. XII, 355 pages. 1987.

Vol. 39: Mathematics and Computer Science in Medical Imaging. Edited by M. A. Viergever and A. Todd-Pokropek. VIII, 546 pages. 1988.

Vol. 40: Theoretical Foundations of Computer Graphics and CAD. Edited by R. A. Earnshaw. XX, 1246 pages. 1988. *(out of print)*

Vol. 41: Neural Computers. Edited by R. Eckmiller and Ch. v. d. Malsburg. XIII, 566 pages. 1988. *Reprinted as Springer Study Edition 1989, 1990.*

Vol. 42: Real-Time Object Measurement and Classification. Edited by A. K. Jain. VIII, 407 pages. 1988. *(ROB)*

Vol. 43: Sensors and Sensory Systems for Advanced Robots. Edited by P. Dario. XI, 597 pages. 1988. *(ROB)*

Vol. 44: Signal Processing and Pattern Recognition in Nondestructive Evaluation of Materials. Edited by C. H. Chen. VIII, 344 pages. 1988. *(ROB)*

Vol. 45: Syntactic and Structural Pattern Recognition. Edited by G. Ferraté, T. Pavlidis, A. Sanfeliu and H. Bunke. XVI, 467 pages. 1988. *(ROB)*

Vol. 46: Recent Advances in Speech Understanding and Dialog Systems. Edited by H. Niemann, M. Lang and G. Sagerer. X, 521 pages. 1988.

NATO ASI Series F

Including Special Programmes on Sensory Systems for Robotic Control (ROB) and on Advanced Educational Technology (AET)

Vol. 47: Advanced Computing Concepts and Techniques in Control Engineering. Edited by M. J. Denham and A. J. Laub. XI, 518 pages. 1988. *(out of print)*

Vol. 48: Mathematical Models for Decision Support. Edited by G. Mitra. IX, 762 pages. 1988.

Vol. 49: Computer Integrated Manufacturing. Edited by I. B. Turksen. VIII, 568 pages. 1988.

Vol. 50: CAD Based Programming for Sensory Robots. Edited by B. Ravani. IX, 565 pages. 1988. *(ROB)*

Vol. 51: Algorithms and Model Formulations in Mathematical Programming. Edited by S. W. Wallace. IX, 190 pages. 1989.

Vol. 52: Sensor Devices and Systems for Robotics. Edited by A. Casals. IX, 362 pages. 1989. *(ROB)*

Vol. 53: Advanced Information Technologies for Industrial Material Flow Systems. Edited by S. Y. Nof and C. L. Moodie. IX, 710 pages. 1989.

Vol. 54: A Reappraisal of the Efficiency of Financial Markets. Edited by R. M. C. Guimarães, B. G. Kingsman and S. J. Taylor. X, 804 pages. 1989.

Vol. 55: Constructive Methods in Computing Science. Edited by M. Broy. VII, 478 pages. 1989.

Vol. 56: Multiple Criteria Decision Making and Risk Analysis Using Microcomputers. Edited by B. Karpak and S. Zionts. VII, 399 pages. 1989.

Vol. 57: Kinematics and Dynamic Issues in Sensor Based Control. Edited by G. E. Taylor. XI, 456 pages. 1990. *(ROB)*

Vol. 58: Highly Redundant Sensing in Robotic Systems. Edited by J. T. Tou and J. G. Balchen. X, 322 pages. 1990. *(ROB)*

Vol. 59: Superconducting Electronics. Edited by H. Weinstock and M. Nisenoff. X, 441 pages. 1989.

Vol. 60: 3D Imaging in Medicine. Algorithms, Systems, Applications. Edited by K. H. Höhne, H. Fuchs and S. M. Pizer. IX, 460 pages. 1990. *(out of print)*

Vol. 61: Knowledge, Data and Computer-Assisted Decisions. Edited by M. Schader and W. Gaul. VIII, 421 pages. 1990.

Vol. 62: Supercomputing. Edited by J. S. Kowalik. X, 425 pages. 1990.

Vol. 63: Traditional and Non-Traditional Robotic Sensors. Edited by T. C. Henderson. VIII, 468 pages. 1990. *(ROB)*

Vol. 64: Sensory Robotics for the Handling of Limp Materials. Edited by P. M. Taylor. IX, 343 pages. 1990. *(ROB)*

Vol. 65: Mapping and Spatial Modelling for Navigation. Edited by L. F. Pau. VIII, 357 pages. 1990. *(ROB)*

Vol. 66: Sensor-Based Robots: Algorithms and Architectures. Edited by C. S. G. Lee. X, 285 pages. 1991. *(ROB)*

Vol. 67: Designing Hypermedia for Learning. Edited by D. H. Jonassen and H. Mandl. XXV, 457 pages. 1990. *(AET)*

Vol. 68: Neurocomputing. Algorithms, Architectures and Applications. Edited by F. Fogelman Soulié and J. Hérault. XI, 455 pages. 1990.

Vol. 69: Real-Time Integration Methods for Mechanical System Simulation. Edited by E. J. Haug and R. C. Deyo. VIII, 352 pages. 1991.

Vol. 70: Numerical Linear Algebra, Digital Signal Processing and Parallel Algorithms. Edited by G. H. Golub and P. Van Dooren. XIII, 729 pages. 1991.

NATO ASI Series F

Including Special Programmes on Sensory Systems for Robotic Control (ROB) and on Advanced Educational Technology (AET)

Vol. 71: Expert Systems and Robotics. Edited by T. Jordanides and B.Torby. XII, 744 pages. 1991.

Vol. 72: High-Capacity Local and Metropolitan Area Networks. Architecture and Performance Issues. Edited by G. Pujolle. X, 536 pages. 1991.

Vol. 73: Automation and Systems Issues in Air Traffic Control. Edited by J. A. Wise, V. D. Hopkin and M. L. Smith. XIX, 594 pages. 1991.

Vol. 74: Picture Archiving and Communication Systems (PACS) in Medicine. Edited by H. K. Huang, O. Ratib, A. R. Bakker and G. Witte. XI, 438 pages. 1991.

Vol. 75: Speech Recognition and Understanding. Recent Advances, Trends and Applications. Edited by P. Laface and Renato De Mori. XI, 559 pages. 1991.

Vol. 76: Multimedia Interface Design in Education. Edited by A. D. N. Edwards and S. Holland. XIV, 216 pages. 1992. *(AET)*

Vol. 77: Computer Algorithms for Solving Linear Algebraic Equations. The State of the Art. Edited by E. Spedicato. VIII, 352 pages. 1991.

Vol. 78: Integrating Advanced Technology into Technology Education. Edited by M. Hacker, A. Gordon and M. de Vries. VIII, 185 pages. 1991. *(AET)*

Vol. 79: Logic, Algebra, and Computation. Edited by F. L. Bauer. VII, 485 pages. 1991.

Vol. 80: Intelligent Tutoring Systems for Foreign Language Learning. Edited by M. L. Swartz and M. Yazdani. IX, 347 pages. 1992. *(AET)*

Vol. 81: Cognitive Tools for Learning. Edited by P. A. M. Kommers, D. H. Jonassen, and J. T. Mayes. X, 278 pages. 1992. *(AET)*

Vol. 82: Combinatorial Optimization. New Frontiers in Theory and Practice. Edited by M. Akgül, H. W. Hamacher, and S. Tüfekçi. XI, 334 pages. 1992.

Vol. 83: Active Perception and Robot Vision. Edited by A. K. Sood and H. Wechsler. IX, 756 pages. 1992.

Vol. 84: Computer-Based Learning Environments and Problem Solving. Edited by E. De Corte, M. C. Linn, H. Mandl, and L. Verschaffel. XVI, 488 pages. 1992. *(AET)*

Vol. 85: Adaptive Learning Environments. Foundations and Frontiers. Edited by M. Jones and P. H. Winne. VIII, 408 pages. 1992. *(AET)*

Vol. 86: Intelligent Learning Environments and Knowledge Acquisition in Physics. Edited by A. Tiberghien and H. Mandl. VIII, 285 pages. 1992. *(AET)*

Vol. 87: Cognitive Modelling and Interactive Environments. With demo diskettes (Apple and IBM compatible). Edited by F. L. Engel, D. G. Bouwhuis, T. Bösser, and G. d'Ydewalle. IX, 311 pages. 1992. *(AET)*

Vol. 88: Programming and Mathematical Method. Edited by M. Broy. VIII, 428 pages. 1992.

Vol. 89: Mathematical Problem Solving and New Information Technologies. Edited by J. P. Ponte, J. F. Matos, J. M. Matos, and D. Fernandes. XV, 346 pages. 1992. *(AET)*

Vol. 90: Collaborative Learning Through Computer Conferencing. Edited by A. R. Kaye. X, 260 pages. 1992. *(AET)*

Vol. 91: New Directions for Intelligent Tutoring Systems. Edited by E. Costa. X, 296 pages. 1992. *(AET)*

Vol. 92: Hypermedia Courseware: Structures of Communication and Intelligent Help. Edited by A. Oliveira. X, 241 pages. 1992. *(AET)*

Vol. 93: Interactive Multimedia Learning Environments. Human Factors and Technical Considerations on Design Issues. Edited by M. Giardina. VIII, 254 pages. 1992. *(AET)*

NATO ASI Series F

Including Special Programmes on Sensory Systems for Robotic Control (ROB) and on Advanced Educational Technology (AET)

Vol. 94: Logic and Algebra of Specification. Edited by F. L. Bauer, W. Brauer, and H. Schwichtenberg. VII, 442 pages. 1993.

Vol. 95: Comprehensive Systems Design: A New Educational Technology. Edited by C. M. Reigeluth, B. H. Banathy, and J. R. Olson. IX, 437 pages. 1993. *(AET)*

Vol. 96: New Directions in Educational Technology. Edited by E. Scanlon and T. O'Shea. VIII, 251 pages. 1992. *(AET)*

Vol. 97: Advanced Models of Cognition for Medical Training and Practice. Edited by D. A. Evans and V. L. Patel. XI, 372 pages. 1992. *(AET)*

Vol. 98: Medical Images: Formation, Handling and Evaluation. Edited by A. E. Todd-Pokropek and M. A. Viergever. IX, 700 pages. 1992.

Vol. 99: Multisensor Fusion for Computer Vision. Edited by J. K. Aggarwal. XI, 456 pages. 1993. *(ROB)*

Vol. 100: Communication from an Artificial Intelligence Perspective. Theoretical and Applied Issues. Edited by A. Ortony, J. Slack and O. Stock. XII, 260 pages. 1992.

Vol. 101: Recent Developments in Decision Support Systems. Edited by C. W. Holsapple and A. B. Whinston. XI, 618 pages. 1993.

Vol. 102: Robots and Biological Systems: Towards a New Bionics? Edited by P. Dario, G. Sandini and P. Aebischer. XII, 786 pages. 1993.

Vol. 103: Parallel Computing on Distributed Memory Multiprocessors. Edited by F. Özgüner and F. Erçal. VIII, 332 pages. 1993.

Vol. 104: Instructional Models in Computer-Based Learning Environments. Edited by S. Dijkstra, H. P. M. Krammer and J. J. G. van Merriënboer. X, 510 pages. 1993. *(AET)*

Vol. 105: Designing Environments for Constructive Learning. Edited by T. M. Duffy, J. Lowyck and D. H. Jonassen. VIII, 374 pages. 1993. *(AET)*

Vol. 106: Software for Parallel Computation. Edited by J. S. Kowalik and L. Grandinetti. IX, 363 pages. 1993.

Vol. 107: Advanced Educational Technologies for Mathematics and Science. Edited by D. L. Ferguson. XII, 749 pages. 1993. *(AET)*

Vol. 108: Concurrent Engineering: Tools and Technologies for Mechanical System Design. Edited by E. J. Haug. XIII, 998 pages. 1993.

Vol. 109: Advanced Educational Technology in Technology Education. Edited by A. Gordon, M. Hacker and M. de Vries. VIII, 253 pages. 1993. *(AET)*

Vol. 110: Verification and Validation of Complex Systems: Human Factors Issues. Edited by J. A. Wise, V. D. Hopkin and P. Stager. XIII, 704 pages. 1993.

Vol. 111: Cognitive Models and Intelligent Environments for Learning Programming. Edited by E. Lemut, B. du Boulay and G. Dettori. VIII, 305 pages. 1993. *(AET)*

Vol. 112: Item Banking: Interactive Testing and Self-Assessment. Edited by D. A. Leclercq and J. E. Bruno. VIII, 261 pages. 1993. *(AET)*

Vol. 113: Interactive Learning Technology for the Deaf. Edited by B. A. G. Elsendoorn and F. Coninx. XIII, 285 pages. 1993. *(AET)*

Vol. 114: Intelligent Systems: Safety, Reliability and Maintainability Issues. Edited by O. Kaynak, G. Honderd and E. Grant. XI, 340 pages. 1993.

Vol. 115: Learning Electricity and Electronics with Advanced Educational Technology. Edited by M. Caillot. VII, 329 pages. 1993. *(AET)*

NATO ASI Series F

Including Special Programmes on Sensory Systems for Robotic Control (ROB) and on Advanced Educational Technology (AET)

Vol. 116: Control Technology in Elementary Education. Edited by B. Denis. IX, 311 pages. 1993 *(AET)*

Vol. 118: Program Design Calculi. Edited by M. Broy. VIII, 409 pages. 1993.

Vol. 119: Automating Instructional Design, Development, and Delivery. Edited by. R. D. Tennyson. VIII, 266 pages. 1994 *(AET)*

Vol. 120: Reliability and Safety Assessment of Dynamic Process Systems. Edited by T. Aldemir, N. O. Siu, A. Mosleh, P. C. Cacciabue and B. G. Göktepe. X, 242 pages. 1994.

Vol. 121: Learning from Computers: Mathematics Education and Technology. Edited by C. Keitel and K. Ruthven. XIII, 332 pages. 1993. *(AET)*

Vol. 122: Simulation-Based Experiential Learning. Edited by D. M. Towne, T. de Jong and H. Spada. XIV, 274 pages. 1993. *(AET)*

Vol. 123: User-Centred Requirements for Software Engineering Environments. Edited by D. J. Gilmore, R. L. Winder and F. Détienne. VII, 377 pages. 1994.

Vol. 124: Fundamentals in Handwriting Recognition. Edited by S. Impedovo. IX, 496 pages. 1994.

Vol. 125: Student Modelling: The Key to Individualized Knowledge-Based Instruction. Edited by J. E. Greer and G. I. McCalla. X, 383 pages. 1994. *(AET)*

Vol. 126: Shape in Picture. Mathematical Description of Shape in Grey-level Images. Edited by Y.-L. O, A. Toet, D. Foster, H. J. A. M. Heijmans and P. Meer. XI, 676 pages. 1994.

Vol. 127: Real Time Computing. Edited by W. A. Halang and A. D. Stoyenko. XXII, 762 pages. 1994.

Vol. 128: Computer Supported Collaborative Learning. Edited by C. O'Malley. X, 303 pages. 1994. *(AET)*

Vol. 129: Human-Machine Communication for Educational Systems Design. Edited by M. D. Brouwer-Janse and T. L. Harrington. X, 342 pages. 1994. *(AET)*

Vol. 130: Advances in Object-Oriented Database Systems. Edited by A. Dogac, M. T. Özsu, A. Biliris and T. Sellis. XI, 515 pages. 1994.

Vol. 131: Constraint Programming. Edited by B. Mayoh, E. Tyugu and J. Penjam. VII, 452 pages. 1994.

Vol. 132: Mathematical Modelling Courses for Engineering Education. Edited by Y. Ersoy and A. O. Moscardini. X, 246 pages. 1994. *(AET)*

Vol. 133: Collaborative Dialogue Technologies in Distance Learning. Edited by M. F. Verdejo and S. A. Cerri. XIV, 296 pages. 1994. *(AET)*

Vol. 134: Computer Integrated Production Systems and Organizations. The Human-Centred Approach. Edited by F. Schmid, S. Evans, A. W. S. Ainger and R. J. Grieve. X, 347 pages. 1994.

Vol. 135: Technology Education in School and Industry. Emerging Didactics for Human Resource Development. Edited by D. Blandow and M. J. Dyrenfurth. XI, 367 pages. 1994. *(AET)*

Vol. 136: From Statistics to Neural Networks. Theory and Pattern Recognition Applications. Edited by V. Cherkassky, J. H. Friedman and H. Wechsler. XII, 394 pages. 1994.

Vol. 137: Technology-Based Learning Environments. Psychological and Educational Foundations. Edited by S. Vosniadou, E. De Corte and H. Mandl. X, 302 pages. 1994. *(AET)*

Vol. 140: Automating Instructional Design: Computer-Based Development and Delivery Tools. Edited by R. D. Tennyson and A. E. Barron. IX, 618 pages. 1995. *(AET)*

Vol. 142: Dialogue and Instruction. Modeling Interaction in Intelligent Tutoring Systems. Edited by R.-J. Beun, M. Baker and M. Reiner. IX, 368 pages. 1995. *(AET)*